George E. Marks

A Treatise on Marks' Patent Artificial Limbs

with rubber hands and feet

George E. Marks

A Treatise on Marks' Patent Artificial Limbs
with rubber hands and feet

ISBN/EAN: 9783337223090

Printed in Europe, USA, Canada, Australia, Japan

Cover: Foto ©Andreas Hilbeck / pixelio.de

More available books at **www.hansebooks.com**

ON

MARKS' PATENT

ARTIFICIAL LIMBS

WITH

RUBBER HANDS AND FEET.

A. A. MARKS,
701 BROADWAY,
NEW YORK CITY,
U. S. A.

PREFACE.

The labor expended in the preparation of this treatise has been much greater than apparent. The subject has been elaborated with a scrupulous regard for originality and a conscientious purpose of presenting the truth shorn of every vestige of exaggeration. Context, illustrations and plates have been especially prepared with the purpose of imparting the subject in its simplicity. The work has rested principally with the undersigned, who for the past ten years has devoted his energies exclusively to the advancement of prothesis.

Having made a tour abroad, visiting the principal cities of Europe and studying thoroughly the methods and peculiarities of the manufacturers of those cities, he feels himself fully competent to cope with the subject from comparative, scientific and professional standpoints.

The name A. A. Marks is the title of the firm, which consists of A. A. Marks, Geo. E. Marks, and Wm. L. Marks. Although the senior member has for a number of years withdrawn from an active position, his judgment is consulted on matters of peculiar importance, and the principles which his labors have so thoroughly established, and which have become such an essential and distinctive part of the profession, are rigorously followed. The undersigned could not resist the impulse of paying a compliment to him in the first pages of this book, being mindful of the self-sacrificing constancy which has marked his years of devotion to the profession.

About thirty editions of pamphlets and abstracts in English, German and Spanish precede this book; in order to avoid confusion in the enumeration of cuts, privilege has been taken of beginning with the number 101. It will thus be seen that any correspondent can refer to any particular cut by simply mentioning the number, and there will be no danger of mistaking his reference with numbers in former editions.

The testimonials are of four classes, in numbers as follows: Awards, 15; press, 50; profession, 140; and wearers, over 700. In all very nearly one thousand. This number may be regarded as super-abundant. An invitation to our friends to express themselves in regard to our work struck such a responsive chord that in a brief time we found ourselves in possession of these glowing evidences of confidence and esteem.

The testimonials from wearers are arranged under eight headings, enumerated in the table of contents.

These eight classes are each subdivided into states.

The object of this arrangement is to enable one to find a case similar to his own very near his own door, with whom he may confer.

The table of contents on page 2 should be consulted for guidance to any particular subject.

The undersigned begs to call the attention of the surgical profession to his article on page 100, and invites criticism on the views therein expressed.

A few pages devoted to statistics may be found of interest to those who attach importance to the subject.

GEO. E. MARKS, A.B.

April 3, 1888.

TABLE OF CONTENTS.

	Page
Preface	2
A glimpse at the past	7
How I came to invent the rubber foot	12
Argument	14
Economy	18
Why an ankle-joint leg is not strong	18
Comparative weight	19
Required weight	20
How long will an artificial leg last	20
Shoes and stockings	21
An indisputable fact	21
Artificial legs	22
The new patent foot	23
Accessories	23
Legs for thigh amputations	24
Lock attachment for knee	27
Hip joint and waist belt	28
Laced thigh	29
Knee-joint amputations	30
Knee-bearing artificial legs	33
Legs for extended and anchylosed knees	36
Legs for below-knee amputations	37
Legs for below-knee amputations with knee bent and contracted	39
Legs for below-knee amputations without thigh support	39
Water-proof legs	40
Natural-crook legs	40
Legs for amputations in or below ankle joints	41
Legs for amputations in or below ankle joints with thigh supports	45
Artificial toes	47
Peg legs	47
Legs, apparatus and extensions for shortened legs, deformities, etc.	50
Rubber feet attached to artificial legs of other manufacture	59
Directions for taking measurements for artificial legs, apparatus, etc.	60–65
Suspenders, roller	66
" old style	69
" belt	70
" for women	72
" for double amputations	73
Artificial arms	74
Rubber hand	77
Ball and socket wrist joint	78
Natural color	78
Arms for shoulder-joint amputations	79
Arms for above-elbow amputations	79
Arms for elbow-joint amputations	80
Arms for below-elbow amputations	80
Arms for wrist-joint amputations	83
Arms for any amputation without hands	84
Apparatus for amputations in the hands	85
Accessories	85
Parts of hands	86
Apparatus for malformations, distortions, exsections in arms	87
Rubber hands applied to artificial arms of other manufacture	87
Suspenders for artificial arms	88
Combined knife and fork	88

Directions for taking measurements for artificial arms	89
How to order an artificial leg or arm	91
How to take a plaster cast	92
Artificial limbs made and fitted from measurements without the presence of the patient	93
Calls made to residence	94
Lady attendant	95
Branches	95
Information for strangers visiting the city	95
Terms of payment	96
Payments on the installment plan	97
Guarantee	97
Artificial limbs supplied to pensioners of the U. S. at government expense	98
Amputations, desirable points, and the kind of operations most suitable for the use of artificial limbs	100
How soon after amputation should artificial limb be applied	106
Dr. Cook's opinion on the subject	107
Children	108
Letter from Dr. Brady	112
Difficulties overcome	113
Our foreign trade	116
Certificate	117
Socks for stumps	118
Supplies for artificial limbs	120
Webbing, buckles, rollers, check straps, lacings, bolts, spiral springs, knives, forks, brushes and hooks, screw drivers, oil cans, grease and felt	121
How to remit	122
Crutches	123
Crutch ferrules	124
Crutches, rubber bottoms	125
do ice spikes	126
Statistics	
Legs and arms	127
Males and females	127
Points of amputations	128
Causes for amputation	129
Ages at which amputations are made	130
Occupations of wearers	131
Letter writing	133
Awards, American Institute	135 to 139
Centennial Exposition, Philadelphia	140
Centennial, American Institute	141
International Cotton Exposition, Atlanta, Ga.	142
World's Industrial & Cotton Centennial Exhibition, New Orleans, La.	143
Notices from the press	144
Practical test of artificial legs	144
Artificial legs on skates	145
Substituted humanity	149
Art practically exemplified	149
Patched-up humanity	150
Lecture by Lewis A. Sayre, M.D.	152
On his legs again	153
A remarkable coincidence	153
A dark cloud with a silver lining	153
A wonderfully successful result, etc.	154
Cripples with improved feet	155
Development of stumps by the use of artificial limbs	156
Translations from the foreign press	158 and 160
False legs and arms	158
Rubber hands and feet	159
Deft rubber hands	162
A survivor from Stoneman's raid	165
Literary amenities on artificial limbs	168
A part of Stewart's body	169

CONTENTS.

A wooden joke	170
Cork legs	171
Endorsements from the medical and surgical profession	173
Letter from Gen. Geo. A. Sheridan	184
Letters of commendation from wearers of artificial limbs	
Double amputations	185 to 207
Above-knee amputations	207 to 254
Knee-bearing artificial legs	254 to 262
Below-knee amputations	262 to 361
Ankle-joint and below amputations	361 to 368
Apparatus	368 to 371
Arms, above elbow	371 to 376
Arms, elbow joints and wrist joints	376 to 394
Cost of transporting an artificial limb to any part of the world	395

ENDORSEMENTS AND COMMENDATIONS CLASSIFIED ACCORDING TO STATES AND COUNTRIES.

The numbers refer to pages in this book.

Alabama, 176, 183, 207, 262, 263, 371, 376.
Arizona, 178, 182, 208.
Arkansas, 185, 377.
California, 179, 185, 263 to 265, 377.
Colorado, 178, 183, 208, 209, 254, 265, 266 to 270. 378.
Connecticut, 175, 180, 185 to 187, 210, 211, 255, 266, 361, 368, 369, 372.
Dakota, 178, 183, 187, 270, 378.
District of Columbia, 211, 255, 271, 378.
Florida, 212, 271, 272.
Georgia, 176, 182, 187. 213, 273 to 277, 362, 372, 375.
Idaho, 177, 178.
Illinois, 176, 177, 182, 188, 213, 214, 255, 277.
Indiana, 176, 188, 214, 215. 278, 279, 362, 379.
Indian Territory, 214, 280.
Iowa, 177, 181, 189, 215, 216, 280 to 282, 372, 379.
Kansas, 178, 216 to 218, 256, 282 to 285, 362, 372.
Kentucky, 218, 285, 286, 379, 380.
Louisiana, 286.
Maine, 219, 286 to 289.
Maryland, 189, 220, 221, 289, 380.
Massachusetts, 175, 221, 222, 290 to 294, 362, 363, 369, 373, 380.
Michigan, 177, 182, 223, 256, 294 to 296, 373, 381.
Minnesota, 177, 182, 294, 297.
Mississippi, 223.
Missouri, 176, 190, 224, 257, 297 to 299.
Montana, 257, 299.
Nebraska, 178, 180, 224, 225, 257, 299, 370, 373, 381, 382.
Nevada, 300.
New Hampshire, 175, 183, 190, 225, 300, 301.
New Jersey, 174, 175, 180, 181, 191, 192, 225 to 228, 258, 301 to 306, 363, 364, 373, 374, 383.
New York, 173, 174, 179, 181, 185, 192 to 200, 228 to 240, 259, 260, 307 to 327, 364 to 367, 370, 371, 383 to 387.
North Carolina, 175, 240, 327, 328.
Ohio, 176, 200 to 202, 240 to 242, 328 to 332. 375, 387 to 389.
Oregon, 178, 242, 243, 261, 333, 390.
Pennsylvania, 175, 181, 183, 202 to 204, 243 to 245, 260, 261, 333 to 344, 368, 371, 374, 375, 390, 391.
Rhode Island, 204, 246, 344, 345, 368.
South Carolina, 246, 261, 345.
Tennessee, 178, 181, 205, 346, 347, 391.
Texas, 176, 205, 347 to 349, 392.
Utah, 178, 349.
Vermont, 247, 349 to 351, 375, 392.
Virginia, 247, 248, 392.
Washington Territory, 178, 179, 182, 183, 248, 351, 352, 376.

West Virginia, 175, 181, 206, 261, 352, 353.
Wisconsin, 177, 181, 182, 206, 207, 248, 249, 353 to 356, 393.
Canada, 179, 183, 249, 250, 356 to 359, 394.
Newfoundland, 250, 251.
England, 251.
Ireland, 360.
Germany, 394.
Holland, 252.
Denmark, 252.
New Zealand, 252.
Mexico, 252, 253, 360.
San Salvador, 253.
Peru, 254.
Cuba, 262.
Porto Rico, 262.
St. Thomas, 359.
Chili, 361.
Costa Rica, 376.

A GLIMPSE AT THE PAST.

Nearly two score years of labor and thought devoted to the development of an industry, calculated to ameliorate the conditions of the crippled and rescue them from a life-long condition of dependence is the boast of Mr. A. A. Marks.

Looking back on those years he has every reason to be proud of them, freighted as they are with tributes to his incomparable genius. Few in this world have the privilege of bearing such honors. Enterprise and thrift alone can not always secure them. An active ingenuity, a soul filled with sympathy, and an indefatigable devotion to his purpose are the attributes to which his success can be ascribed.

Mr. Marks engaged in the artificial limb business in the early part of 1853 in a small and unpretentious way, when but two manufacturers were known to the American people, and at a time when the call for an artificial leg or arm was a matter of very rare occurrence.

There was no encouragement for a man whose aspirations for wealth prompted his actions, as nothing but an existence could be assured in exchange for the devotion of a life of thought and toil; pecuniary emoluments could not be expected; the uncertain "bubble reputation" of having restored the cripple to a condition in which he could walk, labor, and thrive was the reward for the sacrifice. This, indeed, was great, for no aim in life can be more laudable than that of ministering relief to those whom misfortune has placed in a dependent and deplorable condition.

But the bent of human ambition is for the acquisition of money instead of a few plaudits from the world; for this reason we presume genius concerned itself so little with the advancement of the prosthetic*art, and as a consequence the unfortunate cripple was for ages an object of pity, neglected, and entirely at the mercies of the charlatan or the unskilled. He hobbled about in a distressing manner, appealing fruitlessly for amelioration. The grotesque peg of Peter Stuyvesant times offered him the best substitute for the member he had lost. The iron hand of an ancient warrior and the leg of the Holland nobleman were fancies of the imagi-

---

* Prosthetic.—a. of Prosthesis, same as Prothesis, The process of adding to the human body some artificial part in place of one that may be wanting.

nation ; the golden leg of Miss Kilmansegg, that brilliant creation of Hood, proved to be a murderous instrument as much as a fascinating perambulator.

> "But hark ;—as slow as the stroke of a pump
> Lump, thump ;
> Thump, lump ;
> As the giant of Castle Otranto might stump."

The history of artificial limbs begins with very remote times. We have evidences that the Romans and the Greeks improvised some sort of substitute for the limbs lost in battle and the vicissitudes of life. Herodotus tells us of a prisoner who amputated his own foot in order to free himself from the shackle, after which he escaped and returned to his friends, who made him *a wooden foot.*

The treasure-trove that turned up at Capua in 1885 in a tufa tomb is probably the most valuable and indisputable evidence that artificial legs were made in early times. The relic is now on exhibition in the Museum of the Royal College of Surgeons, London. The official catalogue describes it thus :

"Roman artificial leg ; the artificial limb accurately represents the form of the leg. It is made with pieces of thin bronze, fastened by bronze nails to a wooden core. Two iron bars, having holes at their free ends, are attached to the upper extremity of the bronze. A quadrilateral piece of iron, found near the position of the foot, is thought to have given strength to it. There was no trace of the foot, and the wooden core had nearly crumbled away.

"The skeleton had its waist surrounded by a belt of sheet bronze edged with small rivets, probably used to fasten a leather lining.

"Three painted vases (red figures on a black ground) lay at the feet of the skeleton. The vases belonged to a rather advanced period of the decline in art (about 300 years B. C.)."

Gen. H. H. Maxwell in commenting on this further says :

"It is important to add from other sources that the upper third of the leg was hollow, while the lower two-thirds were filled with wood."

From those early times to about the beginning of the present century little or no advance was made in the art ; and, as no evidence exists to prove to the contrary, it is quite reasonable to suppose that for many centuries the manufacture of artificial legs was one of the lost arts.

In the early part of the present century the Duke of Anglesea, being in need of an artificial leg, and possessing an inventive faculty, suggested to an English instrument-maker, what proved to be a very answerable substitute, a decided improvement on the primitive peg of the doughty Peter. The leg received but little improvement until the venturesome Selpho introduced it into this country with some admirable modifications of his own; here it met with American enterprise and began to thrive.

Palmer, one of the pioneers, grasped the opportunity, and with a mind rich with ideas labored creditably; his inventions were meritorious, and we can well understand why Holmes went into ecstasies over his achievements, in his essay entitled "The Human Wheel, Its Spokes and Felloes." Unfortunately Palmer exhausted his ideas at an early date, and on account of his tenacious hold on old principles was soon superseded by his more energetic rival.

The demand for artificial limbs was noticeably increasing; the field was growing larger; the cry for something more durable and more approximate to nature came from every quarter.

Railroad systems were multiplying in all parts of the country; machinery for the rapid production of wares, the tilling of the soil, and the harvesting of crops were making great inroads in the economy of labor.

War-clouds were gathering and conflicts threatening; all these augured the recurrence of accidents and the dismemberment of the human body. Surgery was awakening from its lethargy. Esculapian powers were to be vouchsafed to the new generation. The problem of the preservation of life while undergoing perilous operations promised to be capable of solution by the diligent and thoughtful.

Lister was laboring with the antiseptic problem. Symes, Pirogoff, Markoe, Wood, Sayre, and an army of other brilliant minds were evolving methods which removed diseased parts and gave life and comfort to the suffering. All these conditions augmented the demand for prosthesis, and induced Mr. Marks and others to consecrate their lives to the work.

The early experiments of Mr. Marks were trying. No one could have worked harder or thought more industriously.

At first all the movements of the natural leg were imitated and put in intricate mechanism; movements lateral, anterior, posterior, astraguloid, were introduced in detail; modifications and re-adjustments were indulged in, until the structure passed through all the possible stages from the leg-automaton to the leg-practical.

In 1858 Mr. Marks formulated his ideas and constructed a leg with antero-posterior ankle movement, the lateral ankle movement having been abandoned a few years before by not only himself but other manufacturers, as practically needless. The peculiarity of his ankle joint was its adjustability; the angle of articulation was susceptible of change at the pleasure of the wearer: the tension of the spring was likewise adjustable, and the wear of the joint by attrition was compensated for by the turning of screws. This unique ankle combination was ingenious and met with great favor; the press and the surgical profession commended it highly, and at the American Institute exhibition in 1859 it received the award of a silver medal.

Presumably the ankle joint had been perfected; it seemed to have supplied every requirement; and for several years the Marks leg was made with that characteristic feature.

Mention should here be made of early experiments in endeavoring to utilize some substance aside from wood for the socket. In 1854 Mr. Marks adopted the flexible leather socket, somewhat similar to the method used in France. That part of the socket which encased the stump was composed of leather, so arranged that by tightening up several straps the diameters of the socket could be diminished so as to accommodate a reduced stump. In theory this socket was excellent, but in practice it was found inferior to wood; it did not possess the necessary rigidity to permanently oppose the weight of the wearer; the leather or its lining would absorb the perspiration and become offensive, and worse still, by reducing the socket, the joints would be thrown out of line. The leather socket was then abandoned and the rawhide socket experimented with, which met a similar fate. Vulcanite rubber was afterward used, but that proved to be too friable. Thus convinced by experience that wood possessed the greater advantages, Mr. Marks adopted it, and has since used it to the exclusion of all other material for that part of the leg that surrounds the stump. Nearly all the older manufacturers can recount a similar experience.

In 1861 the ankle joint, which had been the inventor's idol, began to show weakness, although it was calculated to withstand as much strain as ordinary walking and toiling required; yet every now and then some mishap or little thoughtlessness on the part of the wearer would bring undue strain on the working parts, and either break or disorder them; no matter how strong the joints were made, there invariably appeared to be some weakness, always threatening unpleasant consequences; if not a break, there would be a squeak or a grinding noise; some part needed lubricating or some cord needed "taking up," or some spring needed replacing or stiffening; always some little annoying or perplexing matter to aggravate or embarrass the wearer, or exhibit his condition to those from whom he wished to conceal it. From 1853 to 1863 it is safe to say that most of the time of the shop was given to the repairing of ankle joints, either on limbs of Mr. Marks' construction or those of other establishments; a new cord, a new spring, or the bushing of a bolt was the every-day demand. The ankle joint had been reduced to its simplest and strongest form, and yet it was not strong enough; the lateral movement had been abandoned, the antero-posterior movement had been reduced from an angular articulation of a hundred degrees to that of twenty, and still the invariable complaint of instability and lack of control. The poor man could ill afford the constant drain on his scanty means, and the man of affluence, weary from the burden of constant anxiety, craved for something better.

An old patron of the ankle joint tells the following story, which we doubt not is in substance the repetition of the experience of many of the limb wearers who read this book:

"I started from my house one morning to meet a pressing engagement. I had not gone far when the ankle joint of my artificial leg began to call for grease. My first impulse was to disregard it, but the noise increased and became so noticeable that I was afraid I might attract attention, which to a nervous man is something indescribably unpleasant.

"I entered a drug store where I had a passing acquaintance and besought the proprietor to admit me to his private room and furnish me with some oil and a screw-driver. I passed an hour in disjointing the foot, lubricating the parts, and putting them together. I resumed my journey and got within a short distance of my destination, when I made a false step on the toes of my artificial foot and broke the heel cord; this occurred at a moment when I was bearing heavily on the toes, and as a result splintered the front part of my ankle.

"I hailed a carriage, and with the assistance of a passer-by I succeeded in hobbling in the vehicle. The thoroughfare in which this happened being a thickly traveled one furnished a crowd of the curious that looked piteously upon me, much to my mental discomfort. Instead of pushing on to meet my engagement, I dispatched a message of explanation, and directed the driver to take me to my home. Here I was obliged to remain for three weary days until my leg could be repaired and returned to me."

The recurrence of incidents of this kind convinced Mr. Marks that ankle joints were far from perfection, and that improvements of a very decided character were necessary. Several years were spent fruitlessly in experiments. It was possible to make the ankle joint strong, but in doing so the weight would become so greatly increased that to wear it would be burdensome. An increase in strength incurs an increase in weight, is one of the inexorable laws of physics, and no amount of human ingenuity has been able to change it. The addition of weight in the ankle joint was not admissible; here were antagonizing conditions which put

Mr. Marks in a dilemma from which the abandonment of the ankle joint made his escape possible.

The rubber foot was the outgrowth of many months of thought; surrounded in its inception with dubious prospects, few had faith in it, and Mr. Marks himself was somewhat apprehensive of its future; the necessity of an ankle joint had ground itself so firmly in his ideas of the requirements of an artificial leg that to discard the joint altogether was to him more revulsive than otherwise.

In former editions of his pamphlet he replied in the following manner to the often asked question,

"HOW I CAME TO INVENT THE RUBBER FOOT."

"The reader will first impress in his mind that I had made artificial legs for some ten years after the old style, with ankle joints, wooden feet, etc., before I produced the rubber foot.

"I had during the last few years of this time become disgusted with the mode of constructing a wooden foot with mechanical joints at the ankle and toes, and had conceived the idea of a rubber foot, as many to whom I revealed my ideas can attest; but I was in a quandary as to a suitable plan for attachment, clinging as I did to the notion that an ankle joint was indispensable. While thus endeavoring to solve the problem, an old patient of mine called upon me and wanted me to construct a leg for him after a notion of his own. The patient had long been suffering from an irritable and diseased stump, which exuded a substance that saturated and destroyed the cords, joints, and springs of every artificial ankle joint he had ever used. He asked me rather bluntly if I would make him a leg *all solid* at the ankle, at the same time saying that he was poor and could not afford the expense attending the renewing of cords, springs, and joints in his artificial ankle joint. 'O yes,' I replied, 'that can be done by placing the cords on the outside of the leg and sheathing the joint.' He quickly rejoined, 'I mean, make me a leg without any cords or ankle joint whatever, perfectly stiff at the ankle.' To this I made answer 'No, sir, it would be of no use to you.'

"He persisted in arguing with me and finally got me to consent to make the experiment. While I was constructing the leg I was continually reasoning with myself, and recalling the fact that my best operators persisted in tightening their heel cords until they had practically destroyed all movement in the ankles. This being the case, I began to question the utility of an ankle joint. The leg was made for this man after his own ideas. The manner in which he walked, the ease and certainty attending every step, the ecstasy he manifested in the realization of his hopes,—the possession of an artificial leg that would withstand the severe tests of his diseased stump,—convinced me that, with the rubber foot attached, the great problem of constructing a leg strong, light, reliable, and comfortable was in my power of solution.

"I immediately applied myself to the development of the rubber foot, and forthwith put them in operation; first, by substituting them for old wooden feet on legs needing repairs. In every case I met with success which convinced me that the rubber foot was the desideratum. The success which has attended its use is now unquestioned and stands unparalleled as well as defiant against the arrogance of its 'old fogy competitors.'"

The rubber foot in its earliest days was somewhat crude; it possessed merits, but more were undeveloped; nearly a score of years elapsed before all its virtues were patent.

During the period of experiments, many rubber feet were applied to legs of other manufacturers, replacing the complicated ones and rendering the legs of greater utility. In every instance in which the wearer had tried the foot sufficiently long to overcome the novelty, the rubber foot succeeded in winning his admiration and the promise of his life-long patronage.

Manufacturers did not fail to observe the extensive inroads the rubber foot was making in the esteem and confidence of the crippled world, and the disaster the new departure threatened the old methods; they looked with fear and trembling on the multitudes fleeing from their patronage, and seeking the advantages of the new idea. They have at times stemmed the tide temporarily by circulating base rumors and false reports calculated to dissuade those whose fickleness makes them susceptible of being turned from their inclinations. Continuing to print reports from venal and questionable commissions who passed judgment on an undeveloped article years before many of the readers of this book were born is one of the tricks resorted to by some pretentious manufacturers even in this late day, and for the lack of something more recent and tangible we presume they will continue to do so to the end of their time. Like Xerxes commanding the sea to recede, they stand in danger of being engulfed by their own folly.

Notwithstanding the predictions of failure, and in defiance of the bitter opposition the rubber foot has always had to contend with, it has succeeded in making thousands of converts among the wearers of the old style.

Men, women and children walk, run, skate, dance, and toil to the amazement of others: performances regarded as impossible are daily being performed with naturalness. The farmer follows his plow on a rubber foot; the blacksmith works at his forge on a rubber foot; the sailor climbs the rigging, the builder erects houses, men and women of every vocation attend to their affairs with little concern as to their crippled condition; they all feel the assurance that the rubber foot is firm and reliable and will sustain them in their work, no matter what test may be brought to bear. No cords to stretch or break; no springs to weaken; no joints to squeak or make a hideous noise.

Evidences of the advantages of the rubber foot were accumulating, and had already reached such proportions as to command attention from the press, medical profession, and the scientific world; those who in earlier times were pronounced in its disfavor were fast coming to realize their mistake and gracefully acknowledge their errors.

ARGUMENT.

The movements of the rubber foot more closely approximate to those of the natural foot in walking or running than the movements of a mechanical ankle joint leg with wooden foot.

This may seem paradoxical, but if we study thoroughly the action of the natural ankle joint in walking or running under varied circumstances, we will be convinced of the statement, for we will observe that the amount of movement in the ankle joint is in all cases very limited and becomes more so the faster a man walks, until he reaches a very rapid speed, such as running, when the movement of the ankle joint is only such as to throw him from the toes of one foot to the toes of the other. At all times the natural movement is under the control of, and regulated by the mind. The eye telegraphs to the mind just the peculiarity of the surface on which the foot is to be placed. The mind responds by commanding certain tendons and muscles to operate, and the man walks gracefully, naturally, and with safety. Destroy the sympathy between the mind and the foot, and it will not be possible to achieve such results. Suppose a man be blindfolded and told to walk a certain distance on an unknown road; he will instinctively walk slowly, with a measured and feeling tread, and unless he meets with obstacles he will reach the end after much anxiety and concern. Require him to walk fast or run; if his foot strikes an irregularity in the ground he will in all probability fall and injure himself.

A man with an artificial leg with an ankle joint can be compared with the man walking rapidly in the dark, or with one who has lost control over his foot; every time he places the foot on the ground he does it with fear and uncertainty, because he has no will-power over the movements of his foot; a pebble or an uneven surface will throw him off his equilibrium; but with the rubber foot and rigid ankle every step is made with assurance—no rolling or wabbling about in order to conform to irregularities. Watch a man walk on his natural feet at an easy gait:

Fig. 101.

Fig. 102.

As he advances on his left, he elevates on the toes of his right. (See Fig. 101.)

He barely touches the heel of his left to the ground when he gives his body an impetus with the toes of his right (see Fig. 102); the ball of the left foot does not reach the ground until the propulsion given by the right foot has carried the body nearly vertically

Fig. 103.

Fig. 104.

Fig. 105.

over the left foot, at this point (see Fig. 103) his right foot having risen from the ground, is in the act of passing the left; it being carried well in advance of the left, the heel is placed to the ground at the moment the left is well raised on the ball (see Fig. 104); and the right foot rests flat on the ground when the left is taken from the ground and about to pass the right (see Fig. 105.)

This is repeated as the walking continues.

It should be observed that during these movements the plantar surface of the foot is on the ground but a short interval, and only at such times when the body is nearly and directly over the leg. The cuts used to illustrate these five positions have been carefully prepared from instantaneous photographs taken from men while walking at a moderately rapid speed on natural feet. They reveal very curious positions, such as one would scarcely dream of, and appear more grotesque than natural; they are nevertheless true, and present very striking illustrations of the theories embodied in the principle of the rubber foot. They show that on natural feet there is a time when the man stands on the heel of the advanced foot and on the toes of the receded foot, and that the plantar surface of the advanced foot does not reach the ground until the body is carried nearly over the advanced leg; as soon as the body is over the advanced leg, the heel of the receding leg begins to rise and the force of propulsion is obtained from the toes of that leg.

Let us contrast with these pictures the movements of a man wearing an artificial leg with a mechanical ankle joint. Advancing on his artificial leg, he strikes the heel to the ground; the toes almost immediately drop with a thud, and the plantar surface remains on the ground during the entire interval that the body is passing over the foot; the heel does not rise immediately, and the wearer has to exert himself to "get off" the foot; this exertion is an additional tax; it produces an awkwardness and a limp, and tires the wearer more than any other feature of the leg. Some makers of the ankle joint leg remedy these difficulties in a measure by tightening the cords, thus making the ankle joint practically rigid. When they do this they unquestionably improve the conditions; but why not dispense with the movement entirely if it is not to be used?

Having thus made plain the movements of the natural foot in walking, and having contrasted the movements of the mechanical foot, we are now prepared to show that the movements of the rubber foot with rigid ankle more closely approximate those of the natural foot.

The wearer advances on his rubber foot; he touches the heel to the ground first; the weight of the body being gradually applied to the rubber foot causes the rubber heel to compress sufficiently to bring the plantar surface to the ground at the moment when the body is nearly over the leg; as the body is thrown forward the weight is carried from the heel to the toes; the heel being relieved of its weight, its elasticity causes it to resume its shape; this assists in urging the body forward and throws the entire weight on the toes; the heel then elevates and continues to do so until the step is nearly completed, when the wearer is simultaneously placed in such a position as to throw his weight forward of and heavily on the ball of the foot; this gives the body a propulsion and urges the walking.

A comparison of the two methods in artificial legs, with and without an ankle joint, will show that with the artificial ankle joint the interval that the plantar surface rests on the ground is greater than that of the natural foot, while with the rubber foot and stiff ankle the interval is approximately the same, or possibly a trifle less; hence the argument.

If the reader will carry out this thought in detail, he will comprehend fully the many advantages possessed in our method of constructing artificial legs; he will understand why a man on a rubber foot can walk farther and faster than one who has an ankle-jointed leg which allows the plantar surface to remain on the ground longer intervals than nature allows her own ingeniously contrived foot.

In running, the contrast is still more striking, for with either the rubber or natural foot the plantar surface is never on the ground; it is the repeated act of springing from the toes of one foot to the toes of the other; but with the ankle-jointed foot, running is exceedingly awkward and unnatural, as there has to be a slight halt in every step in order to recover from the action of the springs. In standing on the rubber foot the plantar surface rests on the ground; and as there is no articulation in the ankle it supplies a large, balancing surface; hence, men with two rubber feet can stand in an easy, graceful manner, with perfect security and with restfulness; it is not necessary for him to place one foot at right angles to the other in order to brace himself.

The rubber foot affords the laborer a good substantial substitute on which he can rest and relieve his other leg, unaccompanied by uncertain or treacherous movements.

One of the patrons of the rubber foot, a painter by occupation, says: "I can climb a ladder or stand on a scaffold with perfect security. I can give my mind entirely to my work, and forget that I stand on an artificial leg, without risking my life. An ankle-joint leg would make me tottlish, and were I on a ladder I would have to depend more on my grasp than on my foot; but on the rubber foot and rigid ankle I feel absolutely safe."

The farmer who toils in the field can plod along over cobbles and clumps on a rubber foot with perfect safety; the accumulation of mud on his shoe will not cause the toes to drop and trip him; uneven surfaces will not throw him from his balance or bring violent jerks to his stump.

These arguments, we contend, are overwhelming in favor of the rigid ankle and rubber foot. We submit them to the consideration of the careful and thoughtful reader.

A matter of importance to the greater number of artificial limb wearers, those who are not overstocked with the bounties of this world, is that of

ECONOMY.

A leg or arm which requires frequent repairing is not a very desirable article, even for those who can meet the expense without feeling the drain on their purse ; to them it is a loss of time, a tax on their anxieties ; but to the man whose daily toil is his only means of livelihood, the occasional buying of a heel cord or an ankle spring materially affects his finances. It not only robs him of comfort, but deprives his family of many of the good things of this life. A few dollars every month, added to the already large demands, allows the wolf to get nearer his door.

We doubt that there is an artificial leg with an ankle joint made that will not require from $5 to $25 a year to keep the ankle in repair. We do not say this from any prejudice of our own, but from a careful survey of the complaints made by those who have worn them. A rubber foot without springs, cords, joints, or complicated attachments is absolutely free from even the possibility of such annoyances.

WHY AN ANKLE JOINT LEG IS NOT STRONG.

The conditions in an ankle-joint leg are such that weakness in and about the ankle is inseparable. Let any candid mind think of the matter for a few moments and he will arrive at this conclusion. In the first place, the ankle of an artificial leg ought, for appearance and convenience, to be reduced to approximately the size of the natural ankle. In the second place, the weight at and about the ankle must be reduced to the minimum.

It matters little if a pound of weight be added to the thigh of a leg ; it is scarcely felt ; but an ounce added to the foot, which, being removed some distance from the stump, will be burdensome and feel many times its actual weight. Now, in order to have any machinery compact enough to be enclosed in the narrow limits of an ankle, either weight or strength must be sacrificed ; for, if made strong enough to resist the enormous strain and weight of the wearer it must necessarily be made of heavy and strong material ; but this weight being objected to, the maker is compelled to rob those parts of their required strength. We have seen artificial legs constructed with very strong ankle joints, and when placed on the scales would not balance more than the conventional weight ; but examination would show that, in order to get the total weight of the leg reduced to that amount, the thigh piece, joints, and socket had been robbed of their substance and the ankle made heavy.

COMPARATIVE WEIGHT.

Unscrupulous manufacturers of the complicated ankle-joint artificial legs, in their arguments against the rubber foot, compare rubber with wood, and say the ratio which exists between the specific gravities of wood and rubber exists the same between artificial legs made with wooden feet with ankle joints and those with rubber feet. We do not hesitate in branding this as an unwarranted falsehood. We admit that rubber is heavier than wood, but notice should be taken of the iron hinges, bolts, cords, glass balls, screws, and the many trappings required in the attachment of the wooden foot and composing the ankle joint; these attachments are heavier than rubber and add considerably to the weight of the leg, all of which are absent in the rubber foot.

In every case where feet with ankle joints have been removed from legs of other manufacturers and rubber feet applied in their stead, the total weight of each leg has never been increased, but, on the contrary, in nearly every case the total weight has been diminished by the change from one to eight ounces. It should be noticed that this reduction of weight has been made entirely in the foot and ankle, which, being removed so far from the stump, becomes a matter of favorable concern to the wearer.

Our artificial legs with rubber feet, for ordinary adults, weigh from three and a half to six pounds, depending upon the size and requirements of the leg. A leg for a delicate lady of ordinary size should not weigh over three and a half pounds; but for a large, robust, laboring man it can not be made of lasting strength and weigh less than six pounds. These weights are of the leg alone.

The disposition of the weight of a leg can be so made that a leg weighing six pounds will feel lighter when in use than another weighing half as much with the weight otherwise disposed.

If the thigh part and knee of the leg are made strong and heavy, as they should be in severe cases, and the foot made light, better results will follow than if the weight is disposed conversely; although the legs in either case may weigh the same, there will be a great difference in the apparent weight when operating. The use of the rubber foot with rigid ankle renders it possible to dispose of the weight in an advantageous manner.

A strong, heavy thigh piece, with heavy knee joints and a light foot will make the leg lasting, and give the wearer more control over it, and at the same time feel light and secure.

REQUIRED WEIGHT.

The ideas of those wearing artificial legs in regard to weight are variable and can not be taken as a criterion. Some say, "Make the leg as light as possible; if you can reduce the weight to a pound so much the better." Others say, "Do not make my leg too light. I have worn them light and heavy, and I find I can walk more steadily and step more naturally with a leg of moderate weight than with one extremely light. The leg should act like a pendulum, so that in raising it after taking a step its weight will be sufficient to cause it to swing beyond the center of the body without an exertion on the muscles of the stump." These ideas being antagonistic with each other, and both being tenable, throws one in doubt on the subject, and we are compelled to ask the experienced wearer to choose for himself and instruct us accordingly.

When left to our judgment we always make an effort to reduce the weight to the minimum, taking into consideration the sex, weight, age, and the occupation of the wearer. If a man asks us to make him a leg to last him twenty years, we will endeavor to accommodate him, but he must expect to receive a leg more or less heavy, large, and staunch.

HOW LONG WILL AN ARTIFICIAL LEG LAST?

The question is frequently asked, How long will an artificial leg last? Our reply is invariably, "That depends on the care that is given to it." We can boast of patrons who are now wearing, and have continuously worn, an artificial leg made for them twenty-five years ago, and bids fair to last many years longer; but this is exceptional, and should not be mentioned as a criterion, no more than some of our patrons who, through abuse and recklessness, wear their artificials out in a very short time.

An average made of the frequency with which our patrons renew their substitutes fixes the intervals at about every eight years.

Renewals are made as a general thing, not because the artificial is worn out and dilapidated, but because the wearer wants a new one, the same as he wants a new coat before the old coat is worn out.

Men become as proud of their artificials as they do of any article of apparel, and those with abundant means frequently supply themselves with several, and keep them in reserve for changes or emergencies. Then again, changes sometimes take place in the stump, and require a new leg. Taking all these facts into consid--

eration and fixing the average at eight years is actually depriving the leg of much of its deserved credit.

The United States government with its usual liberality has fixed the interval for the issuing of artificial limbs to pensioners at five years.

SHOES AND STOCKINGS.

All artificial feet should be dressed with stockings and shoes or boots the same as the natural. Ankle-joint feet on account of the ankle movement will "chew" a stocking and wrinkle a shoe in a very brief time; they not only wear out a greater number of stockings than the natural foot, but in a short time give the shoe a slovenly and ungainly appearance.

The rubber foot operates quite the opposite; there is no ankle articulation to wrinkle or break the boot or tear the stocking; at the toes the wrinkling is perfectly natural, giving the entire shoe an agreeable appearance. We have heard wearers say that in five years the rubber foot had saved them, in the cost of stockings and shoes, a sum of money nearly sufficient to buy a new leg.

AN INDISPUTABLE FACT.

The most overwhelming argument in favor of the principles involved in the rubber foot leg is the fact that at this writing over eight thousand are in use, distributed in all parts of the world; this vast army of restored cripples testify to the world the satisfactory use and the astounding performances their rubber feet render them capable of doing.

The most enthusiastic of our patrons are those who have worn the ankle-joint legs of various patterns; they invariably say that when the rubber foot and the ankle-joint foot are contrasted with respect to their capabilities of meeting the wants of the wearer the rubber foot possesses overwhelming advantages.

Over eight thousand cripples, representing every nationality, every possible vocation, both sexes, and every grade of life and society, operating with rubber extremities, with naturalness and comfort, with perfect concealment of their loss, make a prestige the rubber foot and hand alone enjoy. Is it possible that the reader can ask for more striking testimony or more convincing argument than this simple fact; is not such evidence conclusive, and sufficient to dispel every vestige of doubt? If it is not, then indeed has reason succumbed to prejudice.

Over seven hundred letters of commendation will be found in this book; each is a witness testifying in favor of our claims; this vast number we regard sufficient to establish our points beyond cavil. We hope the reader will do this book the honor of reading these testimonials and drawing his own conclusions from them. Each testimonial is a story by itself, interesting in portraying bits of individual history.

ARTIFICIAL LEGS.

Ease and comfort to the wearer in the adjustment, naturalness and elasticity in the movements, durability in the construction and safety in the operation, are the paramount requirements of an artificial leg; any artificial leg devoid of any one of these qualities is deficient and should not be worn. We claim that our artificial legs with rubber feet possess every one of these conditions in the highest degree, in contradistinction with those manufactured upon the old principles with complicated ankle joints. The leg is in the first place made to fit the stump so as to secure the greatest degree of comfort; the knee-joint and elastic foot enable the leg to operate with freedom and elasticity; these conditions are so combined as to secure great durability.

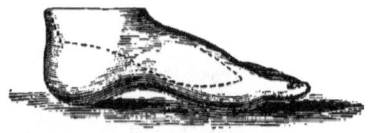

No. 106.

Cut No. 106 represents the rubber foot as originally invented and patented in 1863.

It was mostly made of rubber of a very spongy, light, and elastic character. A piece of willow wood nearly filling the foot at the back and top furnished the medium by which the foot was secured to the leg; this core extended down about two-thirds the distance from the ankle to the bottom of the heel, then downwards and forwards to a point corresponding to the toe movement of a natural foot as shown by the dotted lines. After a number of years it was discovered that, in cases where the wearer bore heavily on the toes, the toes would not always spring back to their proper position; to overcome this objection strips of strong duck were attached to the block as represented in cut No. 107.

On either side of these strips of duck, rubber is chemically attached and vulcanized with the remainder of the foot.

THE NEW PATENT FOOT.

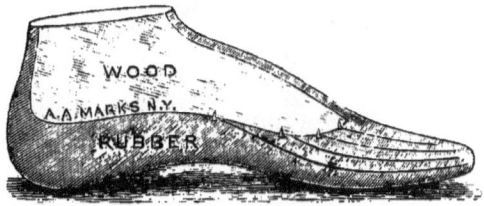

No. 107.

The object of this improvement is not only to add to the great durability of the foot, but give greater spring to the toes and cause them to return to the proper position with certainty.

A little consideration will show that in consequence of these layers of duck two forces are created at every movement of the toes, one operating at right angles to the layers, and the other longitudinal and coincident with them; these two forces combine to make a resultant and a very powerful force which operates as designed. This improvement remedies effectually the only defect originally incident to the rubber foot and the one so much exaggerated and contemned by some of our competitors. Special Letters Patent were issued by the United States for this feature.

Artificial legs herein described are made to fit the person with great care; either with the presence of the wearer, or from measurements supplied by him. In either case each leg when completed and delivered will be accompanied, without extra charge, by the following

ACCESSORIES.

Above the knee or knee-bearing leg: The necessary suspenders attached, one sock for the stump, screw-driver, box of grease, extra spring, and a book of instructions.

Leg for amputation below knee: Necessary suspenders attached, one long and one short sock for the stump, pocket oil can, screw-driver, extra lacing, and book of instructions.

Leg for ankle-joint amputation: Sock for stump, extra lacing.

When desired the leg will be securely boxed and delivered to express or freight office in New York City without additional charge.

LEGS FOR THIGH AMPUTATIONS.

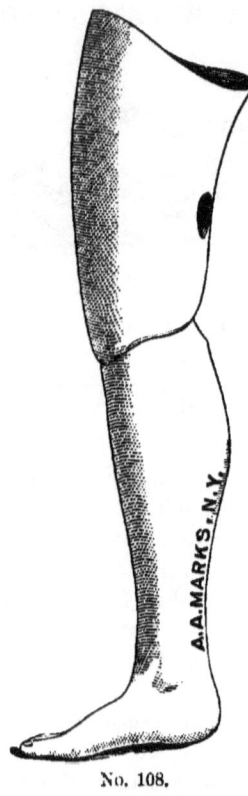

No. 108.

Cut No. 108 presents a side view of a leg, designed for any amputation that has been made at any point above the condyles of the femur, or, as usually denominated, for amputation above the knee. The body of the leg is constructed of willow wood, both upper and lower sections. The leg is firmly attached to a rubber foot at the ankle. The thigh section is hollowed to accommodate the stump comfortably; it is then dressed down on the outside until it assumes a comely and natural appearance, of as near the dimensions of the natural leg as possible.

The calf is but a shell of such character as to combine strength and comeliness.

The end of the stump in cases where the femur has in part been amputated is not allowed to come in contact with either the bottom or the walls of the socket, except in exceptional cases in which the periosteal covering of the extremity of the femur has been preserved, the tissues ample and non-adherent to the bone, forming a comfortable and safe cushion to bear upon.

It is unreasonable to think of bearing on the end of a stump in which these conditions do not prevail.

Generally, the weight is carried on the back section of the rim of the thigh piece, which is left thick and chamfered to receive comfortably a section of the ischium or buttock of the wearer.

Some manufacturers fit the socket for thigh amputations so as to carry the weight on that edge of the thigh piece that contacts with the perinæum or crotch. We are opposed to this method, because, in the first place, it is a very irritable place to take weight; in the second, the act of taking weight at that point tends to influence the wearer to spread his legs and straddle in walking; and in the third place it is not at all necessary.

The seat is partially prepared by nature to bear this pressure, and it seems to us proper to take advantage of the privilege nature has so kindly offered. In cases when the extremity of the stump is well protected with non-adherent tissue, and the wearer can bear his whole weight on the end without experiencing unpleasant sensations, we take advantage of the opportunity and place a soft cushion or pad inside the socket, of sufficient thickness to receive as much of the weight of the wearer as may be found prudent.

Advantage should be taken of this opportunity whenever it is offered.

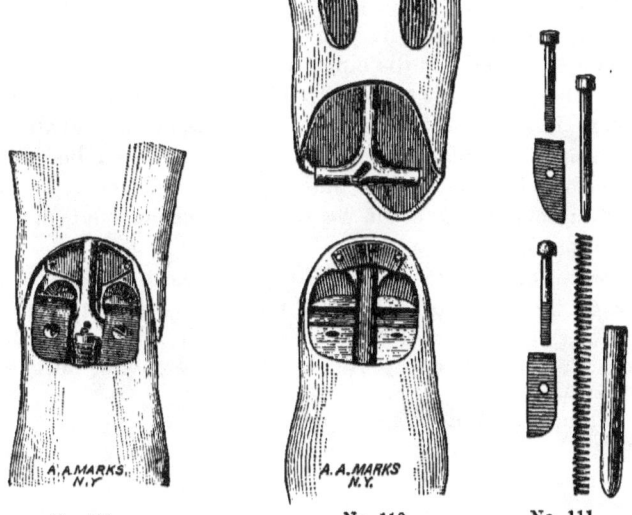

No. 109.   No. 110.   No. 111.

Cut No. 109 represents a back view of the knee joint of all No. 108 legs. Its arrangement is unique and possesses many advantages, for which special Letters Patent have been issued by the United States.

Cut No. 110 presents the same joint disconnected, with all the parts exposed. The joint has the shape of an inverted T, hence its name tee-joint. This joint is made of tough gun steel, forged from one piece of metal. The projecting arms rest in boxes and are held there by two hard wood caps, which are secured by steel screws passing through the leg into steel nuts.

The wearer has command over this joint; he can tighten or loosen the bearings at will, have the joints operate snugly or loosely as he chooses, thus obviating the rattle incident to wear.

The small steel lever with ball on end projecting from the back of the joint operates in the concavity of a hard wood piston; this piston is inserted in one end of a steel spring about seven inches long; this spring is encased with leather and placed in a drawn brass cylinder, the convex end of which rests on a bridge placed in the interior of the leg in the region of the calf. The spring, piston, cylinder, cap, and screws are illustrated in cut No. 111. The operation of the spring is two-fold; it urges the lower leg forward in walking, and, by the automatic reversal of its direction of force, holds the leg back when the knee is bent at right angles as in sitting. The power of the spring can be increased or diminished. If it is desired to increase the power, a little packing can be tamped in the cylinder, and if it is desired to diminish the power, a link or two can be cut from one end of the spring. If the wearer does not want to use a spring in the knee he can remove it from the leg without being required to disjoint the leg or mutilate some of its parts. When the leg is together and in working order the knee movement is arrested by the striking of the vertical shaft of the joint against a pad placed in the knee; this pad can be increased or diminished by the wearer, and the knee movement caused to cease at any angle to suit the wearer or to accommodate a low or high heel on the shoe.

The center of movement of this patented knee is placed back of the line of the center of gravity of the wearer when standing; the purpose of this is to secure the knee against treacherous bending.

Price of this leg, complete, with any style of suspender, each, $100.00.

Measurements required are explained on pages 60 to 65.

Cut No. 112 represents a style of leg for amputation above the knee with a lock attachment in the knee. This arrangement is

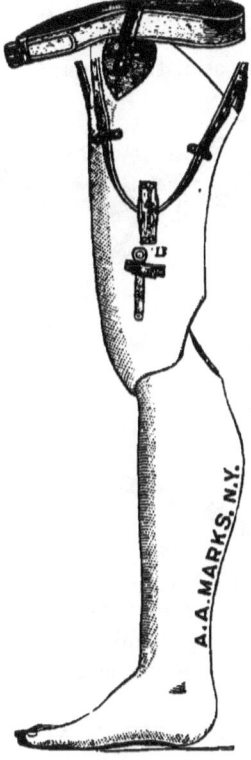

No. 112.

calculated for persons who have become accustomed to a stiff knee leg and desire to have the knee locked when walking or riding horseback. The button B placed on the end of a lever is operated by the hand ; when this lever is placed forward sufficiently to catch in the lever guide, the knee is locked, and can not move; and conversely, when the lever is placed back sufficiently to catch in a second place, the knee is unlocked and at liberty, and will bend naturally for sitting conveniences, as in cut No. 113.

The button B is made large so that it can be readily found through the clothing and operated by the hand without attracting attention or causing inconvenience to the wearer. We do not apply this locking arrangement to every leg, as in most cases it is uncalled for and utterly useless ; we only apply it in cases where we are directed to do so by the ordering party.

We have a Baptist clergymen who finds this locking arrangement of peculiar advantage while performing the rites of immersion, on account of the buoyancy of the lower leg, and the weak knee spring he insists upon wearing; the leg will double under him at the first step unless some similar method is adopted to prevent the knee from yielding to the forces of the water.

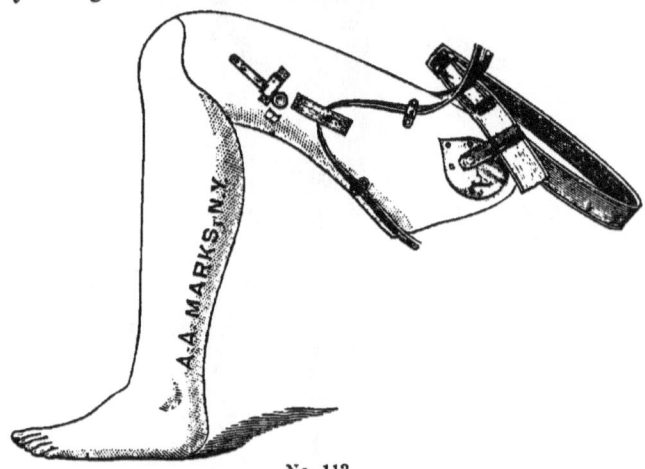

No. 113.

In cases of extremely short or enervated stumps this locking arrangement will be found of advantage. We make no additional charge in the price of the leg for this knee attachment when actually required. The price and measurements required are the same as for leg No. 108.

HIP-JOINT AND WAIST BELT.

Cuts No. 112 and 113 show our hip-joint and waist belt attachment, designed to give the body control over the leg and relieve the stump of some of the burden. It is calculated to be used only where the stump is weak, or force required to overcome objectionable tendencies of the stump; for example, a man going on one crutch for some years will influence his stump so as to hang off from a vertical line. An ordinary leg applied to a stump in this condition would straddle and give the wearer some annoyance; but the hip-joint will force the stump to its proper line and hold it there while the leg is being worn. The socket of the leg is made of sufficient length on the outside to extend nearly to the hip motion; the steel joint is attached at A and works on a plate; a belt passing around the abdomen holds the joint to its place. The hip-joint is applied only when ordered, as it is exceptionally required. We make no additional charge in the price of leg when the joint is actually required. In addition to measurements explained on pages 60 to 65, give circumference of abdomen.

Cut No. 114 represents a leg with laced thigh piece calculated for thigh amputations in which bearing can be taken on the end.

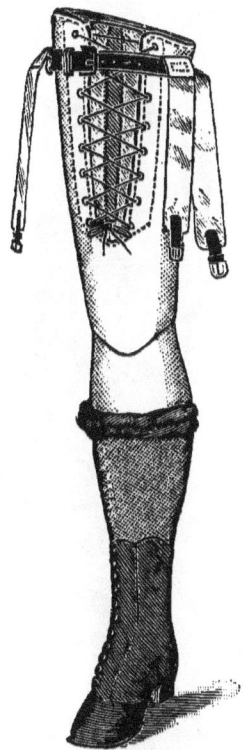

No. 114.

The question may be asked, Why do we not make all sockets for thigh amputations so as to lace and adjust, thus provide for the emaciation that most always takes place in stumps after an artificial leg is worn? Our reply is, that in cases where all the weight must be carried on the top edge of the artificial leg the laced thigh is not resistant enough to oppose the weight of the wearer; when weight can be borne on the end of the stump in whole or in part, it is not necessary to have the top edge so thoroughly resistant, and the leg represented in the above cut can be applied.

Price and measurements required, same as for leg No. 108.

The T-joint used in legs thus far described can not be used in legs for thigh amputations of great length. The mechanism of the T-joint occupies a space of about three inches above the center of the knee movement, if the stump is so long that it requires some of this space, it is either necessary to make the artificial thigh longer than the natural, or to use the bolt joint (described hereafter); the former alternative being objected to compels us to resort to the latter.

No. 115.

Cut No. 115 represents a leg for thigh amputation in which the stump extends very nearly to the knee-joint. The knee movements are analogous to those obtained with the T-joint; its mechanism is illustrated in cuts Nos. 119–120 and described on page 34; when compared with the T-joint it has some disadvantage; for example, the adjustability of the bearings and the method of compensating for the wear; these, however, are nominal, as the wearer can bush the bearing to obtain any desired movement or compensate for the wear. Price and measurements required, same as for leg No. 108.

LEGS FOR KNEE-JOINT AMPUTATIONS.

Knee-joint disarticulations are various; some have the condyles trimmed, others have not; some have non-adherent tissues and others adherent; and as a result some can bear pressure on end and others can not ; on account of these various conditions it is necessary to consider carefully each case and treat it accordingly.

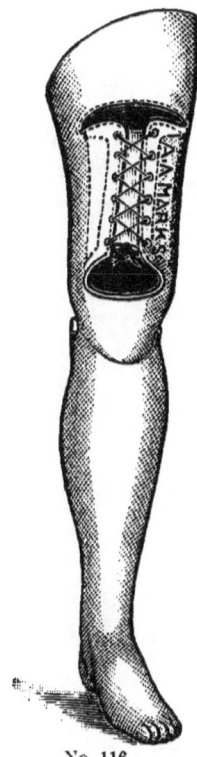

No. 116.

Cut No. 116 represents a leg for knee disarticulation, one in which the articular surfaces of the condyles have been trimmed, but the tubercles or side projections untouched ; it is seldom possible to bear on the end of such an amputation. The bulbous sides give the stump a greater lateral diameter than just above them. In order to hold the stump firm in the socket and prevent irritation it is necessary to make the fitting so that the socket will compress the stump just above the condyles, and at the same time give the condyles absolute freedom from contact.

In leg No. 116 the stump is inserted from the top and prevented from entering too far by the upper annular wooden socket coming in contact with the ischium and pelvis ; after the stump is inserted and in place the socket is laced tightly and the stump held firmly ; heavy shoulder suspension is unnecessary.

Price of this leg, complete, with any style of suspender, each $100.00.

Measurements required are explained on pages 60 to 65.

Cut No. 117 represents a leg for ordinary knee disarticulation in which the condyles have not been trimmed, with the patella removed or not, and the weight of the wearer capable of being

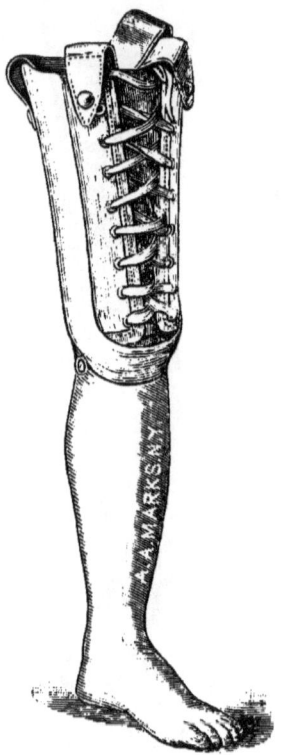

No. 117.

carried in whole or in part on the end. The fitting is made to receive comfortably the end of the stump, so as to give abundant space for the sides of the condyles and hold the stump firmly just above. A soft cushion is placed in the socket on which the stump rests; the stump is then laced firmly in place; the tubercles on the sides of the extremity of the femur afford a means for holding the leg without depending entirely on shoulder suspension. When but part of the weight can be borne on the end of the stump the thigh socket is made to extend well up to the body with flaring posterior top to be opposed by the ischium.

Price and measurements required, same as for leg No. 116.

All the conditions of knee-joint amputations are regarded, and modifications of the various kinds of legs described in this book are made to meet cases to the greatest possible advantage.

KNEE-BEARING ARTIFICIAL LEGS.

The class of legs denominated knee-bearing, include all kinds in which the weight is taken on the knee of the stump while the stump is in a flexed position.

Any one of the following conditions will require the use of a knee bearing leg :

Anchylosis of the knee-joint in a flexed position.

Remediless contraction of the extensors, limiting the knee movement to not more than one half.

Length of tibia insufficient to be of service in controlling the knee movement of an artificial leg.

If there is a possibility of utilizing the stump from the knee down for controlling the knee movements of the artificial leg, advantage should be taken of it, and No. 123 leg, page 37, should be selected instead of the knee-bearing.

We are aware that with inexperienced persons it is sometimes a difficult matter to determine which style of leg should be used, and that certain conditions of the stump make the choice problematic ; the conditions above mentioned will, as a general thing, guide one safely.

It is very frequently the case that from long periods of disuse, or from carrying the stump in a flexed position a great length of time, that the knee extensors become contracted. The contraction is sometimes very great and the recovery of full movement without the aid of the knife a matter of serious doubt ; in such a case a knee-bearing leg should unquestionably be used, but it may be safely asserted, as a rule, that for all contractions of one half the natural movement or less, our No. 123 artificial leg will bring a gentle, constant, and painless tension on the extensors and by degrees force them to relax and thus ultimately reclaim the full knee movement. An artificial leg will almost invariably accomplish this without any assistance, and without occasioning confinement, hindrance, or suffering.

If the length of the stump is a question of doubt in the selection of the style of leg the following test may be used : flex the stump and see if the projection from the back of the thigh or the distance from the popliteal space to the end of the tibia is sufficient to afford an opposing surface ; one and a half inches are usually sufficient.

If the projection is less than that, a knee-bearing leg should be selected.

Cut No. 118 represents a knee-bearing leg. The thigh piece is hollowed to accommodate the stump; the natural knee rests on a

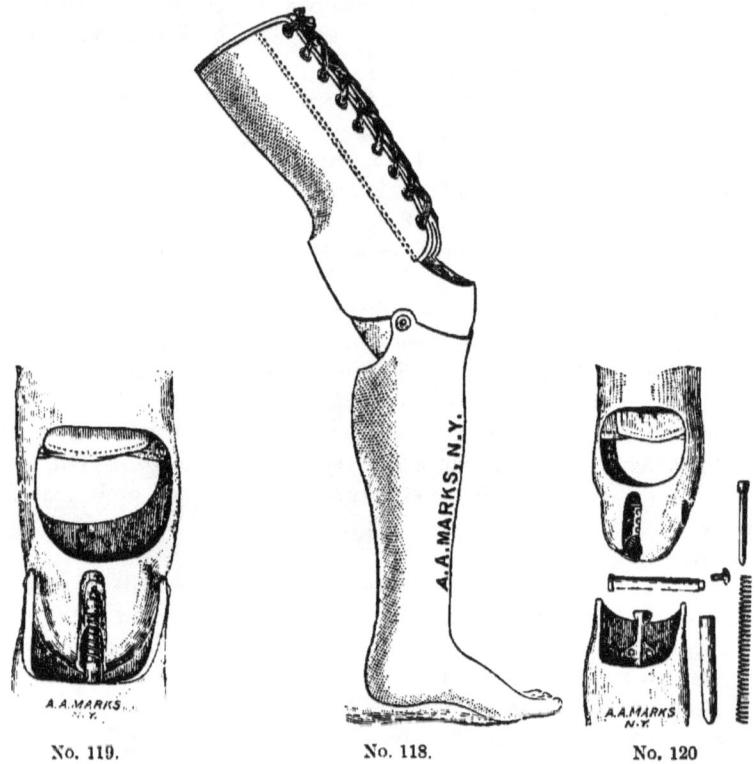

No. 119.   No. 118.   No. 120.

cushion; the weight of the wearer bears on the knee; the projecting stump, if very long, protrudes from the back of the socket; the stump is held firmly in place by a strong lacing.

The cut represents the leg slightly bent at the knee, a slight pressure on the ball of the foot to show the yielding quality of the rubber.

From the knee to the foot the leg is of wood, carved to as near the shape of the natural leg as the construction of the leg will allow; it is hollowed to obtain lightness, and covered with parchment to secure strength. The mechanism of the knee may be understood by the following cuts:

Cut No. 119 presents a rear view of the knee with all the parts together and ready for use.

Cut No. 120 presents the same knee with all the parts separated.

The bolt is the bearing surface; it is made of fine steel; passing through the lower extremity of the thigh, it is secured to the lower leg by steel strips; one end of the bolt is flanged and the other squared; both are received in steel plates, fitted tightly and held in place by a steel screw. It is thus seen that the bolt is held to the lower leg firmly and the thigh section of the leg caused to move about it. The length of this bolt in ordinary cases is four inches; this secures a very large bearing surface, and increases its lasting qualities. The knee movement is stopped at the proper angle by an opposing brace secured to the lower leg; this brace impacts against a rubber cushion; a steel spiral spring assists the knee in its movements. The arrangement of the spring in this joint is similar in its action to that described on page 25 and posses-

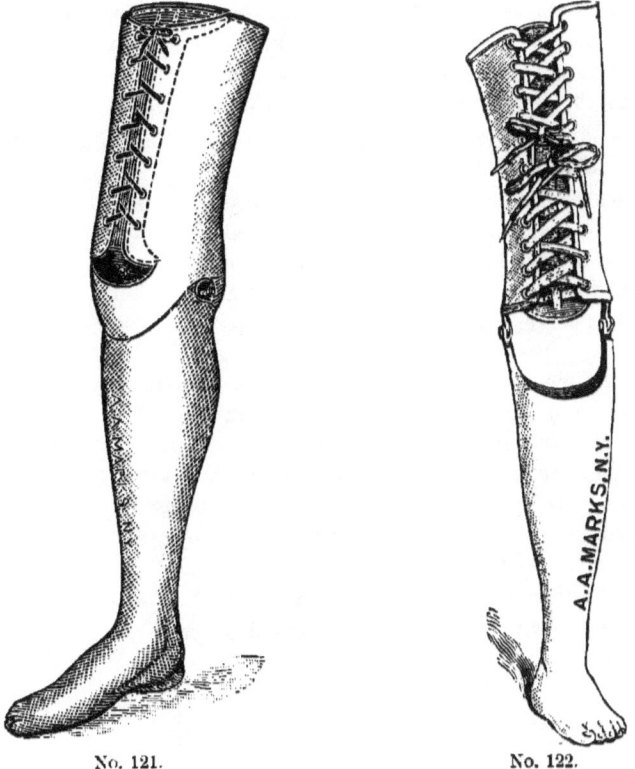

No. 121.   No. 122.

ses the same advantages. This method of constructing a knee-bearing leg secures very great strength and very excellent knee movement; it has one disadvantage, however. On account of the mechanism of the knee being placed below the stump, the thigh is elongated from two to three inches.

Most wearers do not object to this, as it is scarcely noticeable, and the advantage of its durability more than compensates that of appearance, which at the best is but critical; when, however, the additional length of thigh is objected to, and the wearer is willing to sacrifice some of the strength, side joints can be used instead of the bolt; as in Cut No. 121. The center of movement of the joint in this style of leg is placed above the plane of the lower extremity of the knee of the stump; this admits of trimming off the end of socket to very near the knee of the stump, and to about the length of the natural thigh. The mechanism of the knee is fully explained in Cut 124.

Knee-bearing artificial legs are very comfortable to wear, and with persons who take pride in operating their artificials, their movements become quite natural and the results are very flattering.

It can not be expected that the knee movement is as sure and natural as when the stump from the knee down is utilized in controlling the artificial knee movement as in No. 123.

The price of either No. 118 or 121 style, complete, with any style of suspender, each $100.00.

Measurements required are explained on pages 60 to 65.

Cut No. 122 represents a leg calculated for an amputation a short distance below the knee, with stump extended and anchylosed.

The thigh socket is made of wood and leather; it is excavated to receive the thigh of the stump comfortably and to hold it firmly.

All the weight of the wearer is carried on this socket by compression and by the top edge coming in contact with the ischium.

The stump from knee down does not touch any part of the leg.

When sitting the knee of the artificial leg bends naturally; but the stump, being stiff and unyielding, protrudes beyond the leg.

An auxiliary spring is attached to the front of the leg to assist the operations of the knee.

Price, complete with suspender, each, $100.00.

Measurements required are explained on pages 60 to 65.

LEGS FOR BELOW-KNEE AMPUTATIONS.

Any leg designed for an amputation that has been made between the knee and ankle, and the stump from the knee down used in controlling the knee movements of the artificial leg, is included in this class.

Any stump with half or more movement of the knee, and with projection when bent at right angles of one and a half inches or more, measured from the popliteal space to the end, can be properly fitted with a leg of this class.

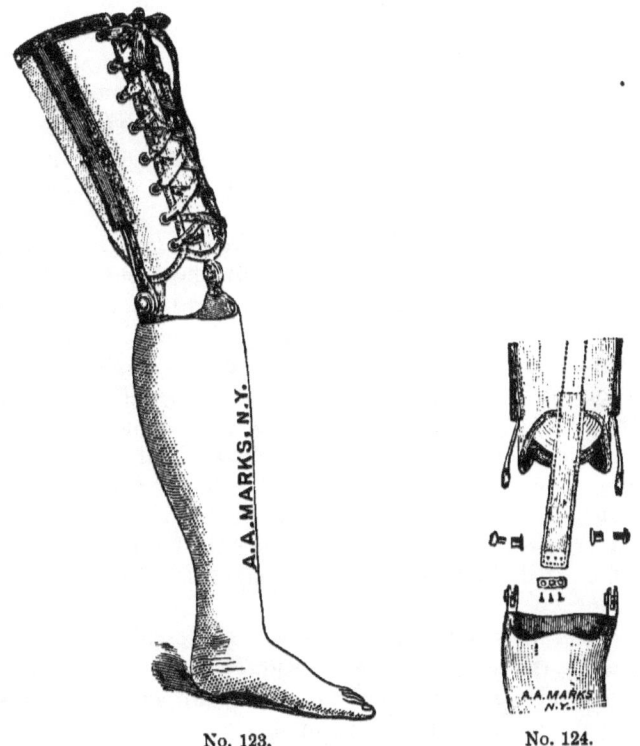

No. 123.   No. 124.

Cut No. 123 represents a leg for amputation below the knee as above described. The leg from the knee to the rubber foot is made of tough kiln-dried willow wood hollowed to receive the stump properly and comfortably; it is then dressed down on the outside to as near the shape and size of the natural leg as possible; the leg is then covered with parchment or buckskin to give it strength. The thigh section is made of strong oak-tan russet leather covered with soft buckskin. The knee joints are made of steel of sufficient strength to stand the wear of years. The cut represents the leg with considerable pressure on the heel to show the compressibility of the rubber. The interior of the leg both above and below the knee has the contours of the stump. The stump is inserted and laced about the thigh sufficiently tight to hold it firmly in place.

Weight is carried in part on the thigh and on the anterior, interior, and posterior surfaces of the stump just below the knee.

In cases of hyperæsthesia or extreme sensitiveness about the stump the weight is carried entirely on the thigh.

It is rarely the case that pressure can be applied to the extremity of any stump in which amputation has been made in the shaft of the bone, unless the tissues are all well preserved and the end of the tibia provided with a good natural non-adherent cushion; under these conditions only can weight be taken on the end with impunity; when such favorable conditions exist advantage can be derived from bearing on the end; we then place a soft pad in the leg. This pad can be increased, diminished, or withdrawn by the wearer as he finds advisable.

Cut No. 124 represents the leg disjointed at the knee with all the parts exposed. The upper joints fit the slots of the lower joints; a bolt passes through each, and held in place by a screw. The strap extending from the thigh piece downward is termed the check strap and is applied to the leg for the purposes of checking the movement of the knee, and avoiding the metallic sound which would result if the stops in the joints were alone depended on. This strap is secured firmly to the thigh piece at the upper end, and screwed to the calf of the leg at the lower end. This strap can be shortened or lengthened as may be desired.

We have said that an amputation below the knee with knee movement of one-half or more should be supplied with a leg of this class.

The object in view being to take advantage of the amount of movement that exists, with the intention of restoring full movement by the influence of the artificial leg. For contraction of not greater than one-quarter, an ordinary leg of this class will usually perform the work of restoration; but for contraction of a greater degree it is necessary to make some modifications.

Cut No. 125 represents a leg especially designed for such purpose.

The leg is constructed so as to receive the stump in the position of its greatest extension; the stump and thigh are firmly held in place by lacing; the shelf on which the stump rests is capable of being inclined at different angles; by changing the angle from time to time a gentle and increasing tension is exerted on the tendons, which causes them ultimately to relax, and thus restore full movement.

Price for No. 123 or 125 complete with suspender, each, $100.00.

Measurements required are explained on pages 60 to 65.

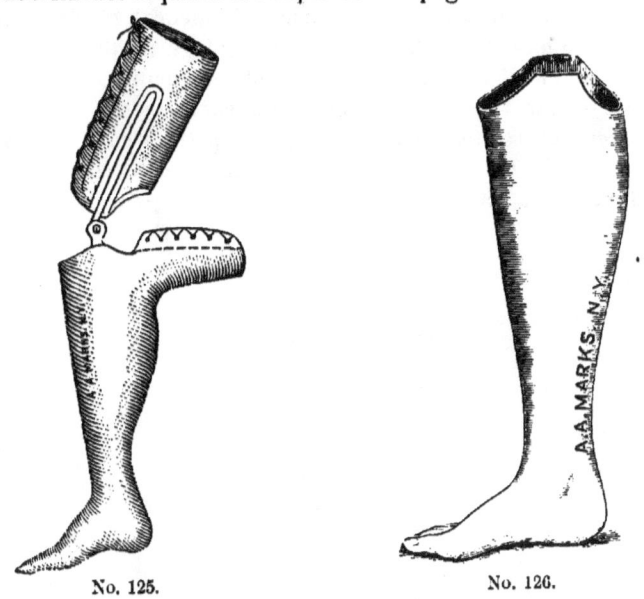

No. 125.   No. 126.

Cut No. 126 represents an artificial leg for amputation below the knee without thigh support. Such can only be worn with long and powerful stumps. If the irregularities of the stump will not hold the leg sufficiently secure, straps are attached, to either pass around the thigh or pass over the shoulder, or both, as may be desired.

Price complete, each, $65.00.

Measurements required are explained on pages 60 to 65.

WATERPROOF LEGS.

Many wearers of artificial legs follow vocations that require them to stand or walk in water for a considerable length of time, and in consequence have been obliged to use peg legs, as there has never been an artificial leg made that would effectually resist this destructive element. Joints, springs, and cords in the ankle would rust, break, or stretch, and all the glued parts would loosen and become detached. Our endeavor has been to construct a leg that would meet this want.

No. 127.

Cut No. 127 is a sectional view of our recently invented waterproof leg. The core in the foot and the body of the leg are cut from one piece of wood, with the grain in the foot at about right angles to the grain in the leg, and continuous with it; this is done to give the leg strength. The rubber foot is secured to this core in the usual manner. It will be seen that there are no glued or attached parts whatever to be affected by water or perspiration. This leg is peculiarly suitable for long stumps, as exudations from the stump will not weaken or destroy it. This natural crook leg is secured by U. S. Letters Patent.

The same principle can be used for any point of amputation.

Price same as quoted.

LEGS FOR AMPUTATIONS IN OR BELOW ANKLE-JOINTS.

Amputations known as Symes', Pirogoff's, Chopart's, Lisfranee's, Hey's, etc., are performed with the purpose of bearing the weight on the end or remaining plantar surface, and with rare exceptions the stump is capable of doing so. The construction of artificial feet for this class of amputations has perplexed the maker more than any other. The limited distance from the end of the stump to the floor debarred the possibility of making an artificial foot light, neat, durable, and helpful, until the rubber foot and natural crook solved the problem. Most manufacturers who pretend to, treat this class of amputations construct a very frail appliance, which merely restores the foot in appearance, but affords no assistance whatever in walking. A person must be able to raise his entire weight on the ball of his foot and elevate the heel in order to walk naturally, easily, quickly, and helpfully; if the artificial foot has an ankle-joint that will not enable him to stand on the ball of the foot, it becomes a worthless appendage, hindering in all its operations; this difficulty is an insurmountable one to all adherents of the ankle-joint. In order to make an ankle-joint foot sufficiently resistant about the ankle to oppose so much strain, the attaching contrivances must extend up the sides of the stump, and in doing this much objectionable weight and bulkiness will be added to the ankle; all the attaching parts would furthermore be insecure and unreliable, as they would be contiguous with the stump, and consequently affected by the exudations of the stump.

Our method of constructing this class of leg is in a very simple manner and meets the requirements in every essential.

The socket which surrounds the stump and the core of the foot are carved from one piece of wood; the grain in the core is approximately at right angles with the grain in the socket; the fibers are thus unbroken and in continuous lines, following the contours of the limb, as shown by Cut No. 127; consequently they are disposed in a manner the most advantageous to oppose the greatest strain.

This is accomplished by cutting the socket and core from the root or branch of a tree in which the natural grain follows a favorable curve. The rubber foot is moulded about the core, and all are secured in the most substantial manner. It is thus seen that there are no attached, glued, or metallic parts to be affected by perspiration. We have two methods of fitting these feet; one receives the stump from the front and the other from the rear.

Cut No. 128 represents the former. The fitting is made so that the stump is comfortably encased and secured by lacing.

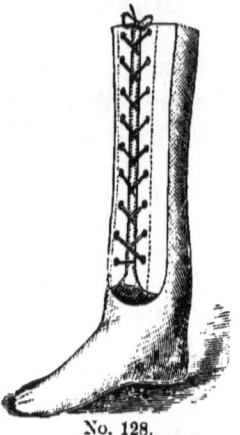

No. 128.

The entire weight is carried on the end in all cases where there is a good flap and there are no objecting conditions.

No. 129.

Cut No. 129 presents a typical Symes amputation; the flap is brought to the front, where it is sutured; the cicatrix is anterior and lateral; the end of this stump is as capable of bearing weight as the heel of the companion foot. The extremity of the stump of any of these amputations is usually bulbous and considerably larger than just above; this condition is fortunate, as it affords a means of holding the foot without resorting to thigh support.

No. 130.

Cut No. 130 presents the same case with artificial foot applied and ready to be dressed with stocking and shoe.

This method of inserting the stump from the front of the foot has some minor objections; all the strain occasioned by rising on the toes is communicated to the sides and rear of the leg; to oppose this strain effectually it is necessary to leave the wood at those places of considerable thickness; this adds to the bulkiness of the ankle. This objection is met by leg represented in Cut No. 122.

Cut No. 131 represents either a Symes or a Pirogoff stump.

Cut No. 132 represents the artificial foot which receives the stump from the rear; by this method we are able to place the resisting part of the leg to the front of the stump and nearer the ball of the foot, thus diminishing the leverage, and consequently allowing the removal of a proportionate amount of material.

As there is no strength required at the sides of the extremity of the stump, the socket can be cut entirely away at those points, thus admitting of a lateral diameter of no greater dimension than the stump itself. This method also admits of a graceful and smooth curve to the front and the instep of the foot and reduces the dimensions of the heel and instep to the minimum; this alone is a very desirable advantage over the former method.

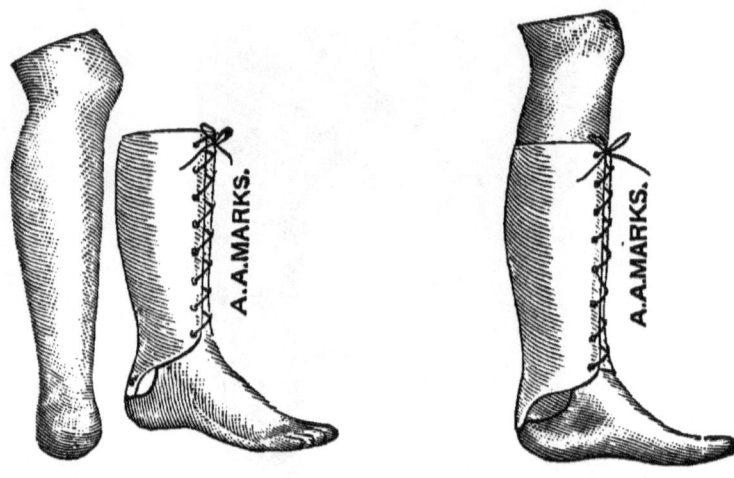

No. 131.   No. 132.   No. 133.

The fitting of the socket is such as to bear comfortably on each side of tibia of the stump; the stump is held in place by a leather case which surrounds the body of the leg and laced in front as in Cut No. 133. In this condition it is ready to be dressed with stocking and shoe.

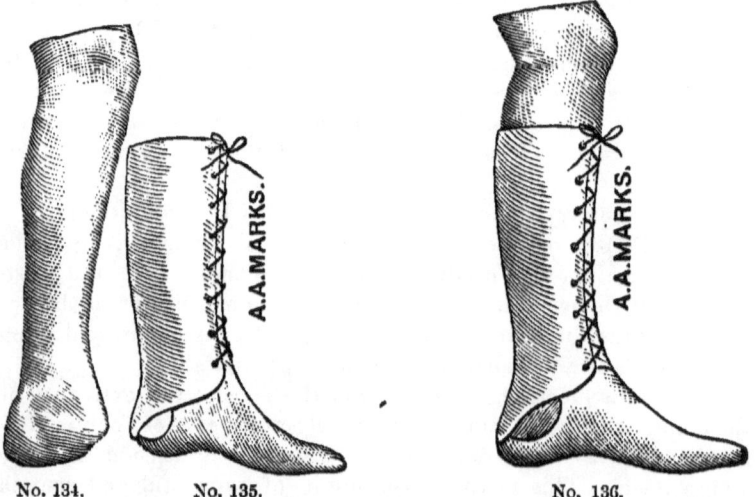

No. 134.   No. 135.   No. 136.

Cut No. 134 represents a Chopart stump; which is fitted with foot No. 135, similar to those for the Symes and Pirogoff, differing from them only in the fact that the stump is placed nearer the floor, as it is required to be. The heel of the stump is held to position by a brace passing up the posterior of the stump; this is done to counteract the tendency of the extensors from drawing the heel backward and the amputated surface downward.

This style of foot can be made so as not to elongate the leg, as the stump is brought adjacent to the plane of the plantar surface. Lisfranc's and Hey's amputations are treated similarly.

Fig. 136 presents the foot applied.

Price for No. 128, 132, or 135 complete, each $50.00.

Measurements required are explained on pages 60 to 65.

It sometimes occurs that in any of the amputations in and below the ankle-joint the weight can not be carried on the end; in such case side joints and a thigh piece are applied and the weight distributed about the thigh and below the knee in proportions to meet the possibilities.

No. 137.

Cut No. 137 represents a double amputation at the ankle-joint; the extremities of the stumps sloughed in healing and left the surfaces of the bones poorly protected; consequently it was not possible to bear any weight on the extremities. The wood of the upper part of the lower leg was left annular and surrounded the stump just below the knee; side joints and thigh piece were applied and the weight carried at advantageous places.

Cut No. 138 represents the artificial legs in position and the wearer ready for walking.

No. 138.

Price of each of these, complete, $100.00, with suspenders if necessary.

Measures required are explained on pages 60 to 65.

There are many appliances made calculated to be worn on feet amputations, but unless they are so constructed as to hold the cicatrix free from contact, and at the same time capable of being held sufficiently firm to the remaining stump as to enable the wearer to rise on the toes, they are practically worthless; it is impossible to treat any tarsal or metatarsal amputation and give the wearer any help with an appliance that does not extend well up on the leg. A simple leather inclosure laced about the ankle and instep, with toes to complete the foot, serves only as a filling for the shoe and does not in the least aid in walking.

ARTIFICIAL TOES.

The amputation of the toes, Cut 140, usually leaves a sensitive surface with an irritable cicatrix, which, if allowed to come in contact with wood, cork, or even the sole of the shoe is in danger of becoming excoriated and troublesome.

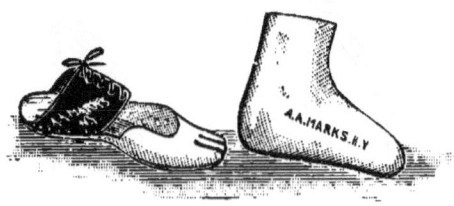

No. 139.   No. 140.

Cut No. 139 is calculated to meet this difficulty. A hard wood sole, extending back to the heel, is formed to receive the bottom of the mutilated foot and fitted to protect all the tender points, it is strapped firmly in place and held free from the cicatrix.

This appliance restores the appearance of the foot, and, on account of the retention of the metatarsal bones, enables the wearer to rise on his toes and receive help from that part of the foot while walking.

Price each, $25.00.
Measurements required are explained on page 65.
Plaster cast also needed.

PEG LEGS.

We are prepared to make peg legs for those who are unable to buy the more perfect leg as described.

We do not advise the use of the peg leg, as it so poorly replaces the lost member, and besides, its use has a tendency to impair the movements of the stump.

An artificial leg with rubber foot possesses so many advantages over the peg that we urge all to exhaust every possible endeavor to buy a good artificial leg with rubber foot, before concluding to wear the peg. Let the peg be the last resort.

Peg legs here illustrated are made of tough wood, well finished, with or without knee-joints, as may be required, and with rubber bottoms, held by ferrules.

With the exception of No. 145, they are calculated to be worn in the pantaloons the same as a regular artificial leg.

Cut No. 141 represents a peg leg for amputation above the knee; it has a knee-joint and will bend in walking or sitting.

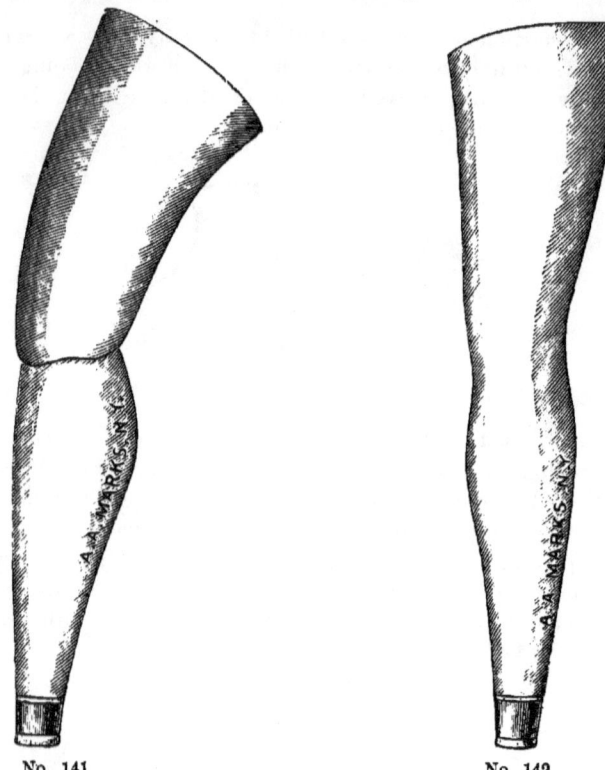

No. 141.   No. 142.

Price, without suspenders, well finished, $50.00.
Measurements required are explained on pages 60 to 65.
Cut No. 142 represents a peg leg for amputation above the knee. It is straight and without knee movement.
Price, without suspenders, well finished, $30.00.
    "   "   "   no covering, finished on wood, $20.00.
Measurements required are explained on pages 60 to 65

Cut No. 143 represents a peg leg for a knee-bearing stump.

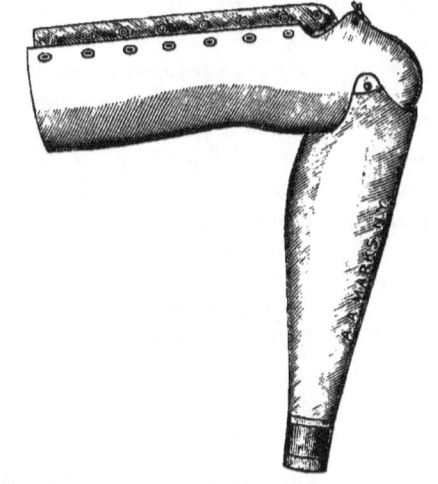

No. 143.

No. 144.

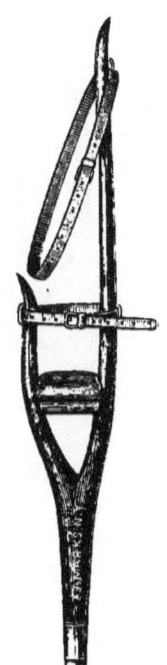

No. 145.

Price, without suspenders, well finished, $50.00.
Measurements required are explained on pages 60 to 65.

Cut No. 144 represents a peg leg for amputation below the knee, with side joints and thigh piece.

Price, without suspenders, well finished, $50.00.

Measurements required are explained on pages 60 to 65.

Cut No. 145 represents the cheapest form of peg leg, to be worn outside the clothing; it is made of strong tough wood with cushioned bearing for the knee to rest upon.

Price each, complete, $10.00.

Measurements required are explained on pages 60 to 65.

LEGS, APPARATUS AND EXTENSIONS FOR SHORTENED LEGS, DEFORMITIES, ETC.

No. 146.   No. 147.

Cut No. 146 represents a case of malformation. The deformed member being a leg in miniature, with all the bones and articulations of a natural leg, but so much dwarfed and distorted as to be of no possible avail except in the control of an artificial leg. The length of the deformed leg from the perinæum to the most distant point did not exceed ten inches.

Cut No. 147 represents the artificial leg constructed for the case; the socket received and held the deformed limb in place;

beneath was placed the knee movement, which operated the same as No. 108 leg. A rubber foot at the required distance completed the structure and supplied the deficiency in all its demands. The wearer was delighted with the results, and has now worn the same leg for at least a dozen years, and with it is able to conceal his deformity and walk naturally and comfortably.

Price complete, with choice of suspenders, $100.00.

Measurements required are explained on pages 60 to 65. Plaster cast also required.

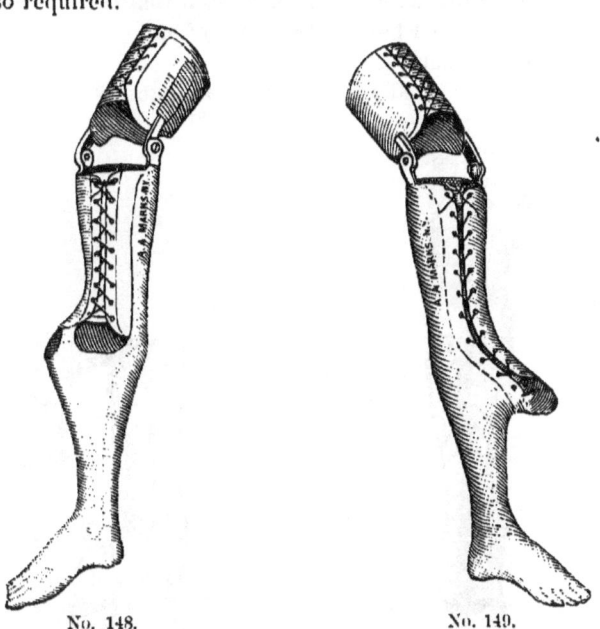

No. 148.   No. 149.

Cut No. 148 represents a leg constructed for a club foot with shortened leg, caused by retarded growth in childhood; the shortness measured about eight inches; knee-joint slightly weak, and entire leg atrophied. The leg was made to take weight on the bottom of the deformed foot; the side joints and thigh piece strengthened the knee. The leg when applied dressed neatly and enabled the wearer to walk with comfort and naturalness without the aid of crutch or cane. We have made a pair of similar legs for a man who had both of his legs deformed, and by the use of the artificials was restored to his proportionate height and appearance, and was enabled to walk perfectly naturally

Price complete, each, $100.00.

Measurements required are explained on pages 60 to 65. Plaster cast also required.

Cut No. 149 represents a leg constructed for a woman; her case was the result of hip disease in childhood. From retarded growth and displacement of the hip joint her leg became ten inches shorter than the companion leg; this deficiency was shared by the thigh and lower leg equally. The artificial leg received the affected leg and was under perfect control by it; with this leg the wearer was enabled to lay aside her crutches, which she had depended on for over thirty years. In a very brief time she was walking as naturally as any one, and with that comfort and relief she had never allowed herself the hope of enjoying.

Price complete, each, $100.00.

Measurements required are explained on pages 60 to 65.

No. 150.

No. 151.

Cut No. 150 represents a leg similar to the above. The deficiency in length of the affected leg amounts to but four inches. These legs can be made for cases where the deficiency in length is but a fraction.

Price complete, each, $100.00.

Measurements required are explained on pages 60 to 65.

In cases where there is no weakness of the knee joint and the knee can be depended on in operating the artificial leg it is not necessary to use side knee joints or thigh piece. Cut No. 151 represents a leg suitable for such a case.

The natural foot rests on a shelf; beneath it is a rubber foot at the required distance to extend to the ground. This leg is only suitable for a woman; her dresses will conceal the projecting upper foot; but for a man the appearance is objectionable; in

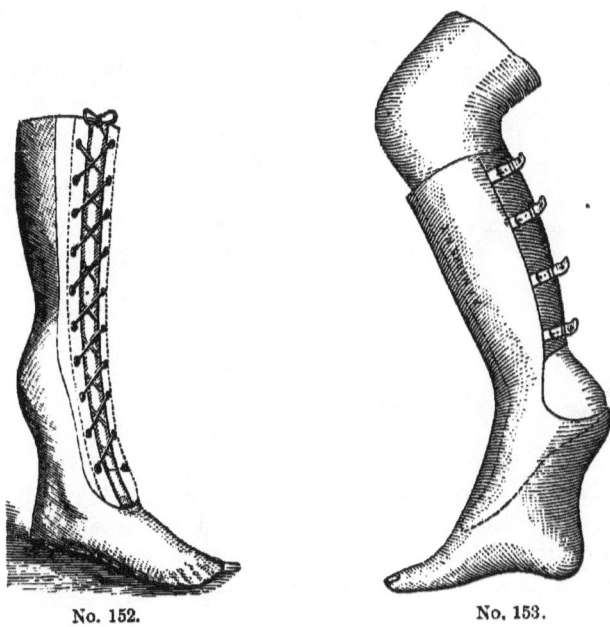

No. 152.   No. 153.

such cases we fit the leg to receive the foot of the short leg at a greater angle, as in Cut No. 152; the angle of the foot is as great as it is possible to have it and not torture the wearer. The weight is taken mostly on the heel and sole of the encased foot.

The rigidity of the ankle in the artificial leg secures perfect safety to weak ankles; the rubber foot supplies all the movement necessary.

This leg will dress very neatly and will enable the wearer to walk naturally, comfortably, and with absolute safety.

Price of No. 151 or 152, each, $50.00.

Measurements required are explained on page 65.

Cut No. 153 represents an artificial leg constructed for the purpose of extending a shortened leg, the results of anchylosis of the knee in a flexed position, as well as for utilizing the affected leg in walking.

The affected leg is received in the artificial leg from the rear; the bottom of the foot resting on a surface prepared for it; most of the weight is taken on this surface. A rubber foot beneath the natural foot, placed at the required distance, completes the leg. The rigidity of the natural knee renders it unnecessary to extend the artificial leg above the knee. This leg enables the wearer to walk without limping and without the aid of a cane.

Price, each, $50.00. Measurements required are explained on page 65.

Cut No. 154 represents an artificial leg constructed for a malformation. The natural leg was perfectly formed in every respect, with the exception of the absence of the foot, from knee down it was six inches shorter in length than the companion leg. The appearance of the stump was that of an ankle-joint amputation.

The artificial leg supplied the deficiency and restored the wearer in every respect.

Price, each, $50.00. Measurements required are explained on page 65.

No. 154.

Cut No. 155 represents a child with the right leg malformed; the thigh and knee were normal, but from the knee down the leg gradually tapered, and at the extremity a single protuberance similar to a toe pointed horizontally and inwardly.

No. 155.   No. 156.

Cut No. 156 represents the boy with leg applied and dressed.

Cut No. 157 represents (on an enlarged scale) the artificial leg constructed for the case; the protuberance referred to was slightly displaced and received into a comfortable pocket. The leg from knee down was encased.

When applied the lad was able to walk and run so naturally that detection was impossible.

Price, each, $50.00. Measurements required are explained on page 65, in addition to which a plaster cast is required.

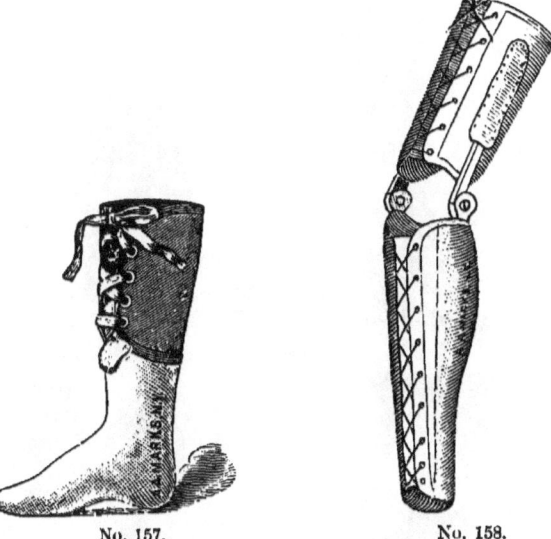

No. 157.   No. 158.

Cut No. 158 represents an apparatus for exsection of the knee-joint, in cases where union of the bones have failed. This apparatus is also advantageous for weakness in the knee or loss of patella.

Price, each, $50.00. For measurements required see page 65.

Legs that have been dwarfed from hip-joint or other affections have until quite recently been treated by thick cork soles or iron frames attached to the bottoms of the shoes; these methods are objected to, as they afford insufficient support, are unwieldy, uncomfortable, and instead of concealing the deficiency make an exhibition of it. The apparatus herein described are calculated to overcome these objections in the greatest possible degree and render locomotion sure, natural, and more of a pleasure than a torture.

Cut No. 159 represents a leg deficient in length only, caused by arrested development or displacement of the hip. Ankle movement full and under perfect control; the amount of shortness, measured from the heel to the floor less than four inches.

It is an ordinary case and often met with.

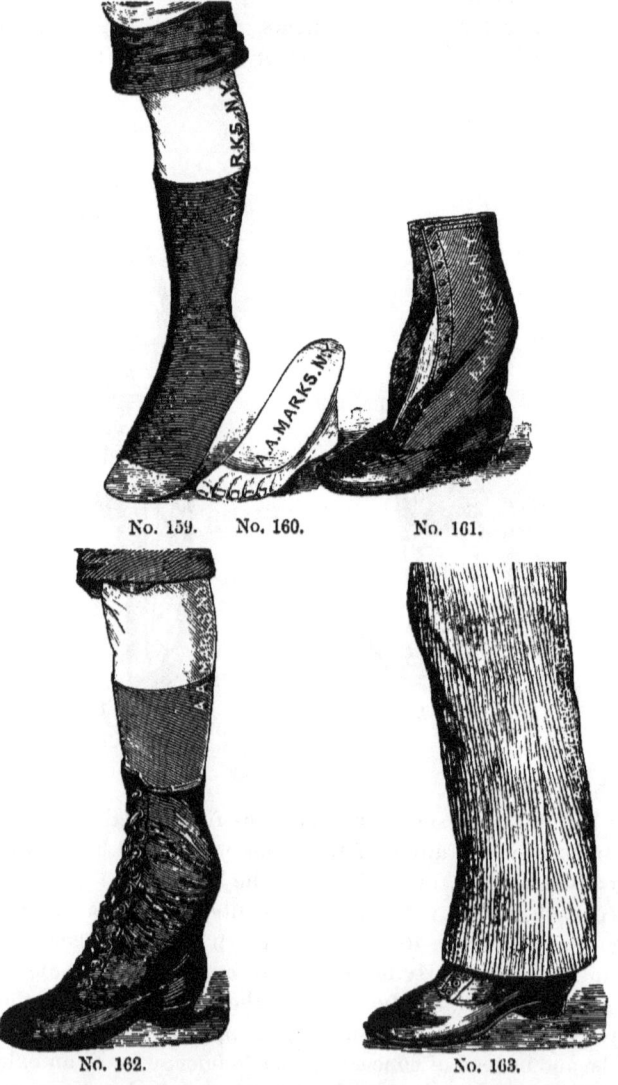

No. 159.   No. 160.   No. 161.

No. 162.   No. 163.

Cut No. 160 represents a suitable extension. The body of which is of light wood, toes of rubber; the bearing surface has a shape to receive comfortably the sole of the foot of the shortened leg; it is placed in a shoe; (Cut 161) made expressly for it, of strong leather with high top to come well up on the leg; when the foot is placed in position, the shoe is laced tightly, as in Cut 162.

Persons with these appliances walk naturally and comfortably, and after a very brief experience become very expert in their use. Cut 163 represents the same dressed.

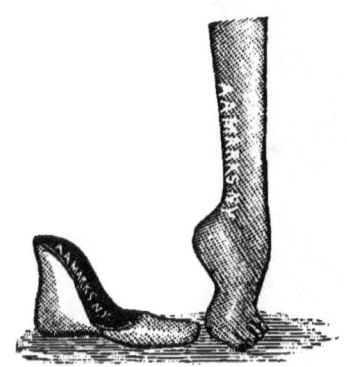
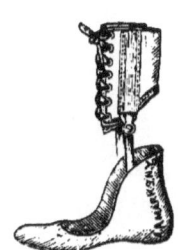

No. 164. No. 165. No. 166.

Cut No. 164 represents a similar extension to be applied to a leg that is short, atrophied, and partially or totally anchylosed in the ankle-joint, as in Cut 165. The subject walks on the ball of the foot; the rigidity of the natural ankle renders lateral movement impossible. If in either of these cases the shoe insufficiently secures the foot to the extension, an additional strap can be fastened to the extension, and pass around the instep of the foot, and be laced securely in place.

If this auxiliary strap can be dispensed with, it is desirable to do so. The weight in either of these cases can be taken on the heel or ball of the foot or both, as may be found most comfortable by the wearer.

Price, each, with shoe and last, $30.00; without shoe and last, $20.00. For measurements required see page 65.

If there is any lateral weakness in the ankle-joint, steel joints are required on the sides of the extension to give security to the ankle movement.

Cut No. 166 represents an apparatus constructed with ankle braces. The point of movement is coincident with the ankle movement of the foot.

Price, each, with shoe and last, $30.00; without shoe and last, $20.00. For measurements required see page 65.

If the shortness of the deficient leg is so great that more anterior-posterior strain is brought on the ankle-joint than the joint is capable of controlling, it is then necessary to encase the heel, ankle and part of the leg, as in Cuts 151–152, thus secure perfect rigidity to the ankle.

No. 167.

Cut No. 167 represents a double shoe, calculated to be worn by a woman; it is rarely made, only in cases where very strong ankle movement is retained or the ankle anchylosed with the foot at right angles to the shaft of the leg. The foot of the shortened leg enters the upper shoe and rests flat on a wooden sole; it is there buttoned or laced securely; beneath this, and at the required distance from it, a rubber foot is secured firmly.

This rubber foot is dressed by an ordinary shoe, a mate to the one worn on the opposite foot. It will be seen readily that this foot is only desirable for women, as with them it can be concealed by their long dresses.

Price, each, with shoe and last, $40.00; without shoe and last, $30.00. For measurements required see page 65.

If in any of the above cases there exists a weakness in the knee-joint, it will be necessary to extend the apparatus above the knee, with side joints to work in harmony with the knee, as in Cuts 149–150.

These side-braces support the knee and prevent any side strain; they can be made to fit sufficiently tight to compress the thigh enough to take all, or a part of the weight on the thigh, thus relieving the lower leg of its burden,—an important provision for cases of fracture or diseased leg.

RUBBER FEET ATTACHED TO ARTIFICIAL LEGS OF OTHER MANUFACTURE.

It has been shown that artificial legs with ankle-joint feet are more or less troublesome on account of their frequent need of repairs, as well as their uncertain movements, disagreeable noise, and unnatural "flop" in walking. We are aware that there are many who possess legs of this description, and who would gladly rid themselves of the annoyance, if it did not entail considerable loss on their part. To such we desire to say that if the legs in other respects than the feet are good, and the fittings comfortable, it will be to their interest to have the ankle-joint feet removed and rubber feet put in their place.

We have done this to a good many legs, and have invariably reclaimed them, and in most cases made them much better than they were originally.

Many of the testimonials in this pamphlet bear us out in this assertion.

Our charge for removing an ankle-joint foot of any style or manufacture, and replacing by a rubber foot, is in each case $20.00.

Persons concluding to have rubber feet applied to artificial legs of any manufacture can be accommodated with a smaller or larger foot if desired, and can have the leg made longer or shorter. Changes of this kind are made without extra charge. This is a very important feature, especially to growing subjects.

The success of the rubber foot depends in a great measure upon the manner and the position in which it is applied to the leg. Considerable experience is required to teach one the most advantageous conditions to be combined in this respect; therefore rather than hazard the chances of a failure we shall decline to sell the foot separate and shall insist upon applying every foot to the leg ourselves. We can apply a rubber foot to any artificial leg, no matter on what principle the leg is constructed or the material of which it is made. Two days' time is all that is usually required to make this alteration.

DIRECTIONS FOR TAKING MEASUREMENTS FOR ONE OR A PAIR OF ARTIFICIAL LEGS OF THE FOLLOWING NUMBERS: 108, 112, 114, 115, 116, 117, 118, 121, 122, 123, 125, 126, 128, 132, 135, 137, 141, 142, 143, 144, 145, 147, 148, 149, 150.

Place a large sheet of paper on a smooth floor or table; divest both leg and stump of clothing; be seated on this paper with both limbs extended; hold a long pencil against the bare person and perpendicular to the plane of the paper; begin at about the hip-joint and carry the pencil down the exterior of the stump, around the end, up the interior to the perinæum, down the interior of leg, around the heel, up the exterior to the opposite hip-joint; when passing around the heel endeavor to hold the foot in a position approximately at right angles to the leg, or in other words, so that the sole will be vertical.

If this drawing is properly taken it will resemble Cut No. 168.

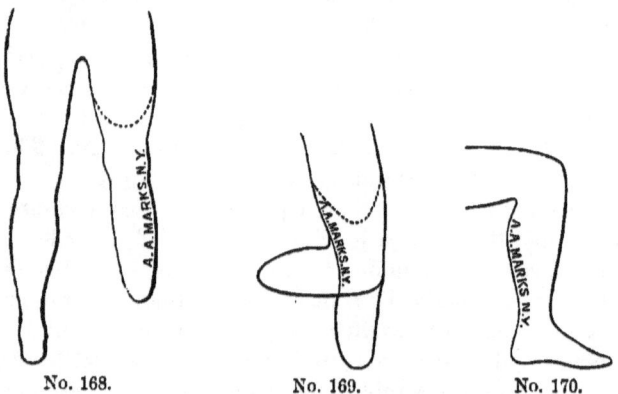

No. 168.   No. 169.   No. 170.

If the knee is contracted it will be impossible to have the posterior part rest on the paper when the patient is in a sitting posture; by lying down, with back on floor, in all probability the entire stump will be able to rest on its posterior surface.

Turn to and lie on the amputated side, with the exterior of stump resting on the paper with stump extended as much as possible; in this position draw a pencil from the abdomen down the anterior of stump, around the end, up the posterior to the body. If the leg is amputated below the knee, flex the stump as near right angles as possible and take side profile of stump, thus showing the stump from body to end in two positions, as near straight as possible for one position, and flexed to about right angles for the other.

This drawing should resemble cut No. 169.

Turn to the opposite side and rest the sound leg on the paper with the knee in a position flexed to about right angles and the sole of the foot on a line parallel with the thigh; draw the pencil around the entire leg while in this position. This drawing, if properly taken, will resemble cut No. 170.

Be seated and place the foot on the paper and mark entirely around it; it should resemble cut 171.

Stand erect, perfectly plumb, supported with crutches or canes, and have some one take the following measurements of the sound leg.

No. 171.

With callipers measure the interior-exterior, or lateral diameter of each knee at articulation; measure the distance from the perinæum to the floor, from the perinæum to the end of stump, and from the end of stump to the floor. Measure the circumferences of the stump beginning on a plane with the perinæum and repeating at intervals of about every two inches to the extreme end. Measure corresponding circumferences of the sound leg as far down as the knee. Measure circumference of leg just below the patella; circumferences of calf, ankle, heel-and-instep, instep, toe-joints, and length of foot; be seated on a chair of proper height to have the leg bent at the knee to about right angles. Measure the distance from upper edge of patella to the floor; the distance from the popliteal space to the floor. If the leg is amputated below the knee measure the distance from popliteal space of amputated leg to end of stump.

The following engravings are explanatory of the foregoing instructions; they are placed here as a guide for those who may regard the above as obscure. If the measurements have been taken according to above instructions, they should compare with those taken by the following, this should be done as a test to see that they are properly taken, and no omissions made.

MEASUREMENTS OF SOUND LEG.

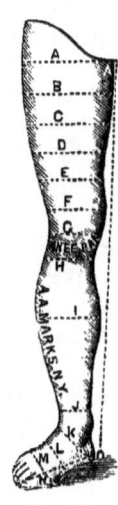

No. 172.

Length from body, or perinæum, to floor			A O
Circumference around leg, close to body			A
" 2 inches from body			B
" 4 " "			C
" 6 " "			D
" 8 " "			E
" 10 " "			F

Lateral diameter through center of knee.... G
That is the distance through the joint from the anterior to the exterior.

Circumference just below knee pan.......... H
" calf of leg.................. I
" smallest part of ankle........ J
" around heel and instep....... K
" " instep........ L
" foot at toe-joints........... M
Length of foot.......................... N

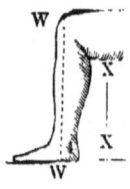

No. 173.

Be seated and take the following measurements, with the aid of a carpenter's square.
Length from top of knee to floor (sound leg bent sitting, see cut No. 173).......... WW
Length from popliteal space to floor (back side on line XX, measured when leg is bent at right angles, as in cut 173).... XX

Diagrams of both sound leg and stump similar to Cuts Nos. 168, 169, 170 and 171 should accompany these measurements.

IF THE AMPUTATION IS ABOVE KNEE or in the knee-joint, give in addition to the foregoing measurements of sound leg, the measurements called for as follows :

Length from body to end of stump...A P
Circum. around stump, close to body.. A
  "   2 inches below................. B
  "   4   "   "   C
  "   6   "   "   .... D
  "   8   "   "   .... E
  " 10   "   "   .... F
Length from the end of stump to the
  floor............................Q Q

No. 174.

IF THE STUMP IS A KNEE-BEARING, that is, contracted or too short to be used, to operate the leg, give the following measurements of the stump in addition to those (cut 172) of sound leg.

Length from body to support of knee. A P
Circum. around stump, close to body.. A
  "   2 inches from body.......... B
  "   4   "   "   C
  "   6   "   "   .... D
  "   8   "   "   .... E
Circumference at the smallest place
  above the knee................... F
Circumference around stump........ S S
The distance the end of stump projects
  back of the thigh................. U
Lateral diameter of knee joint ..... G
Length from knee to floor.......... P O
Length from upper end of knee-pan to
  end of stump..................... R R

No. 175.

NOTE.

Give the "length from knee to floor (P O)" with great accuracy.

IF THE AMPUTATION IS BELOW THE KNEE, and the joint can be used to operate the artificial leg, give the following measurements in addition to those (cut 172) of sound leg.

No. 176.

Length from body to end of stump......				A T
Circum. around stump, close to body....				A
"	2 inches below...............			B
"	4	"	"	C
"	6	"	"	D
"	8	"	"	E
Circumference at the smallest place above the knee..........................				F
Lateral diameter through center of knee................................				G
Circumference at the lower edge of knee pan.................................				O
Circumference 2 inches below...				H
"	4	"	"	I
"	6	"	"	J
"	8	"	"	K
"	10	"	"	L
"	12	"	"	M
Length of stump below knee, measured from back of knee (when bent at right angles) to end				
Distance from end of stump to floor........				T

If both legs are amputated either above or below the knees, give profiles and drawings of both stumps as directed on page 60, together with lateral diameters of each knee and circumferences from body to end, at intervals of two inches. If the patient is desirous of being elevated to a particular height, state the height desired and give the length from the end of stump to the top of head; measured while lying on the floor with stumps extended. Give the size of shoes desired to be worn on the feet, unless the patient is willing to leave that matter to our judgment.

If the leg has been amputated in any of the articulations, or below the ankle articulation, a plaster cast of stump taken from the end upwards eight or ten inches will be of great help. If there are any tender spots or peculiarities on either leg or stump, be careful to note them. Answer the following questions in all cases:

    Name of patient?
    Post-office address?
    Occupation?
    Age?
    Weight?
    Cause of amputation?
    When amputated?
    Which leg amputated, right or left?
    Has the patient worn an artificial limb?
    Whose make?   How long?
    Name of party ordering leg?
    Post-office address of same?

MEASUREMENTS REQUIRED FOR THE MANUFACTURE OF APPLIANCES OF THE FOLLOWING NOS.: 139, 151, 152, 153, 154, 157, 158, 160, 164, 166 and 167.

It is desirable to have the wearer present for the fitting and adjusting of appliances of the above Nos. In cases where this is inexpedient, we will do all we can to reach good results by fitting from measurements, profiles and casts. The measurements and profiles required are as follows: Side and front views of both legs, the sound leg in a standing position and the affected leg held in a position in which the inclination of the foot is the same as intended to be when the appliance is worn.

These profiles should be taken by placing the leg against a piece of paper which has been tacked to the wall or some vertical surface, then marking around it with long pencil held at right angles to the wall. The patient is supposed to be standing erect on his unaffected leg with the foot of the affected leg resting on books or surface elevated and inclined to the desired height and angle. In addition give profiles of the bottoms of both feet. Measure the distance from the heel of the affected leg to the floor, also from the ball of the same foot to the floor; then give circumferences of both legs separately, from the toes upward at intervals of about two inches, extending as far up as it is desired to have apparatus extend. If certain irregularities in the affected leg are not describable, a plaster cast carefully taken with the foot in the position in which it is to be worn, will be required. The most desirable angle at which the foot should be placed is the most comfortable one that will bring the toes the nearest the floor. Supply answers to the questions at the top of this page.

SUSPENDERS.

The methods of suspension for any of the artificial legs thus far described are numerous, and each method seems to possess some advantage peculiarly adapted to the individual wearing it. Persons who have become inured to some peculiar method, and who have found that method to be satisfactory in every respect, are not advised to make a change; by describing definitely just the kind of a suspender they are accustomed to, and by making their request known, they will find us willing to make such for them and apply them to a new leg without additional charge. When we are not instructed in this matter, we use our own judgment and apply suspenders to legs that appear to us to be most suitable.

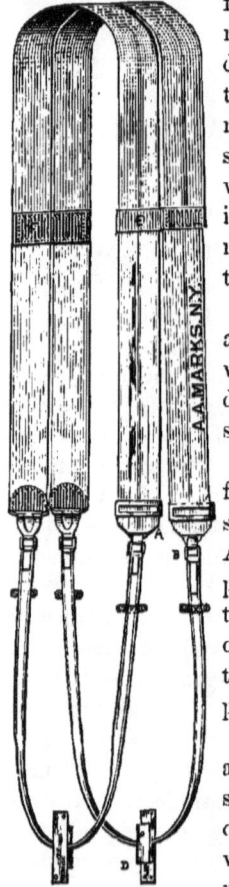

No. 177.

As the result of much thought on the subject, aided by the kindly suggestions of our patrons, we take pleasure in presenting the following devices and commend them as comfortable and secure.

Cut No. 177 represents our new style, suitable for amputation above the knee. The shoulder straps are of two-inch non-elastic webbing. After passing over the shoulders, one strap passes through a loop, E, which is attached to the other shoulder strap; this has the effect of holding the straps in place, and prevents the sliding from the shoulders, so bitterly complained of by wearers of the old style.

The buckles at A (explained hereafter) receive and clamp the shoulder straps at any place to suit the wearer; the snaps at the lower ends of the buckles receive the strong loops B, to which are attached leather straps; these straps pass down the sides of the leg under guides to keep them in place, then through the pulleys D, which are secured to both sides of the artificial leg just above the knee, then passing up the back of the leg through other guides they attach to snaps on the back ends of the suspenders. The suspenders once attached to the clamp buckles always remain so, for in removing the leg from the body the leather straps are unsnapped, front and back, at B; the buckles are not disturbed in removing the shoulder straps from the shoulders; one strap slips from the loop E, and then both are readily removed from the person.

No. 178.   No. 179.

The above cuts represent front and back views of a pair of these suspenders applied to a leg and the wearer; they show the relative position of the rollers, the effect of the front loop and back cross-piece. All the elasticity required for good results is obtained in the piece of elastic webbing extending from back cross-piece to the snaps.

The action of the suspender is illustrated in a side view of the patient while walking. It will be seen that the leather straps move on the rollers very easily, and thus compensate the back and front pull without occasioning any movement of the straps on the shoulders. When sitting, the same effect is obtained; instead of the suspenders being slack in front and uncomfortably tight on the back, as in the old style, the rollers admit of a uniform pull, both front and back, as seen in the following page.

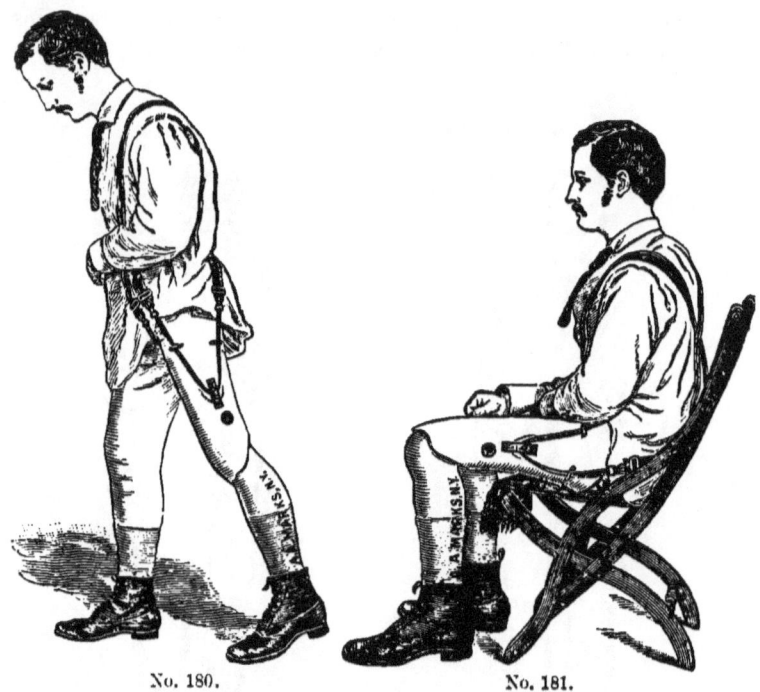

No. 180. No. 181.

When lying down a comfortable effect likewise results; the wearer has not his undergarments pulled out of place. He can throw himself down in an easy position and enjoy a refreshing sleep. Price per pair complete $4.00. Measurements required, distance from top of leg on back over one shoulder to top of leg in front.

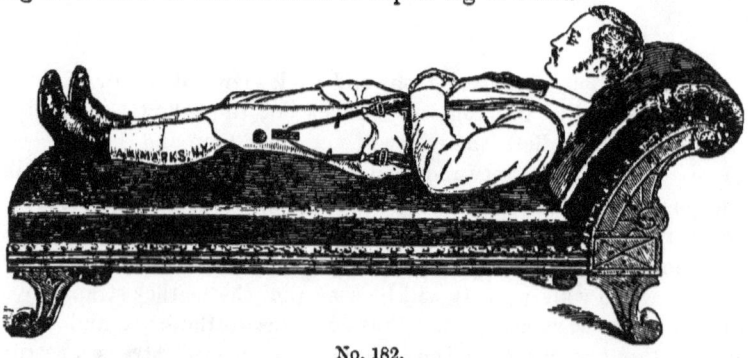

No. 182.

Cut No. 183 represents our new buckle, made of strong rolled brass, nickel-plated, capable of receiving and holding firmly two-inch elastic or non-elastic webbing. The webbing is held by a toothed clamp which does not pierce the web to tear or wear it.

This buckle as shown in the cut has a spring snap which holds the loop securely and can only be released by pressing on the spring.

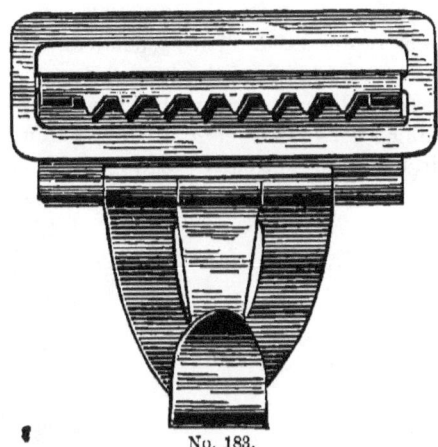

No. 183.

Price each 25 cents.

The rollers used with this Suspender, represented in cut No. 184, are made of strong brass with durable pulleys; they are secured to the sides of the socket of the leg by ordinary screws. The pulleys are absolutely noiseless while in action and will last many years. Price each 25 cts.

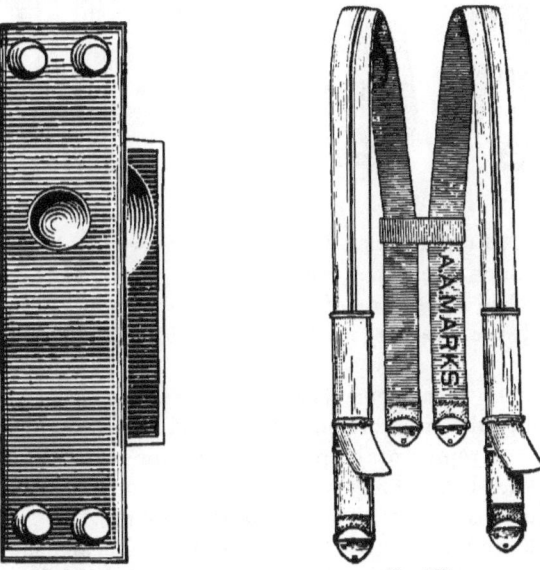

No. 184.   No. 185.

Cut No. 185 represents our old style of suspenders; they do not possess the advantages of the roller suspender, notwithstanding they have many admirers.

The shoulder straps are of fine elastic webbing, two inches wide. The front straps, of two-inch non-elastic web, pass through a link and are buckled as represented. The suspenders are attached to the leg by means of screws holding the leather tags; the webbing is fastened to these tags by plated steel Ds which admit of a direct pull, thus avoiding wear on one edge of the webbing.

Price per pair, $3.00. Measurement required; the same as No. 177.

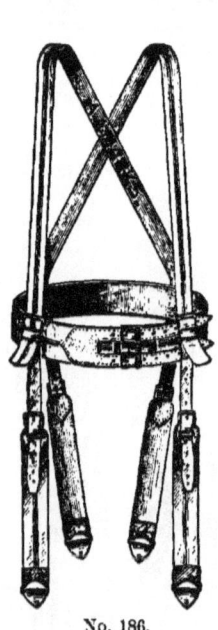
No. 186.

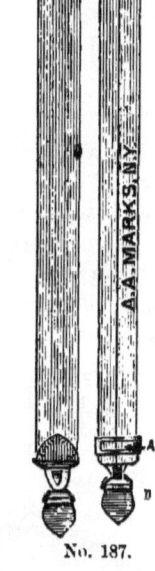
No. 187.

Cut No. 186 represents a belt and suspender combined.

The shoulder straps and waistband are of non-elastic webbing; straps attached to leg are of 1½ or 2 inch elastic webbing; they admit of all the elasticity necessary; are very neat, comfortable, and durable.

Price $5.00. Measurements required are the same as for No. 177, in addition to the circumference of the body about the waist.

Cut No. 187 represents suspender for leg for amputation below the knee, and knee-bearing legs where but one shoulder strap is required. The shoulder-strap is of two-inch elastic webbing.

The front end is buckled to our new clamp buckle, snapped to a metal D fastened to the front upper edge of thigh piece; the back end of shoulder strap is attached to a spring snap, to which is secured a D, fastened to the back part of the thigh piece. This suspender can be adjusted by the buckle once for all time. On removing the leg the suspender can be unsnapped both front and back, thus simplifying the process of taking off and putting on. This suspender, passing over the opposite shoulder, does not have a tendency to slip from the shoulder, except in cases where the wearer has round shoulders. In such cases a piece of webbing should be attached to the back part of shoulder strap, and pass laterally across the back, around the body, under the opposite arm, and buckled to the front strap.

Price $1.50. Measurements required same as No. 177.

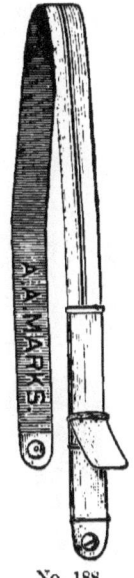
No. 188.

No. 189.

Cut No. 188 represents the old style of suspender for a leg for amputation below the knee. It is similar in material and pattern to No. 185 Suspender, except that it is to go over but one shoulder and adjusted to thigh piece by means of screw buttons which admit of direct pull.

Price, each, without screw buttons, $1.50. Measures required, same as No. 177.

Screw Buttons for suspenders No. 188, made of brass, nickel-plated, represented by cut 189, per pair, 50 cents.

SUSPENDERS FOR WOMEN.

Cut No. 190 represents our roller suspender especially designed for a woman with amputation above the knee. It is provided with a broad yoke fitting the hips neatly.

This yoke makes an excellent supporter for the leg. The leg and shoulder straps are attached to the yoke, and are adjusted by buckles; when women are broad about the hips, the entire weight can be safely carried on the yoke, the shoulder straps loosened or dispensed with. The movement of the straps on the rollers secures all the advantages possessed by style No. 177.

The yoke secures the leg so firmly to the person that the apparent weight of the leg is reduced materially.

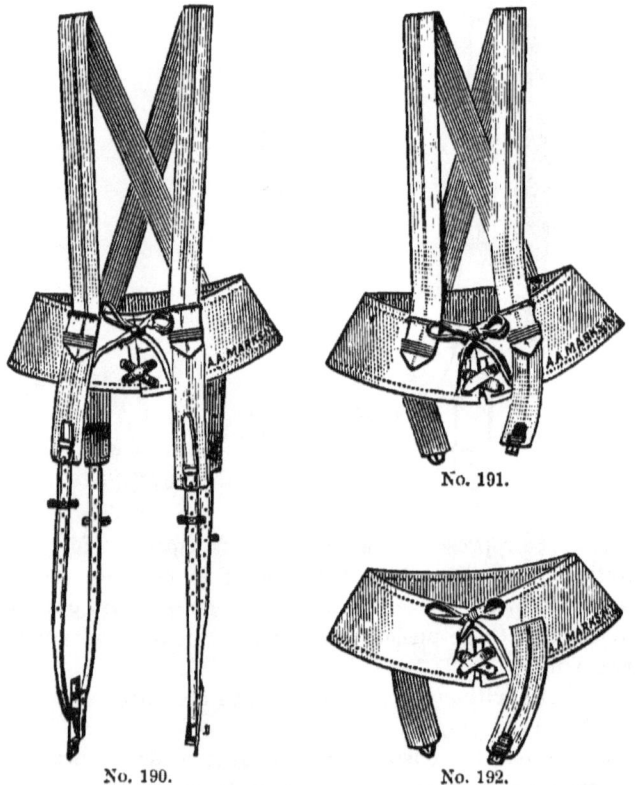

No. 190. No. 191. No. 192.

Price $5.00. In ordering give waist-measurement, or, better still, cut a paper pattern to fit the waist and hips; give measurement from top of leg on back, over the shoulder, to top of leg in front.

Cut No. 191 represents a yoke suspender; calculated for a woman wearing a knee-bearing leg or a leg for amputation below the knee; it is similar to style No. 190, except in its connections with the leg, which the illustration clearly presents.

Price $3.00. Measurements required same as No. 190.

Style 192 is similar to above, except that shoulder straps are dispensed with.

Price $2.00. Waist pattern only required.

SUSPENDERS FOR DOUBLE AMPUTATIONS.

Any of the suspenders described can be so modified as to be suitable for double amputations.

Price, style No. 177 modified for double amputations, $5.00.
" style No. 187 modified for double amputations, $3.00.
" style No. 190 modified for double amputations, $7.00.
" style No. 191 modified for double amputations, $4.00.
" style No. 192 modified for double amputations, $3.00.

In ordering suspenders for artificial legs, designate the style by the number.

Persons ordering artificial legs are entitled to any style of suspenders without additional charge.

ARTIFICIAL ARMS.

A German knight of the 16th century by the name of Goetz von Berlichingen is credited with having possessed an artificial hand which enabled him to engage in battle, and assisted him in many deeds of valor. The hand was of iron, of enormous weight, attached to his armor and operated by some ingenious mechanism which for its initial power, depended on the exertions of the opposite hand. It had a grasping power at such intervals as when the companion hand released certain springs after having placed the object to be held within its clutch. This hand may be regarded as the first artificial hand of which we have any authentic knowledge. Pliny, however, speaks of M. Sergius, 167 B. C., as having made and worn an artificial hand with which he was enabled to render heroic service. B. A. Watson, M. D., in his "Treatise on Amputations and Their Complications," quotes the original Latin: "M. Sergio ut equidem arbitror, nemo quemquam hominum jure praetulerit, licet pronepos Catilina gratiam nomini deroget. Secundo stipendio dextram manum perdidit, ... dextram sibi ferream fecit, eaque religata proeliatus Cremonam obsidione exemit."

This put in our vernacular reads thus: "I suppose every one would admit that M. Sergius, the great grandson of Cataline, had not diminished the fame of his name since he lost his right hand in his second campaign. . . . He made himself an iron right hand, and, with this fastened on, having fought a battle, he released Cremona from siege."

Pliny says: "He prostrated Placentia and took twelve of the enemy's camps in Gaul; all this appears from the speech which he made on his praetorship when his colleagues wished to shut him out of the sacred rites as a mutilated man." (C. Plinii, Hist. Nat. 28, 104-106)

Unfortunately Pliny fails to describe the mechanism of that hand; but from the fact that his colleagues interposed his misfortune as a sufficient reason for his preclusion, we feel justified in concluding that the iron hand which he wore was of little or no value, aside from that for which it was especially designed, viz., the holding of the reins of his horse or assisting in guarding his person by a shield. The hand of Goetz von Berlichingen was in all probability patterned after that of M. Sergius, as it was designed for the same purpose.

Passing to more modern times, we learn of but little advance in this line. The mind of man has indeed devoted an abundance of thought to the development of this branch of prosthesis. We do not hesitate in saying that as much attention in the aggregate has been given to this subject as to that of any branch of invention, the steam engine and electricity not excepted. Paré, Lorrain, Sebastian, Wilson, DeGrafe, and a host of others have struggled with the subject and wrought ingenious contrivances which have merited much admiration, more for their mechanical arrangement than for their utility.

If we give a thought to the mechanism of the natural arm and hand and study its peculiar arrangement we will readily see why so little has been accomplished by the minds of the past and what a gloomy future portends those who are now struggling with the subject.

The anatomy of the human hand. What a marvel of mechanism, what a combination of movements, and what control man has over them! Each finger has its three joints, with every joint under control.

The hand has its wrist, enabling it to conform to any angle.

The forearm has the ulna and the radius, controlling the hand.

Withal, the marvelous strength each finger and joint commands, all operated by sinews and muscles. The parts of this wonderful machine are hinged together with such nicety that the engraver is enabled to etch the finest plate, or the brawny smith to wield the heaviest sledge. Think you that the hand alone does this variety of work, operates voluntarily by an intelligence of its own?

Sever the brachial nerve, and you will have a member as dead and limpsy as an old rag or an empty coat-sleeve.

Remove the arm from the body and irritate the nerves or contract the muscles, and you will have a motion as awkward and spasmodic as you may observe in an artificial arm with jointed fingers.

Hence, all the dexterous movements we observe in the normal hand depend upon some power outside of itself, and that power is the mind. If we look a little deeper in the physiology of the natural arm and hand we will observe that nature has made a curious provision for one of its failings, that of attrition, and were it not for the provision of cushions and lubricating sacs the joints of the arm and hand would soon become loose and rattle as badly as worn-out gudgeons. Every drop of blood that flows through the avenues of the arm carries with it fresh material to replace this waste. From the first beat of the heart of the child, until the being ceases to be, this human repair shop is in active operation and knows no rest.

This cursory glance at the natural arm will fix in our minds the following facts: That the hand is a delicate piece of mechanism of great strength; that it is in concert with and operated by the will ; that it suffers wear, but is constantly undergoing repairs by the action of the circulatory system. With these facts well impressed, we will do well to make a comparison with the artificial arm. What a disparity. It cannot have intimate relations with the mind, nor with the heart. If the joints of the fingers are made strong enough to withstand a small proportion of the strain of the natural hand, it must necessarily be made too heavy for endurance.

If the springs are made stiff enough to have a grasping power of a pound, the exertion to operate them is fatiguing and renders them impracticable. These arguments are presented for the purpose of assisting the reader in thinking for himself and drawing proper conclusions as to the possibilities of artificial arms when compared with the natural, and it is hoped that they will serve to make even the credulous suspicious of the advertisements of those manufacturers who promise to " restore the appearance in full and one-half the usefulness of the natural arm and hand."

The disposition of all conscientious manufacturers has been to produce a hand that would approximate the natural to the greatest possible practical degree. Some have elaborated the ideas of their prototypes; others have ignored the earlier makers and formulated ideas of their own; but when simmered down to actual serviceability we all stand but little in advance of our predecessors ; finger movements controlled by intricate mechanism avail little because of the impossibility of controlling their movements by the mind in order to give them delicate manipulation. Any manufacturer of ordinary ingenuity can make a hand that will hold firmly the reins of a horse in driving or that will carry a valise of some weight ; but if that hand is applied to other more or less delicate purposes its grasp will be either inadequate or too violent and unsuited for the purpose.

In the beginning of our endeavors we naturally fell into the rut of our competitors and made a hand with much complication.

By taxing the remaining arm we could cause the artificial hand to assume various positions, the fingers to flex and extend ; but it did not take us long to learn that it was like the arm of the German knight—an article more to be admired for its complication than for general utility. Until man becomes capable of duplicating nature and harmonizing the artificial member with the nervous system, in short, giving it life, he will fail in supplying the loss in all its detail. Machinery will not accomplish it, and the more complication used the more distantly he approaches the most useful substitute.

After laboring hard in this work and expending much time and thought in its development, and having passed through the most trying and varied experience, we have come to the conclusion that the rubber hand herein represented is the most simple, practical, durable, and useful the market affords.

In 1863 the rubber hand was invented; it was attached to the forearm by means of a spindle held in position by a set screw, easily detached and replaced by a hook, fork, knife, or brush.

The fingers were of soft elastic rubber molded to a graceful shape and yielding to pressure. Its advantages were its naturalness in appearance and to the touch, and its great durability.

It might fall or strike anything without breaking or impairing. These advantages commended it to favor, and many of them were made. In the course of time an improvement was suggested —that of making the fingers ductile. By the assistance of the opposite hand, or by pressing the hand against any resistant surface, the fingers might be placed in any desired position, each one giving the hand a new appearance; thus obviating the monotony of the old style, and making the hand more available for light purposes. The fingers, when bent, are capable of holding a valise or package of considerable weight, or holding the reins of a horse in driving. This feature is secured by letters patent issued by the United States.

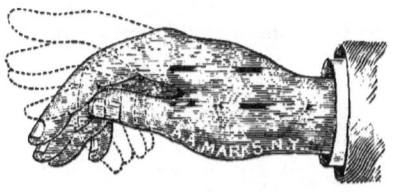

No. 193.

Cut No. 193 represents the rubber hand with ductile fingers; the dotted lines indicate some of the many positions in which the fingers can be placed, through the agency of the opposite hand or the opposition of resistant objects.

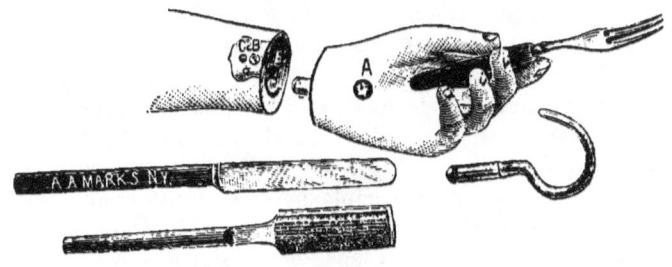

No. 194.

Cut No. 194 represents the hand and part of the forearm detached.

The spindle D is received in the catch E and held securely, admitting of slight rotary motion; pressure applied to the button C will release the hand, which can be laid aside, and a hook, knife, fork, brush, or any implement placed in its stead; by using these implements in the forearm they are brought nearer to the stump and consequently are under greater control. In this manner they will accomplish more dexterously the work of feeding with the knife or fork, washing with the brush, or operating with the hook.

If, however, the wearer desires to have the hand in place while performing these services, he can do so by using the attachment in the palm, which is capable of holding, by a self-acting spring, any of the implements mentioned; by pressing on button A the implements can be released.

The wrist clamp contrivance is ingenious and practical, but on account of the great strain it must necessarily resist in the performance of heavy work it is required to be made strong and consequently heavy. In all cases where the stump is short and weak, or the wearer does not wish to use the arm in heavy labor, by attaching the rubber hand permanently to the forearm, and dispensing with the wrist clamp, depending entirely on the palm thimble for the holding of implements, the weight of the arm can be materially lessened. It may be well to say that any of these implements in the palm of the hand are under good control and can be used to very great advantage.

BALL AND SOCKET WRIST JOINT.

We are able to attach the hand to the forearm by a ball and socket wrist joint, thus giving the hand the ability of being placed at any angle; we do not, as a general thing, regard this of sufficient advantage to offset the additional weight, consequently we place this joint in the wrist only when advised.

NATURAL COLOR.

The hand is always gloved in order to present at all times the most natural appearance. We are frequently asked why we do not give the hand a natural color and avoid the necessity of wearing gloves. If one will consider for a few moments the peculiarities and impermanency of the natural shade, he will not press the question. To be sure, we can paint the hand any shade that may be desired; in fact the wearer can do that himself at any time, and in any manner to suit his taste, purpose, or complexion; but a hand painted in the morning so as to match the opposite or natural hand with the most artistic and critical nicety will look very different to it in the afternoon after the natural hand has gone through some of the daily changes due to work, condition, temperament, or any of the many causes which are constantly changing the hues of the human complexion.

Hence it is desirable to cover the hand with a glove which can be slipped on or off very readily by the wearer.

ARMS FOR SHOULDER JOINT AMPUTATIONS.

For amputations in the shoulder joint an artificial arm serves its least utility. A sheath fitted to the shoulder, held to place by straps, secures the artificial arm. The arm, from the shoulder down, is similar to that represented in cut No. 195.

Price and measurements required are the same as for No. 195.

ARMS FOR ABOVE ELBOW AMPUTATIONS.

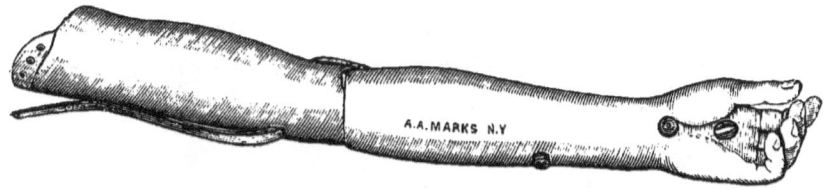

No. 195.

Cut No. 195 represents an arm for amputation at any point above the elbow joint. The arm is made of wood, excavated to make it light, and covered with parchment to make it strong; the hand is of rubber, either permanently attached at the wrist or held in place by

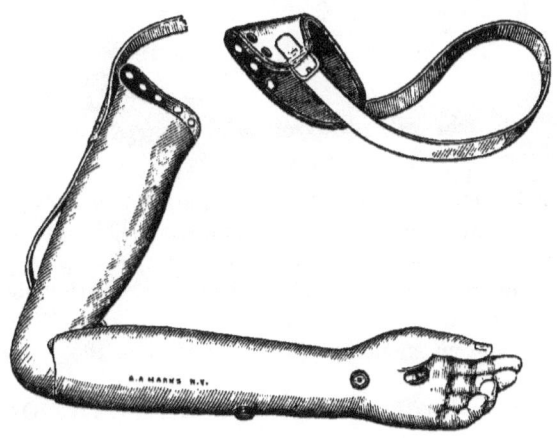

No. 196.

wrist clamp or ball and socket joint, as may be desired by the wearer. The elbow joint is capable of flexion and extension, operated by a strap so arranged that a movement of the stump and shoulder will pull the forearm up to the desired angle. This can only be done, however, on long and strong stumps. When the forearm is brought to about right angles with the upper arm, either by the agency of the stump or by a sudden movement given to it, a lock attachment in the interior of the forearm holds the forearm in position as in cut No. 196.

When held in this position the wearer can carry a shawl, coat, or any loose article on the forearm; thus presenting a very natural appearance when walking. By pressing on the button on the under-side of the forearm the lock can be released and the arm allowed to extend. The hook in the wrist or palm of hand will hold securely any article that may be placed in it.

Price complete, with or without wrist motion, with Hook, Knife, Fork, Brush, 1 pair kid gloves and suspenders, each, $75.00.

Measurements required are explained on pages 89 and 90.

ARMS FOR ELBOW JOINT AMPUTATIONS.

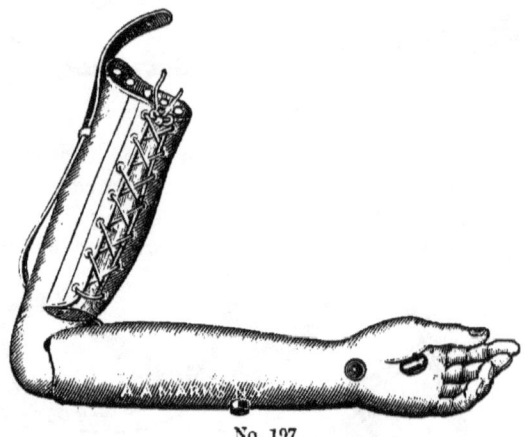

No. 197.

Cut No. 197 represents an arm for amputation in the elbow joint, with the end of the stump larger than above. The upper arm is of wood and leather; the lacing will secure the stump in place and hold the stump in a comfortable position. From the elbow down the arm is made similar to No. 196.

Prices and measurements required same as No. 196.

ARMS FOR BELOW ELBOW AMPUTATIONS.

Cut No. 198 represents an arm for amputation below the elbow, and very close to the joint, so as to leave but a short stump that can be depended on for operating the forearm. The forearm is fitted to receive the stump; steel joints, extending upward on either side with leather socket attached, hold the stump firmly in place; shoulder straps assist in holding the arm to the person and relieve

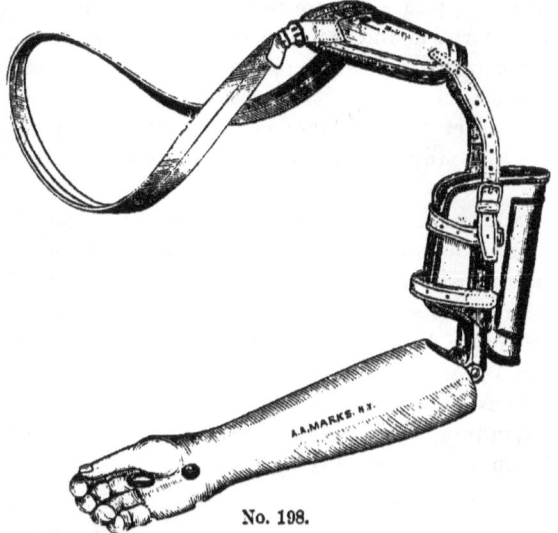

No. 198.

the stump of some of its work. The hand in such cases is usually permanently fastened to the forearm.

Price complete, with or without wrist motion, with Hook, Knife, Fork, Brush, gloves and suspenders, each, $50.00.

Measurements required are explained on pages 89 and 90.

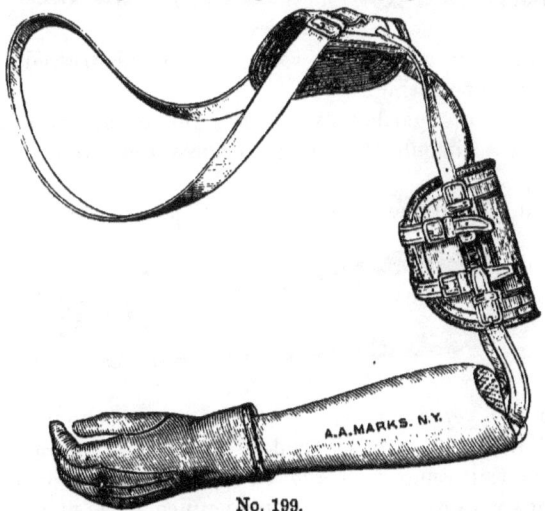

No. 199.

Cut No. 199 represents an arm for amputation below the elbow, with stump of sufficient length to give control over its movements.

The forearm is fitted to the stump and held in place by the upper socket. The forearm and the upper arm are connected by adjustable leather straps ; these are preferred to steel joints, as they admit of rotation of forearm and are more durable than steel joints ; they do not wear or rattle, require no oil, and are less liable to break from strain or concussion. In short stumps, however, the steel joints are necessary in order to hold the socket to the stump rigidly. In long stumps the stump itself can be relied upon for the necessary security.

Shoulder straps are applied to assist the arm in lifting heavy articles. The forearm is carved out of wood and covered with parchment. The forearm can be made of strong leather instead of wood, but we prefer wood, as that material is lighter and not so likely to be made offensive by absorption of perspiration from the stump. Wood when covered with parchment is sufficiently strong for all practical purposes and is not in danger of collapsing.

Notwithstanding, we are not arbitrary in this matter and will yield to the choice of the ordering party.

Price same as No. 198.

No. 200.

Cut No. 200 represents the same, with hand dressed holding a pen in the act of writing.

This has been regarded as a wonderful accomplishment, when really it is less difficult than many services the hand is capable of performing.

Price and measurements required same as No. 198.

No. 201.

Cut No. 201 represents an artificial forearm without the upper arm attachment. The arm is held on the stump by straps attached to the socket, passing over the shoulder and around the body. For persons who wear arms for appearance only and have good length of stump below the elbow this method of attachment is ample and will serve the purpose well.

Price with wrist attachment, suspender, hook, knife, fork, brush, and gloves, each $35.00. Without wrist attachment, with suspender, hook, knife, fork, brush, and glove, each $30.00. Measurements required are explained on pages 89–90.

ARMS FOR WRIST JOINT AMPUTATIONS.

No. 202.

Cut No. 202 represents a wrist joint amputation. These amputations may be divided into two classes: the first in which the osseous processes of the ulna and radius in the region of the wrist are retained, presenting a flattened appearance to the stump, with the greater diameter some larger than above it; second class includes those in which these processes have disappeared, leaving the end of the stump round and smaller than above.

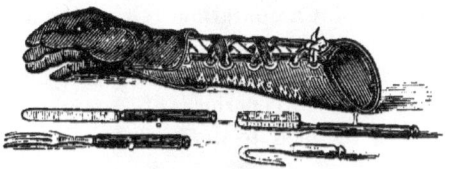

No. 203.

Cut No. 203 represents an artificial forearm suitable for the first class; the stump is encased by a leather sheath which is adjusted and secured by lacing. The processes which distinguish this class afford the means of securing the artificial forearm; if these processes are prominent the arm will be sufficiently secured to enable the wearer to pull and lift heavy objects. The knife, fork, hook, and brush are held in the palm.

Price, with implements complete, each $30.00. Measurements necessary are explained on pages 89–90.

If the processes about the end or wrist are insufficiently prominent or are painful to the touch it will not be possible to depend on them for security.

Cut No. 204 represents an arm for such cases; the stump is encased and laced as tightly as can be endured. The pressure is

No. 204.

taken from the wrist and carried to the upper arm and shoulders as represented.

Price, with suspenders and implements complete, each $50.00. Measurements necessary are explained on pages 89–90.

In either of these cases it will not be possible to use the removable hand unless the wearer is willing to allow the arm to be one inch longer than the opposite or sound arm, the wrist catch requiring one inch of room. On account of this we attach the hand permanently to the forearm and depend on the palm thimble for a means of holding the eating, toilet and laboring implements. The second class of wrist joint amputations, viz., those in which the ends of the stumps are round and smaller than above, are furnished with No. 199 arms and regarded the same as an amputation below the elbow, except that the hand is permanently attached to the forearm, for the same reasons assigned to the first class.

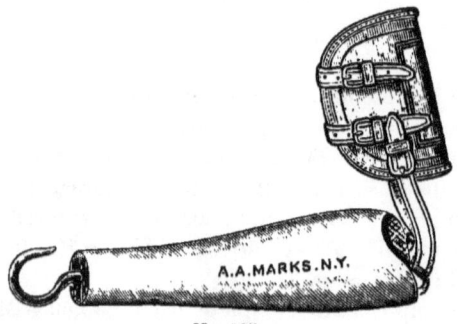

No. 205.

Cut No. 205 represents an arm for amputation below the elbow with hook inserted in wrist; this arrangement secures more utility for the laboring man than any other we know of. If the ordering party desires any of the foregoing arms without a hand there will be a reduction in the price of $10.00.

No. 206.

Cuts Nos. 206–207 represent an apparatus calculated to assist a stump amputated in the metacarpals to grasp and hold articles.

No. 207.

We made a pair of these for a man in New York State, some fifteen years ago; the utility he derived from them was very gratifying; he was able to hold a knife and fork and feed himself. He could grasp almost any farming implement and hold it to advantage.

Price each $25.00.

An order for any of the artificial arms herein described will cover without extra charge the following

ACCESSORIES.

Necessary suspenders attached, sock for stump, knife, fork, hook, brush, pair of kid gloves (except when the arm is ordered without a hand), also boxing and delivering to express or freight office in New York City when desired.

PARTS OF HANDS.

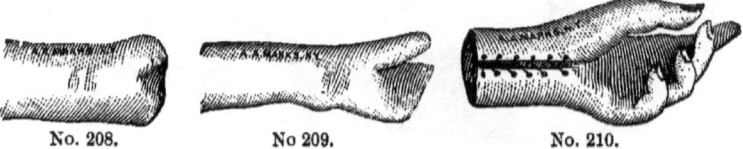

No. 208.   No 209.   No. 210.

Cuts Nos. 208 and 209 represent amputations of the fingers and thumb.

Cut No. 210 represents a rubber hand for the same; the socket extends above the wrist and is held in place by lacing.

The fingers are either ductile, rigid, or flexible according to the purposes for which the hand is to be used. If the wearer wishes to lift considerably, it will be desirable to have the fingers cast in the shape of hooks, and made strong and rigid by a steel skeleton. If the purposes for which the hand is wanted are for appearance and to serve for light work as well, the ductile fingers will be more desirable, and if the hand is for appearance only, and the party wants the rubber hand to be made of the minimum weight, the spongy, flexible fingers will meet his wishes.

As these hands and sections of hands have to be modeled and molded expressly, they are quite expensive, costing $50.00. Duplicates, however, can be had at any subsequent time for the nominal price of $10.00 each.

Plaster casts of both the sound hand and stump, taken well up on the forearm, are required in order to model and fit properly.

No. 211.   No. 212.

Cut No. 211 represents an amputation of the fingers through the metacarpals, thumb remaining.

Cut No. 212 represents a rubber hand for the same. It is attached and held as described in No. 210; the prices and required casts are the same as described for No. 210.

Single fingers or thumbs are made of rubber to fit on the stump, and held in place by the glove or a leather sheath, as may be desired. Price each $15.00.

APPARATUS FOR MALFORMATIONS, DISTORTIONS AND EXSECTIONS OF THE UPPER EXTREMITIES.

We are constantly called upon to make artificial arms and apparatus for malformations, distortions, and a great variety of affections. An exsection of a part of the humerus, or the ulna and radius, or of the elbow joint, can be benefited by an apparatus as represented in Cut No. 213.

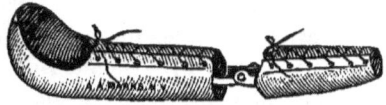

No. 213.

The arm is encased in a manner to give the affected section the necessary firmness to enable the muscles and tendons to act and control the lower sections of the arms.

Price $40.00. Measurements required are explained on pages 89-90.

No. 214.   No. 215.

Cut No. 214 represents an arm distorted by a burn in childhood; the elbow joint fixed; the stump terminated in a bulbous end.

Cut No. 215 represents the arm in which the stump was secured. With this arm the wearer found much comfort; was able to conceal her loss and perform many services.

Price complete $30.00. Measurements required are explained on pages 89-90. In addition a plaster cast of stump required.

RUBBER HANDS APPLIED TO ARTIFICIAL ARMS OF OTHER MANUFACTURE.

Rubber hands can be applied to arms of any method of construction at an expense of $20.00 for each hand, including all the implements.

We will not hesitate to sell the hand separate and allow the wearer to apply it himself.

SUSPENDERS FOR ARTIFICIAL ARMS.

No. 216.   No. 217.

Cut No. 216 represents a suspender for an artificial arm, for any point of amputation. It consists of a shoulder-plate made of stout leather, to which is attached a one-inch non-elastic web strap passing around the body immediately under the arm and buckling to the plate in front. The straps connecting the shoulder-plate with the artificial arm are of leather, adjusted by buckling; if it is desired, these straps can be replaced by a lacing, as in cut No. 217, which makes the adjustment neater though not stronger.

Price for either, $2.00.

A COMBINED KNIFE AND FORK FOR PERSONS HAVING THE USE OF BUT ONE HAND.

Patented March 30th, 1886.

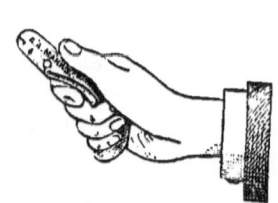 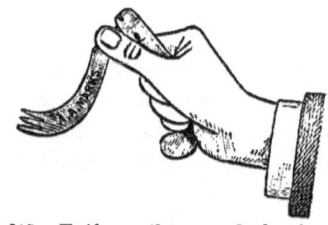

No. 217.—The knife folded as carried in the pocket.   No. 218.—Knife partly opened, showing the manner in which it is done.

No. 219.—Knife open in position for cutting.   No. 220.—Knife inverted and fork brought into position.

The above engravings represent our new device for the convenience of those who have either temporarily or permanently lost the use of one of their hands, and who do not use an artificial hand in eating. It consists of a knife and fork combined, capable of being folded and carried in the pocket. The knife blade is of a crescent shape which, by a rolling movement and a slight pressure given to it by the wrist, will cut meat or any article of food, without danger of sliding from the plate. By rotation of the wrist the fork can be brought into position and the morsels conveniently carried from the plate to the mouth, all accomplished by but one hand, with little exertion, and without attracting attention. The knife blade, in either the opened or closed position, is firmly secured by a locking arrangement which is under the control of the thumb; thus the danger of closing on the fingers when in use, or of opening or cutting or piercing the clothing when carried in the pocket, is obviated. This contrivance is without springs or complication, is simple and effective.

The blade and handle are made of fine steel and heavily nickel plated. The knife can be immersed in hot or cold water for cleansing, without danger of cracking or rusting.

Sent by mail on receipt of $2.00.

DIRECTIONS FOR TAKING MEASUREMENTS AND PROFILES FOR ONE OR A PAIR OF ARTIFICIAL ARMS.

Place a large sheet of paper on a table; undress both arm and stump; extend them on the paper about parallel with each other. Have fingers spread, palm flat on paper, with chest close against the edge of paper; hold a long pencil close to bare person and perpendicular to plane of paper; carry the pencil from the shoulder around each arm and stump to the chest, giving profiles of entire

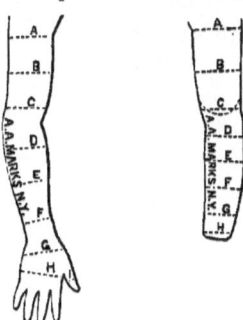

No. 221.

length, including fingers. This, if properly taken, will resemble cut No. 221.

Bend the arm to about right angles at elbow and mark around it in that position as in cut No. 222. Measure the length from point of shoulder to point of elbow, also length from armpit to bend of elbow, as indicated by the dotted lines in cut No. 222.

No. 222.   No. 223.

If amputation is below the elbow, flex the stump at elbow to about right angles and mark around it, as in cut No. 223.

Take circumferences of each arm and stump separately, beginning on a line with the chest, and at intervals of about every two inches, continue as far down as the wrist of arm and extreme end of stump. Take circumference of hand midway between wrist and base of fingers; take circumference of hand under the thumb around the base of fingers.

These measuring places are represented in cut No. 221 by the dotted lines. If the amputation has been at any of the articulations or in any part of the hand, a plaster cast will be required of the stump from end up to the next joint. If there are any peculiarities or sensitive points note them. Answer the following questions:

Name of patient?
Post-office address?
Occupation?
Age?
Weight?
Cause of amputation?
When amputated?
Which arm amputated, right or left?
Has the patient worn an artificial arm?
Whose make? How long?
Name of party ordering arm?
Post-office address?

HOW TO ORDER AN ARTIFICIAL LEG OR ARM.

The data necessary to guide us in the construction of an artificial leg or arm, in the absence of the patient, with positive results, consist of measurements and profiles of both the amputated and sound limbs, as explained on pages 60 to 65 for legs, and pages 89 and 90 for arms. An additional formula with explicit instructions will be furnished upon request. We always send one of these formulæ with every pamphlet; in the event of its becoming separated the directions above referred to can be availed of. These directions should be thoroughly understood and rigorously followed.

When correct measurements are furnished satisfactory results are sure to follow, and all subsequent annoyances of misfit averted. After these measurements and profiles have been made they should be duplicated; the originals placed in a strong envelope together with a letter of instructions and a draft on some banking-house to the amount of the order, sealed securely, with necessary stamps attached to ensure direct carriage, and addressed as follows:

A. A. MARKS,
Artificial Limbs,
701 Broadway, New York City.

If the ordering party resides in a foreign country, and the mail service to New York is attended with the liability of miscarriage,—the duplicate measurements, a copy of the letter of instructions, and a duplicate draft, "good if original is not paid," should be similarly enveloped, addressed, and forwarded by the following mail; one or both of these packets will surely reach us, and should one fail in transmission the other will save the ordering party any serious loss and much delay.

If the patron desires to order through some commission house we suggest that he patronize none but such as are reputably established, and that he give positive instructions that the order be passed to A. A. Marks, New York City, and at the same time write us *directly*, stating the house or party with whom the order has been intrusted.

When the limb is received, see that it has our stamp attached, and do not accept it unless it has.

We desire to guard our patrons against any imposition which might be perpetrated on them by such middlemen as would be unscrupulous enough to place their order with some charlatan in consideration of a large discount, and forward a limb which would neither bear the descriptions in our pamphlet or carry the guarantees of our establishment.

HOW TO TAKE A PLASTER CAST.

Plaster casts are only required in amputations or deformities in which there are irregularities that can not be definitely communicated either by written descriptions or drawings. Usually amputations through any of the articulations are of this character. Plaster casts are never required when the fittings are to be made with the presence of the patient.

The method of taking a plaster cast is simple and can be done by any one of ordinary intelligence.

The simplest plan for taking a cast is as follows : Procure about four or five quarts of the best, finely-ground, quick-setting plaster of Paris. Prepare the stump by divesting it of all covering and by shaving off all the hair. Rub a small amount of vaseline or grease upon it from the end up as far as the cast is to be taken.

Put about a quart of plaster in a vessel and add one pint of water to it ; stir it up thoroughly. (The plaster in this condition should be about the consistency of paste.) Spread the plaster on all sides of the stump, from the end to as far as the cast is to be taken ; if one quart is not sufficient mix up more as quickly as possible and continue spreading it until the entire stump has a coating of about one-quarter inch thickness upon it. When this is done let it rest until it has become thoroughly hard. If the stump will not readily withdraw from the plaster, the mould may be broken in as few pieces as possible in order to remove it from the stump. After the plaster shell is thus taken from the stump the pieces may be put together and tied in their places ; oil the inside thoroughly. Mix more plaster, this time to about the consistency of cream, about one quart plaster and one and a half pints water, fill the mould with it, and let it rest for several hours ; the shell can then be taken from the cast, and a *fac-simile* of the stump will be had. If the stump is very flabby it should be bandaged very tightly with thin cloth, one or two thicknesses only, and the plaster applied on the outside of the cloth.

ARTIFICIAL LIMBS MADE AND FITTED FROM MEASUREMENTS WITHOUT THE PRESENCE OF THE PATIENT.

We claim to be the originators of this very convenient and important feature. At a very early date, after we had had the experience of fitting the person in several hundred cases, we turned our attention to the feature of fitting from measures, chiefly for the accommodation of those residing at a distance and to whom traveling would be inconvenient. We collected all the data we had accumulated, and made ourselves thoroughly acquainted with the anatomy of the extremities, and from them established certain invariable rules which, governed by carefully taken measurements and profiles, established a system by which fitting from measurements became a matter of certainty. This is an achievement for which we claim some consideration. Our competitors viewed our efforts with derision and characterized our motives as ulterior. We are glad, however, to say that results have justified us in our endeavors, and the system which we inaugurated has been a boon to thousands.

It could hardly be expected that persons living in foreign countries, or in our own distant States and Territories, would willingly subject themselves to the fatigue of a wearisome journey in order to get an artificial limb. Such journeys not only incur expense but great sacrifice of time, accompanied with more or less inconvenience. When these facts are taken into consideration the cripple is disposed to forego the purchase of a good leg and buy some make-shift obtainable near at hand, or else resign himself to crutches the remainder of his life.

Our patronage extends throughout the entire world ; within the past few years we have shipped to the following foreign countries : Canada, British Columbia, Newfoundland, England, Ireland, Scotland, Germany, France, Denmark, Sweden, Holland, Spain, Portugal, Italy, Turkey, Japan, U. S. of Colombia, Ecuador, Peru, Chile, Buenos Ayres, Patagonia, Brazil, British Guiana, Venezuela, Guadeloupe, Mexico, San Salvador, Guatemala, Nicaragua, Costa Rica, Santa Domingo, Porto Rico, Trinidad, St. Thomas, Cuba, Jamaica, Bermuda, New Zealand and Australia. With very rare exceptions the limbs for parties in these countries were made and fitted from measurements, and sent to them. The results which followed were generally very flattering. For evidence of our ability to fit persons while they remain at home, we refer to the testimonials printed in this pamphlet. Any one desiring further evidence on the subject can write to any of those parties and receive a written statement from them. It may be noticed that some of our patrons who reside within the short distance of one hundred miles prefer to have the fitting done by measurements, rather than spare the time or submit to the annoyance of coming in person.

We are disposed to encourage fitting from measures, and in order to relieve the ordering party of any responsibility we assume all risks of fit and adaptability, the understanding being,—should a misfit result we will reconstruct the limb or make a new one after new and more accurate measurements; this we do at our own expense, looking to the ordering party to pay expressages only.

Should cases arise in which two or more attempts at fitting from measurements prove unsuccessful, due to peculiarities or irregularities in the stump, incapable of intelligent communication either by measurements, profiles, or plaster casts, then we reserve the privilege of asking the presence of the patient, and will reconstruct the limb to his entire satisfaction. We desire it to be understood, however, that for our own convenience it is preferable to have the patient with us for fitting, and if the patient chooses to come we will never offer the least objection, but will promise to give our earliest and undivided attention immediately upon his arrival. Persons ordering limbs to be fitted without their presence are required to take great care in measuring.

Suitable blanks, with full instructions, are always sent for that purpose. When errors occur, they are usually discovered by a thorough examination before the limb is made, and new blanks returned for new and more correct measures and drafts. The system is such that one can not well make mistakes if he will adhere to the directions that are *plainly* given upon the blank, and repeated in other parts of this pamphlet.

There are some cases, where amputations are performed at the joints, where plaster casts are needed to insure more accuracy; but all usual amputations are treated successfully from measurements only. Printed instructions are always sent with every limb, giving full directions for adjusting, wearing, and caring for the limb.

CALLS MADE TO RESIDENCE.

We will call upon any one desirous of purchasing artificial limbs, residing within the limits of the city, for consultation, measuring, fitting, or advice—free of charge; and upon any party without the city limits, provided they will pay the expense of traveling and a reasonable amount for extra time consumed.

LADY ATTENDANT.

A lady well acquainted with the various departments of the business is employed in the office to give attention to lady patients.

BRANCHES.

We are frequently asked if we have any branches or offices in other parts of the country than in New York City.

To this question we reply, we have not. We have established branches, but have had unpleasant experiences with them; convenient as it would be for our patrons, we are nevertheless compelled to concentrate our endeavors at the headquarters; by doing so we claim to be able to do a greater service to our patrons, give them a better article, and assure them the very best results.

To take the place of branches our system of measurements is found to be sufficient and thoroughly satisfactory.

We have agents established in many parts of the country, who are authorized to solicit orders, take measurements, and apply the limbs; they are required to send all their orders direct to us for execution.

INFORMATION FOR STRANGERS VISITING THE CITY.

We are constantly receiving letters from persons asking for information as to the proper course to take to reach our office, convenient hotel accommodations, etc.

In order to place this information in the hands of all desiring it, we will say that our office, 701 Broadway, is located near Fourth Street, second block above Grand Central Hotel; less than two miles from Grand Central Depot, where the New York, New Haven & Hartford, Harlem, Hudson River, and New York Central railroads terminate in one immense depot. We are located but a trifle over one mile from nearly all the railroad, steamboat, and ferry landings in the city. We mention these distances because the rate of fare to be charged by hacks is governed by a city ordinance, thus: For conveying one or two passengers for any distance not exceeding two miles, $1; for over two and not exceeding three,

$1.50; for over three miles and not exceeding four, $2. This makes it legitimate to charge $1 for conveyance from any of the railroad depots to our office. It is *always* best to make a definite bargain with the hackman before entering his hack, and then hold him *strictly* to it. The Broadway line of cars pass our doors. They can be reached by walking but a few blocks from any depot or ferry, or by taking intersecting line of cars. It is best to make inquiries of a policeman at the depot or landing as to the proper route to take—they are stationed there for the purpose of *directing* as well as *protecting* strangers.

Good hotel accommodations, with or without board, and also restaurants and dining-saloons, are many and near to us, comprising both moderate and expensive rates. One can tarry comfortably in New York at from one dollar per day to any price above that they may choose to pay.

It is often the case that persons upon leaving home wish to inform their friends how to reach them by mail or telegraph. If such communications are directed to them *and* to our care, with our address properly inscribed, the mail will come to us and will be received and held for them.

Our patrons are also welcome to the accommodation of a fireproof safe for the depositing of valuable papers or money. All persons dealing with us and stopping in the city will find us centrally located, and are at liberty to use our premises for their headquarters.

TERMS OF PAYMENT.

Payment is required with every order. If more convenient, one-half the amount can be advanced and the balance paid on completion and delivery. Those who think it unfair for us to exact payment in advance should bear in mind that an artificial limb is made to order and for but one individual; it is not expected that it will fit or can be used by any one else.

Thus is readily seen the necessity of advance payment, or part of it at least, as a guarantee of good faith. The patient can rest confident that just as good a limb and just as good a fit will be secured as though no payment were made until the limb is delivered.

In case any mistake or bad fit occurs we hold ourselves strictly responsible, and will rectify the same with willingness, whether the error can be placed to the carelessness of our workmen or of the patient.

The proposition to place the money on deposit with some business man or in some bank, to be paid to us as soon as the limb is received and found to be satisfactory, is frequently suggested by correspondents. We invariably decline such terms; a little thought will assure any one of the necessity of our position.

A new artificial limb, no matter how well it is made and fitted, or how perfectly well adapted it may be to the case, seldom impresses the wearer favorably at first; there is most always a feeling of disappointment which nothing but perseverance and practice will overcome; if the arrangements in regard to payment are subject to these impressions the maker is pretty likely to have all his labor for nought, and the ordering party, by his hasty conclusion, denied what would ultimately prove to be a blessing. Hence it is obvious, that some obligation on the part of the ordering party must be imposed that will require of him the necessary exertion to overcome the novelty of a new limb. Advance payment is found to be the most efficacious. In view of these facts we shall always insist upon this method; at the same time we obligate ourselves to furnish a serviceable and proper article, and will cheerfully make any alteration that may be necessary to improve matters, at no additional cost to the wearer except expressages.

PAYMENTS ON THE INSTALLMENT PLAN.

We are perfectly willing to allow any one any reasonable length of time in which to pay part of the money for their limbs, and will accept of small payments at periods to suit the convenience of the party, provided one-half the money be paid with the order and the balance be secured by some reliable business house, or by collaterals. Under no consideration will we accept of any proposition that does not fully and amply secure us against any caprice or possible injustice. We propose to deal with all sincerely and honestly, and place our reputation at stake in all transactions. We shall expect the same consideration from others.

GUARANTEE.

Every limb we manufacture and deliver is protected by the following guarantee:

Material, workmanship, and adaptability warranted to be faultless. Should any defects present themselves we obligate ourselves to make them good without charge, provided the limb is delivered to us as soon as such defects are known. This guarantee to be in force for a period of five years from the date of delivery of the limb.

We regard this guarantee consistent and satisfactory to any reasonable mind.

It is well to note that we do not agree to keep the limb in repair for five years irrespective of accidents, improper treatment, or ordinary wear. Nor do we obligate ourselves to reconstruct any limb to meet changes that may take place in the stump.

A written guarantee will accompany every limb when requested. This guarantee printed in our pamphlet will answer every purpose.

ARTIFICIAL LIMBS SUPPLIED TO PENSIONERS OF THE UNITED STATES AT GOVERNMENT EXPENSE.

Artificial limbs have been furnished by the Government to our Nation's defenders, who suffered amputations from injuries received while in service ever since the year 1862. The first law provided but one limb for each amputation; but, in 1870, new laws were enacted which supplied new limbs immediately, and renewed them every *five* years *thereafter*.

The fourth and present general issue commenced about June 17, 1885. The following information, taken from the Surgeon-General's circular, is printed for the benefit of those interested:

"Every officer, or enlisted or hired man, who has lost a limb or the use of a limb in the military or naval service of the United States is entitled to receive once every five years an artificial limb or apparatus. The period of five years is reckoned from the filing of the first application after June 17, 1870, and no arrears accrue previous to each filing.

"Necessary transportation to the manufactory and return, by the most usual and direct route, will be furnished to those desiring it for the purpose of having artificial limbs fitted, but will not be furnished except for this purpose."

Sleeping-car accommodations will be given upon request.

All manufacturers of Government limbs are required to furnish bonds of two sureties of *five thousand dollars each*, for the faithful performance of their work.

Having satisfied this requirement, orders are (and have been for the past twenty years) issued upon us after a proper application has been made by the pensioner. The number of limbs we have made under these laws are in excess of the most extravagant boasting of any manufacturer, and as issue follows issue the applications are constantly on the increase.

Blanks and instructions necessary for applying for government artificial limbs will be sent to pensioners who wish to apply; also blanks for transportation to come and return from any part of the United States for the purpose of having the limb fitted.

Plain common-sense people select plain common-sense articles.

The uncomplicated instruments of war proved the most effectual and most serviceable, and the soldiers know it; the same rule applies with *equal force* to artificial limbs.

Our old soldier patrons need no assurance from us that they will be fairly dealt with, and those who have no practical knowledge of our limbs or of our reputation will do well to correspond with some whose names will be found in the pages of this pamphlet.

Pensioners who reside at a great distance and do not care to travel so far, notwithstanding the fact that the Government will supply them with transportation, can have their Government limbs made from measures and sent to them, same as individuals who were not soldiers, and thus avoid the labor and time of a long journey. Our system of measurements, together with long and extensive experience, insures the very best results. We preserve all our old measurements, as well as a full record of all the limbs made, in a fire-proof safe, and are able to duplicate an order at any time.

Many persons are availing themselves of our facilities and skill, and save their time and money by having their limbs made from measures.

Every pensioner in need of an artificial limb should take advantage of the Government's generosity; by so doing they secure the very best article and are protected by the Government.

Some manufacturers endeavor to have the pensioner draw the money in lieu of the limb and afterwards buy the limb with the money.

As an inducement to follow this plan they offer some rebate; it should be understood that when this is done the manufacturer is relinquished of any obligation his bond has placed him under and the Government has no claims against him.

AMPUTATIONS, DESIRABLE POINTS, AND THE KIND OF OPERATIONS MOST SUITABLE FOR THE USE OF ARTIFICIAL LIMBS.

An amputation that has been made with favorable results for the use of an artificial limb will greatly simplify the problem of supplying the want. On the other hand if the amputation is made regardless of prothesis, the patient is likely to be encumbered with a stump incapable of being supplied with an artificial limb to the best advantage. The latter condition always provokes unpleasant criticism on the ability of the surgeon, and is frequently exhibited as an evidence of his lack of skill.

The surgeon, therefore, can not be too careful in the choice of operation and the point of amputation, not only for the interest of his patient but as well for the protection of his reputation.

Our contact with thousands of amputations, embracing every character and school, ought to place us in a position to give the operator a hint or two that might serve him in the prosecution of his good intentions. We therefore beg to offer a few suggestions.

In the first place the surgeon should acquire some knowledge of artificial limbs. He should know where the points of bearing can be taken in every kind of amputation. He should acquaint himself with the changes that take place in the stump after the application of an artificial limb, so that he can work the stump into a condition that will reduce these changes to the minimum. Under these three heads we propose to discuss this subject.

1st. The surgeon should acquire some knowledge of artificial limbs. This is essential because the successful use of an artificial leg depends in a measure upon the character of the work he has done, and then, too, the surgeon is the first man the patient consults on the subject. If he exposes ignorance the patient is thrown in a state of doubt and worry over the thought that possibly ignorance on the subject had led the operator into errors in his management of the case. And if, on the other hand, to conceal his ignorance, the surgeon has given the patient some wild, fanciful notions concerning artificial limbs, the patient, if of a chimerical disposition, will never be suited with the appliances of the most ingenious maker; he will always be in search for some utopian limb that will bring him to the realization of his expectations, encouraged by his surgeon, who "knows every thing."

Any surgeon can acquaint himself with artificial limbs sufficiently for all practical purposes, in a very few hours; if he can meet a maker who has had considerable experience, an hour's talk with him will suffice; if this is denied, the perusal of the pamphlets of experienced makers will inform him on the subject.

2d. He should know where the points of bearing are taken in every kind of amputation, so as to make the choice of amputation a wise one.

An amputation through the shafts of the bones, or in other words any where between the articulations, leaves the end of the stump insufficiently protected to bear pressure; consequently the weight is necessarily taken in part on the sides of the stump by compression, and in part by opposition of the artificial leg with the enlarging part of the stump. This means: for amputation in the thigh, that the weight is taken on the sides of the stump above the end and about the ischium. For amputations in the lower leg, the

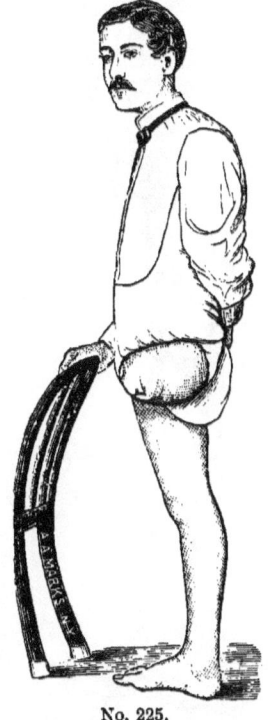

No. 225.

weight is taken on the sides, above the end, and on the surfaces of the interior and anterior tuberosities of the upper section of the tibia.

The exceptions to this rule are too rare to be mentioned.

In disarticulations in which the articular surfaces have not been interfered with and the cicatricial tissues non-adherent, the entire weight of the wearer can be carried on the end with perfect safety and with great relief and comfort to the wearer.

In amputations of the thigh it is a good rule to save all the bone possible; protect the bone with abundant periosteal tissue and carry the flap well to the posterior so as to have the cicatrix distant from the end of the bone.

Cut No. 225 represents an amputation above the middle of the thigh; the stump is held in a horizontal position to show the mobility of the hip. The flap is well carried to the rear and the tissues about the end are free and yielding; although this stump is quite short it can be relied upon for a great amount of work with less danger of irritation than if the femur were several inches longer and unprotected by abundant tissue; this favorable condition may be attributed in whole to the disposition of the cicatrix and the non-adherence of the tissues.

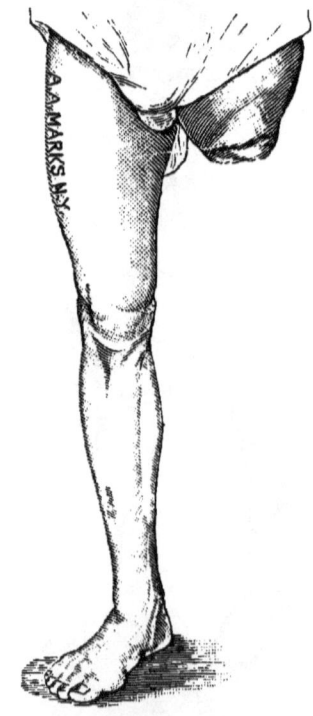

No. 226.

Cut No. 226 shows an amputation above the middle of the thigh in which the tissues, although adherent to the bone, are supplied with accommodating folds, which fortunately protect the cicatrix from danger of laceration.

Without this abundant tissue the stump would be an unfortunate one.

Amputations in the knee joints are very favorable and are preferred to any point above.

An unfortunate practice exists, however, among some operators of trimming the condyles in knee joint amputations; we are very much opposed to this, as the trimming of the condyles in most cases removes the possibility of bearing on the end, as any interference with the condyles has a tendency to remove or impair the natural cushions on the articular surfaces and is likely to render them incapable of enduring the pressure of the weight of the patient. If the patella can be placed in the inter-condylic space and kept there without danger of slipping, it will be quite desirable to do so, but the advantages of having the patella retained are not sufficient to risk any chance of subsequent displacement. The flap for this amputation should be anterior, so as to bring the cicatrix well up on the posterior of the stump.

If this can not be done, let the flap be selected from that part of the leg that will admit of enough tissue to allow the cicatrix to be placed well away from the end.

We advise in all knee-joint amputations to take the weight on the end when it is possible to do so, and find that the best results follow when the wearer is able to take advantage of this condition.

In amputations below the knee it is desirable to save all the length possible down to about the juncture of the middle and lower thirds; between this point and the ankle-joint there can be no advantage in saving length of bone. In an amputation below the knee it is particularly desirable to have the end of the tibia well covered with periosteum, and the flap carried well over the end of the bone so as to avoid adhesion. Teale's method for the lower third amputation is unquestionably one that produces excellent results. The same may be said of his method for thigh amputations.

The most favorable ankle joint amputation for the use of an artificial foot is that known as Symes'; this amputation leaves a stump that combines the greatest number of favorable conditions. In the Symes amputation there is no need of cutting any of the surfaces of the bones; the periosteum should *never* be interfered with and the cicatrix should be located on the anterior surface, a trifle above the end.

The end of the stump carries the weight, and the patient can be supplied with a leg that fills the highest possible conditions and at the least cost. Cut No. 129, page 42, represents a model Symes stump.

Pirogoff's amputation takes a second place to the Symes. There is but little choice between the two, but the preference favors the Symes. Either the Symes' or Pirogoff's amputation commands much respect. They are simple to treat and subject the patient to the least expense in the purchase of substitutes for the lost foot.

Chopart's and Heys' amputations of the foot through the metatarsals leave the most opprobrious of stumps; contrary to the Symes' they are difficult of prothesis; the most practical appliance devised can not compare in utility, comfort, or durability with legs constructed for either of the above tibio-tarsal amputations. The conditions inseparable from the stumps of these amputations leave but little opportunity for the limb-maker.

The natural length of the leg from the knee to the heel is retained, thus allowing no space for attachments or mechanism in the appliance. All the dimensions of the stump from the end to the ankle articulation are either normal or excessive, and as the appliance must encase the stump the diameters about and below the ankle are necessarily very much larger than natural; this gives the appliance an uncomely and clumsy appearance.

The stump from the ankle-articulation will not admit of a firm grasp, as the remaining bones and the neurological complications of the foot are such as to forbid continuous pressure; on account of this the ankle-joint articulation can not be availed of, for, in order to secure an artificial foot to the stump sufficiently firm to enable the wearer to use the ankle joint and rise on the toes without excoriating the stump, the pressure required about the stump would be so great that it would induce unpleasant consequences. On account of this it is necessary to carry the artificial above the ankle, encasing the leg very nearly as far as the knee, depending on the shaft of the leg for security, leaving the stump free and entirely disregarding the articulation of the ankle.

The most serious objection, however, to these amputations, and which ought alone to debar them from license, is the disposition of the amputated surface pointing downward, occasioned by the severance of the flexors, thus destroying all opposition to the extensors. The cutting of the tendo-achilles is occasionally the resort to counteract this tendency, but this is only partial relief at the best.

The Symes' or Pirogoff's amputations secure so many advantages not possible to be attained in the Choparts', Heys', or any of the amputations below the ankle joint, that really we can only see complications and difficulties in retaining parts of the bones of the foot.

Amputations of the upper extremities or arms can be safely governed by one rule,—that is, to save all the length possible with a preference for disarticulations to amputations above. The utility of an artificial hand compared with the natural is almost insignificant, therefore it is desirable to retain every thing possible. Exsection of the ulna, radius, humerus, or of any of the articulations that will leave the hand or even a part of the hand in place and under muscular control, should by all means be preferred to an amputation. A single finger or even the metacarpals will be of more value than any artificial hand ever invented. Our prayer to the surgeon is therefore to save every thing possible in all surgical operations in the upper extremities.

3d. The changes that take place in a stump after the use of an artificial limb, and which in a measure can be obviated by the surgeon.

The almost invariable tendency of a stump immediately after recovery from the amputation is to accumulate fat. This not only enlarges the stump but makes it flaccid.

The effect of an artificial limb on a stump in this condition is to crowd out the fatty tissue and harden and solidify the stump; this change is desirable, as a stump can never control an artificial limb to the best advantage until such a change has taken place; but unfortunately this change when brought about by the use of an artificial limb unfits the stump for the artificial limb—as the stump becomes smaller the artificial limb becomes looser; it is true the wearer can add coverings to his stump or place linings in the socket of the limb, but both of these methods are objectionable, as they add weight and are more or less uncomfortable; the better way, however, is to have a new socket applied to the limb and fitted to the reduced stump.

The surgeon in most cases has it in his power to obviate the occurrence of these changes, by the simple method of bandaging the stump tightly from the end upward and continuing in the same, up to the time of the application of the leg. Tight bandages will not admit of undue growth, and have a tendency to reduce the stump to small dimensions. In addition to tight bandages, frequent rubbing or massage, with occasional bathing with clear water, will keep the stump in a healthy condition.

The frequent movement of the joints, sufficiently violent to bring a tension on the tendons, will preserve full movement and check the tendency to either contract or anchylose.

It will be a fortunate day when the medical and surgical institutions of the land will add to their curriculums the subject of amputations and the treatment of stumps with view to prothesis. Up to the present time the practitioner has to learn from experience; he is thrown entirely on his own resources, and, being usually an occupied man, can ill afford the time to devote to a subject that to his mind is of little gravity. In consequence of this he is very likely to run into errors.

To continue tight bandages after the stump is healed and sound, for the purpose of keeping the stump down to small dimensions, is so unnatural that his mind is slow to comprehend the importance of it ; and the opposite disposition is likely to prevail—that of encouraging growth so as to have the stump assume the proportions of the opposite or sound leg.

HOW SOON AFTER AMPUTATION SHOULD AN ARTIFICIAL LIMB BE APPLIED?

Experience shows that the most suitable time to apply an artificial limb is as soon after the healing and recovery from shock as possible. A little thought will convince any one of the prudence of this. We have already called attention to the fact that stumps immediately after recovery from amputation tend to grow large and flabby, and that the joints become enervated and the muscles tend to contract. To counteract these tendencies we have prescribed bandages, massage, and frequent vigorous movements of the joints, to be persisted in until the artificial limb is applied. As soon as an artificial limb is applied the artificial limb controls these tendencies.

We have applied limbs to stumps within one month after amputation with very excellent results ; this period, however, for the usual case is too brief. A safe rule to govern this matter is, as soon after healing as possible.

Patients are frequently advised to wait until the stump becomes hard and tough ; this advice is an evidence of a lack of knowledge on the subject. Nothing but use will make the members of the human body hard and tough. The bottoms of our natural feet are hard and calloused from constant walking upon them. The hands of a laborer are strong and hard from the constant use he puts them to, while those of the unoccupied are soft, tender, and effeminate ; nothing but use keeps our joints strong and flexible. Allow a sound and healthy arm to hang uselessly by the side for a month and the consequence will be that the arm will become so enervated that it will require a great effort even to move it. A stump hanging uselessly from the body undergoes the same enervating changes ; hence we say, apply a leg as soon as possible after the healing and recovery from the shock. The following correspondence on this subject will, we hope, be read with interest :

STEPHEN G. COOK, M. D.,
          New York City.

DEAR SIR—Your experience as a surgeon and physician, and more especially as United States Government Inspector of Artificial

Limbs, purchased by the Government for the disabled soldiers, enables you to exercise a practical as well as theoretical knowledge upon the important question of what constitutes a proper period to elapse after amputation before applying an artificial limb.

Upon this very important question surgeons differ very widely, and I desire to obtain your opinions for publication, and trust you will contribute a full expression of your views upon the subject.

Yours very truly,
A. A. MARKS.

REPLY.

Mr. A. A. MARKS.

DEAR SIR—Your letter, asking my opinion as to the length of time to intervene between the amputation of a limb and the application of an artificial one, has been received, and in response I would say that I would allow just as long a time to elapse as is necessary for the thorough healing of the stump, and no longer.

In my opinion there are at least three good and sufficient reasons why the interval should be brief, to wit:

First. Because by disuse the muscles left by the amputation, and which in the future are to control the action of not only the stump but also the artificial limb thereto attached, become *undisciplined;* that is to say, they lose the nice co-operation there is naturally between them and the will-power.

That muscles act under the strictest discipline needs no further evidence than to watch the skillful movements of any trained artisan and compare them with the bungling efforts of the unskilled, the untrained, and the undisciplined. After an amputation the muscles left are necessarily for a time unused, and if left too long lose the power of responding to and being governed by the will. The application of the artificial limb is the first impulse that arouses them from their long period of inactivity; hence, in my opinion, it should be applied just as soon as practicable after the stump has healed.

Second. My second reason is based upon the old physiological law that "action increases strength." Compare the muscular development of the blacksmith, the boat-rower, the trained athlete and gymnast, with those of gentlemen of leisure and pleasure, and the adage needs no further proof. The muscles of an amputated limb not only become undisciplined, but they also become atrophied, shrunken, and effeminate, and the longer they are unused the more atrophied they become. The shrinking of the muscular tissues is supplemented by a deposit of adipose tissue (fat), so much so that sometimes when the manufacturer of artificial limbs is applied to, he finds, instead of a hard and firm stump, what has more the appearance of a mass of quivering jelly.

Third. My third reason is applicable to the loss of a lower limb only, and refers to the use of crutches. Under the most favorable circumstances, it is a difficult task to learn to use an artificial leg skillfully and naturally, a task that some learn much more readily than others, the same difference existing between individuals in this respect as in learning a science or a trade. The patient who has learned to balance himself upon a pair of crutches, and to get along as rapidly and almost as easily as before he was injured, is very apt to become both discouraged and disgusted when, on the application of an artificial limb, he discovers he has to learn the art of locomotion all over again. Under such circumstances, unless possessed of more than the usual share of energy and determination, he is too apt to lay the artificial limb one side for intervals too long to enable him to become speedily accustomed to its use.

For these and other reasons that might be mentioned, my experience of over twenty years as surgeon both in civil and military life, as well as inspecting surgeon of artificial limbs for the United States Government, has led me to the conclusion that the period of time that should elapse between the healing of the stump and the application of the artificial limb can not be too brief.

Yours very truly,
S. G. COOK, M. D.,
111 West 12th Street, New York City.

CHILDREN.

Children who lose one or both of their limbs before they attain their full growth are sometimes prevented from applying artificials on the ground that they will soon outgrow them. This appears at first glance sufficient reason, but a little reflection will show that it is ill advised. The child's growth and symmetrical development being paramount, the use of an artificial limb is the only method by which the child's growth can be governed and its development made uniform and symmetrical.

An artificial limb can be lengthened at any time at an expense not exceeding five dollars, and sometimes much less. It may be well to here state that the limbs we manufacture possess a very important advantage over *all* others in this respect, on account of their being free from internal complications of cords and springs, thus saving the largest part of the expense attending the operation of lengthening the limb to keep up with the growth of the patient.

The most important point to be taken into consideration in this matter is, how shall we most benefit the tender sprig of childhood, whether by compelling him to use crutches and grow up round-shouldered, one-sided, or otherwise ill shaped, as frequently results from the long use of crutches, or at once to apply a substitute, and pay proper attention to the lengthening, and thereby avoid the unpleasant sight of a cripple, and the mortifying effect (to say nothing of the great inconvenience) to the patient. Another very important fact should be taken into consideration, and that is that a child growing up without a substitute to exercise the stump impairs the use of it, either by its becoming permanently contracted or enervated. When an artificial limb is applied at the proper time, and the child grows with it, the child never seems to fully realize the loss, and becomes the most skillful of operators. No child that loses a leg at any age should go without a substitute for a single year after the stump is healed. Some are without means to secure limbs, and others will say that they can not afford it. Then call upon your friends for assistance, or do some thing to provide for the necessity of your child and avoid its growing up in your sight a deplorable spectacle of misfortune.

"To clinch the nail of theory with a few blows from the hammer of experience," we present the following cases.

No. 227.

No. 228.

Mabel Thompson, cut No. 227, had her leg amputated very close to her knee joint when she was but nine months old—before she began to creep. The stump, from disuse and for better protection, involuntarily tended backward and upward. There was apparent tendency to anchylosis or stiffening of the knee.

On consultation with the surgeons it was decided that an artificial leg properly fitted, with joints to operate in harmony with the natural knee, would swing and force the stump to move as the child was being carried, thus check anchylosis and restore the full amount of motion. We applied a leg to her when she was about one year old. In a short time she began to creep. A few months after her parents were surprised to find her standing alone. She soon began to walk, and at this writing the child is less than five years old, and walks, runs, and frolics about just like other children of her age. Cut No. 228 represents her with an artificial limb applied.

The leg has been lengthened and enlarged to accommodate her rapid growth, at an expense not exceeding the renewal of crutches. Had this child been neglected in her infancy, instead of the cheerful, healthy, active little girl you see in the picture, in all probability she would now be a weak, helpless object of pity. On examination you would find a stump, contracted, weak, and almost lifeless, which would be a burden to her all her life. As it is, her stump is a model of health, strength, and usefulness, and will never fail in controlling an artificial leg with advantage, comfort, and naturalness.

No. 229.

Cut No. 229 represents a little girl eight years of age, one view exposing her stump and artificial leg; in the other she is dressed and ready for walking. This girl grew up, developed, and at this writing is a lady of graceful proportions.

Would she now be so well-formed, healthy, and competent to occupy her proper sphere in life, had she grown up without the aid of this substitute? Her picture, cut No. 230, shows clearly what she now is.

It is very well understood that young ladies wearing artificial limbs are not over-desirous of having it publicly known; this is not

No. 230.

an exception; nevertheless her name and address will be given, when desired by persons giving satisfactory reasons. She resides in New York City.

Cut No. 231 represents Mr. Thomas Kehr exposing his stumps. At the age of ten the lad was run over by the cars, which caused the amputation of both legs, one above, the other just below the knee. In December, 1875 (just about a year after the accident), we applied a pair of artificials as illustrated in the cut.

In two weeks thereafter he was walking very well without a cane. Two months passed and he was walking and getting about, up and down stairs, and in fact everywhere he wished to go, without any assistance whatever, with such ease and comfort that it was absolutely wonderful for such short and unfavorable stumps as his.

Cut No. 232 shows how he appears with his limbs on and dressed. This case is another which practically illustrates the great importance of applying substitutes to those who are maimed in tender years.

No. 231.   No. 232.

Dr. Brady's letter on this case will doubtless be found of interest.

BROOKLYN, E. D., NEW YORK,
May 16th, 1876.

MR. A. A. MARKS.

DEAR SIR—I have thoroughly examined the case of the boy Thomas Kehr, of this city, who has been wearing a pair of your artificial legs for the past six months. About a year and a half ago he was run over by a train of the S. S. R. R. of Long Island, and both of his lower limbs were so crushed that I amputated them, the one well above the knee, the other about one inch and a half below. At the time of the operation many expressed a wish that death would occur, as the lad being very poor it was thought that his future would not only be a burden to himself but that his future support, should he reach man's estate, would depend upon the charity of the public, as it was considered about an impossibility for him to serviceably use artificial limbs.

I am thankful that I can say that you have made his future worth the living, by giving him the means of good locomotion.

I saw him two weeks after he had put them on for the first time, and it astonished me greatly to see the remarkable use he had already acquired; since then I have seen him *many* times, and have each time seen marked improvement in the freedom of use in walking.

Within the past week I saw him walking on the street without even the help of a cane, and so little lamed that any person seeing him would not for the moment have the least suspicion that he was using legs other than such as nature provided.

I feel competent to say that in this case your artificial limbs have proved a grand success. I have never before seen artificial limbs which in action approached so near that of perfection.

I attribute the wonderful success in this boy's case mainly to the superior results achieved by your inventions.

Especially can attention be called to the use of the rubber foot, thereby dispensing with the ankle joint, thus giving the wearer an *elastic, reliable,* and *sure footing,* which must greatly relieve him from the care and *watchfulness* which must certainly be required by those who wear artificial limbs having jointed feet.

Your plain and simple mode of construction of artificial legs is to my mind *unquestionably* the *best,* and when asked by legless persons as to whose make of artificial limbs would prove the best to secure comfort and utility, I most decidedly say, without any hesitation, Marks'.

Very respectfully,
SAMUEL J. BRADY, M.D.

DIFFICULTIES OVERCOME.

Amputations and deformities are frequently attended by complications that make the adjustment of substitutes very difficult.

We have given special attention to these matters and have always been able to cope with the most perplexing.

This may be surmised from the very peculiar apparatus illustrated in the fore part of this book. There are, however, anomalous cases presented every day that require some unusual method of treatment.

Cut No. 233 represents an amputation a little above the ankle joint. The conditions of the case were as follows: The foot and ankle had been mutilated by a railroad accident. The tibia about four inches below the patella had been injured so that a scale of dead bone of about two inches by one inch was by the slow process of nature disintegrating and separating itself from the living.

The amputation was performed a little above the malleoli. There being scant material at this part of the leg to furnish a copious flap, the extremities of the bones were poorly protected. The dead scale remained on the tibia partly exposed with ulcerations about its border. Examination revealed the facts that no pressure could be taken either on the end of the stump or on the sides of the extremity, and further, that the tissues about the dead bone were sensitive and painful to the touch.

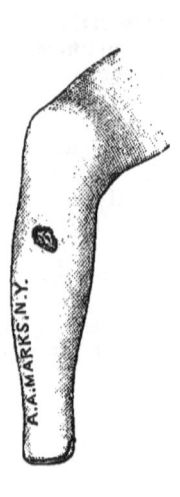

No. 233.

No. 234.

Even slight compression on the calf would irritate the diseased part. The patient came to us in this condition and was very anxious that something should be done to enable him to get about and discard his crutches. The leg we constructed was provided with a laced front, adjustable so that pressure could be taken about parts where it could be endured. Cut No. 234 represents the leg applied.

This gentleman found the artificial leg of great benefit. With it he was able to go about without crutches and attend to his wants.

The following case is one worthy of special notice. The subject met with an accident on an ocean steamer, which mangled his left arm, left leg, and dislocated the left hip joint. The arm was amputated in the shoulder joint, and hip dislocation reduced, but subsequently the leg was amputated in the middle third of the thigh. A short time after, the subject was taken with an epileptic fit and fell out of bed. The fall redislocated the hip, which unfortunately was not noticed until about two months had elapsed. It was then deemed inadvisable to make any attempt at reduction, as the stump had not thoroughly healed. The subject was confined to his bed for several months, when he was permitted to go about the hospital and the grounds in a rolling chair. His stump having become healed, he was placed under our charge. An examination revealed the following complications: Left hip still dislocated, stump about eight inches long, measured from the perinæum; on account of the hip dislocation the stump inclined interiorly several degrees. From disuse and long confinement the right leg became enervated, with considerable contraction of the knee extensors. The patient could not bear any weight on his natural leg. Even with the help of two attendants he was not able to stand erect.

No. 235.

Our first duty was apparent, that of restoring strength to his right leg, and full mobility to the knee of the same. With this in view we directed his attendants to apply massage and to work the knee vigorously; this was continued for two weeks with little perceptible benefit.

We then suggested the Dr. Meigs Case Apparatus, the purpose

being to hold the patient in a vertical position, suspended from all the available parts of his body, and at a suitable height to enable him to barely touch his one foot to the floor. Fig. No. 235 represents the patient suspended in the chair.

The suspension was easy, comfortable, and almost a luxury.

Propulsion was obtained by the right foot touching the floor at intervals. In a brief time he had recovered sufficient strength to command the movements of the chair. Favorable results followed rapidly. Full extension of the knee was obtained, followed by restored strength and a very favorable tendency of the stump to hang vertically. The hip dislocation showed a disposition to reduce. We applied an artificial leg in due course of time with results that justified all our endeavors. The patient returned to his home soon after, and from the latest we can learn of him his progress is flattering.

We commend the Meigs Case Apparatus for cases of unusual weakness and spinal troubles, and will supply them to parties at a reasonable price.

OUR FOREIGN TRADE.

This department of our business has increased rapidly and assumed proportions to require special attention.

We have applicants from all quarters of the world, and are filling orders for foreign countries constantly, more particularly for South and Central America and Mexico. No stronger testimony of the durable and satisfactory qualities of our work can be given than this, from the fact that these parties living at so great a distance choose our work because they are denied access to the manufactory, and require an article that will keep intact and in good working order without frequent repairing.

In view of these facts, we have found it necessary to publish an edition of our pamphlet in the Spanish language, which has been widely circulated and is bringing in large returns.

To introduce us to those with whom we have had no dealings and assure them of our business standing and responsibility the following certificate was prepared and signed by the distinguished men whose names are thereto appended. In addition to this certificate, in other parts of this book we print a translation of some of the letters of commendation, together with a few abstracts from complimentary notices taken from the foreign press. We deem it not out of place to introduce this matter in our English pamphlet, as this book will, in all probability be circulated extensively in foreign countries, and doubtless it will reach some one who would prefer the Spanish edition, to whom it will be sent on application.

CERTIFICATE.

(Translated from the Spanish.)

We certify that the establishment of A. A. Marks, of this city, is one of the oldest and most responsible in the manufacture of artificial limbs.

This establishment is one that offers the best guarantees of any in the United States.

HIPOLITO DE URIARTE, Consul General of Spain, 1883.
JOSE CARLOS TRACY, Consul of Peru.
JACOBO BAIZ, Consul General of Guatemala and Salvador.
HIPOLITO BILLINI, Consul of the Republic of Dominica.
FRANCIS SPIES, Consul General of Equador.
MELCHOR OBARRIO, Consul General of Bolivia.
D. DE CASTRO & CO.
F. PARRAGA.
TELLADO GIBERGA & CO.
A. G. DICKERSON.
JOSE G. GARCIA.
R. & C. DEGENER CO.
JOHN OSBORNE, SON & CO.
P. E. DESVERNINE.
KANE & BEHRENS.
C. JULIAN.
ABRAHAM BAIZ.
WM. R. GRACE, Merchant and Mayor of the City of New York.
J. DE RIVERA & CO.

S. SAMPER & CO.
N. PONCE DE LEON.
EDWARDO AVILA, Official of Uruguay's Legation.
MIGUEL SUAREZ, Consul General of Spain, 1884.
CARLOS FARINI, Consul General of Uruguay.
CLUNACO CALDERON, Consul of U. S. Colombia.
SALVADOR DE MENDONCA, Brazilian Consul General in United States.
LAVANDEYRA BROS.
E. EGNES.
F. MIRANDA & CO.
JOS. F. SPINNEY.
HORATIO R. HAMILTON, Consul of U. S. of Venezuela.
R. MARTINEZ, Consul of Argentine Republic.
JUAN RUIZ.
DAVIS BROS.
PAREZ TRIANA & CO.
J. BARKER READ CO.
FREDK. PROBST & CO.

SOCKS FOR STUMPS.

The question is frequently asked by inexperienced persons, "Is the socket of the artificial limb padded, or what protects the stump from contact with the wood?" Our reply to this question is that padding or lining permanently placed in a socket is found to be objectionable; if of an absorbent material it becomes offensive by the exudations of the stump; it soon hardens, becomes rough, and is attended with other weighty objections. The best method we know of is to draw on the stump one or more woolen or cotton socks, made of fine soft yarn, knit to fit the stump as well as stockings do the feet.

These socks should be frequently removed and washed; by this method the stump will be kept clean and in a healthy condition.

We have a department for knitting these socks, and keep a large stock constantly on hand; they are arranged in eleven different sizes calculated to fit any ordinary stump; should, however, a size or shape be desired different to the sizes in stock, we will knit them to order at no advance in price. They are made of woolen or cotton yarn, white or colored, as may be desired.

Unless otherwise ordered a colored woolen sock will be sent in response to the order.

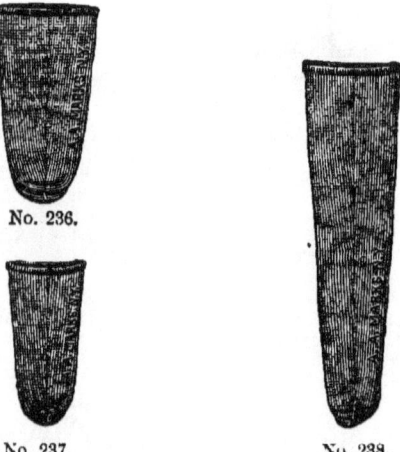

No. 236.

No. 237.

No. 238.

The general appearance of socks can be understood from the cuts.

NUMBER.	LENGTH.	CIRCUMFERENCE AT THE LARGEST END.	PRICE EACH.	PRICE PER DOZEN.
0	1 to 10 inches.	Less than 15 inches.	$ .40	$4.00
1	10 to 15 "	" 15 "	.50	5.00
2	10 to 15 "	Over 15 "	.60	6.00
3	15 to 20 "	Less than 15 "	.60	6.00
4	15 to 20 "	Over 15 "	.70	7.00
5	20 to 25 "	Less than 15 "	.70	7.00
6	20 to 25 "	Over 15 "	.80	8.00
7	25 to 30 "	Less than 15 "	.80	8.00
8	25 to 30 "	Over 15 "	.90	9.00
9	30 to 35 "	Less than 15 "	.90	9.00
10	30 to 35 "	Over 15 "	1.00	10.00

In some cases of amputation below the knee, a short sock in addition to a full length one to come only to the knee joint is desired. For such cases No. 0, 1, or 3 will be suitable. In taking measures for socks, adhere to the following instructions :

First. Take length of stump from body to end, then circumferences at body and at distances of about three inches apart.

In determining the number of size, five inches should be added to the length of stump to allow for turning over the top of leg and the shortening caused by the stretch in drawing on the stump. If the sock is to cover the stump from end to the knee only, commence at the knee, and state length from centre of knee-joint to end, circumference at knee, and so on down. If for a knee bearing stump, take measures as in cases where the knee joint is used and flexible.

One-half and one-quarter dozen sold at the same rates as per dozen. The same furnished in cotton at the same price. Orders for socks filled and sent by mail or express, carriage prepaid by us

SUPPLIES FOR ARTIFICIAL LIMBS.

Webbing.—We have manufactured, expressly for our own use, a superior quality of webbing, which is more suitable in strength and color for artificial limbs than any other in the market ; its color is light, and is not affected by perspiration. We can fill orders for the same at the following rates, and in any quantity desired :

Elastic Webbing, 2 inches wide, per yard, 60 cents.
Elastic Webbing, 1½ inch wide, per yard, 50 cents.
Elastic Webbing, 1 inch wide, per yard, 40 cents.
Non-elastic Webbing, 2 inches wide, per yard, 30 cents.
Non-elastic Webbing, 1½ inches wide, per yard, 25 cents.
Non-elastic Webbing, 1 inch wide, per yard, 20 cents.

Buckles, old style, two-tongue, 2, 1½, and 1 inch, nickel-plated, very strong, each, 5 cents.

Buckles, 5-8 and 7-8 inch, for leather use, single-tongue, each, 10 cents.

Clamp Buckles, see Cut 183, page 69, each, 25 cents.

Rollers, see Cut 184, page 69, each, 25 cents.

Screw Buttons, see Cut 189, page 71, per pair, 50 cents.

Check-straps, for legs for amputation below the knee, made of non-elastic webbing, comprising two or more thicknesses. Two thicknesses, each, 40 cents. Three thicknesses, each, 50 cents.

Lacings, of fine buckskin, average length, 50 inches, each, 25 cents ; $2.50 per dozen, or $1.25 per half-dozen.

Bolts, of fine steel, applied to side joints of below-knee legs, complete with screws, per pair, $2. (The leg must be sent to us to have them properly applied.)

Spiral Springs, of fine-tempered steel, used in knee-joints of above-knee and knee-bearing legs, with cylinder, complete, $1 ; without, 25 cents.

No. 239.

Knives, Forks, Brushes, and Hooks, made to fit palm of hand or wrist of artificial arm, of our own make. Knives and forks, each, 50 cents. Brushes and hooks, each, $1.

Screw-drivers, made of steel sufficiently strong to turn the larger screws in a leg or arm, each, 25 cents.

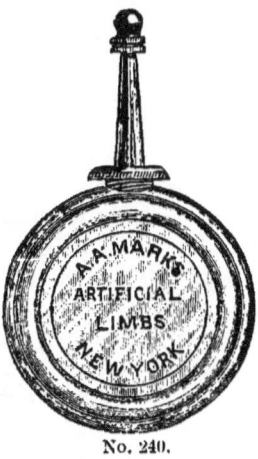

No. 240.

Oil-cans. Cut No. 240 represents a new style of oil-can, neat and compact, capable of being carried in the pocket; oil can not escape; each, 25 cents.

Grease. Above the knee and knee-bearing legs require a substance with more body than oil for their journals. We have a preparation for this purpose. The compound is prepared in small tin boxes, containing enough to last one year. Per box, 10 cents. (Can not be sent by mail, must be sent by express.)

Felt—of fine wool—used for pads and fillings, the best substance for lining a socket when the stump has reduced. Rates: 1-8 of an inch in thickness, per square inch, 1-2 of a cent; 3-16 of an inch in thickness, per square inch, 3-4 of a cent; 1-4 of an inch in thickness, per square inch, 1 cent. Cut a paper pattern so that it will surround that part of the stump desired to be covered, multiply the length by the breadth half-way between the top and bottom, thus ascertaining the number of square inches wanted. Send the paper pattern to us and we will cut the felt to suit.

Socks and any of the above-named articles except grease (which is not mailable) will be forwarded by mail, post-prepaid by us, when orders are accompanied by the money.

The system of sending goods by express, C. O. D. (collect on delivery), is very well and satisfactory when dealing with business houses, but many persons of unbusiness-like principles order articles recklessly, thinking they will be able to pay for them when they arrive, and subsequently, finding it not convenient to do so, allow the goods to be returned, incurring an expense of transportation both ways for which we receive nothing. On account of the frequency with which this has occurred, we will send nothing C. O. D. unless some of the money is advanced to assure us of good faith on the part of the ordering party.

HOW TO REMIT.

In making remittances of large amounts, it is advisable to send by a money order, postal note, registered letter, express, or draft on New York. Fractional parts of a dollar may be sent in postage stamps. In ordering, state the precise article or articles desired, and do not omit giving, together with your name, your post-office address in full, with county and State. Address all communications to

A. A. MARKS,
701 Broadway,
New York City.

CRUTCHES.

Every person who has lost a leg ought to be the possessor of a pair of crutches, whether he wears an artificial leg or not.

It is not intended to be understood that crutches are necessary when wearing artificial legs, or even at the beginning, but there are occasions constantly arising in a cripple's life when a pair of crutches can be used to great advantage.

A sore on the stump, an injury to the sound leg, a sprain in either knee, and a hundred other causes are likely to occur that will render a pair of crutches invaluable. The cost of crutches is trifling, and any one can own a pair at a very little sacrifice. The crutches which we here offer are fine, strong, and tasty. They are made of rosewood, lancewood, and rock maple, as may be desired. Rock maple are the strongest and the most chosen, and are always sent unless other kinds are ordered. If the natural light color of the wood is objectionable they can be had stained, ebony or rosewood at an additional expense of $1 per pair.

The wood in all our crutches is selected with great care. The arm pieces and hand rests for the rock maple or lancewood crutch are of fine grain cherry; the hand rests are secured with long rivets passing from one side of the crutch entirely through the handle and riveted to the opposite side. This is done as a security against accidents which have so frequently occurred with the use of screws as in other styles.

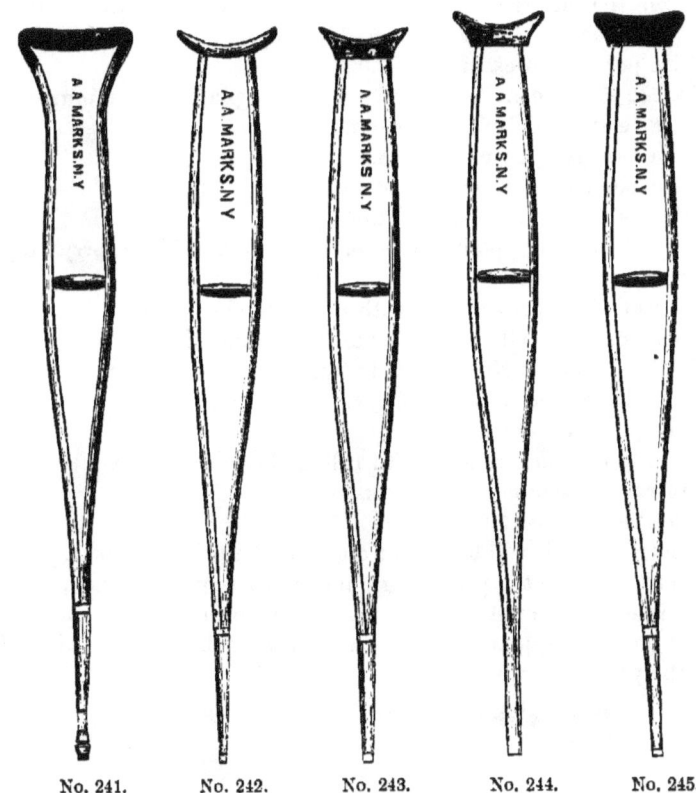

No. 241. No. 242. No. 243. No. 244. No. 245.

The above cuts represent the different style of crutches. Description and prices as follows :

No. 241 is known as the Whitmore crutch; side sticks are steam bent ; top made of genuine Russia leather; stuffed with curled hair secured to side sticks. The yielding soft quality of the top, which is made more elastic by the springing of the side stick, makes a most delightful rest for the arm.

Patented clamp ferrules No. 246 are used for the bottoms.

They hold No. 249 tips. All the trimmings are nickel-plated. The crutch is highly finished.

Price per pair, rosewood, $10.00.

Price per pair, lancewood, $10.00.

Price per pair, rock maple, $8.00.

No. 242 is known as the " cow-horn top " crutch on account of its cow-horn resemblance. They are very light, tasty, and durable. The top is made of cherry, very smooth and highly polished. This top is frequently preferred to the cushion ; they are as comfortable.

and from the fact that they are smooth, do not wear the clothing nearly as much as the elastic or padded top.

Price per pair, rock maple, $3.00.

No. 242½ same as 242, with full nickel-plated trimmings with No. 248 ferrules and No. 249 rubber tips.

Price per pair, rosewood, $6.00.

Price per pair, lancewood, $6.00.

Price per pair, rock maple, $4.00.

No. 243 ordinary plain rock maple crutch with cherry tops.

Price per pair, $2.50.

No. 244, plain split crutch with ordinary cherry tops.

Price per pair, with No. 250 rubber bottoms, $2.00.

No. 245, same as No. 243, with upholstered top made of leather stuffed with curled hair, making an agreeable soft top.

Price per pair, $3.00.

No. 245½, same as 245, with full nickel-plated trimmings, No. 248 ferrules and number 249 rubbers.

Price per pair, $4.00.

A single crutch will be sold at one-half the price of a pair.

In ordering use the preceding numbers to avoid confusion.

Enclose the amount of money with the order. Give length in inches from arm-pit to the floor when arm is hanging by the side and the person standing erect.

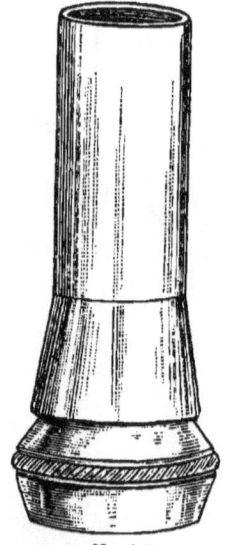
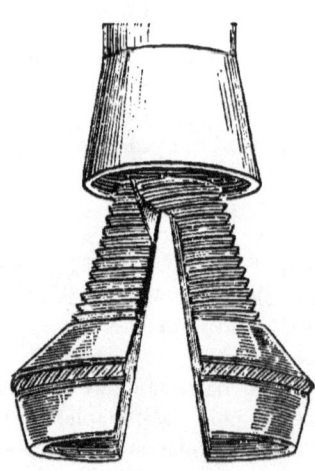

No. 246.   No. 247.

No. 246 represents the patented clamp ferrule without the rubber tip.

No. 247 represents the same with jaws expanded ready to receive rubber tip No. 249, which is secured firmly by screwing the jaws in the socket. These clamp ferrules are made of cast brass, nickel-plated, and can be screwed on the ends of any crutch ¾ inch in diameter.

Price per pair, with rubber tip No. 249, $2.50.

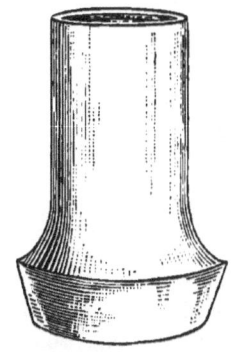

No. 248.   No. 249.

No. 248 represents a heavy brass nickel-plated ferrule capable of holding No. 249 rubber tip. The tip in this ferrule has to be squeezed in place. The operation is a little more difficult than in No. 246, but after being once placed it is held securely. Can be screwed in crutches ¾ inch in diameter.

Price per pair with rubber tips No. 249, $1.00.

No. 249 represents rubber tips to be used with Nos. 246 and 248 ferrules. Size one inch in diameter.

Price per pair 25 cents.

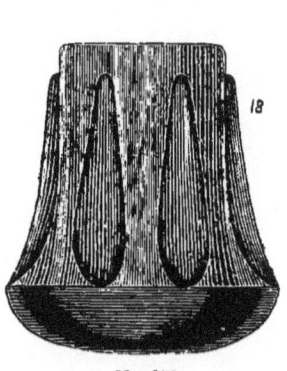
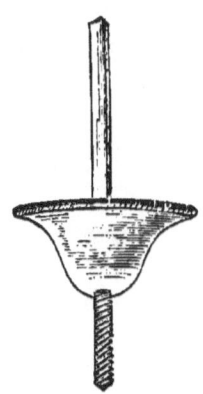

No. 250.   No. 251.

No. 250 represents rubber ferrules calculated to slip on the ends of crutches in order to prevent the crutch from slipping or making a harsh thumping noise as well as marring floors.

They can be applied to No. 242, 243, 244, and 245, crutches; they will take the place of metallic ferrules and answer every purpose. They can be slipped on the end of a crutch that has been shortened, and will protect the wood. They are excellent to use on walking canes, and are so used to quite an extent; they are not, however, as lasting as No. 249 tips.

These tips are of five sizes.

No. 17 fits $5/8$ in. diameter, price per pair 35 cents.
No. 18 fits $3/4$ in. diameter, price per pair 35 cents.
No. 19 fits $7/8$ in. diameter, price per pair 35 cents.
No. 20 fits 1 in. diameter, price per pair 40 cents.
No. 21 fits 1 $1/8$ in. diameter, price per pair 40 cents.

Cut No. 251 represents an adjustable ice spike. It consists of a brass cone with a steel spike passing through it. One end of the spike is inserted in the rubber tip or end of crutch, and the opposite end projects beyond the cone. No. 249 tip is made with a hole through its centre to receive the spike.

The spike can be adjusted to suit the surface with which it is to come in contact simply by turning the cone.

Price per pair 50 cents.

STATISTICS.

At this writing the last order for an artificial leg or arm bears the number of 8600. Records of only about 3,500 of these are found sufficiently full to enable us to tabulate for statistical purposes. With great care and very much labor these 3,500 cases have all been thoroughly reviewed and the following percentages computed. We hope the interest these statistics may provoke will justify us in devoting so much time and space to the subject. It is the only time to our knowledge that such statistics have been prepared.

Of all the artificial limbs made by us 85% are legs and 15% arms. This small percentage for arms may be explained by the fact that fewer persons who have lost their arms supply themselves with artificials than those who have lost their lower extremities, inasmuch as it is easier for a man to go through this world with one arm than with one leg, and besides an artificial arm for amputation above the elbow is of so little service, aside from appearance, that few persons with amputations above the elbow ever use them. Taking these facts into consideration the percentages referring to arms cannot be regarded of very much value in estimating the comparative restorations of the upper and lower extremities.

Of all the legs taken into consideration 49% are right, 46% are left, and 5% both.

We have frequently been asked if there were not more right legs amputated than left. The above figures show that the proportion is nearly even, with the small difference of three per cent. in favor of the right. Seventy-eight per cent. of legs amputated are of males, and twenty-two per cent. of females. They may be separated as follows:

TABLE A.

PERCENTAGES.

	Males.	Females.	Both Sexes.
Right	49.9	51.4	49
Left	45.6	46	46
Both	4.5	2.6	5

An analysis of this table will show that females are more disposed to lose their right legs than their left, and the difference is much greater than that which exists with males.

The proportion for double amputations of males is nearly double that of females. This may be explained by the fact that males are more frequently placed in jeopardy than females.

TABLE B.
Percentages.

	Males.	Females.
Right legs above knee.	16	22
Left " " "	15	16
Right " at knee.	3	2
Left " " "	2	4
Right " between knee and ankle	30	24
Left " " " " "	27	24
Right " ankle and below.	2	2
Left " " " "	3	1
Right deformities	1	2
Left "	1	3

The above table shows that over one-half of all the amputations are between the knee and ankle, with a larger percentage for males.

The percentage of deformity is more than double in females than in males.

ARMS.

Of all the arms manufactured by us ninety-two per cent. are for males and eight per cent. for females.

TABLE C.
Percentages.

	Males.	Females.
Right.	50	46
Left.	49	54
Both.	1	0

TABLE D.
Percentages.

	Males.	Females.
Right above elbow	7	6
Left " "	10	19
Right below "	43	40
Left " "	35	35
Hands	5	0

TABLE E.
CAUSES FOR AMPUTATIONS.
PERCENTAGES.

	Both Extremities.	Legs.	Arms.	Legs. Males.	Legs. Females.	Arms. Males.	Arms. Females.
Disease	14.	15.8	1.5	12.	51.5	1.	8.8
Railroads	26.	28.1	11.	29.5	12.6	12.3	4.5
Wars (including foreign)....	30.	30.4	21.7	33.3		24.4	
Falls	3.	3.3	1.1	3.4	3.	1.3	
Sprains and fractures	4.5	4.3	1.9	4.4	3.5	1.8	4.5
Crushed by falling bodies ...	3.5	2.3	13.5	3.5	2.4	10.4	8.7
Farming implements	2.5	2.3	3.9	2.5	1.8	4.5	
Accidents by firearms	1.5	1.	1.1	.7	3.	1.	4.5
Horses and vehicles	2.5	3.	1.1	3.1	2.4	1.3	
Manufacturing machinery...	2.	.7	11.5	.8		11.3	17.
Mills	2.	1.	10.6	1.		12.2	
Mines	.4	.5		.5			
Boats and accidents on water.	.8	1.		1.			
Elevators	.3	.3		.2			
Sharp-edged tools	.5	.4	1.1	.4		1.3	
Explosions	.8	.5	5.5	.2		6.3	
Frost	1.5	2.	.8	2.	.6	1.	
Malformations	1.5	1.	5.5	.8	3.	2.7	35.
Burns	.2	.4		.2	1.2		
Miscellaneous accidents	2.5	1.7	8.2	.5	15.	7.2	17.

Under diseases are classed: Anchylosis, aneurism, blood poison, bunions, cancers, caries, chicken pox, corns, erysipelas, embolism, felons, fevers, gangrene, inflammation, mosquito-bite, necrosis, paralysis, rheumatism, scrofula, snake-bite, synovitis, tumors, varicose veins, ulcers, elephantiasis, etc., etc.

Horses and vehicles include kicks or bites by horse, run over by vehicles, collisions, and falls from the same.

Boats and accidents in water include all manner of accidents incident to seafaring, including the parting of cables, one case in which the person was struck by a whale, and another in which the person claims to have had his leg bitten off by a shark.

Explosions include blasting and premature discharges.

Malformation includes all forms of congenital distortions requiring or not requiring amputation.

Miscellaneous accidents include the following:

Caught by rope, caught by chain, coasting, cyclone, jammed in logs, needle in leg, kicks from boys, skating, struck by lightning, wrestling.

In analyzing Table E, we may draw some rather curious facts, as follows:

Females lose more legs from disease than all the other causes combined. With men one-third are the results of war and nearly another third the results of railroads. Twelve per cent. only are the results of disease.

Next to disease, females lose more legs from railroads than any other one cause. Over one-third of all the deficiencies of the upper extremities with females are the results of malformation, exceeding the number maimed by miscellaneous accidents and manufacturing machinery combined.

When we consider the vast number of females laboring in the shops and factories of the land, this revelation is startling.

With males the loss of arms from results of war amounts to 24.4 per cent., while that from railroads amounts to 12.3 per cent., and the falling of bodies to 10.4 per cent.

TABLE F.

Percentages.

AGES AT WHICH AMPUTATIONS WERE MADE.

LEGS.

	Both Sexes.	Males.	Females.
Less than 10,	6	5	15
10 to 20,	24	24	31
20 to 30,	37	38	24
30 to 40	17	18	13
40 to 50,	10	9	11
50 to 60,	4	4.5	5
60 to 70,	1.75	1	1
Over 70,	.25	.5	

ARMS.

	Both Sexes.	Males.	Females.
Less than 10,	7	4	47
10 to 20,	33	33	30
20 to 30,	32	34	12
30 to 40,	18	18	6
40 to 50,	7	7	5
50 to 60,	2	3	
Over 60,	1	1	

A review of Table F shows that more men are maimed in their lower extremities between the ages of 20 and 30 than during all their subsequent years. With women the period of the maximum loss is between the ages of 10 and 20.

One-half of one per cent., or one case in every two hundred, occur to men when past the alloted time of life, or 70 years.

This speaks well of modern surgery, as well as the vigor of our septuagenarians. With arms, Table F corroborates Table E in placing a high percentage on the loss of arms with female children under 10 years, as that period includes congenital troubles.

TABLE G.
PERCENTAGES.
OCCUPATIONS.

MEN.

Legs.		Arms.
9½	Sedentary.	22
17	Farming.	20
13	Working at bench.	5
6	Professional.	8½
5	Heavy mechanical work.	2½
8½	Laborers.	8
7	Railroading.	8
7	Work requiring much walking.	9
3½	Work requiring much lifting.	5
3	Salesmen.	1
2	Seamen.	
1	Watchmen.	1½
1½	Men in U. S. military service.	1½
3	Students.	2½
2½	Miners.	3
7	Clerks.	
3½	Proprietors.	2½

WOMEN.

62	Housekeepers.	60
16	Dressmakers.	10
7	Teachers.	20
5 ½	Factory.	10
1 ½	Clerks.	
6 ½	Students.	
1 ½	Nurses.	

Sedentary occupations include aldermen, assessors, auditors, bookkeepers, bank clerks, brokers, coroners, court officers, county clerks, editors, justices, librarians, livery, marshals, musicians, machine operators, postmasters, penmen, recorders, secretaries, speculators, shoemakers, segarmakers, superintendents, telegraph operators, tailors, treasurers, weavers.

Farming includes cattle raisers, cowboys, farmers, florists, gardeners, herders, poultry raisers.

Working at bench includes architects, assayers, bakers, butchers, bottlers, bookbinders, boltmakers, broom-makers, boxmakers, barrowmakers, confectioners, carpenters, cabinetmakers, car builders, cooks, casemakers, combmakers, caulkers, draughtsmen, electroplaters, filers, gunmakers, harnessmakers, hatters, jewelers, lastmakers, laundry, matmakers, mechanics, machinists, needlemakers, potters, papermakers, polishers, piano tuners, printers, photographers, rubber manufacturing, rollermakers, sailmakers, shirtmakers, sawyers, sealers, turners, upholsterers, wool-dressers, wool-sorters, watchmakers.

Professional includes actors, artists, clergymen, civil engineers, dancing masters, dentists, gymnasts, horseback riders, judges, lawyers, nurses, physicians, sculptors, teachers.

Heavy mechanical work includes blacksmiths, coppersmiths, coopers, drop forgings, foundry, ironworkers, iron-pipe makers, plumbers, roofers, tinners, well-borers, wheelwrights, wagonmakers.

Railroading includes baggage-masters, brakemen, conductors, car inspectors, engineers, employees, flagmen, freight agents, firemen, gate tenders, messengers, office hands, overseers, switchmen, signal men, station agents, timekeepers, watchmen, yard-masters.

Work requiring much walking includes auctioneers, book agents, bell-ringers, barbers, collectors, contractors, dealers, examiners, foremen, ferrymen, fanciers, hotel clerks, insurance, junkmen, janitors, liquor dealers, land agents, messengers, milkmen, mail carriers, newsboys, porters, post traders, pedestrians, painters, peddlers, real estate, sanitary inspectors, stewards, sextons, shooting gallery, sheriffs, saloon, street inspectors, scouts, teamsters, target tenders, tollgate keepers, timber surveyors, travelers, undertakers, wood dealers, weighers.

Work requiring heavy lifting includes bridge building, brewers, fruiterers, longshoremen, lumbermen, molders, millers, masons, marble workers, metal dealers, market men, truckmen, stove dealers, quarrymen.

The review of table G will convince any one that a cripple either in the upper or lower extremities is not necessarily a creature dependent on others for his livelihood. The largest percentage for those with artificial legs is for farmers, and the next for workmen at the bench; the two combined nearly cover one-third the entire list. Their occupations are laborious and trying.

Less than one-third of those with artificial arms pursue sedentary occupations, leaving over three-quarters to be divided among occupations requiring manual and physical effort.

Among women more than half with the loss of either extremities are housekeepers. This exhibit ought to strike the reader forcibly of the utility of artificial limbs and the great work they are performing in the economy of labor, to say nothing about the great boon they are in their service of the restoration of appearances.

" *Would ye not think that cunning to be great that could restore this cripple to his legs again?* "—*Shakespeare, King Henry VI.*

LETTER WRITING.

Of the various branches of education called into action in the transaction of business, that of letter writing is one of the most important. The purpose of a letter is the communication of an idea. It must be unencumbered with ambiguities, concise, and to the point. The language should be chosen and technical, and the chirography decipherable.

If the amount of time annually lost to every business man in the endeavor to interpret and decipher illegibly and recklessly written letters were computed the total would be appalling. It is indisputable that most of the mistakes made in the execution of orders are traceable directly to some recklessness in the wording or writing of the order. This recklessness does not belong to the illiterate, for many of the erudite allow themselves to enter deeply into the error. A few suggestions, we trust, will accomplish something by stimulating more consideration and care in this important matter.

Do not indulge in broad generalizations. If you have lost a *leg*, do not write that you have lost a *limb*, for if you do we cannot tell whether you have lost a leg or an arm. In describing the point of amputation use the knee, ankle, elbow, or wrist as points of reference; the " upper third " or " lower third " are surgical terms, and may either refer to points above or below the knee or elbow joint. If others have corresponded or called on us in regard to your case, or if you have had intercourse previously with us, state so, mention time and names, or if you have been referred to us by any one, mention the fact and name the party; this will enable us to trace your case in our books and recall all the transactions we have had directly or indirectly with you, thus avoiding posssible delay in correspondence.

If you have occasion to enclose your measurement or make a remittance in one envelope and write us in another, be sure you attach your name to both. If your name is one that can be spelled in two or more ways, put yourself in the habit of always using but one. You will readily see the importance of this if you consider for a moment the confusion occasioned in our books by indexing the names of correspondents who change the orthography of their names when they write. We have a correspondent who writes his name Smith, Smyth, Smythe; another Stewart, Stuart; another Carnes, Karnes; another John O. Donnell, John O'Donnell; another Snyder, Schneider, Snider, etc., etc.

A needless habit exists among some people in encumbering their letters with excuses for "troubling, etc." This should be avoided; our pleasure is to answer all questions pertinent to our business. Have your inquiries concise and explicit, and never write unless you have something to say. Do not fail to sign your name in full to every correspondence. If your autograph is a confusion of curves and angles, enclose a business card, or write on a sheet with a printed head, or write your name in characters that we cannot mistake. State your post office address in full, town, county, and State, and when you direct your letters to us see the envelope bears the following:

A. A. MARKS,
701 Broadway,
New York City.

AWARDS.

In 1859 The American Institute of New York City awarded A. A. Marks a silver medal for his superior artificial leg; it should be noticed that this was prior to the invention of the rubber foot, and consequently had no reference whatever to it.

The fact that the award was made in the face of competition, is evidence that the old ankle joint of Mr. Marks' model was of more than ordinary merit.

The first industrial exhibition in which the rubber foot and hand were exhibited was the American Institute of New York City, in the year 1865. The following official report and judges' decision show the triumph at that exhibition:

ARTIFICIAL LIMBS.—The judges on these important articles were Prof. J. M. Carnochan, Prof. J. V. C. Smith, and James Knight, M.D., and, after a careful and extended examination and practical testing of the various kinds of limbs on exhibition, awarded the First Premium Gold Medal to Mr. A. A. Marks, for his limbs with India Rubber Hands and Feet.

No. 559, A. A. Marks, New York, for Artificial Limbs, for simplicity of construction and durability. Gold Medal.

No. 252.

No. 253.

The above cuts are *fac-similes* of both sides of the Medal awarded as stated in the above report.

Probably there never was a more searching investigation in to the merits of artificial limbs than at this exhibition, as competition was lively and public interest aroused by pedestrial contests which were repeated many days.

1867, AMERICAN INSTITUTE, NEW YORK CITY, FIRST PREMIUM.

The American Institute held no fair in 1866, but in 1867 it again put forth its energies and held a very successful and brilliant exhibition, known as the 37th Annual Fair.

The contest was again invited. The by-laws of the Institute had been changed in such a manner as to require the judges in their investigations to take into consideration all the different articles of their class of which they had any knowledge, whether on exhibition or not. The chairman of the Board of Managers stated publicly at the close of the fair that the board had determined to elevate the standard of excellence in articles on exhibition, by declining to give the first premium to any article unless it was pronounced by competent judges of great utility and equal or superior to any like article known to them, whether on exhibition or not. The result on artificial limbs is found in the following official report:

No. 254.

No. 255.

No. 238, Marks' Patent Artificial Limbs, have frequently been before the Institute, and continue to sustain their former reputation.

Profs. A. K. GARDNER; J. C. V. SMITH; J. J. CRAVEN, M.D., Judges.

The first premium was consequently awarded, consisting of the large bronze medal (as here shown) and diploma.

1869, AMERICAN INSTITUTE, NEW YORK CITY.

The contest in artificial limbs was lively and the investigation by the judges in testing the merits of the limbs was thorough, searching, and convincing, as would be expected from men of their high standing, being well-known leading professional and learned men of the present day.

Annexed hereto will be found the report of the judges, which was

No. 256.

inserted upon the large diploma accompanying the medal of 1869; it tells its own story:

No. 44, Artificial Limbs, A. A. Marks' Best.—This limb is constructed with an india-rubber foot, which, from its elasticity, does away with the necessity of motion at the ankle joint, and also obviates entirely that *heavy, thumping sound* when the foot strikes the ground in walking, an objection which exists in *all other* artificial legs which the committee have any knowledge of.

The control which the wearer has over it and its movements, so closely resembling those of the natural limb, as well as the small cost of keeping it in repair (almost nothing), entitle it to the highest commendation.

LEWIS A. SAYRE, M.D. ; JAS. R. MCGREGOR, M.D., Judges.

A true copy from the report on file.

JOHN W. CHAMBERS, Secretary.

Upon this very plain, careful, and elaborate report, the Board of Managers awarded the first premium, consisting of large bronze medal and diploma.

1870, AMERICAN INSTITUTE, NEW YORK CITY, FIRST PREMIUM.

The following report of the judges on artificial limbs speaks for itself:

No. 3, Marks' Artificial Limbs, A. A. Marks, New York City, N. Y.

BEST.

The especial point of excellence appears to us to be the india-rubber foot, by the use of which all complications in the construction of an ankle joint are avoided.

FRANK H. HAMILTON, M.D.; HARVEY S. GAY, M.D.; WM. H. VAN BUREN, M.D., Judges.

A true copy from the report on file.

JOHN W. CHAMBERS, Secretary.

No. 257.

Upon this comprehensive report the Board of Managers awarded the *first premium*, consisting of *large bronze medal and diploma*.

1871, AMERICAN INSTITUTE, NEW YORK CITY.

The by-laws were changed, and no medals or diplomas awarded in any case, the judges giving a written report instead, which is embodied in the following extract:

The artificial legs with india rubber feet, are especially recommended for their *simplicity*, *durability*, and *easy movement*.

1872, AMERICAN INSTITUTE, NEW YORK CITY, FIRST PREMIUM.

By-laws again changed and diplomas awarded.
Diploma with the following report inscribed:
The artificial limbs manufactured by Mr. Marks continue to merit approval, and are entitled to *all* the confidence the public have to this time reposed in them.
JOHN OSBORN, M.D.; HARVEY S. GAY, M.D.; FRANK H. HAMILTON, M.D., Judges.

1873, AMERICAN INSTITUTE, NEW YORK CITY.

Artificial limbs. Report of judges:
After full and impartial examination of the articles above described, the undersigned judges make report that they find the artificial limbs on exhibition by A. A. Marks worthy of the confidence heretofore reposed in them. We cheerfully endorse all that has been said of them by former examinations, *their simple construction, easy movement, durability, etc.*
First premium, LARGE SILVER MEDAL.

JOHN OSBORN, M.D.; D. F. FETTER, M.D.; C. D. VARLEY, M.D.

1874, AMERICAN INSTITUTE, NEW YORK CITY.

Report of judges: Artificial Limbs, A. A. Marks.
We consider the artificial limbs of A. A. Marks of great value. A *great improvement—better than any known to us;* and of their grade, entitled to the *highest award.*
A silver medal awarded in 1873, as the *best;* a diploma of *maintained superiority* awarded.

V. P. GIBNEY, M.D.; H. B. SANDS, M.D.; E. G. JANEWAY, M.D., Judges.

1875, AMERICAN INSTITUTE, NEW YORK CITY.

A. A. Marks, Artificial Limbs. No. 13, Dept. 3, Group 5.
Judges' report:
After a full and impartial examination of the articles above described, the undersigned judges make report that the artificial limbs presented by Mr. Marks are the same as those offered by him at former exhibitions. We regard them as *superior to all others* in *practical efficiency* and *simplicity,* and would respectfully recommend the award of a diploma of *maintained superiority.*

FRANCIS A. THOMAS, M.D.; CHARLES W. PACKARD, M.D.; J. R. MCGREGOR, M.D., judges.

CENTENNIAL MEDAL.

The following engravings represent the face and reverse side of the medal of the great Centennial Exhibition, held at Philadelphia, Pa., 1876. Reduced to one-half the actual diameter.

No. 258.　　　　　　　　　No. 259.

First Premium.

Report of judges and award of the commission:

International Exhibition, Philadelphia, 1876, No. 235.

The United States Centennial Commission has examined the report of the judges, and accepted the following reasons, and decreed an award in conformity therewith.

Philadelphia, December 11, 1876.

REPORT OF AWARDS.

Products: Artificial Limbs, with Rubber Hands and Feet. Name and address of exhibitor: A. A. MARKS, New York City.

The undersigned, having examined the product herein described, respectfully recommends the same to the United States Centennial Commission for award, for the following reasons, viz.: UTILITY, WORKMANSHIP, and ADAPTATION TO PURPOSE INTENDED.

HENRY H. SMITH, Professor of Surgery,
(Signature of Judge.)

Approval of Group Judges. H. K. OLIVER, EDWARD CONLEY, B. F. BRITTON, SPENCER F. BAIRD, CHAS. STAPLES, JR., M. WILKINS, J. FRITZ, JAS. L. CLAGHORN, COLMAN SELLERS.

A true copy of the record.

FRANCIS A. WALKER, Chief of the Bureau of Awards.

Given by authority of the United States Centennial Commission.

A. T. GOSHORN, Director-General.

J. L. CAMPBELL, Secretary.　　J. R. HAWLEY, President.

1876, AMERICAN INSTITUTE, NEW YORK CITY, FIRST PREMIUM.

These engravings represent the exact size, form, and inscription (face and reverse side) of the Centennial Award Gold Medal, as fully set forth in the following extract of the printed rules and regulations of the American Institute:

No. 260.

No. 261.

THE CENTENNIAL MEDAL.

This medal (of gold) is to be awarded only for a machine, product, or process exhibited this Centennial year, at the 45th Exhibition of the American Institute of the City of New York.

It can be awarded only for a machine, product, or process of great value, decided importance, and of more than usual merit, and then only by a majority of the whole Board of Trustees, upon the written report of three judges, whose report shall certify to the above requirements, and after said report shall have been approved by a majority of the whole Board of Managers.

Copy of the Judges' Report in Department 3, Group 5, Division A at the 45th Exhibition of the American Institute, held in the City of New York, October, 1876:

NO. 72, ARTIFICIAL LIMBS.

A. A. Marks, Broadway, New York City.

We consider these limbs remarkable for simplicity of construction, durability, efficiency, and comfort to the wearer.

We think them entitled to the highest commendations, and believe that their merits call for an award of the Centennial Medal, which we respectfully recommend.

FRANCIS A. THOMAS, M.D., CHARLES W. PACKARD, M.D.; J. R. McGREGOR, M.D., judges.

The above report was duly confirmed by the Board of Managers and Trustees of American Institute.

JOHN W. CHAMBERS, Secretary.

1877, AMERICAN INSTITUTE, NEW YORK CITY.

Extract from the report of the judges at the 46th Annual Fair of the American Institute of New York City:

NO. 523, ARTIFICIAL LIMBS.

A. A. Marks.—After a full and impartial examination of the articles above described, the undersigned judges make report that we consider this exhibit of great value and entitled to recognition.

CHARLES W. PACKARD, M.D.; FRANCIS A. THOMAS, M.D.; AUGUST VIELE, M.D., judges.

Upon this report the Board of Managers awarded the MEDAL OF SUPERIORITY.

A true copy of the report on file. JOHN W. CHAMBERS, Secretary.

1878, AMERICAN INSTITUTE, NEW YORK CITY.

Having received the Medal of Superiority in 1867, this

DIPLOMA FOR MAINTAINED SUPERIORITY

Is awarded to him at the Exhibition of 1878.

NATHAN C. ELY, President.
G. K. McLEOSER, Recording Secretary.

New York, November, 1878.

1881, INTERNATIONAL COTTON EXPOSITION, ATLANTA, GEORGIA.

REPORT ON AWARDS.

No. 262.

Atlanta, Georgia, Dec. 21, 1881.

Group No. 19, Class 31. Entry No. 1568. Product, Artificial Limbs. Name and Address of Exhibitor, A. A. Marks, New York.

The undersigned, having examined the products herein described, respectfully recommend the same to the Executive Committee of the International Cotton Exposition for award for the following reasons, viz.:

1st.—Simplicity in the mechanism of the knee-joint and for its excellent movement.
2d.—Durability.
3d.—Rubber Foot, possessing many excellent qualities and compensating for the absence of motion in the ankle joint.

We recommend that a gold medal be awarded.
Approval of group judges, CHAS. L. WILSON, M.D.; AMOS FOX.
Approved, H. I. KIMBALL, Director General.

1885. The only first-class medal " which is of gold" awarded for artificial limbs at

THE WORLD'S INDUSTRIAL AND COTTON CENTENNIAL EXHIBITION, NEW ORLEANS, LA.

No. 263.   No. 264.

December 1, 1884, to May 31, 1885, Department of Awards, Jury report:

Application No. 1784, Group 8, Class 809.

Jurors in the above entitled class having carefully examined the exhibit made by A. A. Marks, New York City, and all competing exhibits, concur in recommending the award of the First Class Medal for Artificial Limbs.

S. D. CARROLL,
For Department of Awards.

Since the last-named award we have withdrawn from exhibitions. The long series of *first premiums* for so many years has fully satisfied our desire for that class of encomiums.

We have never been vanquished, but have always been conquerors.

NOTICES FROM THE PRESS.

The public Press has frequently spoken of our artificial limbs in very flattering terms. We print but a few of the many complimentary notices we have been favored with.

New York Times, 1865.

We examined Marks' artificial limbs, and saw some examples of their use that were interesting and satisfactory. These limbs consist of the simplest possible conditions. The ankle is firmly attached, and depends on the elasticity of the india rubber foot for the required facility in walking. The elegance, naturalness, and efficiency of these artificial limbs make them almost perfect.

New York Herald, October 16, 1865.

AMERICAN INSTITUTE FAIR.—The cripple race, which created so much interest on Saturday last, will be repeated to-day. The manufacturers of other artificial legs will compete with Mr. Marks for the laurels he gained on that day. Dodworth's full band will be present.

New York Tribune, October 16, 1865.

AMERICAN INSTITUTE FAIR.—PRACTICAL TEST OF ARTIFICIAL LEGS.—The practical test of the merits of artificial legs on exhibition at the American Institute Fair, on Saturday evening, was both novel and attractive. It consisted of a walking match along the center aisle of the Fair building. Three gentlemen entered the list, and gave a specimen of their facility in walking on these substitutes for natural legs. The first contestant, Mr. Bates, was a tall, heavy man, over six feet high, and weighing over 200 pounds. He wore a pair of artificial legs he had used less than three weeks, and therefore walked somewhat unsteadily. The second competitor, Mr. Augsburger, followed, wearing but one artificial leg. He walked a fourth of a mile without a cane in four minutes with apparent ease, and was warmly applauded. Mr. Frank Stewart closed the performance, wearing two artificial legs, applied just below the knees. He walked a half mile in nine minutes without a cane, with so much spirit, ease, and naturalness that he was frequently obstructed and taken hold of by persons who could not believe that he wore two artificial legs, and he was finally obliged to take the large stand and exhibit the legs and feet to the audience, when he was loudly applauded. All of these gentlemen wore the artificial legs and patent india-rubber feet manufactured by Mr. A. A. Marks; there were two other gentlemen present, each wearing two of Mr. Marks' legs, having lost their own while in the service of their country.

This walking match originated with Managers Carpenter and Ely, and was superintended by the managers in person, the object being to enable the thousands of legless soldiers to avail themselves of the benefits of a fair trial of the real working merits of the many artificial legs constantly thrust upon their attention.

There are several exhibitors of artificial limbs in the Fair, most if not all of whom are expected to give a sample of the walking capability of their respective limbs at the walking match which takes place this evening at 8 o'clock. A prize will be awarded to the most successful maker.

Soldiers' Friend, November, 1865.

*** Several other exhibitions took place during the fair. The gold medal was awarded to Dr. Marks. The "Rubber Foot," manufactured at this establishment under special patents, has an elasticity and durability that must make the limb welcome to every wearer. The award of the Committee, after a careful examination, is a high testimonial in its favor.

American Eclectic Medical Review, August, 1866.

MARKS' PATENT ARTIFICIAL LIMBS.—These Limbs are beyond all question the most perfect and simple ever made, and their indorsement by the American Institute at its last Annual Fair was but a just tribute to their unquestionable excellence. The principle of the india-rubber feet and hands *is the true one;* and the remarkable skill and extensive experience of Dr. Marks in this branch of surgical appliances is unexcelled in this country OR THE WORLD.

We recommend Marks' Artificial Limbs—unqualitiedly—to *all* surgeons and to all who may require the aid of such appliances.

Soldiers' Friend, January, 1866.

"ARTIFICIAL LEGS ON SKATES."—The time has not long passed since it was considered a wonder to see a person walking with apparent ease upon one artificial leg, but when an unfortunate fellow who had lost both of his propellers was enabled to walk, even with two canes, it was thought so remarkable that few would believe it without witnessing the feat with their own eyes. But we have recently seen something far exceeding this in novelty and success. We saw a young man *skating* leisurely along on the Central Park Lake, with both hands in his pockets, and without any assistance of staff or cane. It is true he did not carve out with exquisite neatness and precision an elegantly spread eagle, neither did he leap over the heads of his fellow skaters, but his movements were easy and graceful, and no one would suspect any thing unusual, except that he might be a beginner. This was really the case, as he had then put on skates only a few times. Our attention was called to him by some one who knew him personally, or we should not have thought that among that vast throng there was one who sought the merry sport upon *two wooden legs*. We should not call them wooden, for the quiet skater was no less a personage than Mr. Frank Stewart, who wears the Artificial Legs with Rubber Feet, invented and manufactured by Mr. Marks, of this city. Mr. Stewart ran, or walked, the race at the Fair of the American Institute last year, and made the unprecedented time of half a mile in nine minutes, with no assistance whatever, and was still anxious to proceed, declaring he could make the next half mile in the same time, but was prevented by the crowd.

The Gold Medal for Artificial Limbs was awarded to Mr. Marks, at the American Institute Fair, 1865.

American Phrenological Journal, October, 1869.

ARTIFICIAL LIMBS.—It is but a few years since the person who was unfortunate enough to lose a part of his leg was obliged to stump about, like poor "Tommy Taft," in Mr. Beecher's "Norwood," for the rest of his life, or, what was worse, to swing himself through the world on crutches.

There have been various ingenious and useful devices to obviate the old stump-leg, as well as to do away with the crutches, and these inventions have served their purposes with more or less convenience and pleasure to the wearer and his friends.

Since the beginning of our great rebellion ten thousand maimed soldiers have called upon the inventive talent of our citizens, and now we have the pleasure of presenting, for the consideration of our readers, the Artificial Limbs with India-rubber Hands and Feet, invented and manufactured by Mr. A. A. Marks.

We give also an engraved likeness of Mr. Frank Stewart, who has had both legs amputated below the knees, and wears, of course, two artificial legs. One amputation is within two and a half inches of the knee-joint, the other five or six inches below it; yet with his two artificial legs he walks very briskly and very much better than many men having corns, who would resent the imputation of being lame. The dotted lines across the legs show where the amputations were made. He uses a cane, but can walk without one.

We see nothing in the artificial line which gives so natural a step as this.

We are informed that Mr. Marks has been authorized to furnish artificial limbs, at the expense of the Government, to commissioned officers, soldiers, and seamen of the United States army and navy, who may have been maimed in the service of their country. It is a source of great pleasure to us, and must be to

No. 265.

every body, that the maimed soldier, without special charity from personal friends, should thus be enabled to procure, at no expense to himself, the best possible substitute for the limbs which he has sacrificed for the honor and freedom of his country.

We recommend all persons who are interested to make an investigation for themselves of this work, and we doubt not they would be pleased and profited thereby.

New York Dispatch, September 6, 1866.

ARTIFICIAL LIMBS.—These artificial limbs are the invention and manufacture of A. A. Marks, of this city. We have seen some of these limbs, and examined the peculiar simplicity of their construction; we have also seen them in practical use, and have been truly astonished with the naturalness and grace with which they walk. They remind us of the great advance made in the steam-engine by being shorn of its former and many complicated parts, to its present simple and improved condition. Mr. Marks *dispenses* with the ANKLE *joints* in his legs and its COMPLICATIONS, by substituting a foot made mostly of *india rubber*, of a very tough, elastic, and durable character, thereby giving the wearer a more *reliable, natural*, and *perfect* limb than we have heretofore ever seen.

At the Fair of the American Institute last year, there was a very spirited contest for the Gold Medal to be awarded to the inventor of the best limb, and although there were many contestants, Mr. Marks' limbs carried off the prize.

Mr. Marks is a *pioneer* in this line of *art*, having been engaged in his profession since 1853, and after much study and many experiments has attained to those special improvements, which he patented some *four* years since. The Government adopted his limbs, thus enabling our heroic soldiers who have lost their limbs in defense of their country to secure them free of charge.

We have given these inventions more than a *passing* notice, as we think they effect *important* changes and improvements in the construction of implements for the relief of our unfortunate fellow-beings, and more especially as they emanate from one who has labored for many years in this branch of a noble work, and whose present standing as an *inventor* and *gentleman* needs no further recommendation at our hands.

New York Tribune, September 16, 1868.

ARTIFICIAL LIMBS.—The inventor who can make a machine do its work with the least machinery is considered by all good judges as the best. Simplicity of construction, in every thing, is not only its beauty, but its best recommendation. In nothing is this rule more applicable than to substitutes for lost limbs, especially when applied to our brave soldiers and seamen, who sacrificed their own precious limbs to save our country.

We find the above qualifications well exemplified in artificial limbs invented and manufactured by A. A. Marks, New York, which seem to combine every feature of utility and comfort to the unfortunate wearer, while their simplicity of construction must render them durable and unlikely to get out of order. The soldier or citizen who places himself under the care of Mr. Marks will find a competent, prompt, and reliable friend, a man well known as an energetic, hard worker, of large experience as an inventor and mechanic in a profession both honorable and beneficial to the human race.

New York Dispatch, October 24, 1869.

Very few persons, in proportion to our population, are required to use artificial limbs, yet in looking into the matter a little we find there are many thousands among us needing and using those useful inventions of art, and many persons use them with such ease and naturalness that their misfortune is never known by the public, and often but by very few of their acquaintances. In examining Mr. Marks' large case of artificial limbs at the Fair, our attention was attracted to a very genteel and pretty little girl of about ten years of age, who presented us with a card. Upon one side we found a portrait of the little girl above mentioned, taken in different positions, one of which represented her as she appeared with her sweet, honest face and lovely black eyes, and skipping about apparently as sound in limb as in body and mind, but another view represented her sitting and exhibiting her misfortune, showing that her left leg was amputated just below the knee. She informed us that she had used it for over two years, and with perfect ease. We saw her afterward walking about the Fair without exhibiting any signs whatever of her loss. We are informed that Mr. Marks has hundreds of patients who testify to the great utility and assistance they receive from his valuable inventions—many, too, who have lost both legs, and with these substitutes are enabled to attend to their vocations.

Illustrated Weekly, New York, December 18, 1875.

We have been particularly interested in reading a pamphlet issued by A. A. Marks, explaining the construction of the artificial limbs produced at his extensive factory, which must be placed at the head of all institutions of the kind on this continent.

Established in his business many years, Mr. Marks has succeeded beyond expectation in the endeavor to produce the most perfect substitute possible for a lost limb, either arm or leg. All the limbs manufactured by him are light and strong, elastic and uncomplicated, and admit of such use as is perfectly wonderful. Persons wearing his legs—we intend no joke—find themselves able to walk long distances, to work in the fields or the store, and, in the case of ladies, to perform all their domestic duties, including going up and down stairs, without weariness and want of grace, so that their wearing artificial assistances of this nature may not be known to their associates. This is true even of persons necessitated to wear two artificial legs. The foot is of india rubber—as are the hands. It has been found that children from four years and upwards, wearing legs of Mr. Marks' manufacture, can indulge in their childish sports and grow up in vigorous health, instead of feebly moving by aid of crutches. We need not add that the inventor has achieved a brilliant success in his business, and that persons and institutions of eminence have cheerfully accorded their expression of the utility of his inventions, which those who have used them know best how to appreciate. We cordially indorse the verdict of the judges at the Forty-fourth Fair of the American Institute, lately held in this city: "We regard them (Mr. Marks' Artificial Limbs) as superior to all others in practical efficiency and simplicity." We may add that Mr. Marks has received numerous medals from the judges of this institution, the first dated as far back as 1859.

Toledo Blade, Toledo, Ohio, August 26, 1875.

WONDERFUL IMPROVEMENTS IN PATENT ARTIFICIAL LIMBS.—The limbs manufactured at the establishment of Dr. A. A. Marks, New York, we are warranted in saying, from personal examination, are beyond any question the most perfect ever made, and their indorsement by the American Institute at its last Annual Fair, was but a just tribute to their unquestionable excellence.

The principle of the india-rubber feet and hands *is the true one*, and the remarkable skill, and the experience of Dr. Marks in this branch of surgical appliance, is simply unexcelled in this country or in THE WORLD. They are recommended and fully indorsed by all leading surgeons throughout this entire country.

Grand Army Record.

ARTIFICIAL LIMBS.—Science and the industrial arts present no higher evidence of progress than that observable in the perfection of surgical appliances designed to replace portions of the human form removed by innumerable causes. The requirements of an article of this description are not only to come as near as possible to nature in appearance, but in the uses of the lost part. Take the leg, for example. It should not only look the counterfeit of Nature, but its wearer must be able to walk, dance, run, skate, or do any thing as before his misfortune, and at the same time have the limb conform to his person.

Of the truly ingenious and vastly useful devices for these purposes, examples have recently come under our notice which show conclusively that the best articles of this description ever devised by man's ingenuity, and one which fully meets the requirements, is the Artificial Limbs, with Indian Rubber hands and feet, made by Dr. A. A. Marks, of this city, and which are now in such extensive use throughout the whole country. Consisting of the simplest conditions, availed of with most consummate ability, it is a model of elegance, naturalness, and efficiency, and fully deserves the high encomiums it has received from medical and other scientific sources, from the Government, the press, and public generally.

Of course Dr. Marks' peculiar features in perfecting artificial limbs are secured to him by letters-patent, and he is the sole manufacturer of them.

By Act of Congress, the Surgeon-General of the United States has commissioned Dr. Marks to supply these limbs to commissioned officers, soldiers, seamen, and others, free of charge, under stipulated regulations. Those afflicted, or having friends deprived of their limbs, should communicate with Dr. Marks.

Davenport Democrat, Davenport, Iowa, February 10, 1876.

SUBSTITUTED HUMANITY.—The imitation of portions of humanity with all those movements which are peculiar to the substituted limb has arrived at a perfection which is marvelous. The victim of patriotism or the sufferer from an accident who requires the amputation of a member can now be supplied with hand or foot, arm or leg, so perfect in contour, and so elegant in action, that the sense of loss is reduced to a minimum. Especially is this the case with Marks' patents, which are made with rubber hands and feet so exactly *fac-simile* that none but the wearer is cognizant of the substitution.

Mechanical surgery, carried thus to perfection, ranks in importance with those other inventions and discoveries which have made America the leading nation of the world in the alleviation of suffering humanity. Disabled soldiers and citizens should apply at once to A. A. Marks.

New York Evening Mail, November 15, 1875.

Undoubtedly one of the most valuable features of the whole exhibition is the display of artificial limbs, made by Dr. A. A. Marks, of New York.

The beautiful young lady who attends the case of goods entered by Dr. Marks has been wearing one of his artificial limbs for the last eight years.

A photograph is distributed at the Fair, showing her as she was at the age of eight, and as she now appears, which very beautifully illustrates a specialty in his business in applying artificial limbs to children.

These limbs are constructed with india-rubber hands and feet, and are models of elegance, naturalness, and efficiency ; in short, they are the best articles of this description ever devised by man's ingenuity. They are now in extensive use throughout the whole country, and have received the highest indorsements from medical and other scientific sources, from the Government, the press, and the public generally.

Stamford Advocate, Stamford, Conn.

ART PRACTICALLY EXEMPLIFIED.—While on a visit to the city a short time since, we made a call at the celebrated manufactory of Artificial Limbs, owned and carried on by Mr. A. A. Marks, and although we had known before something of this establishment, we were surprised to see and learn of the real extent and magnitude of what we had always before considered quite an insignificant business. Mr. Marks is, with but a single exception, the oldest manufacturer and inventor in the United States, in this line. He started in the business in a small way nearly a quarter of a century ago, and has gradually increased it until his patrons are numbered by the thousands, and are scattered in almost every part of the globe. While there, he showed us a fine specimen of a full length Artificial Leg made for a gentleman in Buenos Ayres, South America, for whom he had made one a few years ago, and he was so well pleased with it that he had again sent this long distance for a duplicate. Mr. M. showed us another for a young man in the northern part of California. One also for a Miss of twelve years old, who lost her limb by a mowing machine when she was but three. More than a dozen more were shown us either finished or in progress of construction, for persons of various occupations, and scattered widely over the world, some of a peculiar historic character. But more than this, he showed us the practical working of one particular case that was well worth seeing. He was a snugly built boy of eleven years of age. Mr. M. says : "Tommy, let the gentleman see you walk," upon which he started off without a cane, at an easy gait, with a slight limp in the right leg. We thought it excellent walking for any one with an Artificial Leg, and so expressed ourselves, supposing, of course, that he was wearing but one Artificial, but when informed that the solid little fellow was walking on a *pair* of Artificial Legs, and shown his photograph taken with his bare stumps, this told the story so clear that no doubt could be entertained of his actual condition, and that the little fellow had lost one leg just below the knee and the other above, and yet he walks well and for long distances without any cane. This case has excited much wonder and comment where the boy is known.

Mr. M. then called our attention to a young man of about twenty-six years of age, who was walking about the large reception room, and informed us that he was wearing a pair of artificials also. From his easy manner and steady step none would for a moment suspect he was in any way disabled. This personage has been in Mr. M.'s employ for nearly a dozen years, therefore grown from a mere boy in an occupation which accident compelled him to patronize, and in which he steadily labors in assisting others who, from accident or disease, are similarly circumstanced.

The inventor was awarded a Gold Medal for the Best Artificial Limbs at the great Fair of the American Institute, in 1865, and also the *highest awards* of that time-honored institution at every exhibition since.

Mr. Marks has a peculiar faculty of making those who call on him feel interested in his humanitarian work. He certainly has developed this peculiar business to a wonderful extent. Many a brave soldier has had his life made happy by having his missing leg or arm replaced with one of Mr. Marks' artificial ones. The nation owes him a debt of gratitude for his untiring efforts in this department.

Mr. M. is a resident of Riverside. He lives on his fine farm on the banks of Long Island Sound, a short drive from our village, where his life and tastes are beautifully exemplified by his ornamented surroundings on the breezy shore. His orchards and well tilled grounds yield ample harvests. Thus he shows an ardent love for nature's quiet and pure attractions, as well as for the development of art in his singular though necessary profession.

Appleton's Journal, June 19, 1875.

PATCHED-UP HUMANITY.—It is quite appalling how callous we have grown to the tendency of the fair sex to amplify Nature by artificial means. We no longer look upon Sophronia's mass of black hair with suspicious dread. The most gallant of men, the weakest dupe of feminine arts, is not deceived by it; nor does he suppose that it indicates any real deficiency as in the natural supply. He recognizes and sanctions it, not as a snare, but a graceful concession to fashion; and the women themselves do not seek concealment.

I have watched fair girls—girls with sunshiny tresses waved across their brows—enter the store of a *perruquier* on Broadway without a blush—without a moment's care for observers—and I have seen them boldly comparing the shade of their cast-off, lack-lustre braids with new ones, which they have purchased under the very eyes of prying men.

The propriety of thus amending Nature whenever fashion demands seems to be generally conceded, not only in the matter of hair, but also in many other things, and I am much too discreet a person to find fault with that which meets the approval of so many. I will go even so far as to say that it may be partly a good tendency, in the interest of candor and against deceit, for while the custom is extant it is surely better to be honest about it.

If Mrs. B——has the misfortune to be sallow, and finds her complexion improved by the use of anthosmimos, at two dollars a bottle, we should be glad that the prejudices of her neighbor do not compel the poor lady to be hypocritical over it; and the understanding that Fanny's profusion of hair is not wholly her own will spare dear Edgar many a heart-pang after marriage.

But there is also a tendency to substitute as well as to amplify nature. Formerly, a cripple was a cripple, and hobbled through the world an object of pity to sympathetic elders, and of derision to wicked youngsters. An unfortunate with one eye had no means of hiding his defect, and the loss of the arms made a person helpless. Even when artificial legs were first introduced, they were so imperfect that no one was deceived by them. They had movable, clattering ankle-joints, which betrayed their wearer at every step, and his entrance into a parlor was mistaken for the complaint of a broken-down chair, or the squeak of a rat. When he moved in the street, people turned round, expecting to see a wheelbarrow in want of grease approaching, and when—awful moment!—he cast himself on his knees before his adored one, his impassioned utterances were accompanied with rattling noises which suggested the unrest of a fallen spirit in torment. Naughty little boys whistled the tune of the "Cork Leg" in his presence, and his whole life was made miserable by the rude queries of persons who wanted to know all about his misfortune.

Such improvements have been made in late years, however, that, in all but sense of touch, an artificial leg performs the most important duties of a natural one, allowing the wearer to walk, run, or sit with ease, and to endure an astonishing degree of fatigue in an upright position. It is noiseless, and only an expert can detect it.

The foot wears a real boot, which can be removed at pleasure; the knee and ankle joint work without a creak, and the whole mechanism is, as one maker eloquently says, "at once a beauty and a joy forever." The form is perfection, the instep really arched, and the ankle trim. The calf swells with exquisite gradations, and recedes toward a well-shaped knee. The surface is smooth and glossy as satin, and delicately tinged with a color between a soft pink and a luscious creaminess, as unlike the abnormal and offensive redness of a ballet-girl's fleshings as blush rose is unlike a flaunting dahlia.

A wooden leg, pure and simple, is a perpetual reminder of the wearer's bereft condition. It can never be mistaken for any thing more than the shallow mechanism it is. But the modern artificial leg is a complete illusion, and the wearer himself may easily forget its unreality. Coming home in the evening from a day of toil, and throwing himself into an arm-chair for a consoling smoke, he can take off his boots and put on his slippers in the most natural manner possible. His stockings—prosaic necessity—need changing once a week, and I have heard of men who gratified their inordinate vanity by clothing their rubber feet in the softest of silks. Then, if he be of a utilitarian turn, with little care for trappings and seemings, he can discard the limb altogether when he is seated, and put it in a corner like an umbrella or a walking-stick. Or if he has the native habit of sitting with his heels elevated above his body, he can continue to enjoy that delusive pleasure by resting his artificial leg on the window-sill while he sits upon the lounge in a more comfortable posture. A thousand advantages suggest themselves, and therein we find an example of the excellent law of compensation which atones for so many of our grievances.

But, when we glance through the neck of the leg, so to speak, our feelings suffer a revulsion. We see that all the external beauty and tenderness, all the lustre and refinement of tint, only serve to hide a combination of ugly iron bolts, rods, and screws, which give the thing its movements.

The outer case or shell is made of wood, wrought by a carpenter's chisel, and when we rap it with our knuckles it gives forth a hollow, sepulchral sound. The delicate texture of the surface is the result of a coating of some kind of fine enameled leather, which makes the wood more durable and handsome and prevents it from splitting or cracking. So the artificial leg æsthetic is dismissed from our minds, and we have only to consider the practical leg as a thing of mechanical ingenuity and utility.

We have seen what the artificial leg is ornamentally, and we have hinted at its posssibilities, but we have given you no idea of how varied and extensive these possibilities are. We know a gentleman with a passion for pedestrianism, an excellent skater, who moves on two artificial legs, and yet this is nothing.

In a pamphlet before us there are several pages filled with the experiences of crippled men whose infirmities have been relieved, not by the all-potent grace of winking Madonnas, nor by the talismanic touch of sainted hands, but by the dexterity of artisans in human-repair shops.

A brevet major of United States Volunteers, who was cut in two during the war, writes, "I walk six miles every day without a cane or other assistance." Another martyr of gunpowder declares, "I am employed in a locomotive-works, and with the aid of an artificial leg I am able to support a large family." Think of supporting a large family on an artificial leg, and dandling a baby on an artificial knee! And what a sermon and example it is to those who complain that they cannot afford to marry with even the two natural limbs at their service! This is not all, however. "Being fond of sport, I have frequently started from home early in the morning and have not returned until night, spending the whole day in hunting-exploits, and accomplishing altogether about fifteen miles distance." This same hero is member of a fire-department, and is often in active service. If you saw him in the street you could not discover his imperfections, for, beyond a slight limp, his gait is steady and easy.

Still another writes, "With my artificial leg I have visited the Highlands and all the noteworthy scenery of Ireland, Wales, England, Germany, France, and Switzerland, and have ever found it all I desired while on horseback, on foot, or at rest."

A fourth states that he is a farmer, and that he has built a stone-fence while wearing an artificial leg, mowed and cradled, spread and pitched hay, and made himself generally useful.

We imagine that the wearers of these artificial limbs grow attached to them, as to a meerschaum pipe, and it occurs to us that there must be a large amount of satisfaction in taking one's leg off and rubbing it up and down in a fondling way. Some connoisseurs—for there are connoisseurs even in this—have collections of legs—week-day legs, Sunday legs, dancing legs, and riding legs, each expressly made for a distinct purpose. But this is vanity, and leadeth only unto vexation of spirit.

The following lecture is taken from the *Medical and Surgical Reporter*, of April 14, 1877, published in Philadelphia.

LECTURE.

CONVALESCENT CASES.

A Clinical Lecture by Professor LEWIS A. SAYRE, at Bellevue Hospital, February 14, 1877. Reported stenographically for *The Medical and Surgical Reporter*, by N. W. CADY, M.D.

Case 6.—Mary Cashen. Here is a little girl I feel proud to show you. Look at that smiling face, compared with what it was when she came here several months ago. The operation was performed three months ago. You will recollect this girl came here with chronic disease of the knee joint, which she had had ever since she was seven months old. From the age of seven months on, she remained with her knee in a state of chronic inflammation. It was plastered and issued, and fired and iodined, and she took internal remedies all the time, until within a few weeks of the time when she came here, but she never had extension and counter-extension, to overcome reflex muscular contraction. The muscles contracted in such a way as to produce a complete luxation backward of the leg upon the thigh, so that the head of the tibia lay in the intercondylic notch.

You will recollect that the leg and foot were models of symmetry and beauty, never having been stepped upon, or never having worn a shoe. The disease had so thoroughly involved the joint that an exsection alone could not save the limb. If a resection had been performed, the leg would have been too short to walk upon, and on that account I decided to perform an amputation upon the knee joint, leaving the patella to form the end of the stump. You will observe that the cicatrization is complete. There were two or three sinuses at the lower end of the femur and one under the patella, but I preferred to trust to nature for curing the inflammation, and the result has justified my choice. The sinuses soon ceased to discharge, and the girl was sent out from the hospital with a perfect stump.

Mr. A. A. Marks, the instrument maker, has been kind enough to present to this little girl an artificial leg, and I feel under great obligation to him. He makes, as I think, *altogether the best artificial leg I have ever seen*, simply because of its durability and simplicity. The foot has no joint at the ankle, and this is where the great advantage comes in. The core of the foot is a small solid piece of wood in the shape of a foot, only much smaller. This core is covered with a thick and heavy layer of india-rubber, so that from the instep to the toes, and back to the heel, the foot is simply solid spring rubber. The elasticity of the toes and heel compensates for the absence of the ankle joint, and in walking there is none of the jarring, dot-and-go-one walk so characteristic of the jointed leg. With this rubber foot she can walk with the *stealthy, noise-*

less tread of a cat. The spring and elasticity of the foot is a *positive* comfort to the patient.

Hartford Courant, November 5, 1877.

ON HIS LEGS AGAIN.—Lieutenant-Governor Sill's son George, who had his legs cut off at Stony Creek last summer, has returned from New York City, where he has been having a pair of Marks' Artificial Legs fitted to him. Young Mr. Sill finds that he can use his artificial limbs very easily, and manages to move about with little trouble even at the present time. The limbs are really wonderful, and when the young man gets accustomed to their use it is probable that he will be able to move so easily that few, if any, strangers would imagine him deprived of both his natural pedestals. The Patent Legs are *the best invented,* and are made by A. A. Marks, New York. Young Mr. Sill is to be congratulated on his speedy and complete recovery from so severe an accident.

Rock Island Union, Rock Island, Ill., August 23, 1877.

Mr. Marks is one of our oldest and most reliable manufacturers, and his limbs are generally acknowledged to have *no superiors.* They have taken the First Premium at the leading expositions in the world, as *Gold Medals* in Mr. Marks' possession testify.

Quite a number of soldiers living in this and adjoining counties are using these limbs, and speak in the highest terms of their excellence.

Boston Evening Traveller, December, 1881.

A REMARKABLE COINCIDENCE.—A visitor at the Artificial Limb establishment of Mr. A. A. Marks, New York, a little time ago, was shown two sets of drawings and measurements for pairs of artificial legs for two different persons; but although one pair was for a man in Idaho Territory, and the other for a man in Kentucky, and for amputations below the knees, and one stump about three inches longer than the other, yet they were each so near like the other that one pair would fit the other person as well as the one for whom it was made. Both persons lost their limbs from freezing, and both were about the same weight, yet one was ten years older than the other. The circumstance, Mr. Marks says, never occured before in his nearly thirty years' experience in making several thousand artificial limbs, and over one hundred pairs where persons had lost both. These two pairs of limbs were recently made, both orders received the same day, and were made from measurements, have been sent to their destination, and give most excellent satisfaction. The perfection which has been acquired in the manufacture of these artificial limbs is something very wonderful, and the benefits thereby brought to suffering humanity are incalculable. There is at present a young man in Mr. Marks' employ wearing a pair of limbs, one amputation being just above the knee, the other just below, and not one observer in a hundred would, from his manner of walking and his general activity, for an instant suppose he had legs other than those provided by nature. A visit to Mr. Marks' establishment, and observation of the immense business carried on there, will well repay any visitor to New York his time and trouble to call and see for himself.

The Atlanta *Christian Index and Southwestern Baptist,* November 27, 1879.

A DARK CLOUD WITH A SILVER LINING.—One of the saddest things connected with the late war is the fact that so many noble men lost a limb, or limbs; and, saddest of all, the most of them, from loss of time and property, and other terrible results of the war, were seemingly destined to move on through the dark shadows of adversity with an empty sleeve, or upon crutches, dragging their maimed bodies through the rough journey of life,

But thanks to the liberality of an appreciative people, and the wonderful ingenuity of man, the halt and the maimed may take courage, and, looking up and beyond the dark cloud of adversity, may catch the silver lining of hope, with the assurance that the empty sleeve may be filled with an arm that can be used, and the awkward, tiresome crutches give place to limbs both useful and ornamental. Under these considerations, all manufacturers of artificial limbs, who are skilled in their profession and satisfied with reasonable compensation, should be considered public benefactors.

The writer who is a Georgian, justly proud of his native State, fully appreciating the justice and generosity of the late Legislature in making an appropriation to furnish limbs for those who lost them in the late war, and in full sympathy with all these unfortunate sons of the South, while spending some time in the cities of New York and Philadelphia has taken special pains to investigate the standing of the various manufacturers of artificial limbs. While there are many of whom our country may feel justly proud, as skilled artisans, the writer feels constrained to mention specially the name of Mr. A. A. Marks. This special reference is made after a close and critical investigation into his present and past record, covering an experience of over a quarter of a century, during which time he has been largely connected with Government contracts. He can show many flattering testimonials from official sources, as well as from private individuals, together with numerous diplomas and first premiums.

Mr. Marks is a practical mechanic, thoroughly acquainted with every detail of his business. He is not only able to give to it his own personal attention; but has two sons who, by their close training, have also acquired an experimental knowledge of the business, and are fully competent to take charge of the different departments.

Mr. Marks has the most skilled mechanics in his manufactory, turning out frequently a dozen or more limbs a week. It is interesting to see his patrons leave their crutches in his office, and walk off apparently whole—men, too, who had lost both legs and who were brought in by attendants.

Atlanta (Georgia) *Constitution*, January 1, 1882

ARTIFICIAL LIMBS.

A Wonderfully Successful Result of Skill in Their Manufacture.

Prominent among the exhibits in Art and Industrial Hall, which were displayed during the life of the exposition which closed yesterday, were the artificial limbs displayed by Mr. A. A. Marks, of New York. They attracted universal attention, and their beauty and perfection were much commented upon. The display was very elaborate, and embraced the various styles and kinds required by the demands of the trade. They were easily seen to be of superior workmanship and of the very best material. The rubber foot and hand feature has gained much favor, and gives promise of supplanting all other styles. By means of the rubber foot and stiff ankle joint, a natural movement is given to the step which deceives the most practiced eye. Mr. Marks has applied an artificial leg to Master Willie Wilson, the little son of our esteemed fellow-citizen, Dr. H. L. Wilson. This young gentleman had his leg cut off by a train several months ago, but now wears an artificial limb with such natural grace that no one would ever suspect that he had lost a limb.

Mr. Marks has met with wonderful success in his efforts to supply reliable and practical artificial limbs. The limbs that he turns out are equal if not superior to any others. They were carefully examined by the judges at the exposition and compared with the competition. They awarded the exhibit a gold medal.

These artificial limbs are recommended with the assurance that they can not be surpassed in any particular whatever, and all who need any thing of the kind should address Dr. Marks. A prominent Atlanta physician said of him yesterday: "He is the best artificial limb maker in the world. I have seen his work and I have seen it tested. I am prepared to say that it is the best in existence." This was a high compliment but a deserved one.

The Sun, New York City, Sept. 27, 1885.

The house of A. A. Marks, 701 Broadway, established 1853, is the oldest in this country, and owing to its peculiar mode of constructing limbs, with rubber hands and feet, enjoys a trade second to none on both continents. Their widespread reputation for lightness, durability, and naturalness is evidenced by three orders recently filled, one for the son of the Peruvian President, another for a prominent Neapolitan surgeon, and a third for an attache of the Japanese Legation. A simple and reliable system renders it unnecessary for subjects to call in person, the proper filling out of blanks being sufficient to insure a perfect fit. This house furnishes a greater proportion of the limbs purchased by the Government for disabled soldiers. Limbs are supplied to subjects ranging from infancy to old age. In the case of little Mabel Thompson, of New Haven, a leg was applied when she was less than one year old, for amputation below the knee, to prevent stiffening and contraction of the joint, and in a brief time she was walking naturally ; Cleary, a famous pedestrian, wearing two of these artificial limbs, has made a record athletes possessing natural ones might envy.

New York Sun, December 3, 1882.

CRIPPLES WITH IMPROVED FEET.

More Maiming Done by Railway Cars and Machinery than by Wars.

Gen. Hoke, of North Carolina, is credited with remarking on the rapid disappearance, in late years, of the maimed veterans of the civil war, and saying that in a few years men who have lost arms or legs will be rare. A newspaper paragraph to that effect was shown to a maker of artificial limbs, who furnishes more substitute arms and legs than any body else in the United States, and he said : " It is true that there are not so many cripples observable in the streets as there were a few years ago, but it is also true that there are almost as many in the community, and probably always will be as long as we have railroads. So far as the old soldiers are concerned, I don't imagine that they are dying off any faster than any other men who were in their prime when the war ended, seventeen years ago. As for cripples becoming rare, that is true as far as their ceasing to be conspicuous objects, but they are here among us all the same. The difference is that the perfection to which the making of artificial limbs has been carried, especially in legs, prevents the mutilation of their wearers being noticed. Many men wander about with artificial legs whom nobody would ever suspect of being maimed."

In a practical demonstration of what he said he called upon three of his employees—a young woman, a boy, and a middle-aged man—and set them walking to and fro in his large office. There was nothing peculiarly observable in the gait of either—no heavy, wooden thump, no stiffness in the motions of the feet, and no halting in the alternating steps, yet the young woman wore one artificial leg, and each of the others was supported on two wooden limbs.

" There," he continued, with an air of triumph, " is the climax of scientific invention in this direction. Nobody would imagine, seeing them in the street, that they have been crippled. And the young woman will dance all night with that substitute leg without her partner suspecting its existence, the man will skate, and the boy can run a race. This is all attained by the use of a rubber foot that is elastic under the heel tread and bends at the toes like a natural foot. I could point out to you in the street scores of men that wear these rubber feet, not only old soldiers, but victims of railway and other accidents, and you would not recognize in their easy, springy, and noiseless walk that they were not in possession of all their natural members. And that is the greas reason why cripples are disappearing. It is a common error that more men were maimed in battle during the war than during any other time of equal duration in the history of the country, but the fact is that there are as many cripples made by the railroads in each year now as were made by the war in any year of the war. That I affirm from intimate knowledge of more than 6,000 cases. According to the war records there were only about 22,000 cripples made on both sides, North and South, by the war. Of course the exact number has not been, and cannot be, ascertained, for not only were many cases never reported, but in not a few instances injuries received in battle led to amputations a number of years afterward, so long that they could not have been included in the official records or kept an exact account of. There was Henry La Rue, of Pa., for instance, who had a leg amputated in 1877, in consequence of a fracture received in 1865, when he was a member of the Eleventh Pennsylvania Cavalry.

"I have made thousands of legs and arms for soldiers, who are supplied with them free of cost by the Government. They are allowed a new limb every five years. A good leg of willow, well made, with good steel joints and springs and a rubber foot, will last fifteen years, with proper care, and an arm is good for a lifetime. The elasticity of the rubber foot increases the durability as well as the serviceability of the leg. A first-class leg costs $100. I have heard of artificial legs being made to order in France with gold-plated joints and all sorts of fancy business, costing several hundred dollars, but have never been called upon to get up any thing of the kind, and if I had to wear an artificial leg I am sure I would prefer a plain one with that great American invention, the rubber foot, rather than any gold-plated and jeweled one without it. I am called upon to furnish from 500 to 600 arms and legs, comparatively few of the former, every year, and you may say, on my authority, that the railroad system in this country, as at present conducted, and the machinery used in so many branches of manufacture, may be relied upon to make three cripples for every one that would be likely to be made by another war."

A dealer in surgical appliances said : "I do not deal in artificial limbs any more, for the reason that the things I have to keep are multifarious enough to set a man's head whirling, and to prosecute the artificial limb business properly requires exclusive attention to it. But I know all about it, and I often have to repair arms and legs, so that I meet many persons who wear such things, and I give you my word that I have been surprised more than once by men who came into my store and disclosed that they had artificial legs. I had not observed any indication of it in their walk. I know a girl employed in the Fifth Avenue Hotel, who has a wooden leg with a rubber foot, and nobody of all those about her every day, not even the other girls who sleep in the same room with her at night, suspect the fact. She is a very smart, bright girl, and she told me that the secret of her concealing the fact so well is that, when she commenced wearing it, she carefully and systematically trained the well leg to adapt itself to the movements of the maimed one, instead of reversing that process as most persons do. The rubber foot is the invention of an old and experienced American maker, and is acknowledged in Europe as well as this country as the greatest discovery of the age in this direction."

Henry Laurens Bascomb, the actor, who had both his feet amputated in consequence of their being frozen, has had them replaced by rubber ones, and he now walks about almost as well as anybody, well enough, at all events, to enable him to teach elocution and acting.

The following article appeared in the *New York Medical Journal;* it refers to a matter that should be called to the attention of the profession.

THE DEVELOPMENT OF STUMPS BY THE USE OF ARTIFICIAL LIMBS.

The impression seems to prevail to some extent among physicians, that an artificial limb should not be worn after an amputation until the stump has had time to "harden," and with this idea patients are advised to defer the purchase of a limb frequently for months after the immediate effects of the amputation have entirely disappeared.

Undoubtedly there are many cases in which this advice is good, particularly in those of a strumous diathesis in whom an injury or abrasion may be productive of severe local lesions, and in those where amputation has been done in consequence of a necrosed condition of the bones. It is not this class, however, to which reference is made, but rather to those in which amputation is rendered necessary by an injury occurring when the individual is in full health, as in cases of gunshot wounds, and in the almost daily and by far too frequent accidents on the steam and horse-railroad tracks.

It may be safely laid down as a rule that the sooner after an amputation an artificial limb is applied the better it will be for the development of the stump and for the preservation of the symmetry and health of the sound limb. Especially does this seem to apply to cases occurring in young persons, in whom the stump is apt not only to fail in development proportionate to the growth of the individual but becomes atrophied and flabby from disuse.

In a recent conversation with Mr. A. A. Marks, manufacturer of artificial limbs in this city, attention was called to this matter, and the following case was cited in support of this theory.

The subject of the accompanying illustration, when but eight years of age, was furnished with one of Mr. Marks' artificial legs, which has been lengthened, enlarged, or replaced by Mr. Marks as demanded by the increased size of the wearer. The result of this early application of an artificial leg is seen in the

No. 266.

healthy development of the stump. In street dress one would hardly recognize the one-legged gymnast whose feats of strength and whose agility have given a world-wide reputation to "Stewart Dare," as he is known in public. When off the stage and in street attire his easy, graceful walk gives very little evidence of an artificial leg, which is due in part to the perfect adaptation of the socket to the stump, and in part to the flexible rubber foot (invented by Mr. Marks) whose action so closely simulates that of the natural foot, and does away so thoroughly with the tell-tale "*thud*" which always accompanies the use of the ordinary artificial leg that one would hardly suspect that the individual under observation has been subjected to an amputation.—*The New York Medical Journal.*

La Voz de Espana, Mexico, July 29, 1882. [*Translation.*]

MARKS—We have received a catalogue from this famous manufacturer of artificial limbs, and, judging from the weight of evidence, he is the first manufacturer in the world. The limbs of his make are firm, comfortable, natural, and inexpensive.

We shall give more minutely the details in the future, in view of the fact that our notable artist and dear friend, Enrique Guasp de Peris, will in a short time sail for the United States, for the purpose of getting an artificial leg from this distinguished manufacturer.

El Reproductor, Orizaba, Mexico, September 17, 1882. [*Translation.*]

"To-day I have seen myself again complete, thanks to the works of Mr. Marks. I shall immediately begin the practice of the artificial part, which has a precision and exactness to the natural one that at the first sight make it difficult to distinguish the genuine from the false."—ENRIQUE.

El Reproductor, Orizaba, Mexico, October 3, 1882. [*Translation.*]

It is exactly eight days since we had the pleasure of embracing Mr. Guasp and welcoming him to his home.

We feel obliged to say to our readers that the artificial leg which was the occasion of his visit to the United States is an admirable piece of mechanical perfection. It seems to have all the movements of the natural leg and its weight is but a trifle. We congratulate Mr. Guasp on the happy results of his trip.

La Libertad, Mexico, October 11, 1882. [*Translation.*]

ENRIQUE GUASP.—Day before yesterday we had a visit from our appreciated friend, with the object of showing to us his magnificent artificial leg, which was bought in the United States from the famous manufacturer Mr. Marks. It is not possible to ask more of the art. The leg moves to the will of our friend as if it were natural. It has not the deformities which are noticeable in other artificial limbs.

Morning Journal, Friday, March 9, 1883.

FALSE LEGS AND ARMS.

WONDERFUL PERFECTION REACHED IN MAKING ARTIFICIAL LIMBS—WHAT THEY ARE MADE OF AND HOW OPERATED—WRITING WITH INDIA-RUBBER HANDS AND SKATING ON WOODEN LEGS.

Fewer persons are seen on the streets of New York with empty sleeves and using crutches than in any European city with an equal population. The improvement now made in the manufacture of artificial limbs is most marked, and the articles that are supplied to-day are so perfect, both in their construction and action, as to almost defy detection, and many men, women, and children now go about the streets with artificial legs and arms whom nobody would ever suspect of being maimed.

HOW THEY ARE MADE.

To supply the loss of any one limb, or of all limbs, the manufacture of artificial members has been brought to such perfection that they can be used by their wearers with almost as much facility as the natural limbs.

Artificial limbs are now almost universally made of willow wood, as affording greater strength, lightness, and utility than could be obtained with other materials. The materials formerly used were as varied as their mode of construction. Some were of tin, solid wood, and even of iron, while the different joints were worked with all sorts of complicated machinery in the shape of cogged wheels, steel springs, etc., which were not only cumbersome and noisy in their operation, but were constantly getting out of order.

The articles of to-day obviate all this. Over the willow foundation is stretched a covering of leather which is enameled to represent the natural flesh, while the joints are articulated by means of light springs of steel, rubber, and cord, according to the formula of each particular maker.

FALSE LEGS.

Mr. A. A. Marks, of Broadway, is the largest manufacturer in this country. He now has in his employment a man and a boy who are fitted each with two false legs. Both can run and walk almost as well as those possessing their natural limbs. The maker attributes his success to the use of rubber for the feet of his legs and ignores what he terms as having been the bugbear of all makers, the artificial ankle joint. Certainly his legs are entirely noiseless, while the action of the knee joint is as perfect as possible.

FALSE ARMS.

His arms are so constructed that they can be fitted to a stump at the shoulder that is no longer than two or three inches, and yet be made to act. * * * * * * The hands are made of soft rubber, with annealed wire running through the fingers, which allows them to be put into any desired position. Others are made like the feet—of solid sponge rubber, which afford a good grasp if any thing is placed between the thumb and fingers. Patients thus supplied can even write with their hands, in proof of which he exhibits many specimens of their caligraphy. In the palm of the hand is fitted a screw-socket into which can be fitted a knife and fork for the purposes of eating at table. The most useful and strongest appliance, however, is a hook which screws on to the wrist in place of a hand, for with it immense weights can be lifted, parcels carried, and many other things done which the hand would not be capable of.

MARVELOUS EXCELLENCE.

In addition to the useful artificial limbs a large practice is had in extending a shortened or deformed leg to agree with its fellow, and so well is this done that detection is impossible when the wearer is dressed.

From the *National Tribune*, Washington, D. C., June 18, 1885.

RUBBER HANDS AND FEET.

The use of some species of artificial limbs to replace those lost by accident or war is of quite ancient origin. These appliances, before the invention of the rubber foot, were of two kinds, generally speaking. The cripple either stumped about upon a wooden peg, like that worn by Stuyvesant, or he procured, at great expense, a limb so intricate and complicated in its attempt to duplicate every joint and ligature of the departed member, that it was practically worthless, owing to the impossibility of keeping it long in repair.

The rubber foot was invented in 1863 by Mr. A. A. Marks, now the leading manufacturer in the United States.

The advantages of the rubber foot are many. The chief, perhaps, is that it does away entirely with all that entanglement of cords, straps, hinges, bolts, screws, etc., by means of which the maker of the old-fashioned artificial limbs attempts to secure a natural action at the ankle joint. By Mr. Marks' system the elasticity is thrown into the foot, giving ease and evenness of motion, as in the natural gait. There are no sudden thumps or clanks when the ball of the foot reaches the floor, as in the ankle joint style of artificial limb, but the even rise and fall of the foot from heel to toe takes place exactly as in the natural member, creating a motion that cannot be told from that of a person who possesses the feet with which he was born.

A very practical advantage is the durability of this style of limb, saving the wearer the annoyance of constant repairs. Its simplicity is the natural cause of this enduring quality. It is also the most economical limb in the market in the matter of price and quality.

Farrow's Military Encyclopedia contains a full description of the invention, describing it as the superior of any thing yet known.

Mr. Marks took the gold medal over all competitors at the New Orleans Exposition, just closed.

El Canal, Panama, October 13, 1882. [*Translation*.]

READER—Are you in need of a limb? if you are there is no necessity of getting discouraged or putting on a sad countenance, because (we speak from our own knowledge) if you are in need of a foot, leg, hand, or arm, which mortals are likely to lose, you can go to New York, the country of extraordinary inventions, where you will find the king of artificial limb-makers, Mr. Marks, who will supply you with limbs of fine finish and perfection. * * * *

Las Novedades, New York, December 9, 1882. [*Translation*.]

ARTIFICIAL LIMBS.

Quite recently we noticed in the columns of this paper the arrival in this city of the famous actor and writer, Mr. Enrique Guasp de Peris, Viscount of San Roman, who, having been deprived of one of his limbs, came to this city to have it replaced by one of the mechanical and ingenious products of North America, only inferior to the works of nature.

Having succeeded in gratifying his wishes with perfect and full satisfaction, the Viscount returned to the Mexican Republic, where he is at present, devoting himself more to the tasks of the journalist than to those of the stage. * * * *

We have had the pleasure of interviewing the manufacturer of the Viscount's artificial leg—Mr. Marks—and also of examining the artificial limbs which he makes. We were surprised at the perfection which he has achieved in this line. We saw arms and legs, with their suitable hands and feet, in a great variety. The legs manufactured by Mr. Marks have the peculiar feature of the india-rubber foot, and to this is due the superiority of the limb. The patient is able to walk with a firm, natural, elastic step, and can balance himself in any position without much effort. At the office of Mr. Marks we were eye-witness to four persons to whom artificial legs were applied below and above the knees, and one of them wore a pair of legs; it was necessary to be informed of this fact or we would not have suspected it.

A communication from Mr. Enrique Guasp de Peris we here publish by the permission of that benevolent person; it is a most eloquent testimonial, more so than any thing we could say. We print it as follows:

MR. A. A. MARKS.

DEAR SIR:—I have the greatest pleasure in addressing you these few lines in order to express the satisfaction which I have with the artificial leg you manufactured for me. To its comfort and stability I owe the invaluable treasure of walking almost naturally. I am pleased with its lightness as well as its easy movements, which so closely approximate nature. You may also take these lines as an expression of my appreciation of the many attentious and kindnesses which in your establishment were paid to your affectionate

Obedient Servant,

EL VIZCONDE de SAN ROMAN.

NEW YORK, September, 1882.

* * * * * * * * * *

Las Novedades, New York, December 11, 1882. [*Translation*.]

ANOTHER PERSON GRATIFIED.

In the establishment of Mr. A. A. Marks, the famous manufacturer of artificial limbs, we have had the pleasure of saluting the Mexican General, Mr. Genaro Gonzalez, who lost one of his legs in the last struggle of the Mexican Empire, and who came, like many others, to this city to solicit the services of the eminent inventor, Mr. Marks. The brave general is highly pleased with the kind, or system, of apparatus of this gentleman, and speaks of Mr. Marks in the same laudatory manner as did Mr. Guasp de Peris and Colonel Federico Larranaga.

Prairie Farmer, Chicago, September 5, 1885.

MARKS' ARTIFICIAL FEET AND HANDS.—The greatest improvement yet made in artificial limbs is the rubber foot, invented by Mr. A. A. Marks in

1868. This was at a time when maimed soldiers were being sent home by thousands, and it came like a boon from above. With its aid these crippled veterans were enabled to engage in the various active vocations of life, which otherwise would have been closed to them. The advantages of this foot are many ; but perhaps the chief one lies in its doing away with all entanglements of cords, straps, hinges, bolts, screws, etc, found in the older inventions. This foot is elastic, giving ease and evenness of motion similar to that of the natural limb. It is also exceedingly durable, and thus far cheaper than other styles.

The rubber hands manufactured by the same parties are also the best substitute known for that member.

The Catholic Review, New York, April 26, 1885.

MARKS' ARTIFICIAL LIMBS.—We very strongly commend to all who need such aids ; the Marks Artificial Limbs, designed, patented, and made by A. A. Marks of New York. Dr. Marks is very widely known in the United States and in various countries of North and South America. Perhaps these lines may serve to make him known to some other unfortunates needing his services. Were they to consult any of our more prominent American surgeons as to the artificial limb-maker most likely to be serviceable to them, the most experienced would probably suggest Dr. Marks first.

The eminent orthopedist and surgeon Lewis A. Sayre, in one of his lectures says of Dr. Marks : "He makes, as I think, altogether the best artificial leg I have ever seen, simply because of its durability and simplicity."

In supplying lower limbs Dr. Marks achieves a perfect success.

He does not claim much for arms except that his are the best the *simplest* and the most useful made. If the amputation is *below* the *elbow* he makes a fair substitute, one with which the patient can write. For cuts above the elbow little can be done. Still, we have seen where even in that cruel suffering Dr. Marks' limb has brought some assistance and great comfort to the victim. The great merit of his limbs, we may repeat, is their great simplicity, in that they do not attempt too much, more than is possible or likely to be permanent ; that they are very strong, light in weight, and graceful to the eye.

Irish World, New York, January 1, 1887.

ARTIFICIAL LIMBS.—Of the many establishments devoted to the relief of the injured and mutilated, we doubt that any have ever reached so near perfection as that of A. A. Marks of New York City.

The manner in which this house repairs the mutilated by replacing those members which accident, disease, war, and various causes have forever severed from the human body is but another name for magic.

Men, women, and children, limbless, helpless, pitiful objects, dependent on the attention and aid of their sympathizing friends or a pair of crutches for their locomotion, are, by this establishment, in a very brief time enabled to go out in to the world relieved, restored, and practically as useful as before misfortune befell them. It has taken years of close study and devotion to the work to be able to achieve such results. Genius has given to the world the man who has successfully mastered this task, and it is but right that men and the press should commend him to those in need of his aid.

Mr. A. M. Forrester, an associate editor of the *Irish World*, had learned of the Marks establishment from experience, and writes as follows :

Office of *The Irish World*, No. 17 Barclay St.
PATRICK FORD, Editor, Publisher and Proprietor.
NEW YORK, December 13, 1886.

MY DEAR MR. MARKS : Somewhere about four months ago you undertook to build up a foot for me to replace one that I had lost in 1874. I allowed you to experiment on the stump of my leg with some misgivings and doubts lest you were going to make bad worse.

I am sorry for my suspicions. The foot which you have supplied me has done its duty nobly. It clings to me with the stern affection of a parent, never slips, always responds to the movement of the ankle, and generally behaves as if it were acquainted with me intimately since my birth. My best friends fail to recognize my magnificent stride, so different from the crutch hop that formerly marked my march ; my foes don't know me at all.

I can safely defy any one not aware that I am minus a foot to take exception to my physique. I gladly testify to the success of the limb with which you have supplied me. You may remember that I feared a failure. It is, therefore, with the more pleasure that I admit a success. If I ever lose my other foot I shall look to you to replace it.

Yours faithfully, A. M. FORRESTER.

The Baptist Weekly, New York, April 29, 1886.

The name of Mr. A. A. Marks is familiar to all who need artificial limbs. Every possible improvement has been brought into service, and hundreds of people give testimony to the admirable adaptation of his manufactures to supply the place of their lost members.

Rural New Yorker, May 1, 1886.

MARKS' ARTIFICIAL LIMBS.—This book is an argument, if such a term may be allowed, in favor of artificial limbs ; that is, it shows how easily such limbs may be secured and how comparatively comfortable they are.

It is well known that artificial eyes and teeth can be made so true to nature as to deceive even a close observer ; but it is quite surprising to know that there are persons in our midst wearing artificial legs and arms who very seldom betray their unpleasant secret. This book is interesting and well written.

Such a work would be incomplete without the old song "The Cork Leg," a parody on which is given in full. We hope none of our readers will ever have the misfortune to lose a limb.

Should they be so unfortunate, we can only hope they may secure as comfortable substitute as those described in this book.

The Weekly Tribune, July 27, 1887.

154 NASSAU ST., NEW YORK, July 25, 1887.

MR. A. A. MARKS.

DEAR SIR :—It is now about sixteen months since you fitted me with one of your rubber foot legs. My experience with the old kind had disgusted me so thoroughly with artificial legs that I was not disposed to try any other, and especially your rubber foot with a rigid ankle. Only by the solicitations of kind friends was I persuaded to give yours a trial.

I am happy to inform you, however, that I can walk with ease, naturalness, and comfort. The elasticity of the foot accommodates itself to all the angles necessary to natural and comfortable walking, and at the same time contributes wonderfully to the sense of security and self-control, so that one feels almost as though he were upon his own legs again. My friends say it has made a new man of me, and I never found any thing so near the natural limb in its feeling and sense of security in walking, especially on uneven ground.

Very truly yours,
JOSEPH H. PATTERSON.

New York Herald, Sunday, 1887.

DEFT RUBBER HANDS—UNFORTUNATE WALTER ALEXANDER AND HIS NEW HANDS.

TO BECOME A STENOGRAPHER—GRATEFUL TO THE HERALD FOR ITS AID IN GIVING HIM A CHANCE IN LIFE.

A boy with rubber hands is a freak that not even a dime museum can offer. But Belleville, New Jersey, can.

It's no joke, either.

No, indeed. It's the sternest kind of reality, and a very sad fact to poor Walter E. Alexander, to whose arms they are attached.

Still, rubber hands are very much better than no hands at all, especially as they can be used to a certain extent, and with that comforting thought he keeps up his good spirits, and is quite proud of the deftness that he infuses into his gutta-percha fingers.

Ever since that direful day in June last when the accident happened the public has known of Walter E. Alexander. From an ordinary factory boy he unwittingly and unwillingly became the object of public sympathy and public aid as well.

It was through this same public sympathy and aid and the instrumentality of the *Herald* that young Alexander is taking the bright view of life that he now seems to, and that he is swinging his rubber hands that he wished for so long.

THE BLACK FRIDAY.

It was on Friday—and a very black Friday indeed for Walter—June 17 last, that the accident occurred that deprived him of his hands. He was employed as a "feeder" in the Riverside Rubber Works, at Belleville, N. J. It was his duty to stand behind the iron rollers of a grinder and keep their ever-hungry maw supplied with a mass of rubber scraps.

Walter was standing on tiptoe, leaning forward and pushing the pasty mass of rubber down into the narrow crack between the rollers, where it snapped and spluttered as it was ground through. Whatever went in between the shining sides of those rollers was found to come out mashed to a pulp. The rollers were revolving slowly and steadily on their mission of pulverization.

Thousands of times had Walter been in the same position. There was no danger. He never let his hands go down with the—

A shout of anguish!

DRAWN IN TO BE CRUSHED.

The time had come at last. The fingers of both hands had got caught, and slowly and surely were being drawn in between the cruel steel and crushed to a jelly. There was no pulling them out. They were embedded in the mass of rubber. There was no help for it in any way but to let the rollers grind on and draw down inch by inch his arms and body.

He could not reach with his feet the brake that by a simple kick would stop the machine.

Meanwhile he did not neglect to shout for help. A lad working at a similar machine at the other end of the mill heard him and ran to Walter's assistance. He kicked the brake, stopped the machine, and, with a horror-stricken face, pulled the mashed arms of the victim from between the rollers and out of the sticky mass of rubber.

All the while young Alexander kept his presence of mind and positively refused to faint. It is that same kind of pluck that has carried him through so successfully. There is no chicken to him.

Not a groan did he let escape, even while bumping over the rough road in the wagon to the hospital.

After his arrival at St. Barnabas' Hospital both arms were taken off half way between the wrist and the elbow by Dr. Clark.

Four days afterward Walter was up and around the building. It was only four weeks afterward—nearly the middle of July—that he left the hospital altogether.

A GRAVE QUESTION.

Then he went home, and the very grave question arose as to what he was to do for a living. It was absolutely necessary that he should earn his own living somewhere. He always had, and with his hands back there was no doubt that he always would, for the lad was a bright fellow and very apt at any thing he turned his attention to.

Then it was that the *Herald's* interest in all unfortunates came into good play. A fund was started that was liberally subscribed to. It came in very opportunely, for the boy was sadly in need of money. When he saw the *Herald's* practical way of expressing sympathy, and that it was with him in his trial, he took new hope and concluded that his life was not quite blasted after all. He determined to find some way of making himself useful and earning his living in the future. Of course he was utterly helpless. He could not even feed or dress himself, and had to be taken care of as a baby would.

PERHAPS TO WRITE EVEN.

Then came the scheme of the rubber hands. He was greatly elated when he learned to what perfection the art of making artificial arms had been carried. He might be able to write even! That was a great consolation.

Before his affliction his penmanship had been noted all over Belleville, and he took no little pride in the graceful way in which he could dash off his autograph. But with only his stumps he could not dot an "i" or cross a "t."

Then, again, it was a pretty hard strain on his boyish pride to go around with the empty ends of both sleeves flapping at his side.

Then came the proposition for the rubber hands. They were made and paid for out of the fund, and a few days ago they came. The lad held up his arms to have them strapped on with such a feeling of satisfaction as he had never known before.

THE NEW HANDS.

The hands are made of rubber, covered with kid gloves. From the wrist up the artificial limb is of willow. It is attached at the elbow. There are also straps that lead up to the shoulder.

The first use to which he put them was to try and write his name with a pencil. After a little practice he took up a pen and wrote a letter of thanks to the *Herald*. It was certainly a success, all things considered. There are many boys of sixteen, who have been to school, too, with real hands of flesh and bone, that can not write as well.

BESIEGED FOR AUTOGRAPHS.

When the *Herald* reporter called on young Alexander he was busily employed in writing his autograph on the sheets of a little pad of paper. He has become quite the curiosity of the place. Hundreds of people have asked him to write his name for them, and all his spare time is now taken up in that occupation that is such a bore to great men.

The girls are the most persistent of the lot, and want verses and quotations written as well as the autograph. Alexander had wasted a whole pad in his attempts to write the following verse neatly:

> "There is a wild but lonely flower,
> That twines around the shepherd's cot,
> And in the silent, midnight hour
> It sweetly sighs 'Forget me not.'"

Alexander can even pick up a pen himself. The fingers are made of stiff rubber that will hold any thing put between them. They are slightly bent, as on the fingers of a hand in repose. In picking up a pen he presses down on it with the back of the fingers, and the springlike quality of the rubber holds it fast. Of course he cannot move them, except by pressing them against something. In writing he uses the whole arm movement and writes from the shoulder.

HOPEFUL AND AMBITIOUS.

"Oh, I am getting along first rate with them," said he. "I think in time I shall be able to write a good, legible hand and quite rapidly. I have to write from the shoulder, and after once having learned how to do it I am told that it is the easiest way to write. I have lots of time to myself, and so have a good chance to practice."

"Are you still employed at the works?"

"Yes, I am acting as timekeeper now, and doing any thing that I can to make myself useful. Ever since I came out of the hospital I have been around the office, running the errands and doing such things to save other people time, but now, with my hands, I can do more valuable work."

TO LEARN STENOGRAPHY.

"Have you any other ideas of occupations that you can follow?"

"Yes, sir, lots of them. Mr. Marks is making me a new pair, with some improvements, so that I can use a typewriter. I have no doubt of being successful with that. Then my friends here have suggested that I learn stenography. I am going to try it anyway. If I can get to be a stenographer and a type-writer I will be pretty sure of always being able to earn a living. The other night I was introduced to a couple of young men. They both shook hands with me and never noticed the difference. People who don't know me would never suspect that the hands are not natural."

"Can you feed yourself?"

"Very nicely. I have a special knife and fork that are made to fasten on to the wrists. I have to get some one to fasten them on for me, and then I am all right and can cut the toughest kind of steak. When I wish to lift anything I use this hook here on the arm. I can lift 150 pounds with it."

THEY SEEM LIKE HIS OWN.

"Does it seem strange to have the hands there?"

"No, it does not. It does not seem unnatural at all. I imagine I can feel my hands all the time, and to a certain extent it seems as though these rubber arrangements were my own hands. It's a little singular, too, but the sense of touch is in a slight degree transferred through the rubber to the nerves in my arm. For instance I can tell with my eye closed whether my fingers are touching a wooden surface or wood covered with cloth."

"My greatest feat yet," he continued, "was in driving the other day. Another young fellow was out with me. I took the reins to see if I could hold them, found that I could get along very nicely indeed, and drove all the way from here to Elizabeth and back without any trouble. You should have seen how people who know of my accident stared when they saw me drive by. There are no pains at all in what is left of my arms."

BUT HE CAN'T PLAY BALL.

And so, although an unkind fortune had robbed him of enough to discourage the bravest of men, this stripling of a boy keeps up his spirits and is bound to make the best of things and succeed in the world yet, even though he has to sign his name with rubber fingers and cannot enjoy that delight of all boyhood, baseball. That is one of his severest trials. But he can strike a match, pull a coin out of his pocket, sharpen a lead pencil, and do a great many things that to others might seem trivial enough, but that to him mean a great deal. The joy of little things can only be fully appreciated when one has rubber hands.

"I'm not much of a success as a knocker-out," he said, laughingly, "but in other respects I'm doing quite well, thanks to the *Herald* and my friends."

Minonk Blade, Minonk, Ill. July 8, 1886.

A SURVIVOR FROM STONEMAN'S RAID.

BRIEF REMINISCENCE OF THE REBELLION.

In introducing to an acquaintance, some time ago, our much-esteemed and sympathetic friend, Mr. January, as perhaps one of the most notable human monuments now surviving of the horrors of our civil war, what if we had announced him as having both feet in the grave? What an expression of mingled wonder and inquiry the countenance of the former would have assumed! Yet the affirmation were no less truthful than astounding.

This reflection prompted us that a brief record of the incident that suggested it would serve at once to gratify and interest the readers of the *Blade*, and bear testimony of our sincere regard for a staunch friend and worthy citizen.

"To noble hearts the Native Land is dear."

So, too, is the memory of those who fell in the battles fought for the preservation of her integrity. Nor can we be indifferent to the lot of such as survived from the field but to pine through captivity and hardships which, when not ending in death, not infrequently resulted in the loss of limbs to the sufferer, as in the case of the subject of these lines.

John W. January, born in Clinton Co., Ohio, on the 29th of November, 1847, passed the first seven years of his life in his native State, the following seven near Henry, Ill., and, still with his father's family, well-to-do farmers, removed, in the spring of 1861, to their farm one mile south of Minonk, and two years later to their present comfortable homestead in the western part of the city of Minonk, in the last mentioned State. One of the promptest respondents to the call for 300,000 men, he enlisted in company B of the 14th Illinois Cavalry, and on the 7th of February, the lad having scarcely entered upon his sixteenth year, quitted for the first time the parental roof and proceeded to his regiment, then organizing at Peoria. The corps, under the command of Colonel Horace Capron, was transported by rail into Kentucky, and marched thence across the Cumberland Mountains to unite with the main body of the army. History chronicles some sixteen battles in which the 14th was engaged between that time and the midsummer of 1864, and in all these Mr. January took part. On July 27, his command, detailed for service in the ill-starred expedition known as Stone-man's raid, set out from Atlanta for Macon, Ga., for the fourfold purpose of harassing the enemy, cutting off and destroying their supplies, diverting their attention from Sherman's division, and releasing Union prisoners at Andersonville. By August 1, the youth having already been promoted to the rank of corporal and with fair prospects of further advancement; but five men returned of the fifty-five which Company B mustered at the start. Twenty-three were killed, and twenty-seven captured, among the last January himself, who a few days later, after the usual transfers had been effected, was imprisoned at Andersonville. On the fall of Atlanta he was sent to Charleston, S. C., and ten days later to Florence, S. C., where he remained until the end of the war. The trials and hardships of prison life and Confederate prison fare now began to tell sadly upon January's constitution; from the hale, robust stripling of 165 pounds at the time of his capture, three months further of all but starvation at Wilmington, N. C., after his release, found him reduced to forty-five pounds! But the end was not yet. After a tedious and fatiguing journey he was landed at David's Island near New York Harbor, and there, at the end of seven months, dwindled to a skeleton by the

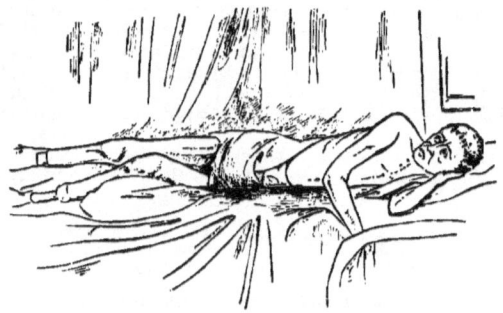

No. 267.

ravages of a loathsome disease, was mustered out of the service on the 15th day of October, 1865. The last sad scene of this harrowing drama had now to come. A prey to scurvy and gangrene, which had all but separated his feet from the legs; unaided by the surgeons; despairing but yet desperate, for his native fortitude had not forsaken him, his own hand guided the knife that severed the meagre thews, the only remaining attachments of those feet!

As convalescence progressed, his chief preoccupation was the thought: should he ever be able to walk again? His feet were gone. How might he replace them? Agents from the several manufacturers of artificial limbs paid daily visits to the hospital, each seeking to secure the preference of the maimed soldiers for his special system of apparatus. But one particular day Frank Stewart was announced, as representative of the already well-known inventor A. A. Marks, of New York City, the fame of whose patent legs and arms with rubber feet and hands is now universal, for they have been introduced by thousands in every country in the civilized world. Mr. Stewart's canvass was more eloquent than wordy, more experimental than theoretical; for to demonstrate the superiority of his principal's system, he himself, with the Marks apparatus, set to pacing lustily up and down the ward before surgeons and patients. It was pitiful to observe the divergence of opinion among the men of science when asked which of the pedestrian's legs was the artificial one, some opining the right and some the left, until utterly discomfited by the assurance that the case before them was one of amputation of both legs! The wild hilarity of the patients beggars description; as for the agents aforesaid, they saved the situation by laughing with the rest. Mr. January and every other man in the ward—half a dozen in all—that was similarly afflicted with

Mr. Stewart's condition, desired to be furnished with the Marks limbs, and their desires were granted at the expense of a bountiful Government. The beam of hope that burst upon our friend that day was the forerunner of returning happiness, which reached its fulness the moment he found himself again upon his feet. But who is so wise as to know when he is happy enough? Our friend January is human like the rest of us, and under the influence of one or two attacks of discontentment, he made trial of other apparatus, which, however, to do him justice, were each time no sooner tried than rejected, for one cause or another, but above all, we understand, because of the absence of the rubber foot. Some wonderful charm there must be in this said rubber foot, a charm which he delights to dwell upon, when he finds a sympathetic ear into which he can pour his praise. For our own part we have learned from him of its lightness, and softness, and the easy gracefulness with which it adapts itself to every possible movement of the natural foot, and that without betraying its artificial construction by the irritating THUD characteristic of all other

No. 268.   No. 269.

mechanical limbs that we have so far seen. Then the airy lightness of the whole apparatus—4 pounds—yet a strength equal to double his weight, for with his present 180 pounds he trips along with a firmness and elasticity of step that would put to shame many a man of like proportions with natural means of locomotion. Indeed, he assures us that he frequently forgets that his feet are those made by Marks, and not those that nature gave him.

The extremes of this most interesting case will be more clearly appreciated with the aid of the appended illustrations. The first of these, exhibiting the patient upon his hospital couch, and emaciated almost beyond recognition, shortly after the operation in which he figured at once as subject and surgeon, is an exact reproduction from an illustrated article published in *Harper's Weekly* at the time. In the next engraving what a change! Eleven years have elapsed. Eleven years of activity and bread-winning, thanks to the twin apparatus standing either by the side of the limb in which their friendly efficacy is respectfully developed. Then the lusty proportions of the man, now in the plenitude of his physical power, and that comely rotundity of contour suggestive, indeed, of his 180 pounds of genial flesh, blood, bone, and sinew. We would now ask who, without knowing the man or his story, and by the mere contemplation of the third and last figure, would suspect he was looking on the original of the picture first referred to ?

We had almost forgotten to mention that Mr. January, in his intervals of leisure (alas, too frequent at times), has of late years taken to lecturing in some of our Western States. Such of our readers as have the advantage of his acquaintance, and consequently know his versatility and his turn for eloquence, will not be surprised to learn that he has achieved no little success and popularity in that field.

From "A Descriptive Catalogue of Manufactures from Native Woods as Shown in the Exhibit of the U. S. Department of Agriculture at the World's Industrial and Cotton Exposition at New Orleans, La., 1886," page 54.

ARTIFICIAL LIMBS.

EXHIBIT.—One sample willow lumber, with leg carved in relief; artificial limbs in parts and complete, from A. A. Marks, New York.

Mr. Marks states that artificial limbs are also made from bass-wood. Most of the wood used comes from Fairfield County, Connecticut, only thrifty, large trees being selected, the trunks alone being used. The wood is secured in winter. Bass-wood from Ohio and willow grown in New York have also been used, but they find no superiority over the Connecticut-grown lumber. From the irregular shapes and hollow forms of limbs the waste often amounts to 90 per cent., the lumber costing from $150 to $200 per thousand feet. It comes to the factory in blocks 4 to 8 inches square, and from 1 to 4 feet long, bored out in the center when green, and seasoned for three years. It is also stated American willow and bass-wood are not excelled for this purpose by any of the many foreign woods that have been experimented with. The different processes of manufacture are interesting. The tree is cut into lengths of from 1 to 4 feet, split into square pieces of from 4 to 8 inches, dressed on a circular saw, bored the entire length with 1 or 1½ inch auger, allowed to season in a dark, dry place for from two to three years. Carved into shape, hollowed out to a thickness, smoothed outside and inside, hooped to give it additional strength, covered outside with skin, a water-proof coating applied to the covering. Inside of leg is smoothed and polished. Feet are made by carving a block of willow wood into the shape of a small last of about two-thirds the diameter of the natural foot; about this sponge rubber is vulcanized, alternated by layers of canvas. Some of the wood-work is done by grinding and sand-papering machines; otherwise the work is done by hand. The leg will pass through at least a dozen hands before finished.

There are about fifty manufactories of artificial limbs in the United States; capital not estimated.

The Chemist and Druggist, London, England, June 6, 1886.

We have received a volume from Mr. A. A. Marks, of Broadway, New York, describing very fully and apparently with the utmost fairness his patent artificial limbs and india-rubber hands and feet. The principle of these limbs is that the limbs are manufactured with india-rubber feet and hands, so constructed as to yield to the movements of the body without any complicated arrangement of joints, cords, etc. These limbs seem to have given much satisfaction to many who have had occasion to buy them, and to any such in this country we would advise at least a careful perusal of Mr. Marks' book. He supplies, besides, full directions for measurements, with diagrams, etc., enabling patients to give exact details " in absentia."

LITERARY AMENITIES ON ARTIFICIAL LIMBS.

General Maxwell, in his clever little book on the Beaufort leg, says: " A leg which ends in a point is always subject to curious adventures. A story told by a Norfolk ostler, in the coaching days, will go far to prove the assertion. He said he was never in such a " precadiment " in all his life as when he helped down an old peg-legged woman from the top of his coach; she gave a slip and the end of her wooden leg was thrust into his breeches pocket."

A story is told of a wealthy merchant who possessed more than the usual share of vivacity; he was jocose and pranky under all circumstances, and once in a while his jokes would take a rather unexpected turn, and make matters uncomfortable for himself as well as others, but he enjoyed life all the same.

His confidential clerk, Smith, wore an artificial leg and was accounted an exceptionally fine operator on the rubber foot; in fact no one would ever suspect that Smith was a cripple.

One day when the merchant was entertaining one of his congenial friends in a hilarious sort of way, Smith stepped from the office, and as he did so, the merchant said to his friend: "Did you notice Smith as he left the office? He is one of the curiosities of this world; although he walks as well as you or I, he has no more feeling in one of his legs than you have in your false teeth. Why, I can plunge my knife up to the handle in the calf of his leg and he won't budge an inch." "No! you don't mean it," incredulously replied his friend. "I'll show you when he comes in," said the merchant. Presently Smith returned and took his position by the side of his high desk. The merchant with great deliberation took his knife from his pocket, opened it carefully, winked at his friend, and with a desperate lunge thrust the knife into the calf of Smith's leg. Smith jumped nearly to the ceiling and uttered words that could not be found in the dictionary. He turned on his employer, and but for the timely interference of his friend would have dealt him some severe blows.

When matters quieted down, it was found that the merchant had made a miscalculation, and plunged the blade into the natural leg instead of the artificial.

One day as Worcester was strolling leisurely down Second Avenue an irritable dog ran after him, barking and snarling furiously. Worcester struck at him with his wooden leg; the dog snapped at it and set its teeth deeply into the wooden shell; withdrawing his teeth from the unfleshy substance, the dog looked Worcester in the face, turned and ran away as though he was pursued by cudgels.

A PART OF STEWART'S BODY.—A practical joke is told on Tom Stewart, who in an engagement in the early part of the rebellion met with the loss of both legs.

It would seem as though one deprived of both legs had enough to keep him quiet at home instead of *running* about and getting into all sorts of deviltry; but Stewart's disposition was not lugubrious; he was naturally active, vivacious, and always ready for any thing that could be termed sport.

After supplying himself with a pair of those marvelous instruments invented by the world-famous Marks, he soon became able to walk on his rubber feet with an elastic step, just like a dude.

He could walk tiptoed, flatfooted, with a high or low heel, narrow or broad toes, just as the law of fashion demanded, and, no matter how hideous or uncomfortable the custom was to other people, Stewart was in the same happy peace of mind.

He had neither corns nor bunions to annoy him, and could go to the extreme and have as much comfort as his companions who were shod in moccasins. He had another advantage—he could waltz with the Chicago girl and his rubber feet would be insensible to any danger. Stewart got so he could run, skate, play billiards, drink "Sec.," and spend money as well as any of the boys. He was naturally free and had plenty of money, and thus he became quite a lion among his associates.

One thing would annoy Stewart, and that was if any one found out that he wore wooden legs. His new companions were kept in ignorance, and his old ones were sworn to eternal silence.

If any one wanted his bitterest enmity, all they had to do was to intimate that he wore wooden legs.

Stewart belonged to a club of young bloods who seemed to have nothing to do but to indulge in every thing of a sporting nature.

They were known as the "Eccentrics," and a more fitting title could not be chosen. They went fishing in the summer, pigeon shooting in the fall, sleigh riding in the winter, and drank beer all the year round, and Stewart was always with them.

About the time when the whole world was astir over the desecration of the grave of the millionaire A. T. Stewart, and the papers were full of rumors as to the whereabouts of the stolen body, and large sums of money were offered for the return of the same, the Eccentric Club indulged in one of their hilarious fishing exploits. On the evening of July 3 they arrived at one of those happy spots on the south side of Long Island where several hotels, plenty of beer, and the wide ocean lay before them.

The Eccentrics retired early that evening and all were up bright and early in the morning, except Stewart. The boys were somewhat exercised at his delay, as all were ready and eager for the fishing grounds.

Myles, who always carried his jokes to a distressing degree, rushed up stairs into Stewart's room for the avowed purpose of hauling the sleeping Eccentric from his couch.

There was Stewart fast asleep. A chair by the side of his bed contained his clothing, and by the side of his chair were standing his two wooden legs as natural as if they were of flesh and blood instead of wood and rubber. Myles grasped the situation, and in a moment had a leg under each arm, rushed down stairs, entered the bar-room almost out of breath, and shouted so every one could hear : "Boys, I'm in luck this morning, I've found Stewart's body, and here is half of it. Now for the reward." The legs were placed on the counter and thoroughly baptized with several rounds of beer, and placarded "Part of Stewart's Remains." It is needless to say that when Stewart awoke and became conscious of the situation all the beer in Babylon could not drown his wrath to keep him from taking the first train to New York. The Eccentrics have not had the pleasure of his company since, and Myles has been wise enough to keep his distance.

Farm and Fireside, April 5, 1886.

A WOODEN JOKE.—Speaking of wooden legs, there is an old soldier employed in the government office in this city who has had some experience with an artificial limb, his meat one having been taken off at the knee. Among the most amusing was one with a sleeping-car porter.

This pampered railway tyrant rarely earns his quarter all around by his pretence of blacking shoes and flipping dust from his victim's back, but it is the habit of this wooden-legged man to utilize the darkey in taking off that leg and making him earn his hire. On the train he struck an uppish sort of a porter—a brother to the insufferable swell who sings out, "Last call for dinnah in the dining-cah." That darkey stood around with a languid dignity that would make a street-corner dude sick at heart.

The man with the wooden leg made up his mind he would "wake that nigger up" before he chipped in his quarter.

He told a couple of men in the car his purpose, and they joined in with him. He wears his shoe firmly fastened to the rubber foot, having no need to remove it, and having fallen once from a loose shoe. After his berth had been made up he went to the dressing-room and unstrapped his leg, keeping hold of the strap, and then got to his berth. Then he called to the porter : "I've got rheumatism and can't bend over," he said, "and I wish you'd pull off that shoe." The porter untied the shoe and tried to pull it off, but it wouldn't come. "Pull hard," said the passenger. The darkey gave it another pull.

"Oh, brace against the berth and pull," said the passenger.

The porter had blood in his eye. He put his foot against the berth and pulled like a dentist. The passenger let go the strap, and the darkey fell back with the shoe and the leg.

"My God, you've pulled my leg off," shrieked the passenger.

The porter dropped it, and with his eyes bulging and his teeth chattering, he broke from the car. He concealed himself in the corner of the baggage car, and pretty soon the two other conspirators came in, pretended they didn't know where he was, sat down on a trunk and talked over the awful condition of the man whose leg had been pulled off, and about the penalty the darkey would have to suffer if he should be caught. The porter was of no service to anybody that night, even after they had explained the joke to him.

Mr. Marks in the earlier edition of his pamphlet published the following article together with the "Song of the Cork Leg." It is reproduced here for the benefit of those who may find it of interest.

CORK LEGS.

The wonderful power of song has been well exemplified in the old song of the "Cork Leg." When but a mere lad, I remember with striking clearness of going off for a long way through a lonely woods, on a clear autumn night, to visit what is termed in old Connecticut a burning coal pit (a process of converting wood into charcoal by fire and heat):

One of the watchers was a noted singer, and frequently entertained his nightly visitors with some favorite songs.

On that night, among others, he sang the song of the "Cork Leg," which was then entirely new to me, and made a very lasting impression; indeed, all the way home it kept ringing in my ears, how the Cork Leg started off at break-neck speed, taking the wearer with it around the world, as it were, until the poor man was knocked to pieces, and nothing left but the cork leg itself, and that was still going. Well, I reckon it is going yet, for that old song is still ringing in my ears, and ever since my first entrance into this so-called "Cork Leg" business, it really seems as if it was continually ringing in every body's else ears, for hardly a day has passed during the last twenty years but one or more have asked, either by voice or letter, if I made "Cork Legs," and although I have answered that question thousands of times, I will here say that, although there is sometimes cork used to a very limited extent in the construction of artificial legs yet with a tolerable degree of perseverance I have exercised all the inquisitive powers I have had to spare to get hold of a cork leg or find something authentic about it. All my efforts have proved a failure, and I give up in utter despair of ever ascertaining to a certainty that one single artificial leg was ever made of cork. If any body has one, I should be glad to see it, and would gladly purchase it as the most valuable of all my trophies of ancient and modern inventions of artificial legs. I don't suppose there is any body living who has not heard this old song, but there may be some who will, as a matter of course, be glad to get hold of this mythical old invention, so I will here print the real original thing itself, that all who read it may know just exactly what a vagary the cork leg is.

Should this have the effect to satisfy those inquiries about cork legs, and at the same time dispel the illusions created in the minds of many, the object of this explanation shall have been accomplished.

THE CORK LEG.

I.

I'll tell you a tale now without any flam,
 In Holland there dwelt Mynheer Von Clam,
Who every morning said, "I am
 The richest merchant in Rotterdam."
  Ri tu, di nu, di nu, di nu,
   Ri tu, di ni nu, ri tu, di nu, ri na.

II.

One day, when he had stuff'd him as full as an egg,
 A poor relation came to beg;
But he kick'd him out without broaching a keg,
 And in kicking him out he broke his leg.
  Ri tu, di nu, *etc.*

III.

A surgeon, the first in his vocation,
 Came and made a long oration;
He wanted a limb for anatomization,
 So he finished his jaw by amputation.
  Ri tu, di nu, *etc.*

IV.

"Mr. Doctor," says he, when he'd done his work,
  "By your sharp knife I lose one fork;
But on two crutches I never will stalk,
  For I'll have a beautiful leg of cork."
    Ri tu, di nu, *etc.*

V.

An artist in Rotterdam, 'twould seem,
  Had made cork legs his study and theme;
Each joint was as strong as an iron beam,
  And the springs were a compound of clock-work and steam.
    Ri tu, di nu, *etc.*

VI.

The leg was made, and fitted right;
  Inspection the Artist did invite;
Its fine shape gave Mynheer delight,
  As he fixed it on and screw'd it tight.
    Ri tu, di nu, *etc.*

VII.

He walk'd thro' squares and pass'd each shop,
  Of speed he went to the utmost top;
Each step he took with a bound and a hop,
  And he found his leg he could not stop!
    Ri tu, di nu, *etc.*

VIII.

Horror and fright were in his face!
  The neighbors thought he was running a race;
He clung to a lamp-post to stop his pace,
  But the leg wouldn't stay, but kept on the chase.
    Ri tu, di nu, *etc.*

IX.

Then he call'd to some men with all his might,
  "Oh! stop this leg, or I'm murder'd quite!"
But, though they heard him aid invite,
  In less than a minute he was out of sight.
    Ri tu, di nu, *etc.*

X.

He ran o'er hill and dale and plain,
  To ease his weary bones he'd fain;
Did throw himself down, but all in vain;
  The leg got up, and was off again.
    Ri tu, di nu, *etc.*

XI.

He walk'd of days and nights a score;
  Of Europe he had made the tour:
He died—but though he was no more,
  The leg walk'd on the same as before;
    Ri tu, di nu, *etc.*

ENDORSEMENTS FROM THE SURGICAL AND MEDICAL PROFESSION.

The following letter was forwarded to a limited number of physicians and surgeons with whom we have had relations, with a request that, if in consonance with their convictions, they might sign and return the same to us. A few objected to sign on account of the publicity, at the same time writing us very flattering letters, commending our work in the highest terms.

Those whose names are appended to the endorsements have had, in most cases, extensive experience with artificial limbs, and will gladly confer with any one desirous of penetrating the subject more thoroughly.

January 10, 1888.

Mr. A. A. MARKS,
    New York City:

We, the undersigned, are professionally interested in the subject of artificial limbs. We have witnessed the operation of the rubber hand, foot (or both), and acknowledge that they possess exceptional merit. We cheerfully endorse them, and give you permission to refer to us in your pamphlet.

LEWIS A. SAYRE, M.D.,
    285 5th Ave., N. Y. City.
  Consult. Surg. Charity and Bellevue Hosp.

GEO. F. SHRADY, M.D.,
    247 Lexington Ave., N. Y. City.
  Consult. Surg. Hosp. Rupt. & Cripp led, N. Y. Cancer Hosp. Vist. Surg. St. Francis Hosp. Editor *Medical Record.*

R. B. GRANGER, M.D.,
    3 Bond St., N. Y. City.
  The New York Medical Journal.

ALFRED K. HILLS, M.D.
    465 Fifth Ave., N. Y. City.
  Editor of the *New York Medical Times.*

RUEL S. Gage, M.D.,
    400 West 22d St., N. Y. City.

HENRY RUHL, M.D.,
    East 164th St. & Delmonico Place, N. Y. City.

G. A. ROMERO, M.D.,
    232 East 27th St., N. Y. City.

THOS. CLELLAND, M.D.,
    354 West 22d St., N. Y. City.

D. D. Stevens, M.D.,
   252 West 38th St., N. Y. City.
S. R. Ellison, M.D.,
   266 West 43d St., N. Y. City.
G. M. Edebohls, M.D.,
   198 Second Ave., N. Y. City.
J. W. Metcalf, M.D.,
   642 Gates Ave., Brooklyn, N. Y.
J. E. Richardson, M.D.,
   125 So. Oxford St., Brooklyn, N. Y.
John Ball, M.D.,
   124 So. Oxford St., Brooklyn, N. Y.
F. G. Winter, M.D.,
   18 Patchen Ave., Brooklyn, N. Y.
J. Densmore Potter, M.D.,
   Delphi, Onondaga Co., N. Y.
Geo. C. Hubbard, M.D.,
   Tottenville, Richmond Co., N. Y.
H. D. Brown, M.D.,
   Potsdam, St. Lawrence Co., N. Y.
M. Cavana, M.D.,
   Oneida, Madison Co., N. Y.
Thos. M. Johnson, M.D.,
   309 Main St., Buffalo, N. Y.
A. S. Zabriskie, M.D.,
   Suffern, Rockland Co., N. Y.
B. A. Watson, A.M., M.D.,
   94 Fairview Ave., Jersey City, N. J.
   Author of "Amputations and their Complications."
Romeo F. Chabert, M.D.,
   Hoboken, N. J.
   Surg. St. Mary's Hosp.
G. K. Dickinson, M.D.,
   63 Wayne St., Jersey City, N. J.
J. Henry Clark, M.D.,
   26 E. Kinney St., Newark, N. J.
   Surg. St. Barnabas' Hosp.
Jos. W. Taylor, M.D.,
   Long Branch, N. J.
John L. Taylor, M.D.,
   Succasunna, Morris Co., N. J.

J. W. Silvara, M.D.,
  Ringoes, Hunterdon Co., N. J.
F. H. Milliken, M.D.,
  3614 Walnut St., Philadelphia, Pa.
B. F. Dilliard, M.D.,
  East Bangor, Northampton Co., Pa.
I. C. Gable, M.D.,
  York, York Co., Pa.
D. E. De Ross, M.D.,
  7 Washington St., Corry, Erie Co., Pa.
W. P. Snyder, M.D.,
  Spring City, Chester Co., Pa.
A. Le Bar, M.D.,
  Stroudsburg. Monroe Co., Pa.
J. M. Strohm, M.D.,
  Fredericksburg, Lebanon Co., Pa.
Julius Stricker, M.D.,
  Portage, Cambria Co., Pa.,
W. C. Foster, M.D.,
  Petrolia, Butler Co., Pa.
D. C. Waters, M.D.,
  Arnot Mines, Arnot, Tioga Co., Pa.
J. Finley Bell, M.D.,
  Osceola Mills, Clearfield Co., Pa.
Henry P. Geib, M.D.,
  Stamford, Fairfield Co., Conn.
  Ex. Surg. General, State of Conn.
Julian N. Parker, M.D.,
  So. Manchester, Hartford Co., Conn.
E. R. Wheeler, M.D.,
  Spencer, Worcester Co., Mass.
F. E. Sanger, M.D.,
  Littleton, Grafton Co., N. H.
B. F. Page, M.D.,
  Littleton, Grafton Co., N. H.
John McDonald, M.D.,
  Washington, Beaufort Co., N. C.
F. P. Gates, M.D.,
  Bayboro, Pamlico Co., N. C.
Jno. D. Myers, M.D.,
  Huntington, Cabell Co., W. Va.

E. C. Goodrich, M.D.,
  817 Broad St., Augusta, Richmond Co., Ga.
J. S. Todd, M.D.,
  74 Marietta St., Atlanta, Fulton Co., Ga.
W. Duncan, M.D.,
  Savannah, Ga.
Thos. J. Charlton, M.D.,
  Savannah, Ga.
J. W. Farill, M.D.,
  Farill, Cherokee Co., Ala.
P. B. Greene, M.D.,
  Ft. Payne, De Kalb Co., Ala.
J. D. Carpenter, M.D.,
  Rolla, Phelps Co., Mo.
O. St. John, M.D.,
  Mo. Pac. Hospital, St. Louis, Mo.
Geo. R. Kimbrough, M.D.,
  Emory, Rains Co., Texas.
  Member Med. Examining Board, 8th Judicial D. S.
  Local Surgeon, M. O. P. R. R.
H. F. Pahl, M.D.,
  Brenham, Washington Co., Texas.
C. L. Kinnaman, M.D.,
  1463 Cedar Ave., Cleveland, Ohio.
T. J. Barton, M.D.,
  Zanesville, Muskingum Co., Ohio.
Edmund C. Brush, M.D.,
  Zanesville, Muskingum Co., Ohio.
  Surgeon C. & M. V. Ry. Co. and B. Z. & C. R. R.
O. W. Ward, M.D.,
  Duncan's Falls, Muskingum Co., Ohio.
James L. Dickens, M.D.,
  La Fontaine, Wabash Co., Ind.
Chas. L. Wilson, M.D.,
  Indianapolis, Ind.
J. W. Willis, M.D.,
  Woodhull, Henry Co., Ill.
J. R. Gamble, M.D.,
  Blandinsville, McDonough Co., Ill.
M. Cassingham, M.D.,
  Roberts, Ford Co., Ill.

F. B. STRAUSS, M.D.,
  Gibson City, Ford Co., Ill.
C. C. HUCKINS, M.D.,
  Greene, Butler Co., Iowa.
J. W. REED, M.D.,
  Lime Springs, Howard Co., Iowa.
CHAS. L. LATHROP, M.D.,
  Lyons, Clinton Co., Iowa.
WIN. WYLIE, M.D.,
  Wausau, Marathon Co., Wis.
D. B. WYLIE, M.D.,
  Wausau, Marathon Co., Wis.
ALLEN ROBERT LAW, M.D.,
  Belmont, Lafayette Co., Wis.
P. O'KEEFE, M.D.,
  Oconto, Oconto Co., Wis.
W. C. BEDFORD, M.D.,
  Fergus Falls, Otter Tail Co., Minn.
W. D. LITTLE, M.D.,
  Mazeppa, Wabasha Co., Minn.
R. CHAREST, M.D.,
  Perham, Otter Tail Co., Minn.
JOHN R. BAILEY, M.D.,
  Mackinac Island, Mackinac Co., Mich.
  Late acting assistant surgeon U. S. Army, surgeon 8th Mo. Infantry Volunteers, and Brevet Lieutenant-Colonel U. S. Volunteers.
W. T. DODGE, M.D.,
  Marlette, Sanilac Co., Mich.
ALFRED DAVID, M.D.,
  Atlantic Mine, Houghton Co., Mich.
  Physician and surgeon to the Atlantic Mine Co.
JAS. JOHNSTON, M.D.,
  Sault Ste. Marie, Chippewa Co., Mich.
H. M. HASKELL, M.D.,
  Palmer, Marquette Co., Mich.
F. KELLY, M.D.,
  Alba, Antrim Co., Mich.
GEO. A. KENNY, M.D.,
  Salmon City, Lemhi Co., Idaho.
  Examining Surgeon for Pensions.

S. P. Hunt, M.D.,
  Salubria, Washington Co., Idaho.
J. W. Dysart, M.D.,
  15th and Douglas Street, Omaha, Neb.
  Surgeon Omaha Smelting Works Co.
J. C. Russell, M.D.,
  Exeter, Fillmore Co., Neb.
D. W. Hershey, M.D.,
  Nebraska City, Otoe Co., Neb.
G. H. Simmons, M.D.,
  Lincoln, Neb.
L. J. Abbott, M.D.,
  Fremont, Dodge Co., Neb.
Henry Wisner, M.D.,
  Sharon, Barber Co., Kansas.
Sarah C. Wisner, M.D.,
  Sharon, Barber Co., Kansas.
J. A. Jeannotte, M.D.,
  Clyde, Cloud Co., Kansas.
A. G. Saxton, M.D.,
  Clyde, Cloud Co., Kansas.
Dan'l K. Dickinson, M.D.,
  Lead City, Lawrence Co., Dak.
  Surgeon H. G. M. Co.
W. A. Taylor, M.D.,
  New Market, Jefferson Co., Tenn.
Robert McDonald, M.D.,
  527 East 8th Street, Leadville, Col.
Wm. T. Dalby, M.D.,
  St. Johns, Apache Co., Arizona.
J. S. Courtney, M.D.,
  Lebanon, Linn Co., Oregon.
W. F. Anderson, M.D.,
  255 Second East Street, Salt Lake City, Utah.
John P. Taggart, M.D.,
  Salt Lake City, Utah.
H. R. Garner, M.D.,
  Carbonado, Pierce Co., Wash. Ter.
J. F. Cropp, M.D.,
  Walla Walla, Walla Walla Co., Wash. Ter.

Raymond Mitchell, M.D.,
   Puyallup, Pierce Co., Wash. Ter.
Geo. P. Lee, M.D.,
   Merced, Merced Co., Cal.
C. S. Marshall, M.D.,
   Mill Village, Nova Scotia, Canada.
I. F. Black, M.D.,
   Halifax, Nova Scotia, Canada.

NEW YORK, March 20, 1866.

A. A. MARKS, ESQ. :

SIR :—I have examined with great care your patent Artificial Limbs, and cheerfully bear testimony as to the simplicity and efficiency of the invention.

From their peculiar mechanism they perfectly fulfil the purpose for which they were intended, and in my opinion have *no superior* at present in use.

Very respectfully, JOHN J. CRANE, M.D.,
    Surgeon to Bellevue Hospital.

---

285 Fifth Avenue, NEW YORK CITY, N. Y.

A. A. MARKS, ESQ. :

DEAR SIR :—I have had frequent occasion to apply your most valuable Patent Artificial Leg, in cases where I have unfortunately been compelled to mutilate my patients by amputation, and the admirable imitation which your substitute has given of the original limb, and the perfect satisfaction to the wearer, is the highest possible commendation that I can give it.

LEWIS A. SAYRE, M.D.,
Professor of Surgery, Bellevue Hospital Medical College.

---

22 East 18th street, NEW YORK, March 22, 1866.

A. A. MARKS, ESQ.:

DEAR SIR :—Having been well acquainted with your Artificial Limbs and various improvements which you have made for the last ten years, and from the great success which has attended the application of your limbs, and the utility of the same, I have no hesitation in saying that their accomplishments have not been surpassed.

The ease and facility with which persons move and walk about, and run, as it were, is such that in many cases the Artificial Limb cannot be detected.

Yours truly, ROBERT S. NEWTON, M.D.

No. 80 Irving Place, NEW YORK, May 24, 1866.

A. A. MARKS, ESQ.:

DEAR SIR :—I have carefully examined your Artificial Limbs, and believe, because of their simplicity and strength, that they will be sought for by those who may be so unfortunate as to require them.

Very truly yours, etc., JAMES R. WOOD, M.D.
Surgeon to Bellevue Hospital, Professor of Operative and Surgical Pathology, Bellevue Hospital, Medical College, etc., etc.

COCHECTON, SULLIVAN COUNTY,
NEW YORK, March 14, 1865.

MR. A. A. MARKS :

DEAR SIR :—I have worn your Patent Leg for the last year. I am well pleased with it. It has not required the least repairs. I can walk better with it than any leg I ever used, *except the natural one*.

I consider your India-Rubber Foot a valuable improvement to Artificial Legs.

Respectfully yours. W. L. APPLEY, M.D.

FLEMINGTON, NEW JERSEY, March 1, 1876.
MR. A. A. MARKS:

DEAR SIR:—It is now more than two years since you fitted my son with one of your Artificial Legs, and sufficient time has elapsed to form an opinion as to its merits.

I think your claim for "superiority of your Artificial Limbs over all others, in practical efficiency, simplicity of construction and durability," is well founded, and cannot honestly be denied. I will also add that for ease and comfort in use they cannot be surpassed.

Yours truly,
W. H. SCHENK, M.D.

ELIZABETHPORT, NEW JERSEY.
MR. A. A. MARKS:

DEAR SIR:—Having for the last eleven years used in my practice your Patent Artificial Limbs, with India-Rubber attachments, I feel it my privilege as well as duty to acknowledge my favorable appreciation of them.

Several of the cases have been under my daily observation while in pursuance of their various avocations, the majority being employees of the Central Railroad of New Jersey, with which I have been a long time connected as surgeon. I will only mention a single case, that of Patrick Liddy, of this place, whom you supplied with a pair of limbs for the lower extremities, sixteen months ago. Fortunately both knee joints had been preserved, and he has since the application been able to perform a considerable amount of walking, and usually without any cane, regarding it as an encumbrance. I met him yesterday, and although he does not fully conceal his infirmity, his movements are easy and do not call up the unpleasant sympathy which observers so often have to feel for the unfortunate.

I may, if desired, by consent of the parties, refer to others having lost one lower extremity, who almost or wholly succeed in their natural desire to escape observation; another remark is due, that the India-Rubber Foot does *not* produce that wooden leg sound so often noticed on the street from *less* modern appliances. I have not yet heard a patient express dissatisfaction, and feel well sustained by experience in giving this approval.

Yours truly,
J. S. MARTIN, M.D.,
Late Surgeon 14th Reg. New Jersey Vol.

FORT SIDNEY, CHEYENNE CO, NEBR., Nov. 1, 1887.
A. A. MARKS, New York:

DEAR SIR:—In reply to yours of the 26th ult., I can reply that I have purchased your artificial limbs for patients, and that they invariably have given entire satisfaction.

Yours truly,
C. EWER,
Asst. Surgeon U. S. A.

From HON. HENRY P. GEIB, M.D., *Member of the Legislature, State of Connecticut.*

STAMFORD, CONN., March 27, 1883.
MR. A. A. MARKS:

DEAR SIR:—The persons to whom you furnished artificial appliances for amputations of the feet (one Symes' and the other Pirogoff's operations) express themselves as being perfectly satisfied.

The appliances are light, easily applied, and do not produce excoriation or tenderness at the end of the stump.

I consider that your appliances fulfill all the indications called for in providing artificial support after amputations.

Very truly yours,
HENRY P. GEIB, M.D.

26 E. Kinney St., NEWARK, N. J., Jan. 10, 1888.
A. A. MARKS, Esq.:
DEAR SIR :—I cheerfully and fully endorse your rubber hands and feet. I have several patients using them and with perfect satisfaction.
Sincerely,
J. HENRY CLARK, M.D.

A. A. MARKS, New York:
MY DEAR SIR :—In matter of finish, durability, simplicity of construction, completeness of action, and perfect adaptation to stump, your artificial limbs are far superior to any thing I have ever seen.
W. H. TAYLOR, M.D.,
Jan. 11, 1888. New Market, Jefferson Co., Tenn.

OSCEOLA MILLS, CLEARFIELD Co., Pa., Jan. 12, 1888.
I ordered an artificial hand and arm for a patient, and it has given good satisfaction.
J. FINLEY BELL, M.D

642 Gates Ave., BROOKLYN, N. Y., Jan. 13, 1888.
DEAR SIR : You are always welcome to refer to me as to the merits of your limbs, and I shall always be glad to send sufferers to you.
Yours truly,
J. W. METCALF, M.D.

The *New York Medical Journal*,
3 Bond St., NEW YORK, CITY, Jan. 10, 1888.
I know of no artificial appliance that so nearly simulates nature as those of your manufacture.
R. B. GRANGER, M.D.

DELPHI, ONONDAGA Co., N. Y. Jan 21, 1888.
I have waited till now ere I endorsed your work, because I wanted to see Mrs. K. E. Cardner, who obtained one of your limbs a short time since. I have seen her and find that the leg works to a charm.
She can get about without even a walking-cane. Does her housework without any difficulty.
I am, etc., J. DENSMORE POTTER, M.D.

HUNTINGTON, CABELL Co., W. Va., Jan. 12, 1888.
I have used the "Marks Artificial Legs" with rubber feet, and they give more complete satisfaction than any others I have ever seen. Have one case of double amputation (thigh and leg) ; the man walks with ease and comfort simply with a cane.
JNO. D. MYERS, M.D.

BELMONT, LAFAYETTE Co., Wis, Jan. 1888.
The pair of artificial legs I ordered of you about three years ago for Jno. Nodolf are wearing well and give perfect satisfaction.
ALLEN ROBERT LAW, M.D.

GREENE, BUTLER Co., IOWA, Jan. 17, 1888.
MR. A. A. MARKS, New York.:
DEAR SIR :—While my relations with you have not been very extensive, I have observed the matter of artificial limbs very closely, and as a result of my observation can truthfully say that my bias is very strongly in favor of the solid "Rubber Feet and Hand Limbs," on the grounds of, first and foremost,

durability, in the case of the foot solidity and firmness of footing, with sufficient pliability and no side motion, and in the case of the hands pliability. I have yet to find the person wearing either who finds any fault, which I can not say in regard to many rattle-traps.

Yours respectfully,
C. C. HUCKINS, M.D.

FERGUS FALLS, OTTER TAIL CO., MINN., Jan. 16, 1888.
Your rubber hand has been especially satisfactory,
W. C. BEDFORD, M.D.

SAULT STE. MARIE, CHIPPEWA CO., MICH., Jan. 14, 1888.
I have no idea of ever recommending a jointed limb again. The rubber foot fully meets the wants.
JAS. JOHNSTON, M.D.

CARBONADO, PIERCE CO., WASH. TER., Jan. 24, 1888.
A. A. MARKS, ESQ.:
SIR :—I am pleased to add that the leg I procured from you for my patient works to perfection. He does any thing that is to be done on a farm, and has lately learned to dance.
H. R. GARNER, M.D.

WAUSAU, MARATHON CO., WIS., Jan. 13, 1888.
You make by all odds the best artificial limb made. I have a number of patients wearing your limbs who would not accept any other maker's artificial limb as a gift.
WIN WYLIE, M.D.

SAVANNAH, CHATHAM CO., GA., Jan. 12, 1888.
A. A. MARKS, ESQ., New York:
DEAR SIR :—I endorse your artificial limb with pleasure. My associate, Dr. T. I. Charlton, who rendered me very valuable assistance in taking the measurements for the two last artificial legs ordered from you, also endorses them.

Some ten or twelve years ago I procured an artificial arm and hand from you for an employee of the Savannah, Florida & Western R. R. which gave perfect satisfaction up to the time of the man's death about a year ago. No complaint has been made to me by any persons for whom I have procured your artificial limbs, and they seem fully adapted for all that is required of them.
I am, respectfully yours,
W. DUNCAN, M.D.

BLANDINSVILLE, McDONOUGH CO., ILL., Jan., 1888.
DEAR SIR: The endorsement of patent articles, of whatsoever kind and description, is something I very seldom do, but your artificial limbs with rubber hands and feet meet my unqualified approval, as being the *best* I have ever had occasion to recommend to those desiring artificial limbs.
J. R. GAMBLE, M.D.

ST. JOHN, APACHE CO., ARIZ., Jan. 20, 1888.
A. A. MARKS, Manufacturer of Artificial Limbs, etc., New York:
DEAR SIR : I have had various opportunities of testing the merits of your artificial limbs with rubber hands and feet, and can cheerfully recommend them to be superior in every respect to any other which has come under my observation, and that the operation of your rubber hand and foot will prove to possess exceptional merit to any who will try their virtues.
Very truly,
WM. T. DALBY, M.D.

LEAD CITY, LAWRENCE CO., DAK., Jan. 1, 1888.
DEAR SIR : I have ordered several of your artificial limbs for patients who had lost their limbs above and below the knee, and in every instance they have given perfect satisfaction
       Respectfully,
          D. K. DICKINSON, M.D.,
          Surg. H. G. M. Co.

       ARNOT, TIOGA CO., PA., Jan., 1888.
I have bought one arm. In a few months shall call on you for a leg.
          D. C. WATERS, M.D.

    LITTLETON, GRAFTON CO., N. H., Jan. 11. 1888.
The leg bought of you is perfectly satisfactory.
         F. E. SANGER, M.D.,
         B. F. PAGE, M.D.

      YORK, YORK CO., PA., Jan. 14, 1888.
A. A. MARKS, ESQ.:
 DEAR SIR :—I have recommended your very valuable patent artificial limbs to a number of my patients who are wearing them with perfect satisfaction, and I have no hesitancy in saying in my judgment they fulfill their purpose better than any others that have come under my observation.
        Very respectfully,
          I. C. GABLE, M.D.

---

    527 E. 8th St., LEADVILLE, COLO., Jan., 1888.
Being the oldest pioneer of Colorado, I can say your limbs are the best in the market.
        ROB'T MCDONALD, M.D.

    FARILL, CHEROKEE CO., ALA., Jan., 1888.
I have experienced the worth of the A. A. Marks artificial arm, and would say it is a perfect Godsend and worth its weight in gold.
         J. W. FARILL, M.D.

    PUYALLUP, PIERCE CO., W. T., Jan. 31, 1888.
MR. A. A. MARKS, New York City :
 DEAR SIR :—I would state that actual observation has clearly demonstrated the superiority of your artificial leg with rubber foot. I had occasion to order one for a patient more than a year ago, which was duly received and applied, and the patient left for the scene of his labors some thirteen miles distant. In less than two weeks thereafter I met him on the street walking rapidly with no perceptible limp, and he assured me that he had covered the above distance in about three hours without even the aid of a stick or cane. This I thought was very good, considering the short time he had worn the limb.
       Respectfully,
         RAYMOND MITCHELL, M.D.

   MILL VILLAGE, QUEENS CO., NOVA SCOTIA, Feb. 6, 1888.
A. A. MARKS, ESQ.:
 I thoroughly believe your make of limbs with rubber hands and feet are superior to any other make.
 The leg purchased by me for Miss Aggie Holland is giving good satisfaction. I can heartily recommend your make of artificial limbs.
        Yours truly,
         C. S. MARSHALL, M.D.

LETTER FROM THE DISTINGUISHED ORATOR, GENERAL GEORGE A. SHERIDAN.

MORTON HOUSE, NEW YORK CITY, July 1, 1885.

MY DEAR DOCTOR: The last leg you made for my son came promptly, and is, if possible, more satisfactory than the one he had from you heretofore. The boy is now fifteen years old; he has worn a leg of your make for the past five years, and *always with comfort and satisfaction.* Visiting him at his school a while since, I found he was out for a day's fishing; when he returned and stated where he had been, the teacher remarked he had walked at least twelve miles. I asked the boy if he was not used up; he replied: "No, papa; thanks to the good old doctor (that's you), I don't get used up any more than boys who have two legs of their own." George skates on steel or roller skates, rides a bicycle, and in short enjoys to the full the usual sports of boys of his own age. For this we have you to thank more than any one in the world.

Refer to me at any time. A letter will always reach me if sent to the Morton House, New York.

Yours truly,
GEO. A. SHERIDAN.

To DR. A. A. MARKS,
Broadway, N. Y.

COMMENDATIONS.

The following pages contain about seven hundred testimonials from wearers of artificial limbs.

With few exceptions these testimonials are responses to the following circular letter:

DEAR SIR: We are preparing a new pamphlet calculated to present all the new features we have recently added to our limbs.

As you have had some experience with our work, we invite you to express your opinion for publication.

The especial points we desire to present are the superiority of the rubber hand and foot; their durability and advantage, compared with the old style; and particularly our success in fitting from measurements.

A reference to your experience in these matters will be greatly appreciated.

Kindly state your occupation, if laborious or otherwise.

How long you have worn artificial limbs. Point of amputation.

The comparative cost of repairs, and what other information you may regard of interest.

We are, respectfully yours,
A. A. MARKS.

The original plan of this pamphlet did not provide for more than three hundred testimonials; we regarded that number as sufficient for all purposes, but the responses to our invitation came so heartily and liberally that we find ourselves in possession of over seven hundred, which, to respect the courtesies of our patrons, we feel obliged to print. Most of these cases, it will be observed, are patrons whom we have never seen, all transactions having been conducted through the mails, the limbs fitted from measurements and sent to them by express. Many have also worn limbs of other construction, and make their comparisons from experience.

What stronger testimony can be asked to substantiate the claims set forth in this book?

The arrangement of the testimonials is made according to amputations and sub-divided into States. Readers are at liberty to write to any of these parties. Should their letters fail to reach, on account of removal, etc., a note addressed to us, stating the fact, will receive in response the latest address we have.

DOUBLE AMPUTATIONS.

BOTH LEGS AMPUTATED, ONE ABOVE THE KNEE AND THE OTHER BELOW.

FULTON, HEMPSTEAD CO., ARK., Dec. 12, 1887.

To WHOM CONCERNED: On the 13th of January, 1884, I had the misfortune to lose both my legs in a railway accident, one four inches above, the other three and one-half inches below the knee. The following October I applied a pair of A. A. Marks' artificial limbs with rubber feet, which enabled me to walk with but little difficulty, with only the use of one cane, and without that when walking about the office.

The rubber foot prevents an unnatural sound while walking on the floor; also prevents the uncomfortable jarring of the stumps which is experienced in the wooden feet of other manufactures.

I will cheerfully reply to any inquiry in regard to what I consider the best artificial limbs made, viz., A. A. Marks'.

Yours respectfully,
D. M. ALKIRE,
Opr. St. L. I. M. & S. Ry.

BOTH LEGS AMPUTATED BELOW THE KNEES.

Fitted from Measurements.

OAKLAND, CAL., Nov. 1, 1887.

Mr. A. A. MARKS:

DEAR SIR: I take great pleasure in testifying to the merits of your artificial limbs. I have used them for about four years.

They were fitted from measurements, with the exception of a few alterations when I first received them. I have worn them constantly without any trouble. I am by profession a lawyer, and probably walk on an average of several miles a day.

In my opinion your leg is the best made, and particularly the best for cases similar to mine.

Yours sincerely,
S. B. McKEE.

BOTH LEGS AMPUTATED, ONE AT THE ANKLE, THE OTHER BELOW THE KNEE.

Nov. 1, 1887.

Mr. A. A. MARKS:

DEAR SIR: I wish to say through your pamphlet, to all whom it may concern, this is to certify that I have had constantly in use two of Mr. A. A. Marks' patent artificial limbs since 1878, and I am glad to state they have come up to my greatest expectations on account of their simplicity of construction and great strength. The patent rubber feet give elasticity and naturalness of movement that can not be had in other kinds.

I am in the oyster business, and have not lost any time on account of wearing two artificial limbs. I cheerfully recommend them to all requiring artificial substitutes as the best, as they are the safest and most natural of any there is

No. 270.

made, so far as my knowledge extends. During my nine years of experience on artificial limbs I have worked hard seven years at the oyster business, doing the raking myself. I have had but very little repairing done.

Yours respectfully,
ALBERT W. MILLS,
Rownyton, Fairfield Co., Conn.

BOTH LEGS AMPUTATED BELOW THE KNEES.

Law Office of GEORGE F. SILL,
345 Main St., HARTFORD, CONN., Oct. 28, 1887.

A. A. MARKS, Esq. :

MY DEAR SIR :—It gives me great pleasure to be able to testify to the great excellence of your artificial limbs, for I know what they are, and can not see how they can be improved upon in any way. It is now ten years that I have worn your limbs, and during all that time I have never had the least trouble with them, and the longer I wear them the more impressed I am with their serviceability and great simplicity. The foot being of rubber, there is no "click" made in walking, which I have noticed in feet that are full of springs and joints, and which must be very unpleasant to the wearer. But the great beauty of your patent is that it is so simple that the foot seldom, if ever, gets out of repair. I have worn your patent since November, 1878. I know I have not paid ten dollars for repairs in all that time, and, for all I know, these rubber feet will last for years.

As I am a lawyer I do not, of course, give the artificials very hard usage, but while at college at Amherst I gave them about as hard a trial as could be given them, and they never went back on me once. Having worn your patent for ten years, and both amputations being just above the ankle, I get along remarkably well, but I must confess that I think the great secret of my success is owing to the excellence of your patent rubber foot, and would not change to any other patent for a good deal of money.

In closing, permit me to say that your patent artificials have more than satisfied me, and I hope you will refer to me at any time, so I may be able to tell other sufferers about what I consider to be the best artificial limbs made.

Yours very truly,

GEORGE ELLIOT SILL.

LEG AMPUTATED BELOW THE KNEE, AND ARM AMPUTATED BELOW THE ELBOW.

GRANDVIEW, DOUGLASS CO., DAK., December 1, 1887.

MR. A. A. MARKS:

DEAR SIR :—Your letter requesting me to write a report of my experience in wearing artificial limbs of your manufacture was received. I am well pleased with them, and think they are much better than any I have heretofore used. Those that you made for me one year ago were a perfect fit and have not been out of repair since I put them on in your factory, October, 1886.

I have worn artificial limbs since May, 1865. My foot was amputated at the ankle joint, hand at the wrist. I have worn one leg more than five years; no repairs.

Yours truly,

OSCAR DUNLAP.

BOTH LEGS AMPUTATED BELOW THE KNEES.

Fitted from Measurements.

ELBERTON, ELBERT CO., GA., December 12, 1887.

MR. A. A. MARKS, New York City:

SIR :—I have been wearing artificial legs for twenty-one years, and have had three different kinds, and am much better pleased with the pair received from you eight years ago than any others I have ever used. They fit better, notwithstanding they were made from measurements. I walk with more ease. Fifteen dollars cover all expenses for repairs up to date, on both, and I now have a good pair of limbs. They enable me to superintend my farm of one hundred acres under cultivation, and to attend three churches as a minister of the gospel. My legs are both amputated below the knees, four inches.

I am sincere in recommending your artificial rubber feet and legs to all cripples.

Yours truly,

REV. E. B. HIGGINBOTHAM.

BOTH LEGS AMPUTATED BELOW THE KNEES.

Fitted from Measurements.

(*Walked Four Miles in One Hour and Twenty-five Minutes.*)

NAPIERVILLE, DU PAGE CO., ILL., November 7, 1887.

A. A. MARKS:

DEAR SIR:—Yours of October 26 just received. In reply will say that I have worn a pair of your artificial feet for nearly three years and am well pleased with them. Three years ago I was employed by the New York, Ontario and Western Railroad Co. as brakesman, and while doing switching (through the neglect of the company not having their road in safe condition, and the neglect of an employer) I was run over. My right leg was amputated six inches below, and my left eleven below the knee.

Through a friend's advice I purchased a pair of your limbs, and am not sorry that I did so, for I don't think they can be beat. I am now following operating, and very often I have occasion to deliver messages to conductors on through trains. I think nothing of jumping on and off a train running twelve or fifteen miles per hour, and can pick up any thing, and put it on my shoulder, that don't weigh over one hundred pounds. As far as walking is concerned, I think that I can keep up with the most of them that have two sound legs. One day last summer a party bet me five dollars that I couldn't walk four miles in two hours; so I took him up. I made it in just one hour and twenty-five minutes, and it was on a fearfully rough road, rocks and hills lots of them, and didn't even chafe the skin on my stump. They fit so perfectly, from the measurements I sent, and they haven't been any expense to me since I got them. The rubber foot is, I think, as near to the natural foot as it is possible to get it.

I can put my hands on any thing that is breast high and spring upon it. Now, these stories look big, but I can bring proof to all of them. For references ask any of the employees on Middle Division Ontario and Western Railroad. I will close, hoping that all the unfortunates will come to you to be helped in their trouble.

I am, yours truly,

W. J. HARMES.

BOTH LEGS AMPUTATED BELOW THE KNEES.

Fitted from Measurements.

ATLANTA, LOGAN CO., ILL., Nov. 15, 1887.

MR. A. A. MARKS:

DEAR SIR:—I take pleasure in writing to inform you of the fact that your artificial limbs with rubber feet have given me entire satisfaction. I can wear them with comfort.

I make use of a cane when walking, but can as well dispense with it. I was accidentally run over by the railroad cars, whereby I lost both of my limbs when I was seven years old, and have been walking on my knees till four years last New Year's, when I got a pair of your artificial limbs. I have had them repaired once, and think that they will wear many years.

Yours respectfully,

MISS A. PRANGE.

BOTH LEGS AMPUTATED, ONE KNEE BEARING AND THE OTHER SYMES'.

PILOT KNOB, CRAWFORD CO., IND., Dec. 1, 1887.

DR. A. A. MARKS, New York City:

DEAR SIR:—Replying to yours of the 26th ult., I would say that three years' wear of a pair of your make of artificial legs makes me stronger in the belief that your rubber foot is the best substitute for nature yet found. In superintending general farm work I walk considerably, and sometimes use one cane, and for short, smooth walks seldom use any cane. So far there has been no repairs to make, and all I have been out was to occasionally insert a piece of gum in the back of the knee, cost, all told, 40 cents for three years. When I again buy I will take a pair of your make beyond a doubt.

Yours etc.,
DAVID T. STEPHENSON.

BOTH LEGS AMPUTATED BELOW THE KNEES.

GARDINER, BATCHELDER, & WELLES, Manufacturers of Lumber,
LYONS, CLINTON CO., IOWA, Oct. 28, 1887.
A. A. MARKS, ESQ., New York City:

DEAR SIR: Some five years ago I wrote you, expressing the highest satisfaction with the pair of artificial limbs you made for me. I have at this time nothing to retract from what I then said, and cheerfully renew my recommendation of your "rubber feet" to all in need of "wooden legs."

Very truly yours,
SILAS W. GARDINER.

BOTH LEGS AMPUTATED BELOW THE KNEES.

BALTIMORE & OHIO RAILROAD COMPANY,
Sup't of Motive Power Office, Nov. 10, 1887.

MY DEAR MR. MARKS: So many persons with like affliction to my own whom I meet in my daily vocation say to me, "How is it that you get along so well and perform your work with so much ease and comfort?" My answer is, "Go to Mr. A. A. Marks, the friend and benefactor of the unfortunate, and secure the comfort obtained by the use of his patent rubber feet."

In this connection I desire to say your idea of fitting by measurements, thereby saving your patients great inconvenience, loss of time, and unnecessary expenses, is unique and your success simply wonderful. My thirteen years of experience affords me ample opportunity to judge and appreciate the merits of your patent and workmanship, and I do not hesitate to pronounce your devices superior to any in the market, the durability and advantages of which as compared to the old styles are beyond question, the repairs being a mere bagatelle. While my occupation is not what you would term laborious, I am constantly on the go.

Thinking a word from me might benefit some brother or sister in like affliction (to whom I am always glad to impart information), I beg of you to use this letter as you see fit, for no one deserves more praise in their endeavors to make the afflicted comfortable than yourself and sons. Again thanking you for the many kindnesses to me while under your care, and wishing you God speed, I remain

Yours sincerely,
H. M. ETCHISON,
Secy. to Supt. M. P., 1325 Lombard St., Baltimore, Md.

BOTH LEGS AMPUTATED BELOW THE KNEES.

Fitted from Measurements.

176 EAST LOMBARD ST., BALTIMORE, MD., Nov. 30, 1885.
A. A. MARKS:

DEAR SIR:—Not having any complaints to make with the pair of artificial legs you made for me, I could see no reason why I should write you, but after thinking over the matter and reminding myself that there might be some one in this world whom I might benefit by a word or two of advice, I concluded to write.

I find after three weeks' trial that the legs you made for me are far ahead of my greatest expectations. With these legs I have carried breakfast, dinner, and supper daily up a flight of stairs without the aid of a stick, both of my hands being full of dishes. I have not yet made a misstep or a trip. When I first got them they felt decidedly better than the pair I had worn before. In a very brief time I was able to walk up and down stairs, to and from the room of my sick wife. I can say no more than that the legs are as near perfection as human ingenuity can contrive. With them I can stand erect, straight as a soldier, which I never could do with the other kind. I have walked with them over a mile in fifteen minutes, with little or no exertion. The rubber feet please me immensely.

Yours Resp'y,
CHAS. KRIDENOFF.

BOTH LEGS AMPUTATED BELOW THE KNEES.

Fitted from Measurements.

STANBERRY, GENTRY CO. MO., Nov. 14, 1887.

MR. A. A. MARKS':

DEAR SIR :—The pair of artificial limbs you made for me some two years ago from measurements has given entire satisfaction. I have not been out one cent for repairs.

Yours truly,
J. M. ROGERS.

BOTH LEGS AMPUTATED BELOW THE KNEES,

Fitted from Measurements.

NO. SPRINGFIELD, GREENE CO., MO., Nov. 5., 1887.

A. A. MARKS, Esq :

DEAR SIR : The pair of limbs you made me two years ago from measurements I have worn constantly ever since, and I can say they have given me unbounded satisfaction in every respect.

I am a clerk in the car accountant office of the Frisco R. R. Co. I walk from two to three miles a day. Besides, I do the biggest part of my day's work standing, and that with as much ease as I ever could. When walking I carry a light cane, but I hardly need its assistance. This may seem incredible, considering that both of my limbs are amputated two inches below the knees : but it is so. Lots of people that I am personally acquainted with and have walked the streets with do not know that I am wearing artificial limbs. I will close by saying that anybody who may be unfortunate enough to need artificial means for locomotion can come no nearer, in my estimation, to getting a duplicate of their lost member than with your limbs.

Yours respectfully,
D. J. MCSWEENY.

BOTH LEGS AMPUTATED BELOW THE KNEES.

Fitted from Measurements.

NEW BOSTON, NEW HAMPSHIRE, May 10, 1866.

MR. A. A. MARKS :

DEAR SIR :—Nearly a year has passed since you fixed me up upon my legs again, and it occurs to me that, my case being rather an extraordinary one, you would like to give it to the public through your pamphlet.

When I decided to take your legs from the government, I had examined all the various kinds that the government had adopted, and concluded to take yours, for the reasons which I will give.

Having been in the hospital for some time, I had seen many soldiers who had been provided with artificial limbs, and witnessed the many troubles and annoyances as well as expenses to which they were constantly subjected in most kinds of limbs, and saw that your patents were clear from all these tormenting trials, and at the same time discovered that your patients walked with more ease, comfort, and natural step than the other kinds with their clattering ankle joints. My experience has only added to the high opinion I formerly had gathered of your limbs.

My weight is over 200 pounds ; and, although both legs are now artificial, I can do almost every thing that I formerly could—can take a pail of water in each hand and walk off readily, and do work generally required about the farm.

I earnestly advise all my unfortunate friends to purchase your plain, substantial, and *always* reliable patent limbs.

Yours very truly,
CALVIN BATES,
Late Corp'l 20th Reg't Maine Vols.

April 11, 1887.
The new pair of legs just received, fitted from measurement, are perfectly satisfactory.
CALVIN BATES.

BOTH LEGS AMPUTATED BELOW THE KNEES.

ELIZABETHPORT, UNION Co., N. J., Oct. 29, 1887.
DEAR SIR : I would wish to state that I am and have been wearing your limbs for the last thirteen years. They have proved entirely satisfactory to me, and of all the limbs that I have ever seen of other make I would recommend Marks, to be the best, in fitting and durability.

My limbs are amputated six inches below the knees. My limbs have not cost me more than fifteen dollars for ten years.

I can walk so well with the rubber feet that no one that don't know me would believe that I had artificial limbs.

My work is very hard ; it takes an able-bodied man to do it.
My work is polishing steel.

I remain, yours,
PATRICK LIDDY.

BOTH LEGS AMPUTATED BELOW THE KNEES.

NEW BRUNSWICK, MIDDLESEX Co. N. J., Oct. 27, 1887.
MR. A. A. MARKS :

DEAR SIR :—After four years' constant use in wearing a pair of your artificial legs with rubber feet, I gladly bear testimony to their superior merits. Having well-trimmed stumps, as prepared by a humane and skillful surgeon, and supplied with your patent artificial legs, I am able to work all day and then walk a mile in eighteen minutes. My work being block-cutting, I am on my feet very often. My prior experience with other kinds tells me of the difference between the comfort and the durability of each, and places your make far ahead of any other in every essential respect. You are at liberty to publish this and refer whomever you wish to me, as I wish to see all my fellow-unfortunates secure all they can to assist them. I remain,

Yours truly,
ELIJAH RHINE.

BOTH LEGS AMPUTATED, ONE IN THE KNEE AND THE OTHER BELOW THE KNEE.

HAMBURG, SUSSEX CO., N. J., Jan. 15, 1888.
MR. A. A. MARKS :

DEAR SIR :—I have recently been reminded of the fact that you made two legs for a patient of mine, Wm. Day.

One leg amputated at knee joint and the other four inches above ankle. Last summer I saw him on a ladder sixteen feet from the ground painting a barn.

Yours,
J. B. PETTET, M.D.

LEG AMPUTATED BELOW THE KNEE AND ARM AMPUTATED ABOVE THE ELBOW.

SOMERVILLE, SOMERSET CO., N. J., Dec. 31, 1887.

In 1859 I suffered the amputation of my right leg and right arm from an accident on the Central Railroad of New Jersey. As soon as practicable thereafter I had Mr. Marks apply his artificial limbs to me. At that time he was manufacturing artificial legs with ankle joints. In 1863 I had one of his rubber feet applied. In 1865 I procured a new leg, and in 1871 I renewed the leg which I have worn ever since, during a period of seventeen years. My experience with the old style of ankle joint and the rubber foot is of such a character as to compel me to speak in high praise of the rubber foot. Its durability is beyond question, and is one of the virtues that commend it to all laboring people. I weigh two hundred and fifty pounds and am on my feet most of the time.

During the seventeen years the repairs on my artificial leg have not exceeded $10.

MORRIS FORCE

BOTH LEGS AMPUTATED BELOW KNEES.

NEW YORK CITY, November 8, 1887.

I have worn artificial legs of A. A. Marks' pattern for the past twenty-six years. The first pair I had were of the old style with ankle joints. When the rubber feet were invented I was one of the first to have a pair put on my legs.

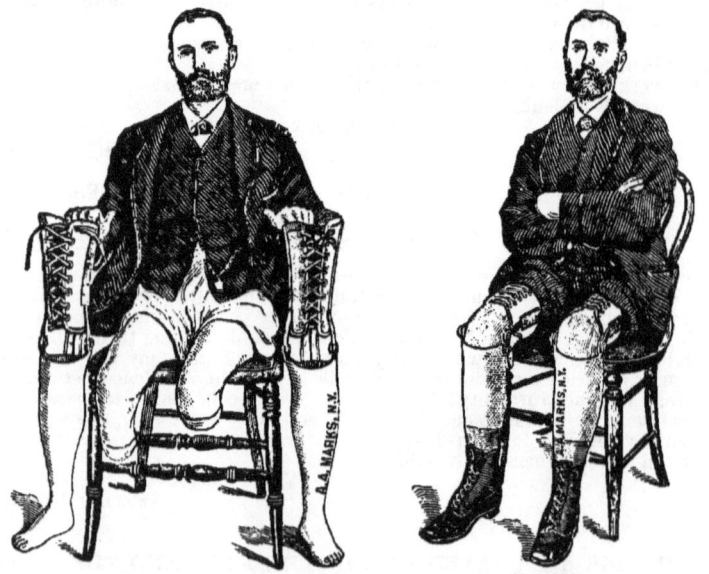

No. 271.   No. 272.

I have worn the rubber feet continually since then. Both my legs are amputated below the knees. With the rubber feet I am able to do about as much as any one. I am a laboring man and work at the bench ten hours a day. Quite frequently I am obliged to ascend a ladder to take articles from the shelves. I find no inconvenience in doing so. The rubber feet and rigid ankle make every step reliable, and my footing, no matter where I am, absolutely sure.

I walk a great deal and have passed many evenings about the billiard table, having become somewhat expert in that fascinating game. Sundays when at home I can be found lying on a lounge, with my legs crossed in an easy and comfortable position, reading some agreeable novel.

I find no hindrance in whatever I wish to do, and firmly believe that the Marks rubber feet have fully restored me.

No 273.

No. 274.

It is so long since I had my naturals that I have entirely forgotten them, and feel about as well off with the Marks' substitutes as I would had I those which nature gave me.

No. 275.

Anybody wishing to correspond with me will please address as below in your care. You will please forward the same to me. Respectfully, F. A. S.

LEG AMPUTATED ABOVE THE KNEE AND ARM AMPUTATED ABOVE THE ELBOW.

Corner Orient and Liberty Avenues,
East New York, N. Y., June 10, 1885.
Mr. A. A. Marks, 701 Broadway, N. Y. City:

Dear Sir:—I write you this simply to say that my experience with your artificial limbs, together with considerable experience with other kinds, induces me to prefer yours by all odds, and I herewith send application for gov't leg and arm for the issue of 1885, knowing the reliability and superior qualities of

No. 276.

your make above all others of which I have known about for over twenty years. The special point I desire to mention is the simplicity of construction in your leg, whereby I can take it apart, lubricate and adjust with my one (natural) hand, and put together again without any help. My good solid weight of 240 pounds gives the leg a good trial, and yet I feel a confidence in it that I have never had in any other kind.

Yours sincerely,
John J. Winn.

LEG AMPUTATED ABOVE THE KNEE AND ARM AMPUTATED ABOVE THE ELBOW.

Binghamton, New York, April 9, 1876.
Mr. A. A. Marks :

Dear Sir :—I learn that you are going to print a new pamphlet; if so I would like very well to tell my story: In October, 1867, I was accidentally caught on a large circular saw four feet in diameter, and my right arm and right leg were so fearfully mutilated that both had to be amputated above the elbow and knee. In March, 1868, after looking around very thoroughly I purchased my artificials of you, and am now compelled to say that after eight years of constant use I feel confident that I made no mistake in taking your patent. The repairs have been comparatively small, and the limbs are in very good condition now. I often walk to church, over a mile, in company with others, and have no difficulty in keeping up with them; and although my walk is slightly defective, many persons whom I frequently meet have no idea of my being so *largely* artificial.

I am rather over medium size and, weight, and having a stump but eight inches from the body, feel well satisfied with my getting about. The arm is not of very much service, the stump being less than eight inches long; but I would not be without it for the price of two or three; it certainly has exceeded your representation in regard to utility. I go all over my farm, climb fences, and see to all the work, and do considerable myself, get in and out of my wagon very comfortably, and transact all my business. When walking about I generally use a cane, but often forget it and go about for hours without any, and get around much better than any one would suppose under the circumstances.

Yours, etc.,
B. W. LAWRENCE.

BOTH LEGS AMPUTATED BELOW THE KNEES.

WALTON, N. Y., November 11, 1881.

A. A. MARKS :
DEAR SIR :—In reply to yours of the 9th inst. In the year 1877 I had the misfortune to lose both my feet on the railroad, and after a year and seventeen days I applied a pair of Mr. Marks' limbs, and the only trouble with them is that they are too near like my natural feet for my own good. I do almost every thing that I did before losing my limbs. They give the very best satisfaction.

Yours truly,
A. SEYMOUR WADE.

BOTH LEGS AMPUTATED BELOW THE KNEES.

2357 Sixth Avenue, TROY, N. Y., November 15, 1887.

MR. A. A. MARKS :
DEAR SIR :—It gives me great pleasure to testify to the value of the artificial limbs furnished by you. As the result of a railway accident ten years ago, both of my legs were amputated, one just below the knee and the other just above the ankle. Since then I have worn artificial limbs of which you are the manufacturer. My gait is so nearly natural that many will not believe without actual inspection that art has in my case pieced out nature. My occupation makes me a traveling man, and I assure you I appreciate the rubber feet, whose easy, springy motion takes away half the terrors that come from the loss of limbs. For repairs the cost has been absolutely nothing.

If I could write a stronger recommendation I would gladly do it.

If I cannot have my own legs I must have your limbs.

Truly yours,
WILLIAM H. ANDERSON.

BOTH LEGS AMPUTATED, ONE ABOVE AND THE OTHER BELOW THE KNEE.

BALLSTON SPA, SARATOGA CO., N. Y., Nov. 3, 1887.

A. A. MARKS, ESQ.:
DEAR SIR :—In regard to your note I would say that the legs that I purchased from you give the most complete satisfaction, and I hope ere long, with their aid and the blessing of God to be able to walk about among my fellowmen with ease and naturalness.

I lost both of my legs by a railway accident, one of them above and the other below the knee joint, and until I procured the legs that I have from you I was a helpless cripple.

At the time I was injured I was the foreman of a gang of hands on a railroad in the southern part of this county.

Hoping that you will meet with the success that your articles justly merit, I sign myself, Gratefully yours,

D. H. KELLY.

BOTH LEGS AMPUTATED BELOW THE KNEES.

Fitted from Measurements.

To Whom it may Concern :
I would state that I have worn a pair of Marks' artificial legs continuously for about five years.

The cost for repairs has not exceeded $5, and that has been mostly for suspenders. These legs have rubber feet, and were fitted for amputation below the knees from measurements taken by myself according to Mr. Marks' instructions. The elasticity of the rubber foot gives all the side movement that seems necessary to enable one to walk easily on uneven ground.

My occupation is that of a mechanic, and is somewhat laborious ; therefore I feel persuaded that for utility, durability, and simplicity the rubber feet are much superior to the old style of wooden feet.

EDWARD P. LAWTON.
SARATOGA SPRINGS, SARATOGA CO. N. Y., Nov. 1, 1887.

LEG AMPUTATED BELOW THE KNEE AND ARM AMPUTATED BELOW THE ELBOW.

Oct. 30, 1887.

MR. A. A. MARKS :
DEAR SIR :—As you are to publish a new pamphlet, I wish to add my name to your long list of patients who use your patent limbs and testify to their merits. I have used yours now for three and one half years, and they have never cost me one dollar yet. I am a very heavy man, weighing 200 pounds, I am working on the railroad. I could not be induced to exchange for any other. I have used your leg and arm. My leg is off below the knee.

HENRY E. LOWELL,
CHATHAM, COLUMBIA CO. N. Y.

BOTH LEGS AMPUTATED BELOW THE KNEES.

ITHACA, TOMPKINS CO., NEW YORK, Jan. 15, 1888.

MR. A. A. MARKS, New York City :
DEAR SIR :—As far as the rubber feet are concerned, I shall say they are the best in my opinion. The rubber foot is one of the wonders of the world. They are to-day without an equal. I do hereby challenge any other maker in the world to produce a man that has a pair of artificial feet to walk with me. I can walk a mile in 13 minutes and not hurry myself any. I do not take a back seat for any man that has got two good natural feet in a one-mile race. I will answer all communications sent to me by others in regard to the durability of the rubber feet.

I am trying to get up five walking matches out here. I have sent five letters to-day to the following places, Syracuse, Auburn, Cortland, Binghamton and Scranton City, and by next Friday I will expect an answer from them. If successful I will write you again. Hoping to hear from you in the near future,

I am, respectfully yours,

THOMAS CLEARY.

(Extract taken from a local paper.)

WALKING WITHOUT FEET.

THE BEST RECORD BEATEN.—A fair-sized audience assembled at Ithaca Rink last night to witness the effort of Thomas Cleary to beat the best mile walking record made by a man with artificial feet. Cleary, it will be remembered, suffered the loss of both feet some two years ago.

At 9 P. M. "the man without feet" made his appearance upon the floor and began his task of endeavoring to beat the best record heretofore made, 19 minutes and 30 seconds, at Atlanta, Ga., in 1881. Messrs. S. G. McKinney and C. J. Vivian were selected as time-keepers. The distance of one mile had been accurately measured, and consisted of 16 1/2 laps.

No. 277.

Mr. Cleary without apparent effort began his walk, going quite moderately at first, but as he neared the conclusion of the mile he quickened his pace and passed the mile-post in fine style in 16 minutes and 50 seconds, thus beating the best record by 2 minutes and 20 seconds, and making 17 laps in 17:10.

BOTH LEGS AMPUTATED BELOW THE KNEES.

MAMARONECK, WESTCHESTER CO., N. Y., Dec. 20, 1887.
MR. A. A. MARKS:

DEAR SIR:—Over twelve years ago I met with the misfortune of having both my legs crushed by the railroad cars, which necessitated amputation below the knees. I was then a mere lad, and did not fully realize the gravity of my misfortune. By the advice of my surgeons and my many advisers, I placed myself under your care for restoration. Your reputation as the one most competent in the land had so impressed me that, from the first, I felt that I was soon to realize the most that skill and ingenuity could possibly do for me. In this I have not been disappointed, for your labors have restored me to my feet, and I am, for all practical purposes, myself again. I well remember how proud I was when your genius placed me in a position in which I could indulge in youthful sports, how I availed myself of every advantage, playing ball, boating, fishing, and hunting in summer, and skating in winter. I even went so far as to swing my partner, on several occasions, in rural dances. I became quite an expert on the skates, and relished the applause my antics on the ice would excite. I have always felt that your artificial legs were wonders, and ought to be known throughout the land. My obligations to the pair that you made for me placed me in a position to feel a sense of duty to put them to the severest test and boast of my accomplishments. For this reason I have indulged in many sports that really belong to the sound and rugged.

No. 278.

My latest prank is that of riding a bicycle. I found the task considerable at first, but, being determined, I succeeded, after repeated attempts, to ride toler-

No. 279.

ably well. I do not regard it as a fascinating indulgence for one situated as I am, and probably shall not continue in the practice long. My purpose was to prove that riding a bicycle is possible with one wearing two artificial legs, and I am proud that I have accomplished so much. Enclosed find my photograph "in the act."

No. 280.

I shall be only too happy to commend your rubber feet, and will do all I can to encourage their sale, believing, as I do, that they are incomparable.

Respectfully yours,
JAMES McDONALD.

BOTH LEGS AMPUTATED, ONE ABOVE, AND THE OTHER BELOW THE KNEE.

Oct. 27, 1887.

MR. A. A. MARKS:

DEAR SIR :—I learn that you are going to print a new pamphlet, and, if so, I would like to tell my story. In March, 1884, I boarded a train for the purpose of going to Rome. When the train arrived at a point, I jumped, and accidentally fell, and was thrown under the wheels. My injuries were so severe that it was found necessary to amputate the right limb above the knee, and the left between the knee and the ankle. With best medical attendance, I pulled through—but this is not telling what I can do with your artificial limbs. It is with great pleasure I bear testimony to the efficient use of your artificial limbs. I have had them in daily use for a period of two years. They have required no alterations nor repairs. I am now so accustomed to them that I walk without a cane. I travel everywhere and anywhere. I think the rubber foot is the king of all other feet.

      Yours truly,
         JOHN ROBERTS,
       85 Steuben St., Utica, Oneida Co., N. Y.

BOTH LEGS AMPUTATED, ONE IN THE KNEE JOINT AND THE OTHER BELOW THE KNEE.

         LEIPSIC, PUTNAM Co., OHIO, Nov. 2, 1887.
Mr. A. A. MARKS, New York City, N. Y:
 DEAR SIR :—Having quite recently learned that you contemplate the publishing of a new pamphlet, and knowing that therein your patrons may have an opportunity to give their opinions of, and experiences with, the artificial limbs manufactured by you, I will avail myself of this opportunity to say what I have learned in more than ten years' practice with a pair of artificial limbs made at

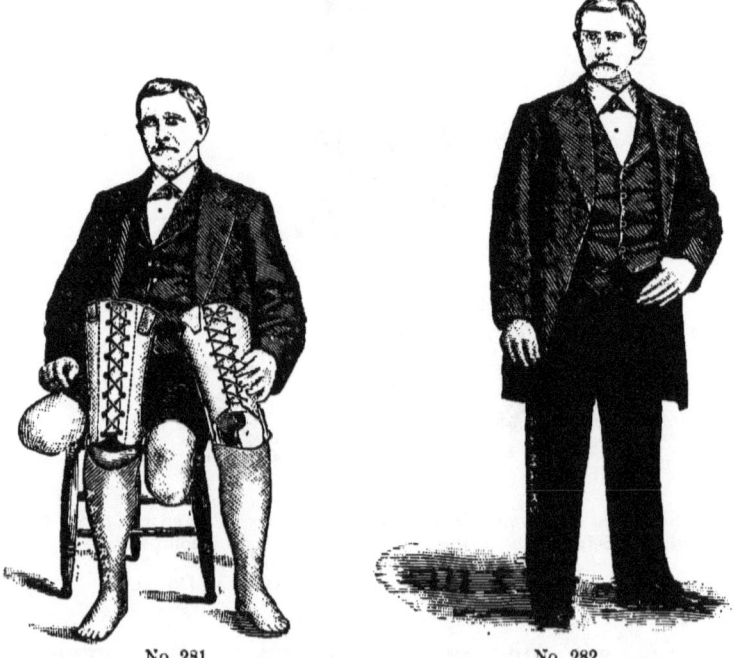

No. 281.   No. 282.

your establishment. On the 12th of April, 1875, I had the great misfortune to lose both my feet in a railroad accident, and after the stumps had healed up I began to look about for a substitute. My attention fell upon you, and I was at once impressed with the belief that, owing to the rubber feet, your make of limbs would be just what I was in need of. To-day I am fully convinced of the wisdom of my choice, for I am walking far better than I or any of my friends thought I would ever do.

 Since one of my limbs was amputated at the knee joint, and the other an inch and one-half below, it was the general belief of myself and my friends that I could not handle myself well enough to walk with any degree of safety or satisfaction.

 But that we were most agreeably disappointed is a fact patent to all to-day.

I now walk wherever I want to go, and am filling a responsible position in a railroad office, and giving as good satisfaction as any one.

You have already been informed that I am a member of the Knights of Pythias, and frequently parade on foot with my lodge; this is a proof that I am well able to take my part in the battle of life. My weight is now two hundred pounds, but with this excessive weight I have little or no trouble in walking, even in extreme hot weather. I have lately become a member of the Accident Insurance Company, whose general agent assured me that they had nothing to fear from my inability to take care of myself.

I remark these things that you may know how well I am doing, and that my fellow unfortunates may, like myself, be fully convinced that there is no use

No. 283.

lamenting while there is an artificial limb manufactured which so successfully counterfeits nature as does the Marks limb. I could not be induced to wear any other kind of a limb. The grandest feature of your limbs is certainly the rubber foot. Of this I can speak from experience, and that experience has forced me to the conclusion that there is no artificial leg complete without it. It is more durable than any other, and a person can walk with as much ease and comfort as with the natural. As you are aware, the limbs that I am now wearing I purchased four years ago, and in that time I have not been at any expense at all for repairing, nor do they now make the slightest noise when I am walking. Hoping that this slight testimonial of the true merits of the artificial limbs manufactured by you may be instrumental in deciding my fellow unfortunates in securing the best limb made, and assuring you that I will cheerfully answer all questions relative thereto,

I remain, very truly yours,

A. A. WEAVER.

BOTH LEGS AMPUTATED BELOW THE KNEES.

Fitted from Measurements.

CLEVELAND, OHIO, January 27, 1876.

Mr. A. A. MARKS:

DEAR SIR:—Having used a pair of artificial limbs of your manufacture for a period of five years, I am happy to testify that they are the best limbs that have come to my notice. I am able to walk comfortably without the aid of a cane. My experience in the use of limbs of different manufacture enables me to judge of their superior qualities and efficiency. I defy any one wearing two of any other kind to walk as well as I do.

Yours respectfully,
WILLIAM MOLHERIN.

BOTH LEGS AMPUTATED BELOW THE KNEES.

EAST BANGOR, NORTHAMPTON CO., PA., Jan. 11, 1888.

Your rubber feet in Mrs. Weidman's case have given perfect satisfaction. I claim they have no equal.

B. F. DILLIARD, M.D.

BOTH ARMS AMPUTATED BELOW THE ELBOWS.

SILVER CREEK, SCHUYLKILL Co., PA., October 31, 1887.

Mr. A. A. MARKS:

DEAR SIR:—Yours of the 25th instant at hand. In reply I will state that I am getting along very well with the artificial hands received from you. I am now using them since the 31st of August, and am fast getting used to them. My hands were lost above the wrist, and I can cheerfully recommend your artificial limbs to any one so unfortunate as to require them.

I remain, yours respectfully,
JOHN ROAN.

BOTH FEET AMPUTATED, ONE CHOPART'S AND THE OTHER BELOW THE KNEE.

57 NORTH HANCOCK ST., WILKESBARRE, LUZERNE CO., PA.
Nov. 1, 1887.

Mr. A. A. MARKS:

DEAR SIR:—I take pleasure in testifying to the satisfaction I have derived from the use of your artificial limbs.

I have worn your make of leg and foot for six years.

I believe your rubber feet are easier to walk upon, more durable, and much more natural than any other kind. I was eleven years of age when I had my leg and foot taken off, and it was a year and fourteen weeks before I could go on crutches, and I wore a peg leg about thirteen years. I then engaged in learning the cigar trade, and in the year of 1881 was in New York, and there I looked around for an artificial leg and foot, and I came to the conclusion that your rubber feet were what I wanted. I have worn them ever since and would not be without them. I am glad to testify that your new foot for Chopart's amputation is far better than any I ever expected to get. I got it February 17, 1887. It has not been out of order at all, and is as perfect now as the day it was made. I cheerfully recommend it to all in need. Hoping you will get a large share of public patronage,

I remain, yours respectfully,
GEORGE UNBEWUST.

BOTH LEGS AMPUTATED BELOW THE KNEES.

3614 WALNUT ST., PHILADELPHIA, PA., Nov. 22, 1887.

MR. A. A. MARKS.

DEAR SIR :—I may state for your benefit that Louis Thomas is very well pleased with his legs.

Very truly yours,
F. H. MILLIKEN, M.D.

BOTH LEGS AMPUTATED ABOVE THE KNEES.

107 No. WATER ST., YORK, YORK CO., PA., Nov. 3, 1887.

A. A. MARKS:

DEAR SIR :—As you are about to print a new pamphlet, a few words from one that has used a pair of your artificial limbs for about eight years may be of some use to you, and to all those who have been unfortunate enough to need artificial limbs.

After eight years' use of the pair of artificial limbs you made for me with the rubber feet, I must truly say that I think you make the best artificial limbs made, because they never cause me any trouble, in all that time, and have not cost me anything for repairs, and they are in good order, and look as if they were good for eight years more without any repairs. I wear them every day, and have not lost one day from the time I got them on account of their getting out of order. My work is not hard on limbs, but I am on my feet the most of the time. As my case is a bad one, I think I am doing very well.

Yours very respectfully,
ROBERT S. LOVEGROVE.

BOTH LEGS AMPUTATED BELOW THE KNEES.

Nov. 19, 1887.

A. A MARKS:

DEAR SIR :—I would most cheerfully recommend your artificial limbs as in my judgment being superior to any I have ever seen. I have worn my pair for seven years, and although my position requires a good deal of walking, I have never expended one penny to keep same in repair or had them away for repair, while several of my companions who wear the old style are not only constantly at an expense to keep them in repair, but are obliged to keep an extra one to wear while they are having them repaired.

Would further state, they have from the first fit me perfectly, and give me comfort in walking, which I can do with ease.

My right foot is off nine inches below the knee and my left six inches below the knee. With my weight over two hundred pounds, I know there is no man of my acquaintance of anywhere near the same weight, with only one limb gone, who can get along nearly as satisfactorily to himself as I do.

Yours truly,
CHARLES W. GLENN,
Train Starter, Pennsylvania Railroad, Broad St. Station,
Philadelphia, Pa.

P. S. It will be a pleasure to refer any one desirous of limbs to me, as I consider your make by far the most economical and serviceable in the market.

BOTH LEGS AMPUTATED BELOW THE KNEES.

ALLENTOWN, LEHIGH CO., PA., Oct. 31. 1887.

MR. A. A. MARKS:

I will inform you that my brother-in-law George Miller is getting along very well. He is working now two months by Nov. 1 for the Philadelphia and Reading Railroad Co., as a watchman on a street-crossing at Macungie. He feels very proud with his legs, and is proud of them. He recommends everybody in need of legs and hands to call on your firm, and I do all in my power to advance your interests.

ALLEN CHRISTMAN,
220 Union St.

BOTH LEGS AMPUTATED BELOW THE KNEES.

MACUNGIE, LEHIGH CO., PA., Nov. 2, 1887.

Mr. A. A. MARKS:
DEAR SIR :—I am very well pleased with the artificial legs which I received from you. In two months I walked without a cane; on the 4th of July I walked one mile. The 1st of August I commenced work, and I have not lost a day since. I am on my feet from morning till night. I will cheerfully answer any letter addressed to
GEORGE MILLER.

BOTH LEGS AMPUTATED BELOW THE KNEES.

(From the Comedian Henry Laurens Bascomb.)

FOREST HOME, SPRINGBROOK,
HOLMESBURG, PHILADELPHIA CO., PA., Oct. 28, 1887.

A. A. MARKS, ESQ:
DEAR SIR :—I am very glad to testify to the comfort and durability of your artificial limbs. Mine have been worn since July, 1882, and, being perfectly adjusted, they have enabled me to walk easily and naturally.

The ladies and gentlemen residing here have examined and commended your work. The Forest Home estate is extensive, and I walk with the same ease the country roads or streets of Philadelphia.

Concluding, let me add that you sent me a perfect work, and I am indebted to you for many kindnesses. In my present " Home," and under the care of Superintendent Wilson, a quotation from " Othello " will explain sufficiently :

" My bark is *stoutly timbered*,
And my pilot of very expert and approved allowance."

Yours,
HENRY LAURENS BASCOMB.

BOTH LEGS AMPUTATED BELOW THE KNEES.

May 13, 1887.

MR. MARKS:
DEAR SIR :—Thos. Connolly, from Ashley, near Wilkesbarre, Pa., got a pair of artificial legs from your manufactory. I recommended your patent legs to him, because he could not get along with his old legs. Yesterday he sent word to me to come and see his new pair of legs from your manufactory, and I must say you made a good fit for Thos. Connolly. Mr. Marks, I recommend your patent artificial legs when I get a chance to do so, because they are better than any I have seen yet. I wear a pair myself, and know of what I say.

Respectfully,
J. SENGHAAS,
141 Scott St., Wilkesbarre, Luzerne Co., Pa.

BOTH LEGS AMPUTATED BELOW THE KNEES.

PROVIDENCE, R. I., November 10, 1875.

A. A. MARKS, N. Y. City:
DEAR SIR :—Having worn a *pair* of your patent artificial legs for over five years, and had an abundance of experience of other kinds prior to using yours,

have no hesitation whatever in pronouncing yours by far the best in every essential point. I do a variety of labor on my *pair* of legs with ease and comfort, and take much pains to recommend your patent limbs to all I see needing artificial ones.

Yours respectfully,

H. F. HICKS.

BOTH LEGS AMPUTATED, ONE KNEE BEARING THE 'OTHER BELOW THE KNEE.

Fitted from Measurements.

333½ Union St., MEMPHIS, SHELBY Co., TENN., Nov. 8, 1887.

MR. A. A. MARKS:

DEAR SIR:—I have been wearing a pair of your artificial limbs with rubber feet ever since 1884; they were made by measurements, and give full satisfaction in every respect. I am flagging for the M. & C. R. R. at Union St. crossing, and have not lost a day on account of my limbs, and have not had any repairing done to them since I got them. I get around so spry and fast that people don't want to believe that I wear artificial limbs; I can go up or down stairs, three stories, get on and off trains, go anywhere I want, and need no help. I have a lifetime job as flagman with the same company I was working for when I lost my limbs. My left leg is off one-half inch below knee, with joint stiff; right leg between knee joint and foot.

Yours truly,
J. E. PATTERSON.

BOTH LEGS AMPUTATED BELOW THE KNEES.

Fitted from Measurements.

HOUSTON, TEXAS, Nov. 5, 1887.

MR. A. A. MARKS:

DEAR SIR:—Your letter came to hand and it found me in good shape on the legs. I received the limbs on the first of Feb., 1886, and put them on, and can say that my health is better, and I can walk anywhere I want to, night or day. I can go upstairs any height I want to.

I can walk three miles per hour; they never hurt me. I am a laborer, and my work is sitting a great deal. The length of the left stump is about five inches. Right about four inches long. You could not have done better if I had come to you.

And as a poor colored man, and the first, I think, in the State ever in this condition, I can say I am more than pleased with your work. I walked on my knees three years and ten months, and walked on the artificial legs one year and nine months, and have not had a day's sickness. I can kneel down and get up just like any other man.

BEN. NICKERSON,
39 Dart St.

BOTH LEGS AMPUTATED AT THE ANKLE JOINTS.

Fitted from Measurements.

BELTON, BELL Co., TEXAS, Nov. 10, 1887.

A. A. MARKS, New York:

DEAR SIR:—It affords me great pleasure to testify to the comfort and enjoyment I now take in wearing a pair of your rubber feet, which I have been using for six months.

I lost both my limbs from " frost bite "(Symes' and Chopart's amputation), in November, 1880, and since that time I have examined the advertisements of several different artificial limbs, and I could find none that had the appearance of durability and comfort that yours have. Mine were made from measurements and

are a perfect fit, just as good as I could possibly have procured had I gone to the expense of visiting the factory. They are as easily applied almost as shoes ; can be worn without pain. I am now Assist. P. M. at this place, and to perform my duties I am standing most all the time, and I defy any one that sees me walking around in the office to detect that I am a cripple. I use no cane, neither do I need one. I have just as perfect use of my limbs as it is possible for any one to have, laboring under a like misfortune. In conclusion I cheerfully recommend your rubber foot to all those who have been, like myself, unfortunate to have lost their limbs. Hoping you every success,
I remain, yours, etc.,
G. W. TATUM.

BOTH LEGS AMPUTATED BELOW THE KNEES.

Fitted from Measurements.

Dec. 12, 1887.

MR. A. A. MARKS :

DEAR SIR :—I am attending the Platteville State Normal School at Platteville, Wis. In order to get to school I am obliged to walk a distance of about one-half a mile. I have had two pairs of artificial limbs, one pair from a firm in Chicago and the other from you ; but yours are far superior in comfort, and I think in durability. My feet were amputated about half-way between the ankles and knees, but as long as I have had your limbs, I have had no trouble of any kind with my limbs, not having needed any repairs as yet, although I have had your limbs over two years. Altogether I have worn artificial limbs over eight years. One great advantage in your limbs is that there are no springs or complex contrivances in the ankle joints. As I have worn such a pair, I can say that they caused me no little annoyance in getting out of order as well as making disagreeable noises. I walk a little lame with my right leg, otherwise a person not acquainted with me would not think that my feet were amputated. I seldom use a cane, preferring to walk without one.

Your limbs have no superior. They fitted perfectly from the first measurements. They are very comfortable and never make my stump sore. They are more durable than all other limbs, as there are no springs or complicated joints to get out of order. As the feet are made of rubber, there is not the annoyance caused by feet with a complicated spring attachment in the ankle. I say that your feet have no superior. Address all further communications from date to June 21 as follows :

JOHN CONRAD NODOLF,
PLATTEVILLE, Grant Co., WIS.

BOTH LEGS AMPUTATED, ONE ABOVE THE KNEE, AND THE OTHER BELOW THE KNEE.

NUTTALLBURGH, FAYETTE CO., W. VA., Dec. 20, 1887.

MR. MARKS :

I like your legs better every day ; they are comfortable. I can stand on my feet ten hours a day and not become very tired. I have never had the least sore from wearing the legs from the start, they fit me so well.

My legs are as good now as when I got them. I have had them eighteen months, having got them in August, 1886, and they have not cost me any thing yet for repairs. When I am walking they never make any noise, and the rubber feet are durable, and work fine.

I can go about the store without any stick or aid of any kind.

When they were building my store I went up the ladder from one story to the other with very little trouble. My left leg is off four inches above the knee, and my right leg is off four inches below the knee. I had no hope of ever having any comfort any more until I got the legs you sent me, and I can not praise you too much for the good you have done for cripples like me.

Wishing you all the success, I am

Yours truly,
WILLIAM HORROCKS.

BOTH LEGS AMPUTATED BELOW THE KNEES AND PART OF ONE HAND.

Fitted from Measurements.

MODENA, BUFFALO CO., WIS., Nov. 3, 1887.

MR. A. A. MARKS:

DEAR SIR:—I take pen in hand with the greatest of pleasure to testify in regard to your limbs. I have worn them now for two years and am well satisfied with them. I can walk right along with them. I have astonished a great many of my friends, and I have met strangers that never suspected anything of me being artificial. I can walk to school and walk to my class without my cane. I don't know what I would do without them. I am a poor boy, and if it wasn't for the good heart of the people I would be on my knees yet. But I have got these legs of yours, and they are almost equal to the natural ones. I hope that your rubber feet will always be in use and that every one that needs an artificial limb will give them the preference.

But I hope there will never be any one in my fix or have the misfortune that I have had. I lost both of my feet at the ankle, and part of my left hand, three years ago in the western part of Minnesota in a snow storm. They were taken off in St. Paul in St. Joseph's Hospital, and there I found an advertisement of your artificial limbs, and the good will of the people got me a pair, and I hope they will last me forever.

Yours truly,
WILLIAM J. MCDONOUGH.

ABOVE KNEE AMPUTATIONS.

LEG ABOVE KNEE—WEARS NO. 112 LEG.

Fitted from Measurements.

The American National Bank of Birmingham,
BIRMINGHAM, ALA., Nov. 2, 1887.

A. A. MARKS, ESQ., New York:

DEAR SIR:—I have steadily worn the artificial leg you made for me some eight or nine months ago.

My occupation is such as to require me to walk a mile or more almost daily. This in cool weather is easily performed, but in very warm weather the stump is likely to become chafed.

Most artificial legs produce a soreness of the stump during active use in summer; this I have found out conclusively after an experience of sixteen years. During that time I have worn legs of four different makers, exclusive of yours, having spent many hundreds of dollars and got nothing satisfactory in return until I got one from you. My left leg was amputated at the upper third, leaving nearly three and one-half inches of stump from the body.

The operation was badly performed by rural doctors, who were somewhat inexperienced. As a result I have not a favorable stump for the most advantageous use of an artificial leg. The fit you gave me was as complete as though I had been present in your factory, and I could suggest no alteration. The main advantages I conceive that your patent possesses over others I have tried are, first, the rubber foot, which gives the artificial limb all the movements of the natural, especially when walking on rough or uneven ground. The other improvements possessed by legs of your make, and which I consider essential to those having very short stumps, consists in the knee lock, enabling the wearer to bend or straighten the leg and lock it. This is a decided advantage.

I wish you to preserve my leg measure, for I may hereafter have to order a new leg, and I should wish it to be exactly the same dimensions as this one.

Very respectfully yours,
R. RANDOLPH.

LEG ABOVE KNEE.

Fitted from Measurements.

FORT GRANT, GRAHAM CO., ARIZONA, Feb. 11, 1887.

A. A. MARKS, Esq :

SIR :—I am happy to say that I am very much pleased with the *cork* leg you sent me. I am around daily without the assistance of a stick, and can ride horseback as well as ever.

I get around just as fast as if I had both natural legs.

You can hardly tell the difference in my walk. After using it about a month the stump decreased about a quarter of an inch.

It did not decrease so much that I had to use other padding.

I use nothing but the socks. The stump has never been sore since I have been using the leg.

Respectfully, etc.,
EDWARD SCOTT,
Corpl. K Troop, 10th Cavalry.

LEG ABOVE KNEE.

GLENWOOD SPRINGS, GARFIELD CO., COLO., Oct. 31, 1887.

MR. A. A. MARKS :

DEAR SIR :—I have worn limbs of your patent over twenty years, and I think none that are made will compare with yours.

I wore three other kinds before getting yours. All the first three had ankle joints that kept me busy repairing. Since I have been wearing yours I have no repairing to do. I am running a ranch, digging sage brush, and all other kinds of rough work.

I do not have to repair my limb. My stump is about three inches long. The fact of my wearing a limb of your patent tells more than I could write in a week.

Respectfully yours,
W. H. ROYSTON.

LEG ABOVE KNEE.

Fitted from Measurements.

BERTHOUD, LARIMER CO., COLO., Nov. 5, 1887.

A. A. MARKS:

DEAR SIR :—I take pleasure in recommending your artificial legs with rubber feet, as I think they are the best made.

I received one made from measurements, on or about the first of April last, and it is a first-class leg in every respect, and a good fit. I am an engineer in a saw-mill, and am on my feet most all of the time. I thought when I lost my limb that I never would be able to wear an artificial limb, as my stump was so short, only being six inches long from the hip joint ; but I now think nothing of walking a half or three-fourths of a mile without a cane. I have had no repairs and do not need any ; the rubber foot is perfect, and I think superior to all others in every respect. Yours,

W. E. DICKERSON.

LEG ABOVE KNEE.

Fitted from Measurements.

"I have nothing but praise to offer."

519 West 5th St., PUEBLO, COLO., Nov. 11, 1887.

A. A. MARKS, New York City :

DEAR SIR :—When I purchased my artificial leg of you two years ago I said that I would write you my opinion of it when I had made what I considered a sufficient test of it. I have nothing but praise to offer. You followed my measurements in making it with such exactness that I can't see how it could fit better if I had gone to New York in person.

I am farming out here, and can harrow, mow, and do all manner of farm work, although my stump is but eight inches long.

The rubber foot is especially serviceable in that kind of work, as it is elastic enough, and has stability. The only repairs I have had, have been done to the shoulder strap.

I will take great pleasure in recommending your leg when occasion offers.

Yours very truly,
THOMAS BARBER, Jr.

HAS WORN THE RUBBER FOOT 24 YEARS WITHOUT REPAIRS— AMPUTATION SIX INCHES FROM HIP JOINT.

"Fitted from measurements and couldn't fit better."

BOX 104, GUNNISON, COLO.

MR. A. A. MARKS:

DEAR SIR :—After wearing your artificial leg for the last 24 years I am well satisfied to state that I don't think a better leg can be made. The length of my stump is only six inches from the hip joint, and you will hardly believe me when I tell you that I have to work hard every day in the year, and that the artificial leg never gets out of repair. I am a ranchman.

I think it is the rubber foot that makes your leg so easy to the wearer. I have to thank you for the admirable fit you gave to my last leg from measurements ; in fact it couldn't fit better if I went to your office in New York. I can recommend your artificial legs to my brother soldiers as giving them the best satisfaction.

Yours respectfully,
AUGUST BIEBEL.

LEG ABOVE KNEE.

Fitted from Measurements.

"Can get on or off a train going eight miles an hour."

EXCELSIOR, via GRAND JUNCTION,
MESA CO., COLO., Nov. 11, 1887.

A. A. MARKS, Esq.:

I have worn a leg of your make since 1880, and it has given me the best of satisfaction. My leg is amputated four inches below the body. I do considerable hard work, can carry 125 pounds on my shoulder, get on or off a train going eight miles an hour, ride horseback, get thrown off occasionally, and am not in constant dread of breaking my leg as I have seen wearers of other legs. I especially recommend your rubber foot, as it sounds so much more natural than others. To those who are so unfortunate as to need an artificial leg I will take pleasure in answering any communication which I may receive. I sent my measure by mail, and I do not see that I could have done any better if I had gone to New York ; I got a perfect fit.

Yours truly,
EDWIN BULPIN.

LEG ABOVE KNEE.

Oct. 28, 1887.

MR. MARKS:
Having been using one of your artificial limbs for some time I feel quite pleased with it, and would always recommend them to any one in need of such. I lost a leg about 11 years ago by a running sore, and have only six inches of stump left.

About one year ago I made up my mind to try one of your limbs, and although a good many said that I could never walk with it, yet I am able to walk well. Of course I do not walk perfectly, but I do not limp but very little. I walk a quarter of a mile to and from my work twice a day, and then do not feel tired.

I have never had any repairing done on it, and it is as good as the first day I wore it. I do not think the rubber foot has any equal. It does not give that dull, heavy thump so common in all other makes, but instead gives a light, soft step, which cannot be detected from the step of my own foot. It also gives a nice bend across the toes and does not wear the shoe as fast as my other foot. In fact, I would not part with it if I could not get another like it.

MATTHEW WHELAN,
Torrington, Litchfield Co., Conn.

LEG ABOVE KNEE.

Nov. 11, 1887.

A. A. MARKS, Esq.:
DEAR SIR:—Yours of Oct. 26 received. The limb you made for me about four years ago has proved satisfactory.

My natural leg was amputated at the thigh, leaving only about one-third of its length. The rubber foot seems to be superior to any other. I am a mechanic and am obliged to stand at my work constantly. Yours was the first artificial limb I wore.

Very respectfully,
AUGUSTINE LEJENNE,
Plainville, Hartford Co., Conn.

LEG ABOVE KNEE.

BRANFORD, NEW HAVEN Co., CONN., Oct. 27, 1887.

A. A. MARKS, Esq.:
DEAR SIR:—The limb which I purchased from you recently is giving entire satisfaction, and is in every way as recommended.

I am now doing my regular day's work, and am improving very fast in strength and gaining in flesh. I expect after a few months to be able to do any ordinary work with the aid of your artificial limb and will not feel the loss of the old one.

Most respectfully yours,
JOHN DALEY.

LEG ABOVE KNEE.

Worn a rubber foot for twenty-two years.

MARBLEDALE, LITCHFIELD CO., CONN., Oct 31, 1887.

MR. A. A. MARKS:
KIND FRIEND:—I wish to say a few words in regard to your artificial limbs. I have worn them from childhood up. I can truthfully speak of their merits. The second limb you made for me was in November, 1863. That limb I wore until two years past.

This was wearing a limb with a rubber foot for twenty-two years and doing ordinary housework. The rubber feet are the most durable. The cost of repairs for that limb was a trifle.

Your rubber feet are a success. They are superior to the old style of wooden feet with heel cord.

Respectfully yours,
MRS. A. FLEEZER.

FATHER AND SON—THE FORMER ABOVE THE KNEE AND THE LATTER BELOW THE KNEE.

869 Main St., Bridgeport, Conn., Nov. 2, 1887.

Mr. Marks:

Dear Sir:—I was in the employ of the Housatonic R. R. as switchman for sixteen years when I caught my right foot in a frog. An engine backed on me and crushed my leg. The amputation was made three and one-half inches above the knee. I had an artificial leg made by ——; it seemed as though I was having it repaired all the time; after a while I heard of your rubber feet legs, and had you put a rubber foot on the leg for me. I afterwards had you make me an entire new leg, which I am glad to say has given me great comfort and much satisfaction. I have taken great pleasure in recommending your legs to others, and have always been thanked for so doing.

There is a saying, "It runs in the family." The wooden leg mania seems to have no exception. My boy Willie was ten years old when he lost his foot by the cars on the N. Y., N. H. & H. R. R. The amputation was made three inches below the knee.

He is now eighteen and works every day selling papers on the railroad. He runs and jumps on the trains, and is as active as any one with the naturals. He is frequently asked if it was not his brother that lost his leg. Through your great invention he is almost able to forget his misfortune. Willie says there is no one in the world that makes as noiseless a limb as you do. He and I both agree that your legs with rubber feet are without equals to build a poor fellow up after he has been mashed to pieces.

Respectfully,

Patrick Bray.

LEG ABOVE KNEE.

Applied when a Mere Child.

Jan. 21, 1888.

Mr. A. A. Marks, New York:

Dear Sir:—I desire to offer you a slight testimonial of my gratitude for the comfort that my daughter has derived from the use of the artificial leg which you adjusted for her in May, 1882, and to say here, for the enlightenment of many who are as ignorant in such matters as I once was, that no one should ever hesitate to have a limb adjusted in childhood, as it is by far the best plan, though many persons advise cripples to wait until they have attained their growth. My daughter lost her leg in 1879, about three months prior to her sixth birthday, and she has worn the artificial leg made by you constantly since 1883, when she first realized the advantage to be derived from its use.

She is a powerful child in frame, and when her leg was removed no hopes were held forth that she would ever be able to wear an artificial limb, owing to the amputation being made so close to the hip joint. The trouble was caused by blood-poisoning after a severe attack of chicken-pox, and a double amputation was made, leaving about one and one-half inches of bone. The case is considered a remarkable one, and your success in adjusting a leg satisfactorily to so short a stump speaks volumes for your work, which can not be surpassed; and not only has the leg given absolute comfort to the child, but she has grown to the age of fourteen years and developed to large and graceful proportions.

Ever gratefully yours,

Maggie V. Benner,
945 T St., Washington, D. C.

LEG ABOVE KNEE.

Oct. 31, 1887.

My Dear Mr. Marks:

It affords me great pleasure to add my testimony to the excellence of your artificial limbs. I know whereof I speak, not only having had an experience of over twenty years in wearing an artificial leg, but also being a close and

interested observer of the work turned out by other manufacturers in this branch of industry, and my experience and observation lead me to the conclusion that for comfort, durability, and the many advantages (including the slight expense of repairs) arising from simplicity of construction, yours are pre-eminently the limbs for those so unfortunate as to need an artificial for the natural limb. Trusting that all who require artificial limbs may come to know as I have, by actual test, the boon your benevolent and indefatigable talent has conferred on suffering humanity, I remain,
Yours very faithfully,
WILLIAM GRIFFIN,
Clerk Adjutant-General's Office, WASHINGTON, D. C.

LEG ABOVE KNEE.

WINTER HAVEN, POLK CO., FLA., Nov. 2, 1887.

Have worn artificial limbs for five years with an amputation two inches above the knee. Have been constantly walking as housekeeper and clerk in grocery store during this time.

For nearly three years I have been wearing a limb made by you with rubber foot. I find it durable, noiseless, and light, needing no repairs except belt and shoulder straps, which are furnished by you at very low prices, and serve nicely as skirt-supporters as well as holding the limb in place. My limb is superior in *every way* to any I have tried, especially the rubber foot, being in shape and pliability similar to the human foot.

MRS. F. A. K. HARRIS.

LEG ABOVE KNEE.

Fitted from Measurements.

FERNANDINA, NASSAU CO., FLA., Nov. 2, 1887.

A. A. MARKS, New York City:

DEAR SIR :—Permit me to say that your artificial leg with rubber foot attached, which I have been using continuously since September, 1886, is all that you have claimed for it.

I have but seven inches of thigh stump. My occupation is U. S. Light House Keeper, North Beacon Ranges, Amelia Island, Fla., and I have to go up and down in one of the ranges 45 feet high, on iron-rod steps, at least twice a day; so I have good reason to say your limbs are all you claim for them. You are at liberty to use this as you wish.

Respectfully yours,
JOHN MILES.

LEG ABOVE KNEE.

Fitted from Measurements.

LITESVILLE, BRADFORD CO., FLA., November 10, '87.

A. A. MARKS, New York:

DEAR SIR :—In 1875 I bought my first artificial leg from you. I am now wearing my second. Both were fitted from measurements, according to your instructions. I consider your make of artificial legs the best I have seen or worn, and with good usage would last eight or ten years.

When I bought my artificial limbs I was living at Blackstock, S. C. South Carolina being my native home, I was the cause there of several getting your make, and since I have been here, nearly four years, several more, one by letter from Pittsburg, Pa. He selected me from your last pamphlet, as the length of our stumps were nearly equal, his being the longest, as you know I have only 5½ inches from hip joint; therefore, you see, I must think your make go d, to recommend them so much. The rubber foot is a great improvement, and there is no clanking about the leg, which, if there was, would give me a case of the jim-jams, for I am very sensitive about my loss anyway. I can stand as well as any of them, walk three and four miles without halting, ride horseback very well in any gait. I hope you will keep improving in your make until the poor maimed can forget that they are subjects of artificials.

Yours truly,
J.O. CARROLL.

LEG ABOVE KNEE.

Fitted from Measurements.

NEWNAN, COWETA CO., GA., Nov. 14, 1887.

MR. A. A. MARKS:

I have used one of your artificial legs with rubber foot for two years. It is one of the best inventions of the kind. I can do any thing with this leg. After ten days it became natural to me; it never troubles me any more.

C. L. COOK.

LEG ABOVE KNEE.

Fitted from Measurements.

Buena Vista & Ellaville Railroad Company,
JAMES M. LOWE, Vice President.
BUENA VISTA, MARION CO., GA., Nov. 24, 1887.

A. A. MARKS, New York:

DEAR SIR:—Replying to yours of recent date, I do not know how to give you a stronger endorsement of the superiority of your limbs than to say I have used them constantly for twelve or fifteen years. I cannot say now how long.

I lost my leg at the second battle of Manassas, in 1862, and for several years after I got well I used several other makes before I procured one of yours. Since then I have worn your make exclusively. During this long term of years I have had many business transactions with you, and it is a pleasure for me to express the uniform fairness which has characterized your dealings.

Yours truly,
JAS. M. LOWE.

LEG ABOVE KNEE.

Fitted from Measurements.

FLOVILLA, BUTTS CO., GA., Nov. 10, 1887.

MR. A. A. MARKS, Broadway, New York:

DEAR SIR:—In the spring of 1876 I received from you an artificial limb, which you made for me by measurement. It proved a comfortable fit; nearly eleven years' constant wear; the india-rubber foot and every part of the limb are still in good condition. No repairs have been necessary, only a renewal of the suspenders once. It affords me great pleasure to offer my testimonial of its great merit.

Very truly yours,
A. E. CHANDLER,
Presbyterian Minister.

LEG ABOVE KNEE.

GENESEE, HENRY CO., ILL., Oct. 29, 1887.

A. A. MARKS:

DEAR SIR:—I received your letter of Oct. 26. My business is manufacturing harness. I have worn artificial legs for twenty-three years. The first was a worthless patent. If all of the legs but yours are of the same style I would not take them as a gift. Point of amputation, seven inches from thigh. Cost of repairs on the one of your make, about three dollars. I have worn this one over six years, and it is as good to-day as when I left your office six years ago. I have boarded with parties six months, and they did not know that I had an artificial leg; the rubber foot fooled them; men that have traded with me for fifteen years get deceived the same way. For ease and comfort give me the rubber foot. I wish every man that has had the misfortune to have lost a leg would try one of your make.

I remain, yours,
EDGAR CRONK,
Late private, Co. C., 21st Missouri Volunteers.

LEG ABOVE KNEE.

HARVARD, McHENRY CO., ILL., Oct. 29, 1887.
A. A. MARKS, New York City:

DEAR SIR:—For over nineteen years I have worn continually an artificial limb, of your make. I can cheerfully say that it has given perfect satisfaction. I am a dentist; my stump is but five inches long. I can stand at my dental chair and operate six hours a day with comparative ease.

The cost of repairs on my limb for nineteen years will not exceed $15 (suspenders excepted). I most heartily recommend your limbs for comfort, durability, and perfect fit from measurements.

Yours respectfully,
ROBERT F. TAGGART.

LEG ABOVE KNEE.

Fitted from Measurements.

WEBBER'S FALLS, CHEROKEE NATION, IND. TER., Nov. 11, 1887.
MR. A. A. MARKS:

DEAR SIR:—I learn that you are going to print a new pamphlet; if so I would like very well to tell my story.

In July, 1884, I accidentally split my right knee joint with a chopping axe, which limb three days later was amputated four inches above knee joint, leaving me an eight-inch stump.

In January, 1886, after looking around very thoroughly, I purchased my artificial leg of you, by sending measurements taken by one of my neighbors and myself. I am now compelled to say that, after about two years of constant use, I feel confident I made no mistake in taking your patent.

The repairs have been very small so far; I often walk to church, over a mile, in company with others. My chief occupation is farming. I often saw wood all day, or I can pick a hundred pounds of cotton in a day, and that is about the amount I picked before my leg was amputated. To all persons who may wish to purchase artificial limbs by sending measurements, I will say that A. A. Marks' style of measuring, if closely and carefully observed, is as good for a neat and easy fitting limb as a dime is for a ginger cake.

Yours truly,
J. D. CLUCK.

LEG ABOVE KNEE.

Fitted from Measurements.

919 W. Ohio St., EVANSVILLE, IND., Nov. 16, 1887.
MR. A. A. MARKS:

DEAR SIR:—On my return home I found your letter, and in reply I will have to say that the artificial leg you made me from measurements fits as perfectly as possible.

If I had come to the shop and you had taken the measurements yourself, I doubt that results would have been better.

I have worn it for about ten months. I put it on the next day after I got it, and have worn it every day since, from early in the morning till late at night.

My occupation is circular and band saw filer; I keep up all the saws for a large circular and band saw mill. I have to be on my feet most all day. I get around almost anywhere without a stick. As to the rubber foot, I think it is the finest thing out. Mine has only worn out two light socks in ten months, and it does not jar me when I make a misstep. I only have six inches of a stump, and I get around better than others I see that have worn other make of legs.

JAMES M. PRITCHETT.

LEG ABOVE KNEE.

Fitted from Measurements.

Worn four different styles, and likes the rubber foot the best.

WOLCOTT, WHITE CO., IND., Oct. 29, 1887.

A. A. MARKS, New York:
DEAR SIR :—In reply to your letter of the 26th, I take pleasure in saying that your limb with rubber foot improvement is the best and most durable limb made. I had tried four different make of limbs before I procured yours, and your limb with rubber foot is the only one that has given satisfaction.

I have given it a fair test for over two years, and during that time my total expense amounts to 75 cents for one yard of elastic webbing, while the limb I used before purchasing yours would either break at the ankle or snap the cords walking on the uneven ground in this locality, which kept me repairing it once a month at least. The principal advantage of your make over all others is its simple construction; no cords or ankle joint to break, which causes me to feel perfectly safe in using it. I am considered hard on a limb; my friends frequently remark that I get round on it as if I had not lost a leg. I weigh 154 pounds, and have what is called an upper thigh amputation, and my duties here require me to be on my feet an average of twelve hours a day.

Limbs of other make may be all right for those who have no idea of the great improvement you have made in the manufacture of artificial limbs, but give me the limb with the rubber foot as the best substitute for the limb left on the battle-field.

Respectfully,
JNO. T. BRADY,
Co. C, 71st Regt. Pennsylvania Vols.

LEG ABOVE KNEE.

FAIRFIELD, JEFFERSON CO., IOWA, Oct. 28, 1887.

A. A. MARKS, ESQ.:
DEAR SIR :—As it has been some years since I purchased my leg of you, I think I ought to let you hear from me again.

It is now about ten years since I got the leg that I am now wearing, and have worn constantly since (I think it was 1877 when I got the leg), and it appears to be perfectly sound and good yet, never having to be repaired, the rubber foot being firmly attached to the leg. The knee joint does not rattle or make any noise, and appears to be as good as when new, ten years ago.

I own a small piece of ground in this city (Fairfield) on which I cultivate small fruit (strawberries, raspberries and blackberries, currants and gooseberries). I do all the hoeing, pruning, and a good part of the picking of the fruit.

I am a carpenter by trade, and work at the business when not engaged in my fruit garden. I climb up and down ladders when at work on houses. Point of amputation at the middle third (or eight inches from the body). My weight is about 132 pounds.

The leg I am now using is the second leg of your make, and the third all told since 1864; my limb was amputated 1863.

I am very well satisfied with your make of leg, especially the rubber foot, and if this one gives out before I do I will surely have you make the next.

R. STEPHENSON.

LEG ABOVE KNEE.

(A Coal Miner by Occupation.)

VAN METER, DALLAS CO., IOWA, Oct. 29, 1887.

MR. A. A. MARKS:

DEAR SIR:—I have used one of your patent limbs for six years, and am well satisfied with it. I am a coal miner by occupation. I think that your rubber

No. 284.

foot is a splendid success; it suits me A No. 1. I never tried any other, or do I wish to, as long as I can get one of your make. Mine is an upper amputation; I have nine inches of a stump; I can walk almost as fast as any ordinary man. I would advise persons needing artificial limbs to buy them from you.

S. T. AKERS.

LEG ABOVE KNEE.

Fitted from Measurements.

SALINA, SALINE CO., KANSAS, Nov. 1, 1887.

A. A. MARKS, New York:

DEAR SIR:—I have worn one of your legs for the past two years, and it has given entire satisfaction; it has never been out of repair and is now nearly as good as new.

Its especial excellence is the india-rubber foot.

I had worn four legs in the twenty-four years from 1865 to 1885, and although well made for their kind, not one of them ever lasted over two months without the ankle-cord giving way and the inside machinery breaking, leaving nothing but a rattle-trap to walk on. Your india-rubber foot so completely remedies this that, although my leg is amputated within two inches of the body, people generally do not observe that I wear an artificial leg.

You made my limb from measurements I sent you from this place, and it fits me just as well as if the measurements had been taken by you in your office. I am in the abstract and loan business, and do a large amount of walking, and believe the "Marks Leg" will stand twice the wear of any other leg made.

Yours truly,
SWAYZE T. CRISS.

LEG ABOVE KNEE.

SALINA, SALINE CO., KANSAS, Nov. 14, 1887.

MR. A. A. MARKS:

DEAR SIR:—I am very glad to put my stump on to brighten the fire. After having worn one of your artificial legs with the rubber foot for more than fifteen years I have no hesitation in saying it is the best leg in use, as it is simple and the most durable of any I have seen, and I have examined the ———, the ———, the ———, and worn one of the ———, but would not use any other now if I can get the rubber foot with stiff ankle, as it never drags at the toe

No. 285.

from weight of mud or other matter on the toes, and is so simple a child can adjust it.

I can heartily recommend the rubber foot as the most durable and easy to handle, and to any unfortunate one in need of such appliance I would say by all means try the rubber foot. I have worn artificial legs since 1862 and do all kinds of work.

I am a blacksmith, and have shod horses, and I refer you to Mr. D. B. Powers, Aug. Bellport, and a score of others.

I have dug wells and quarried stone, and other heavy work.

I can walk farther in a given time than any man can on any other kind of a leg with the same length of stump as mine; it is only three inches from center of hip joint.

Yours, etc.,
E. LINCOLN,
Late of Co. I, 12th, Ill. Vol. Infantry.

LEG ABOVE KNEE.

WINFIELD, COWLEY CO., KANSAS, Nov. 7, 1887.

A. A. MARKS, Esq.:

DEAR SIR:—It affords me much pleasure to bear testimony to the excellence of your artificial limbs. I have worn an artificial leg for twenty-five years, having suffered an amputation at the thigh in June, 1862. I tried three different makes before using one of your make, and give yours the preference over all others. My experience with artificial legs having metallic springs in the feet was not satisfactory, for the reason that the springs became gradually relaxed, letting the toe drop and catch on obstacles, causing an occasional fall and requiring frequent renewal of springs.

Legs made with these springs may be said never to be in order after a few days' wear. I have found your rubber foot sufficiently elastic, and there being nothing to get out of order, it stands hard and long service. Living on a farm and walking over rough and often ploughed land is a trying test to artificial legs, and none that I have used will compare with your make for strength and durability.

Yours respectfully,
ARTHUR H. GREENE.

LEG ABOVE KNEE.

NICHOLASVILLE, JESSAMINE CO., KY., Nov. 8, 1887.

MR. A. A. MARKS, New York City:

DEAR SIR:—This is to certify that I have been using your artificial legs for twelve years, and have also used two different patents before I commenced using that of yours.

I think that the legs you make are superior to all others I have used or seen; the rubber foot beats all the click-clack of other patents. My stump is only four inches long from the body; weight 210 pounds.

I have been superintendent of national cemeteries for eighteen years, and am now constable of this county. I can ride a horse as good as any man, and with perfect control. Trusting that the soldiers may use your limb, or give it a satisfactory trial, I remain,

Yours truly,
E. SCHNEIDER,
Formerly of Co. H, 5th N. Y. Art.

LEG ABOVE KNEE.

GREENUP, GREENUP CO., KY., Nov. 4, 1887.

A. A. MARKS:

DEAR SIR:—I have worn an artificial leg made by you for twelve years without having any repairs done to it. Having worn other makes of legs I consider yours far superior for comfort to any other leg made, and the rubber foot is far ahead of any I have ever seen. My present occupation is a farmer, and I have done some plowing. My leg is amputated about five inches above the knee.

Yours respectfully,
HARRISON RIGGS.

LEG ABOVE KNEE.

Fitted from Measurements.

RANGELEY, FRANKLIN CO., ME., Nov. 22, 1887.

I have had considerable use for artificial legs, and will say that the A. A. Marks is the best and most durable that I have ever used. They are more easy and simple than any that I have tried.

J. H. ORBETON.

LEG ABOVE KNEE.

Fitted from Measurements.

LIMERICK, YORK CO., ME., Nov. 28, 1887.

MR. A. A. MARKS:

DEAR SIR:—I have been using one of your patented legs with the rubber foot for something over four years. My step is perfectly easy. I have been using the leg every day since I received it, and am well pleased with it. I go to school every day and walk over one-half of a mile.

I play ball with the boys. I can skate, and in fact I can do any thing the other boys can do. I can get about so well I never notice but what I have got two sound legs, and in the future you may be assured of the heart-felt gratitude I have for what you have done for me. Hoping you will continue as successful in the future, I remain,

Yours truly,
FREDDIE D. HOLLAND.

LEG ABOVE KNEE.

LEVANT, PENOBSCOT CO., ME., Nov. 2, 1887.

MR. MARKS:

DEAR SIR:—A word to you in regard to your artificial limbs. Your first artificial leg I got sixteen years ago last March. I wore it constantly for ten years. Your last one I got in January, 1886, and have worn it with perfect ease every day.

My weight is 180 pounds. My business is farming, driving teams, which is all laborious work. I am very sorry to say that once in a while I visit the ball room, and the ladies all wonder how I can get around so nicely on an artificial limb.

What I have seen of other artificial limbs, it is my best judgment that yours are the best on earth.

Yours respectfully,
A. O. WING.

LEG ABOVE KNEE.

Fitted from Measurements.

BELFAST, WALDO CO., ME., Oct. 30, 1887.

MR. A. A. MARKS:

DEAR SIR:—I am glad to give my testimony in regard to your artificial leg, which I have worn for the last three years.

I can say of its merits that it is one of the best the Government provides for its soldiers. My first leg was made by Dr. ——. The leg was a source of trouble to me. I was most of the time with a broken leg, and had to wear a peg leg of my own make.

I have worn an artificial leg for 22 years. Three years ago when I applied to Mr. Marks for a leg, Mr. Marks sent me blanks for measuring for one of his with rubber foot; I took my own measurements and sent them to him. He made the leg without my presence, and sent the leg to me.

As soon as I received it I put it on, and have worn it ever since; that was three years and a half ago; it fits me the best of any leg that I have ever had; it is the best and easiest leg that I have ever seen. I can say that he can fit better from measures sent him than the others did when I went to their places.

His leg is easy and safe. I am a farmer, and have some hard work which tries a leg.

Yours truly,
WM. J. BROWN,
Private Co. D, 19th Me. Vols.

LEG ABOVE KNEE.

Fitted from Measurements.

N. E. COR. TREMONT AND PATTERSON AVES.,
BALTIMORE, MD., Dec. 2, 1887.

A. A. MARKS:

DEAR SIR:—I will say as near as I possibly can what I know about your artificial legs. Superiority over others I know nothing about, for I never wore any other but yours.

I will say this, that I had my leg amputated above the knee 21 years ago, and directly after got one of your limbs, which lasted me 14 or 15 years with little expense to me, only ten or twelve dollars in that time, which was my own fault for want of proper care. In fact I might say I have only had two of your limbs in twenty years, and it cost me but a trifle in that time for repairs or any thing else. As to the rubber foot, it can not be excelled. I would have no other, and never will have any other. I must say that as to measurements and fittings I have never had any trouble. Both my legs were fitted from measurements. My occupation for the last twenty years has been in the grocery business. This business is laborious for one who undertakes to load and unload wagons, as I am frequently called upon to do. In fact, I might say that I do every thing that is required of me, the same as others with natural limbs.

It is no task for me to climb ladders, which I had to do when I had men building for me.

Yours respectfully,
JEREMIAH KEADY.

LEG ABOVE KNEE.

No. 407 NORTH MOUNT ST., BALTIMORE, MD., Nov. 7, 1887.

A. A. MARKS, New York City:

DEAR SIR:—I take pleasure in recommending your make of artificial limbs. I have been wearing one since December 10, 1880. It is an excellent fit, and well shaped, so that few are aware that I have an artificial limb. It has cost nothing yet for repairs, and seems to be as strong as the day I received it.

I have been engaged at manual labor most of the time (repairing furniture and upholstering). My amputation is above the knee, with about six inches of stump.

I am respectfully yours,
P. J. COLE.

LEG ABOVE KNEE.

Fitted from Measurements.

ALTAMONT, GARRETT CO., MD., Dec. 15, 1887.

MR. A. A. MARKS:

DEAR SIR:—Your letter of the 26th ult. to hand. I wish to say to my fellow unfortunates I had my right leg mangled in a quarry; it was amputated above the knee in June, 1882. One year after I purchased one of Mr. A. A. Marks' patent limbs with rubber foot. I commenced wearing it shortly after getting it, and have worn it every day since. I was very prejudiced against the stiff ankle at first, but after a little patience I got along better than I ever expected to, as this was the first artificial limb I ever wore. The leg has far exceeded my expectations.

It has proved to be just what Mr. Marks said was the beauty of the limb; it does away with a lot of machinery that I have seen in other artificial limbs. It is not accompanied with rattling or an unpleasant noise when walking; there are no springs, hinges, or bolts to get out of order. My leg has not cost me but twenty-five cents for repairs in four years. I have given my leg some hard trials; I have done a great deal of walking; I have been on my feet sometimes from seven o'clock in the morning till eight and nine o'clock at night. My occupation is a laborer. People have been surprised when I told them I wore an artificial limb. Mr. Marks is worthy of patronage; what he says can be relied on. I cheerfully recommend his limb to all in need.

Yours truly,
P. CLINE.

LEG ABOVE KNEE.

MOUNT SAVAGE, ALLEGANY CO., MD., Oct. 30, 1887.

MR. A. A. MARKS:

DEAR SIR:—Having lost one of my legs on the railroad some years ago, I applied to you for assistance, and received one of the most valuable limbs made. I consider Mr. Marks' limbs without a rival, and any person wishing to purchase a leg can not do better than give you a call. Any person wishing my testimonial can have it by sending a stamped addressed envelope to,

Yours truly,
JOHN HENRY PAUL.

LEG ABOVE KNEE.

717 BAKER ST., BALTIMORE, MD., Nov. 5, 1887.

A. A. MARKS:

DEAR SIR:—I take pleasure in writing a testimonial for your make of legs. By occupation I am a stone-cutter and work every day at setting mantels, vestibules and tiles and wainscoting. I go up and, down ladders. My leg is off above the knee. My stump is but eight inches long. I have to fare the same as all the men in the shop. As much is expected of me as the rest, and I get as much pay. I have seen all other makes of legs, and yours exceeds them all. The rubber foot leg can not be beat for durability. I am wearing your leg seventeen or eighteen years, and it has only cost me about $2.50 outside of straps. I would wear no other make if they were given to me. I remain,

Yours respectfully,
GEORGE SMITH.

LEG ABOVE KNEE.

PLYMOUTH, PLYMOUTH CO., MASS., Nov. 4, 1887.

DEAR SIR:— I have used one of your artificial legs with the rubber foot, for amputation above the knee, for the last fifteen months, and it has proved satisfactory. I am also using a pair of your new suspenders, No. 4, which I think are the best that can be obtained.

Very respectfully,
JOHN WASHBURN.

LEG ABOVE KNEE, GIRL SEVEN YEARS OLD.

Fitted from Measurements.

14 Sudbury Street, Boston, Mass., Nov. 6, 1887.

A. A. Marks :

Dear Sir :—My daughter, seven years old, has been wearing the artificial leg furnished by you about seven months, and I am pleased to say that it has given entire satisfaction.

Although the amputation was above the knee, and the little patient had not used the limb for more than three years previous to its amputation, she was able (greatly to our astonishment) to walk across the room *without a cane* within an hour after the application of the artificial. I consider the rubber foot the best substitute for the natural one that can be provided, and am happy to confirm all that you have said in its favor. As you are aware, the leg was made by measurements, taken by myself and forwarded to you by mail. The fit was perfect, showing that your workmen were as careful in executing the order as I was in giving it. Shall be pleased to recommend persons desirous of procuring artificial limbs to patronize you, as I have found you as honorable in your dealings as the articles of your manufacture are satisfactory.

Yours very truly,
George C. Beckwith.

LEG ABOVE KNEE.

Fitted from Measurements.

17 Exchange Street, Harrison Square, Dorchester,
Suffolk Co., Mass., Nov. 8, 1887.

A. A. Marks, Esq. :

Dear Sir :—I have been wearing one of your artificial limbs for eleven years, and I feel as though I ought to thank you for your great invention. I had my leg amputated just above the knee, and thought I should be useless the rest of my life, but if you could see me go about my house and do the work for a family of five you would be astonished yourself. I have never worn any other kind of artificial leg, neither could I be induced to even try them, as I believe there can be nothing more natural than the rubber foot. I thought of course I should surely have to go to the manufactory, but was spared the journey by your excellent method of self-measurement. I believe I have just as good a fit as if I had gone to the manufactory. About two years ago I had it repaired after wearing it nine years, and it is now in as good repair as ever it was, and it bids fair to last nine years longer, if I live to keep it going.

Long may you live to see your great invention walk, run, skip, dance, and skate.

Yours, very respectfully,
Mrs. I. Kierstead.

LEG ABOVE KNEE.

Mattapan District, 18 Richmond St., Boston, Mass., Oct. 27, 1887.

Mr. A. A. Marks :

Dear Sir :—Yours of the 26th inst. received this day. I must say that I am more than willing to testify in regard to your artificial limbs. In April, 1886, I was injured at Somerville, Mass., by a runaway horse so that amputation was necessary five inches above the knee. I sent for one of your pamphlets, and then started for New York, November, 1886, and that same month and year began to wear your artificial leg, and have not missed a day in wearing it since the first day I had it. I am a carpenter by trade, and in May, 1881, just twelve months after being hurt, began to work at the bench and have worked about all summer and am surprised to know that I ever could get around so well. I walk to my work, and stand all day, and am not any more tired at night than if I had both my legs. Without it I could do nothing, but with it can get along almost as well as before I lost my leg. My leg was very large when you.

measured it, so I had to get a new socket, and thought I would try and save time and expense, and had it done in Boston, but have been sorry ever since, for I have taken very little comfort since, for Boston parties do not have such a line of business, and therefore do not understand fitting a socket, for I suppose you fit ten to their one, and the one that they made for me is just like putting my leg into a lard pail, for the edge is so sharp it almost cuts the flesh, but the one I got from you was very comfortable and fitted like a glove. Just as soon as I need to make another change I shall come to you, regardless of time or money; for give me your leg and no other.

Yours very truly,
CHARLES C. MOULTON.

LEG ABOVE KNEE.

LINDEN, GENESEE CO., MICH., Nov. 7, 1887.

MR. A. A. MARKS, New York City:

With pleasure I endorse the rubber foot as the best artificial foot manufactured. In my opinion it has no equal for durability and stillness, and for my use is far ahead of any ankle joint limb I ever saw; and I have seen a good many different men's make and worn one about two years which cost me $50 for repairs. The limb I am wearing now was made by A. A. Marks thirteen years ago last winter, and has been in constant use ever since, and has not cost more than one dollar a year for repairs.

Yours truly,
WM. H. MEAKER,
Late of Co. G, 5th Mich. V. V. Inft.

LEG ABOVE KNEE.

Fitted from Measurements.

CALUMET, HOUGHTON CO., MICH., Nov. 1, 1887.

MR. A. A. MARKS:

DEAR SIR:—According to your request I pen you these few lines in the way of recommendation. This is to certify that I, John N. Fezzy, have worn Mr. A. A. Marks' artificial leg for over nine years, and can say it has given me perfect satisfaction. I can highly recommend them to any person that is in need of an artificial leg. In regard to walking, I cannot speak as those who have a longer stump, for mine is but six inches from the body. I walk half a mile to and from my work, and I have never missed a day through the severest storms, and I have gone through some pretty heavy snow-drifts off Lake Superior. Dr. Niles of Calumet came to me for advice. I recommended to him your artificial limbs. There are three of us in this town wearing your legs, one machinist, one carpenter; I am an engineer, and have been running the engine for the Calumet Mining Co. for over twenty years, and get around the machines all right without the assistance of a cane. I can climb ladders without fear of slipping.

From yours truly,
JOHN FEZZY.

LEG ABOVE KNEE.

Fitted from Measurements.

CRYSTAL SPRINGS, COPIAH CO., MISS., Nov. 14, 1887.

MR. A. A. MARKS:

DEAR SIR:—I have been using one of your patent artificial legs for over six years, and I have found it to be all you claimed it to be. I have done a great deal of heavy work on my farm since I have been using your artificial leg; as I have never used any but yours, I can not say any thing about any other, but I can recommend your limbs to any one as being good and durable legs. I

would not use any other, as I know the rubber foot is a great improvement on artificial legs. My leg fits well. It has given perfect satisfaction. My leg was amputated just above the knee.
THOMAS GRAVES.

LEG ABOVE KNEE.

ROLLA, PHELPS CO., MO., Nov. 5, 1887.
A. A. MARKS, ESQ., New York City:

DEAR SIR:—I take great pleasure in recommending your artificial limbs, especially for their durability and superiority of the rubber foot over all others. My left limb is amputated just above the knee joint. I have worn one of your limbs since April, 1884, and it has not cost me one cent for repairs to this date. I walk easily without a cane, and have no difficulty in following my profession. Your style of measurements is perfect, and by following your instructions any one can just as well be fitted at home as to go to the city. I have taken measurements for limbs, and among others when double amputation had been performed. In all cases perfect satisfaction has been obtained.

Very truly yours,
J. D. CARPENTER, M.D.

LEG ABOVE KNEE.

FAIRBURY, JEFFERSON CO., NEB., Nov. 18, 1887.
MR. A. A. MARKS, New York:

DEAR SIR:—Yours of October 26 at hand. In reply would say I think the rubber foot is just the thing, as it is very durable, never getting out of repair. I am farming and have done some very hard work, but have not paid for or done any repairs yet, now over two years.

I am yours, etc.,
W. P. SQUIRES.

LEG ABOVE KNEE.

WEEPING WATER, CASS CO., NEB., Nov. 19, 1887.

DEAR SIR:—As far as your limb is concerned, I am glad to recommend it. It is a delight to use it. After wearing a limb for nine or ten years I know how to appreciate it. The foot movement is so noiseless and easy that I'd not think of going back to my old style. At first I thought I *never* could use it, but in a very little while (a day or two) I found I could. It has grown better and better right along. And now rather than go back to the old style I'd pay you $50 a year just for the use of yours, and I'm not rich either. Again it pleases my friends; they say I walk better, easier, etc. Then there is your new strap; it seems to me it is of equal value with the limb. It is as much an addition to comfort in sitting, reclining, and walking, lifting, etc., as the limb itself. Oh, how straps used to drag, and how burdensome when hot and tired and hurried. But this is so no longer. Some one may think that I had a poor limb to start with. Well, last winter I wrote to the *Scientific American* asking them to recommend to me the best inventor of artificial limbs, and they sent me your address and the address of the manufacturer whose limb I already had. That limb *was* a good one as far as a limb can be, I believe, that does not infringe on your patents. I would not take that limb now as a gift, even though I had to pay $500 down for yours and $50 a year royalty. Now don't you raise the price because I say this. Your straps move so freely through the little pulleys on the limb that the strap is not dragged back and forth over the shoulders in the least. Only those who use your strap can appreciate its value.

Yours truly,
REV. C. H. DALRYMPLE.

LEG ABOVE KNEE.

ROGERS, COLFAX CO., NEB., Dec. 4, 1887.

DEAR SIR: Your limb has given me good service.

Respectfully,
JAMES HILL.

LEG ABOVE KNEE.

Fitted from Measurements.

BRADSHAW, YORK CO., NEB., Oct. 31, 1887.

MR. A. A. MARKS:

DEAR SIR: Your letter of inquiry duly received. I am happy to inform you that the artificial leg you made for me nearly four years ago proves perfectly satisfactory in every respect. I cheerfully recommend it to any one. My left leg is amputated above the knee, and I have worn the leg you made for me ever since I first got it. I have not paid out a particle for repairs yet, with the exception of a pair of suspenders. I think the leg is good for four years more. It is getting a little short now, because I have grown some in the last four years, but this is not the fault of the limb. I am a harness-maker by trade, and any one wanting information may write to me.

Yours truly,
ALBERT BROKER.

LEG ABOVE KNEE.

Fitted from Measurements.

Nov. 1, 1887.

MR. A. A. MARKS:

DEAR SIR:—I have worn one of your artificial limbs nearly three years, and although I can not say how they compare with limbs made by others, as I have never worn any other kind, I think the rubber foot is a good thing, as it is perfectly noiseless, and up to this time has not cost anything for repairs.

I have had to have a new socket made, as my stump has shrunken since the limb was first applied. I can vouch for your success in fitting from measurements given.

My occupation is that of a carpenter, some parts of which have been very trying to an artificial limb.

Point of amputation, half way between the knee and thigh.

Yours very truly,
HERBERT W. FICKETT.

ERROL, COOS CO., N. H.

LEG ABOVE KNEE.

508 Grove Street, JERSEY CITY, N. J., Nov. 8, 1887.

A. A. MARKS, ESQ.:

DEAR SIR:—I am well satisfied with your leg; don't want any thing better, and don't think there is any thing better. I am now using limb made for me last summer ('86); this is the second one. The one previous was in continuous use for fifteen years, and with very little work could be fixed so it would go for several years yet. I never had any thing done in the way of repairs in all this time, only what I did myself, which was very little.

Yours,
E. J. BUXTON.

LEG ABOVE KNEE.

Fitted from Measurements.

ELBERON, MONMOUTH CO., N. J., Nov. 2, 1887.

MR. A. A. MARKS:

DEAR SIR :—I can hardly find words to express myself in regard to the artificial limb I purchased of you. I can go most everywhere, upstairs and down. I do for five in family, without crutches or cane. I can climb up step-ladders and wash windows and work as well as any other woman.

Yours truly, MRS. REED.

LEG ABOVE KNEE.

HACKENSACK, BERGEN CO., N. J., Oct. 28, 1887,

A. A. MARKS, ESQ :

DEAR SIR :—I take pleasure in testifying to the satisfaction I have derived from the use of your artificial limb. About eight months ago I had my leg amputated above the knee, and have worn Mr. Marks' artificial leg now for three months with entire satisfaction. I wish particularly to recommend the rubber foot. It makes walking more natural and easy on account of its elasticity than a wooden foot, and more confidence can be placed in it. In my opinion it can not be too highly recommended.

I am, yours, etc.,
ARTHUR CHRISTIE.

LEG ABOVE KNEE.

NEWARK, N. J., Oct. 31, 1887.

Mr. A. A. MARKS :

DEAR SIR :—I am pleased to give my testimony in regard to your artificial leg, which I have worn for the last four years.

I have worked on it every day since, at my trade as Currier, in a leather factory, where I have worked over thirty years.

I was greatly discouraged at first, thinking I would never be able to wear it. I can do as much work as I ever did.

It is a strong, durable leg.

Truly yours,
ARTHUR JOHNSON.

LEG ABOVE KNEE.

Nov. 5, 1887.

Mr. MARKS :

DEAR SIR :—In regard to limb I have of your make, words cannot express the satisfaction it has given me. I have worn it five years constantly, and to-day can walk five miles, which is wonderful, I think, considering my limb is off above the knee joint. I have had no repairs except for lengthening in that time. The rubber foot has no worthy rival. I take great pleasure in recommending your rubber feet to those that use artificial feet.

Yours respectfully,
J. C. GREEN.

Ticket Agt. D. L. & W. R. R., ROCKAWAY, MORRIS Co., N. J.

LEG ABOVE KNEE.

WESTFIELD, UNION CO., N. J., Oct. 31, 1887.

A. A. MARKS:

DEAR SIR :—I have worn your limb since 1867. I think the india-rubber foot is the greatest of inventions. It gives ease to the stump. No clicking in the

ankle. I have a seven-inch stump above the knee; left leg. I walk eight miles a day.
My occupation is a farmer. I can walk without a cane.

CHARLES HENRY HOLMES.

LEG ABOVE KNEE.

TESTIMONIAL.

1st. Occupation since wearing your artificial leg: Book agent. Justice of the peace eight years; township collector of taxes; light ordinary work; cutting wood; gardening; gathering fruit, etc.

2d. How long worn: Since July, 1879.

3d. Point of amputation: Left leg; thigh; eight inches below hip.

4th. Comparative cost of repairs: No cost except for suspenders.

5th. Other information; Worn constantly with great comfort, because of its light weight and soft, flexible rubber foot. I can truthfully testify with pleasure as above.

Yours very truly,
JAMES HOFF,
QUAKERTOWN, HUNTERDON CO. N. J.

LEG ABOVE KNEE.

PERTH AMBOY, MIDDLESEX CO., N. J., Oct. 28, 1887.

A. A. MARKS:

SIR:—Yours of the 26th inst. at hand. In reply would say it affords me great pleasure to testify to the durability of the rubber foot and the ease in walking, especially over rough roads. The artificial limb I now have has been in constant use nearly six years and is in good condition yet. I walk a mile and one-half to my place of employment, morning and night, and am on my feet the greater part of the day. The limb has at all times given the greatest satisfaction and there has been no cost for repairing, only for suspenders, etc. which must necessarily wear out. Of course the ease and comfort to be derived from an artificial limb is in the fitting of same to the stump.

I can say you have well pleased me in this respect, which was done from measurements taken on but one visit to your office; and as my limb is amputated eight inches above the knee, the fitting is all that can be desired. Thanking you for past courtesies, etc., I remain,

Gratefully yours,
JNO. P. KENNA,
Train Runner L. V. R. R.

LEG ABOVE KNEE.

Oct. 31, 1887.

I have been wearing one of A. A. Marks' artificial legs for twelve years and find it superior to any other in use.

I wore one of———. The simplicity of the springs and durability of the Marks leg places it above any that I have ever come in contact with. I am a man over 200 pounds and if not for its durability it would not last so long.

I am a carpet weaver.

HUGH MULHOLLAND.

LONG BRANCH VILLAGE, N. J.

LEG ABOVE KNEE.

Nov. 28, 1887.

Mr. A. A. MARKS:

DEAR SIR:—A little more than twenty-three years ago I lost my right leg above the knee from a gun-shot wound.

When the surgeon examined it and told me that it would have to come off, my first word was, "I wish the ball had gone through my heart," for I thought I would be a dependent the rest of my life.

Being in Washington, D. C., I went to the patent office and looked over the different models. I chose what I thought was the best. For three years I worried along with it, most of which time the leg was on the sick list, and you may well think that I had but little hope for the future. Twenty years ago next March, I think it was, I got one of your artificial legs with rubber foot. I had no faith in it at first. In 1870 I got another of the same kind, and I wore the two until 1885, with an expense of but a few dollars on both.

In 1885 I got another, and am still wearing it, and I do nearly all kinds of work. I think nothing of starting out in the morning and spending the whole day gunning or fishing. I spent last winter canvassing and collecting as an insurance agent, but perhaps the best test was about two years' working in a factory, when I made packing boxes, put them under a press (when packed), nailed down the covers, put them on the scale, weighed them and put them away.

The cases weighed from 300 to 500 pounds each.

And not only that, but there are scores of people with whom I have been acquainted for fifteen or twenty years who do not know that I have lost a leg. If any person can make me a better leg than yours I would like to see it.

Respectfully yours,
E. D. SCOFIELD.

PASSAIC, N. J.

LEG ABOVE KNEE.

Oct. 28, 1887.

A. A MARKS, ESQ.:

I am still wearing the leg you furnished six years ago. I have worn it comfortably with less than six dollars cost for repairs. My occupation (house painter) gives it a good test. I can and do work on scaffolds, ladders, in fact anywhere. I have but a three-inch stump. I am well satisfied.

Yours truly,
ROBERT H. PERRY.

PAMRAPO, HUDSON CO., N. J.

LEG ABOVE KNEE.

129 Liberty St., NEW YORK CITY.

MR. A. A. MARKS:

I have worn your make of artificial leg ever since the rubber foot was invented, and gladly testify to its many superior qualities. Enrol me as one of your lifelong patrons.

JOSEPH TROW.

LEG ABOVE KNEE.

Nov. 1, 1887.

A. A. MARKS, ESQ.:

DEAR SIR :—Your new kind of suspenders are of great comfort to me. Designer by profession, I can work easier while sitting, and get up without strain. I am so satisfied with them that I do not hesitate to recommend them to all afflicted as I am.

My leg was amputated August 25, 1886, by the eminent surgeon, W.T. Bull, four inches above my right knee. I have been using the natural shaped artificial limb you made for me in October, 1886, ever since. I thought to express to you my sincere admiration for your work. You can very well be proud of it. The rubber foot is in excellent order. It has kept its graceful original form, and usage has improved it. The joint above the toes being more flexible, its motion now is even more natural that it was when new. The mechanism under the knee is also in perfect order and as strong and sound as it was a year ago. Thanks to your successful manner for measuring and fitting with such a

small amount of trouble as I have experienced, I can say that you have given me almost another natural leg. Remembering with pleasure the courteous treatment I met with at your rooms, I remain,
Sincerely yours,
J. H. SAUER,
147 West 16th St., NEW YORK CITY.

LEG ABOVE KNEE.

354 West 22d St., NEW YORK CITY.
A. A. MARKS, ESQ.:
DEAR SIR:—I talk the Marks leg every opportunity I have. I consider it by all odds the best, most reliable, and most durable leg made.
Your truly,
T. CLELLAND, M.D.
July 7, 1877.

LEG ABOVE KNEE.

532 11th Ave., NEW YORK CITY.
Patrick J. Monaghan wishes us to write his endorsement of the Marks artificial leg. He says he can testify to its many good qualities. The rubber foot and fit are perfect and highly satisfactory. M.
Nov., 1887.

LEG ABOVE KNEE.

Oct. 27, 1887.
MR. A. A. MARKS:
DEAR SIR:—I had the misfortune to have my leg cut off by being run over by a train some seven years ago. I was recommended by a friend to get one of your artificial limbs, and I did so. I have worn the same for the past six years. It has given me perfect satisfaction. It has cost me but little for repairs. I highly recommend it to any one having use for same. As for me, I would wear no other. I am now employed on road and get around well.
Yours respectfully,
JOHN J. MURPHY,
859 11th Ave., NEW YORK CITY.

LEG ABOVE KNEE.

Oct. 27, 1887.
MR. A. A. MARKS:
About three years ago I had the misfortune to lose my left leg by amputation, to save my life, and for the space of three months I had to use crutches. My hands and arms became almost paralyzed, so that I could not lift them over my head. Then I thought I would try one of your limbs, and since then I have the use of my hands and am able to do my work satisfactorily, or as near as can be done in the grocery business. I am working in the store from five A. M. to nine P.M. every day. I do not know what I would do without it now. I have seen the limbs with wooden feet, but I prefer Marks' rubber foot. It has not got that click-clack sound so often heard from others. Another advantage it possesses is that it is so simple in its construction that a child can take it apart; consequently it is not so apt to get out of order. In the three years that I have worn your valuable limb it has cost me about two dollars for exchange of braces.
WILLIAM A. KELLY,
20 Bedford St., NEW YORK CITY.

LEG ABOVE KNEE.

A Boy 8 Years of Age.

321 East 117th St., NEW YORK CITY, Nov., 1887.

MR. A. A. MARKS :

DEAR SIR :—At first I thought it impossible to be able to use one of your artificial limbs, but after six months' trial I now find it gives me entire satisfaction. I can now run and walk nearly to perfection without my stick. I earnestly recommend any one who should be so unfortunate as to lose a limb to get one of your artificial ones.

Respectfully,
EARNEST HESSE.

LEG ABOVE KNEE.

Wearing a Leg Nine Years Without Repairs.

Oct. 26, 1887.

MR. A. A. MARKS :

DEAR SIR:—I have worn artificial limbs for the last twenty-five years. My right leg is amputated about six inches from the body. I have worn legs of three different makers, but for durability and simplicity of workmanship I prefer yours above all others. It makes no noise in walking, and is very easily taken apart. I have worn one of your legs for nine years constantly, without spending a cent on it for repairs.

Yours respectfully,
WM. A. DOYLE,
754 8th Ave., NEW YORK CITY.

LEG ABOVE KNEE.

218 E. 38th St., N. Y. CITY, Oct. 28, 1887.

MR. A. A. MARKS :

DEAR SIR :—I am greatly pleased with my limb, and am improving very rapidly. I do not use my cane. Miss Rosa Eagan, who has one also, is in the same house with me. Miss Eagan walks splendidly. I shall walk as well in time. As a testimonial, I will gladly state all that is possible, that I am much pleased.

MISS MARY A. GIBSON.

LEG ABOVE KNEE.

BROTHERS DARE, American Pantomine and Specialty Company.
TONY PASTOR'S THEATRE, FOURTEENTH ST.,
NEW YORK CITY, Dec. 8, 1887.

MR. A. A. MARKS :

DEAR SIR :—Allow me to say a few words in praise of your artificial leg with rubber foot. I consider it the best I have ever had. Having worn other makes for a number of years and as I thought the best, I was persuaded to have you make me a leg, and I am thankful that I did, for I can now walk with more ease and comfort and a greater distance with less fatigue than I ever could, with the other so-called best make of artificial legs.

I consider the rubber foot a great advantage over the old style, as it makes a person walk with a nice easy motion. I believe my stump is as short as could be and wear a leg, amputation having been made two inches and one-half from the hip joint. I am a gymnast by profession, and known as Frank S. Dare of the Dare Brothers, and I do a great amount of walking around, and use the leg very rough, but I must say I have less trouble and less repairs with your leg than any other I have ever worn.

FRANK MELROSE.

LEG ABOVE KNEE.

Nov. 1, 1887.

MR. A. A. MARKS:

DEAR SIR:—I have been using one of your artificial legs for the past fourteen years, during which time they have given entire satisfaction. The last one I got about three years ago, and have not had to have it repaired in any shape since.

The rubber foot acts splendidly. I think it is near perfection as any one could wish for. My occupation, that of gate-keeper, requires me to be on my feet pretty much all the time, and I do a great deal of moving around, which I am happy to say I can do without much difficulty. My leg was amputated about six or eight inches below hip joint, so I have but a very short stump to work on.

I shall cheerfully recommend any one who is so unfortunate as to need an artificial leg to call on you.

I remain yours respectfully,
CORNELIUS MORRISON,
Gate-keeper Brooklyn Hospital, Brooklyn, N. Y.

LEG ABOVE KNEE.

Oct. 27, 1887.

MR. MARKS:

DEAR SIR:—I have worn your artificial legs for about seventeen years.

I have a thigh amputation, a five inch stump. I have worn five other legs of different makes, and I would not accept of any other leg, if I had to wear them if they were given to me,

They are always creaking and out of order and eating the stockings at the ankles; also the shoes, and in a short time they eat themselves away at the ankle joint.

I am a carpenter and work at my trade. I have worn one of your legs for ten years, and I could have worn it longer.

They never get out of order. The first one I wore seven years.

I am now wearing the third leg I have had from you, and I have always recommended your artificial leg in preference to all others.

Respectfully yours,
ABRAM D. CLARK,
397 14th Street, BROOKLYN, N. Y.

LEG ABOVE KNEE.

Nov. 15, 1887.

MR. A. A. MARKS:

DEAR SIR:—In May, 1882, I was so unfortunate as to lose my right leg above knee. In September, 1882, I was advised to procure one of your patent artificial limbs with rubber foot.

It now gives me sincere pleasure to be able to inform you that the artificial leg which you made for me has more than realized my expectations. The durability of your patent has, I think, been fully established. The foot appears to be as good now as when I first commenced to wear it, over five years ago.

I cheerfully recommend your legs to all needing them. I remain,
Dear sir,
LEONARD MANZ,
115 Grand Street, BROOKLYN, N. Y.

LEG ABOVE KNEE.

The First Artificial Leg Made to Supply the First Leg Lost in the Late Rebellion.

399 Fifth Ave., BROOKLYN, N. Y., Dec., 1887.

A. A. MARKS, ESQ., Artificial Limbs, etc.:

DEAR SIR:—Having lost my right leg four inches from the hip joint in defence of the Union at the battle of Bull Run, July 21, 1861, as 1st Sergeant of Co. I, 79th N. Y. Vols. (Highlanders), and coming home a paroled prisoner of war from Richmond, Va., October, 1861, the Hon. Simon Cameron was then President Lincoln's Secretary of War, who, when he saw me, most feelingly authorized me to procure the best artificial leg made and send the bill to him. There was formed a committee of gentlemen, of whom Capt. H. A Ellis, late of the 17th U. S. Army, was one, who examined several artificial legs of the day, amongst them yours, ——, ——, etc., and wisely decided that I should have one of your make, as in their opinion best for my purposes.

I was measured, fitted, and received the leg from you in December, 1861 (Gen. Simon Cameron sending his check in payment for same. This was before the Government provided limbs for its crippled defenders). Mine, I believe, was the first artificial leg made to supply a loss caused in the Rebellion. You remember that this leg, your own make, had an ankle joint; well I remember its "clap, clap," every step I took. Your patent rubber foot came soon after. I had the rubber foot applied to my leg, and no person but those afflicted as I am can appreciate such a magical change. In fact, I felt like a whole man again.

So much so that my friends, acquaintances, and strangers whom I met in my traveling would not be convinced until I exhibited your leg, so near was it to perfection and nature. I wore that leg for some twelve or more years, doing some "tall" walking, riding over rough roads, being attached to the 9th army corps, army of the Potomac, as sutler, etc., in that corps, campaign in Virginia, Kentucky, Tennessee, etc., and in all those years I wore the rubber foot which was substituted for the ankle joint foot. I have had two legs from you since. I am now wearing the third with the same perfect satisfaction, and I am willing to testify to its usefulness in a two-mile walk with any wearer of a different make of artificial leg with the same length of stump. I have tried other makers' legs, hoping to better myself. This experience has convinced me that your rubber foot has no superior. My business is clerical, with a considerable share of standing and walking.

It is with pleasure that I make the above statement and permit you to make what use you think proper with it.

I am respectfully, etc.,
JNO. MCKENZIE.
Late 1st Sergt. Co. I, 79th Regt.

LEG ABOVE KNEE.

GEORGE W. PINCKNEY, Attorney and Counsellor at Law,
26 Court St., BROOKLYN, N. Y., Oct. 28, 1887.

A. A. MARKS, ESQ.:

MY DEAR SIR:—I have used one of your legs since 1868.

It serves me well. I have become so accustomed to it that it has become a part of me. In 1866 I used one of ——'s legs, but I got so "strapped" with that that I gave it up.

Since you have allowed me to walk on your leg it has only visited you once a year, and that for the renewal of shoulder-straps.

My leg is amputated above the knee. Your rubber foot is a great invention, and the longer I use it the more I wonder when I see people stumping along on one leg when they can use one of yours. I hope, for the benefit of the legless and footless, you may not fall short of a broad and extensive patronage.

Yours, etc.,
GEO. W. PINCKNEY.

LEG ABOVE KNEE.

"Your leg served me for seventeen years."

137 Walton St., BROOKLYN, N. Y., Nov., 14, 1887.

MR. A. A. MARKS:
I, Peter Schwartz, invalid from the U. S. Army, 46th Regt. Co. F., N. Y. Vols., had my leg amputated four inches from hip, and am wearing one of your legs which has served me for seventeen years, I have found your rubber foot to be the best.

I have had a great deal of walking to do in my former years through rain, snow, and ice, and have never had any trouble. I remain,
Yours,
PETER SCHWARTZ.

LEG ABOVE KNEE.

FLATBUSH, KINGS CO., N. Y., Nov. 1, 1887.

A. A. MARKS:
DEAR SIR :—I think it but just as a tribute to your skill and ingenuity in the manufacture of artificial legs to state my experience of your make as compared with other manufacturers.

I have worn artificial legs for fourteen years, previous to obtaining one of your make, and must say that yours far surpasses any thing I have ever had as to ease, durability, and comfort.

It is therefore with much pleasure that I assure all in need of help in that line that they will find it to their advantage to give you a call. I may state that I have worn your rubber foot now four years and it has not cost me any thing for repairs.

My occupation is that of barber and hairdresser, which necessitates a good deal of walking and standing.
Yours respectfully,
JOHN STOLL.

LEG ABOVE KNEE.

Oct. 29, 1887.

MR. A. A. MARKS, New York:
DEAR SIR :—While a policeman in New York City Aug. 26, 1874, I had the misfortune to have both of my legs broken while on duty at the French dock, foot of Morton St. After being in the hospital nearly a year, I had to have my right leg amputated four inches above the knee. In the spring of 1876 I got of you a leg with a rubber foot. I think the leg and foot are the best made. All the leg has cost me is for suspenders. I have been wearing the leg every day since I received it. I remain,
Yours very truly,
JASPER G. TERRY.
Asst. Postmaster, RIVERHEAD, SUFFOLK CO., N. Y.

LEG ABOVE KNEE.

WOODSIDE, QUEENS CO., N. Y., Nov. 4, 1887.

MR. A. A. MARKS:
DEAR SIR :—In August, 1887, I lost my leg by an explosion in a drug store at Winfield, L. I. Being young and my stump very short, I did not think that I could wear an artificial leg at all. When I grew to be of age my friends and neighbors begged me to try one. In the spring of 1882 I received one of your full-length legs, which I now use and have been using every day since without any trouble. My occupation is a flagman and gateman on the Long Island R. R., which requires me to be on my feet walking across three railroads changing signals every three minutes for twelve hours every day. I must say your leg does not make the noise that I have heard from other kinds. In fact,

it has brought life back to me again. I would not be without one of your legs. Any body wishing any information of me I will cheerfully answer any letters addressed to me on the subject. I am,
Yours respectfully,
JOHN H. SCHAEFER.

LEG ABOVE KNEE.

OZONE PARK, L. I., Oct. 29, 1887.

A. A. MARKS, ESQ. :

DEAR SIR :—I have been wearing one of your limbs for nearly five years, and am fully persuaded that they are the best made. When I first wore one I was in the employ of the Long Island R. R. Co., as an operator, and very little on my feet, so did not have a good chance to test the merits of it as I have since done ; under the pressure of business I wore the leg for one week, day and night, without having it off. At present I am in the lumber business, and find not the least trouble in getting over lumber and on to the highest piles we have in the yard. My leg is off above the knee, and I have considerable collecting to do and find no difficulty in walking any distance. This summer I walked four miles in one hour and fifteen minutes, which I thought good for a one-legged man. Few who have known me since I am wearing your leg know that it is artificial, unless I tell them. My ease in walking is owing, in my opinion, to the rubber foot. The amount I have paid for repairs does not amount to more that $5. You are at liberty to use this in any way you may see fit. I am,
Yours truly,
F. T. NEWCOME.

LEG ABOVE KNEE.

MOUNT VERNON, WESTCHESTER CO., N. Y., Oct. 31, 1887.

A. A. MARKS :

DEAR SIR :—I had the misfortune to lose my right leg when I was six years old. At the age of eight I tried my first artificial limb. I do not remember the name of the maker, nor do I care to, inasmuch as it was worthless so far as usefulness is concerned. It would probably have been my last if my father's attention had not been called to the Marks artificial limb with the wonderful rubber foot. He decided, after considerable deliberation (for he had come to look upon artificial limbs as mere ornaments), to give your leg a trial, and I can testify to its merits. I am a photographer and my business compels me to be on my feet the greater part of the time. I feel no fatigue whatever. I can say this, that having once used the Marks artificial limb I feel that I can never get along without one.
Yours respectfully,
WM. B. DAVIS.

LEG ABOVE KNEE.

Office of DR. H. PEARCE & Co., Druggists, Main St.,
PAWLING, DUTCHESS CO., N. Y., Oct. 31, 1887.

DEAR SIR :—I have worn an artificial leg for about twenty years, and one of Marks' patent for about fifteen years.

I regard it far preferable to any other I have ever seen.

My amputation is above the knee, and I don't meet any one that wears any other leg that can walk as well as I can.

It is so simple and durable that there is no chance for any thing to give out except the suspenders. So the cost of repairs is very trifling.
Respectfully yours,
HENRY PEARCE, M.D.

LEG ABOVE KNEE.

Fitted from Measurements.

CHESTER, ORANGE CO., N. Y., Oct. 28, 1887.

MR. A. A. MARKS:
In reply to your letter of Oct. 26, would say I purchased of you ten years ago last February an artificial leg which has been in constant use ever since. My work is in a creamery and cheese factory. The work is very heavy, and I am on my leg at least 12 hours every day. For straps, and all other expenses, I have not paid over $1 a year. My limb was amputated within six inches of my body. Before purchasing this limb of you, I had two of another manufacturer, which only lasted about four years each. The cost of repairs for the two first limbs was $49. I have been wearing an artificial leg for 19 years, and when I have worn the one out I purchased of you, shall give you an order for another. I am more than pleased with it.

Very truly yours,
JOHN ROACH.

LEG ABOVE KNEE.

Fitted from Measurements.

MOUNT LIVINGSTON, STILLWATER, SARATOGA CO., N. Y., Nov. 4, 1887.

DEAR SIR:—I spent six weeks in Jersey City and was so thankful to find that I could take long walks, one in particular of forty-three blocks, get on and off boats, cars, etc., without even the assistance of a cane, and the day I returned walked from Stillwater out to my home, a distance of two miles. While on Broadway I thought of you and would like to have called, but I could not. My limb was amputated above the knee about eight inches from the body. I have used one of your artificial limbs for six years and am perfectly satisfied with it. As it is my first and only one I cannot compare it with the limbs of other makers, but firmly believe that there is an ease and elasticity about the rubber foot that others lack. I know that the less machinery in them the better they are.

My occupation is not laborious, as I live at home in my father's house, and only assist in the housework. With the exception of two yards of elastic for suspenders, the limb has cost me nothing so far, and is now in good order.

I was fitted from measurements sent from my home.

Hoping all your patrons are as well pleased, I am,

Very respectfully yours,
EVA S. RODGERS.

LEG ABOVE KNEE.

"Worn the leg nine years without one dollar's repairs."

CEDAR HILL, ALBANY CO., N. Y., Oct. 31, 1887.

MR. A. A. MARKS:
DEAR SIR:—It gives me great pleasure to recommend your artificial leg, as I am conscious that in doing so I am not overestimating its value. I have given mine a thorough trial, having worn it every day for over nine years without one dollar expense. I can say I would not exchange it for any leg I have ever seen of other manufacture. The elasticity of the rubber foot is as natural as the real one, and the simple mode of construction makes the leg proof against getting out of order.

I have never felt the need of an ankle joint. I can go up and down hill without the joint better than with it.

I can walk on uneven ground almost as good as any one.

My amputation is ten inches from body. I was fitted from measurements sent to your manufactory. The fit is remarkably good. There has not been any alterations needed.

The rubber foot is a grand invention. There is no jar in walking and no getting out of order.

I can do almost all kinds of work with ease. My occupation is house carpenter, going up and down ladders, in fact doing all kinds of work, so that the durability of your patent has been fully tested by me. The rubber foot is about as good now as when I first commenced to wear it over nine years ago.

I can cheerfully recommend your limbs to all.

Yours respectfully,
WM. SELKIRK.

LEG ABOVE KNEE.

ANDOVER, ALLEGANY CO., N. Y., Nov. 1, 1887.

A. A. MARKS, New York City:

DEAR SIR :—I take pleasure in recommending your make of artificial limbs to those in need, having worn one to my satisfaction for over two years, without any repairs. My work has been heavy, a carrier of mail from post office and transfer from one train to another at Malvern, Ark., sometimes lifting and carrying as heavy as 200 pounds. My leg is off near the hip, or a thigh amputation. I weigh 240 pounds. My leg was made from measurements sent to the shop. I went to have it fitted.

I tried the leg on and had it fitted in about 20 minutes.

I have worn it continually, never chafing so as to have to leave it off for any length of time, as with other limbs I have worn. My leg is now to all appearances in good order. I will also say the rubber foot is a grand improvement, as it is easy in walking and does away with the thumping and clattering of all other kinds that I have tried. I can stand on my feet for hours with perfect ease. I can walk about houses, stores, etc., as still as a man with natural feet. My experience is that many do not believe I have a leg off, and if I ever need another I shall get a Marks if possible.

Respectfully,
V. D. SACKETT.

All communications cheerfully answered.

LEG ABOVE KNEE.

MONTICELLO, SULLIVAN CO., N. Y., Nov. 2, 1887.

I have for the past three years used one of A. A. Marks' artificial legs with rubber foot. The finish, fit, and durability of these legs are, I have no doubt, superior to any other make, so much so that the expense for repairs during that time has been nothing. The amputation is above the knee, and although my work is rather laborious, so perfect is the fit and so suited the leg that I have had very little trouble.

D. M. SCRIBER.

LEG ABOVE KNEE.

Three-Inch Stump.

Nov. 15, 1887.

MR. A A. MARKS:

DEAR SIR :—I have worn artificial legs for about thirty-three years of different manufactures. My leg being taken off very close to the body, only three inches of stump, makes it very hard to fit a limb so that it can be operated at all (so manufacturers say). I was persuaded to try one of your make by a man wearing one, and sent measure to you. The limb you sent fitted and operated far easier than any other I have tried.

My business is traveling agent, and is very trying to an artificial limb, but I find the Marks leg more durable, less liable to get out of repair, and far less

tiresome to wear than any I have tried ; in fact I would have no other, and think I am capable of judging the merits of the limb, having worn one for years.
Yours truly,
F. A. WEBB.
Academy St., WATERTOWN, JEFFERSON CO., N. Y.

LEG ABOVE KNEE.

Fitted from Measurements.

McDONOUGH, CHENANGO CO., N. Y., Nov. 1, 1887.

MR. A. A. MARKS:

DEAR SIR :—I have worn one of your artificial legs for nearly five years, and am exceedingly well pleased with it.

The rubber foot is a grand invention, no squeaking or getting out of order. It can be depended upon, and the knee joint is the strongest and best I ever saw.

No. 286.

I am farming and do all of my work, such as plowing, sowing, cradling and every thing that a farmer has to do. I have a farm of 100 acres of land and do not keep any one to work for me. I can recommend you very highly in fitting from measurements. You could not have fitted mine any better if I had come there to have had it fitted. I use a cane so little that I forget it and often leave it in the field where I have been to work.

Yours respectfully,
CHARLES E. WEBB.

LEG ABOVE KNEE.

CHENANGO BRIDGE, BROOME CO., N. Y., Oct. 30, 1887.

DEAR SIR:—In the month of June, 1874, you made for me an artificial leg above the knee with a rubber foot. I wore the leg for the first seven years, with only twenty-five cents expense for repairs.

It is now fast approaching fourteen years since it was made, and during that time its use has been severe, constant, and protracted. With the exception of six weeks of illness in the spring of 1877 it has been in daily use. My occupation has been largely that of gardening, and that requires me to be moving about most of the time. Besides that, I have picked most of my apples, going into the tops of the trees on a ladder, and picking from 50 to 75 bushels every fall. I have worn artificial legs for 35 years, and ought to know something about them, and think that, excepting your improvements, there has been but comparatively little improvement made on the old Anglesea leg. It is true that for a short time some of the later styles worked well, but their mechanism is too complicated to last long, and their bearings would soon become worn and loose, and it seemed to the wearer as though they rattled, and made nearly as much noise as an old-fashioned horse-power threshing-machine; and here is where your leg beats them all,—it has only one joint in the knee, and that never gets loose and rattles like other kinds, the rubber foot doing away with ankle and toe joints, thereby reducing the mechanism to a minimum, which in artificial legs is no small point in their favor. I would not knowingly lead any one wrong that was unfortunate enough to need an artificial leg or arm, but so far as my knowledge extends, and I have had some experience myself, besides noting that of others. I would say to unfortunates that I think they would consult their best interests by going to you for a leg or arm.

Yours truly,

H. W. PARKER.

To A. A. MARKS, ESQ.

LEG ABOVE KNEE.

"Worn one leg over sixteen years."

Oct. 27, 1887.

A. A. MARKS:

DEAR SIR:—Having heard that you were about to prepare a new pamphlet, I wish to say a few words in behalf of your artificial limbs. I have been wearing one of your legs for over sixteen years, and I would recommend them to any one in need. With your rubber foot there is no rattle in the ankle joints as there is in every artificial leg that has an ankle joint. As for comfort and natural walking, they cannot be excelled, and for durability they certainly cannot be equaled. I have had but two legs in nearly seventeen years, and the one I am now wearing is good for four or five years yet, from all appearances. My limb is amputated four inches above the knee. I am on my feet about ten hours every day, and it never gives me any trouble. I have never laid out one cent for repairs on my leg. My occupation is an engineer. I am now chief engineer of the Wagner Palace Car Works, at East Buffalo, and if any one wishes to see one of A. A. Marks' limbs with rubber foot in use, let him call and see me or write for information.

Respectfully,

F. M. PALMATIER,
381 South Division St., Buffalo, N. Y.

LEG ABOVE KNEE.

Nov. 7, 1887.

MR. A. A. MARKS:

DEAR SIR:—I would like to testify as to the merits or your artificial leg with rubber foot, if by so doing it would help one in like circumstances as myself. After wearing two different make of legs, each with ankle joint (one of them I did not get ten dollars' worth out of), I got one of your make with

rubber foot about seventeen years ago, and have worn it most of the time, and it is now about as good as ever. The amount of repairs on it has been light. I have worked at farming, pioneered on the western frontier, and hunted in the north woods, and it has always stood by me. I seldom use a cane, and friends remark how well I get around with it. My occupation is wool-sorting, which requires constant standing. I consider your make of legs a godsend to any one who has to wear an artificial leg. For comfort and durability it has no equal.
CHAS. McDOWELL.
CLAYVILLE, ONEIDA CO., N. Y.

LEG ABOVE KNEE.

PIERMONT, ROCKLAND Co., N. Y., Nov. 1, 1887.
I am very well satisfied with the artificial leg you made for me and take great pleasure in recommending it to others.
JEREMIAH HANGLON.

LEG ABOVE KNEE.

Nov. 1, 1877.
A. A. MARKS:
DEAR SIR:—Having worn your limbs for over twelve years, and being well pleased with them, I would not do without the rubber foot. I never saw a limb that equaled yours. I always got a good fit from you. My limb is amputated nine inches from hip joint. My business is traveling on the road selling stationery. I am on my feet a good deal and do lots of walking. There are three gentlemen living here with legs off, and I am doing more walking than the whole three of them. I haven't in twelve years seen but one gentleman with a limb off out on the road selling goods, and his leg was off below the knee instead of above the knee. I find it difficult to make men believe I have a leg off, they wont believe it until they have placed their hand on my artificial limb and felt for themselves. I hope that those requiring artificial limbs will find you and get them. The expenses for repairs can't exceed five dollars in ten years. All the expense I have is a spring, once in a while, and new webbing. You have my thanks and best wishes.
Respectfully,
EDGAR S. KELLOGG.
ONEIDA, MADISON CO., N. Y.

LEG ABOVE KNEE.

Fitted from Measurements.

SOUTH OTSELIC, CHENANGO Co., N. Y., Nov. 3, 1887.
MR. A. A. MARKS:
DEAR SIR:—I have worn your artificial legs for about fifteen years, and they have done me first-rate service.
They have all been fitted from measures. I have never been to your shop. My right leg was amputated at the thigh. I am a farmer and do all kinds of farmwork, except plowing. I mow, cradle grain, hoe, etc., on one of your make of legs. I think the rubber foot is better than any other leg or foot with an ankle joint. I shall always wear one of your legs as long as I wear any.
Respectfully yours,
WOODAL EASTMAN.

LEG ABOVE KNEE.

Fitted from Measurements.

MASONVILLE, DELAWARE Co., N. Y., Oct. 28, 1887.
MR. A. A. MARKS:
DEAR SIR:—I willingly add my testimony to the merits of your artificial leg. I believe yours to be one of the best if not *the* best manufactured. My opinion

is based upon my experience in wearing one of your full-length legs with rubber foot from, I think, about 1867 to the present time; previous to that time I had worn one manufactured by ——, of Baltimore, and repaired by ——, of Rochester, but it was continually giving out and its noise and rattle was a great annoyance. The rubber foot is much more durable, inasmuch as it does away with the necessity of so many cords and bolts and at the same time imparts a more natural and elastic step; it also sounds more natural when walking on the floor or pavement. My business heretofore has been farming and harness making. As good a fit as I ever had was made by you entirely by measurements. My leg was taken off at the upper third, leaving a stump about 7½ inches in length from my body. The expense of repairs has been merely nothing, unless you take into account the wear of the suspenders.

Yours, etc.,
J. A. CRAWFORD.

LEG ABOVE KNEE.

POTSDAM, ST. LAWRENCE CO., N. Y., Oct. 31, 1887.
A. A. MARKS, New York City:

I have worn your make of artificial leg for little more than a year past, and I cannot speak too highly of the rubber foot. Although my work is not laborious I walk a great deal. I would recommend your make in preference to any other.

Very respectfully,
HATTIE BROWN.
79 Market St.

LEG ABOVE KNEE.

Fitted from Measurements.

NEWTON, CATAWBA CO., N. C., Oct. 31, 1887.
MR. A. A. MARKS, New York City:

DEAR SIR:—The leg I purchased from you in 1876 has given me entire satisfaction. The fitting from measurements was perfect. My limb was amputated at the lower third of thigh. As I have used no other make of legs, I cannot speak comparatively, but were I to purchase another I would certainly give you my order. I think from experience and observation that the rubber foot is greatly superior to the old style. I am a farmer by occupation. The cost of repairs on my leg has been twenty-five cents since 1876.

Yours truly,
GEO. W. ROBB.

LEG ABOVE KNEE.

Fitted from Measurements.

CROTON, LICKING CO., OHIO, Nov. 20, 1887.
MR. A. A. MARKS, New York City:

DEAR SIR:—Yours of the 26th at hand. I will say that I have been wearing one of your limbs for the past year and a half, and like it very much. The "rubber foot" is very natural and easy. My limb was returned from being lengthened, and I must say it was fixed much nicer than I had expected, and it worked as nicely as a new limb. My limb was fitted from measures and is a perfect fit. I am telegraph operator and am often compelled to handle heavy trunks and freight. My limb has cost me but a few dollars for repairs, and that was for lengthening and for a new pair of suspenders. I think the rubber foot is perfection. It is absolutely noiseless.

I would cheerfully recommend your limbs to all who may need them.

Very truly yours,
LEONARD COWLES.

LEG ABOVE KNEE.

Fitted from Measurements.

SMITHVILLE, WAYNE CO., O., Nov. 7, 1887.

MR. A. A. MARKS:

DEAR SIR :—I lost my foot by a mowing machine over seven years ago. My foot was amputated three inches above the ankle. I was induced to get one of your limbs with a rubber foot, which I did, and am wearing it yet, which has been about six years.

It has cost me about two dollars for repairs. I ordered it from your measurement blank, and it was a perfect fit. I hope I shall be able to give you another order in the near future. I am,

Yours truly,

J. E. CRAWFORD.

LEG ABOVE KNEE.

Fitted from Measurements.

GUSTAVUS, TRUMBULL CO., OHIO, Nov. 8, 1887.

To DR. A. A. MARKS :

MY DEAR SIR :—You desire a testimonial from me in regard to the merits or demerits of the Marks artificial leg.

My opinion is based on actual observation by comparison with legs of different patterns in walking over rough and icy surfaces as well as on the smooth floor. The Marks leg is by far the safest and easiest managed. I do not fall any more in using it than I did when I had two good natural legs.

There has been no repairs needed on my leg in the three years' constant use. And the simple construction of the leg leads me to think that it is going to be lasting. I am a farmer fifty years old. I can and do make a full hand most of the season.

There are legs that cost much less than the Marks, but I look at it like this. The best artificial leg made is mean enough, and if one is so unfortunate as to need an artificial one, and is fortunate enough to have sufficient means to obtain a Marks leg, do it by all means ; then you'll own the best I've seen.

Yours very truly,

FRANK A. CLISBY.

LEG ABOVE KNEE.

DAYTON, MONTGOMERY CO., OHIO, Nov. 18, 1887.

A. A. MARKS, New York :

DEAR SIR :—Yours of Oct. 29 at hand. I lost my leg at Chancellorsville May, 1863. June, 1864, I received and began to wear an artificial made by Mr. Marks, and wore it every day for ten years. During these ten years I worked as helper to a blacksmith at forge, as herder on the plains, as street car driver, etc. Repairs during the life of this leg were about $5. Dec., 1880, I received my second leg from Marks ; this leg lasted five years without repairs. Dec., 1885, I received a leg made by —— of N. Y., and have worn it nearly two years and find it much the worse for wear. If it reaches the end of five years it will be only by extensive repairs. My work for the last two years has been very light on the leg. If I live until Dec., 1890, I expect to ask for an order on Marks for another leg, who in my opinion makes the best leg offered to invalids in this or any other country for "general superiority," durability, natural sound of footfall, and ease to the wearer.

An advantage beyond comparison with the iron-jointed styles, with all their side motion, double back action, and other infernal contrivances with which artificial leg makers afflict the poor fellows who survived the ravages of war, who with one leg are limping on toward the grave on some kind of support, the best of which after twenty-three years' experience I believe to be the Marks leg with the rubber foot. I am,

Very respectfully yours,

ENOS P. ROBINSON.

LEG ABOVE KNEE.

Fitted from Measurements.

Mr. A. A. Marks :

Dear Sir :—I have been wearing your artificial legs for the last seventeen years. I have been working on a farm most of the time; I can plow and do all kinds of work on a farm. I am well pleased with the rubber foot. I can walk over rough ground with ease. I am working from sunrise to sunset most every day.

I get along wonderfully, considering that my leg was amputated six and one-half inches from body. There are some of my neighbors who will hardly believe that I wear an artificial leg.

I think that the leg with the rubber foot is the very best that is made. My leg was made by measurements and it fits me perfectly. The expense of keeping the leg in repair is very small, considering how rough I have used it.

Yours truly,
D. W. Pritchard.

Delaware, Delaware Co., O., Nov. 5, 1887.

LEG ABOVE KNEE.

Philo, Muskingum Co., Ohio., Oct. 30, 1887.

Mr. A. A. Marks :

Dear Sir :—I have worn artificial legs for twenty-two years, and think I ought to be a pretty good judge of them by this time. After wearing your artificial leg with patent rubber foot attached for over twelve years, it gives me great pleasure to recommend them to any person or persons wanting anything of this kind. I have not had a cent's worth of repairs on my leg since I received it. There is one advantage this leg has over all other kinds. It never cries for grease like a dry wheelbarrow.

The rubber foot saves all jarring. I walk with a great deal more ease and satisfaction to myself with your leg than any other I ever used. I expect to use your artificial legs as long as I shall need them. I would not exchange for any other manufactured in the United States. Hoping this may be of some benefit to you and your patrons. I am,

Yours truly,
Silas W. Fickel.

LEG ABOVE KNEE.

Fitted from Measurements.

Dec. 10, 1887.

A. A. Marks, Esq. :

Dear Sir :—I received my leg in due time. I think after a few days it will be a splendid fit. I get along admirably well.

With my sincere thanks I remain, your friend,

Fred Legler.

Portland, Multnomah Co., Oregon.

LEG ABOVE KNEE.

Dec. 31, 1887.

A. A. Marks :

I have worn one of your legs ten years, and am still wearing the same one, and am well pleased with it. My weight is 270 lbs.

Yours respectfully,
F. P. Jones.

Philomath, Benton Co., Oregon.

LEG ABOVE KNEE.
Fitted from Measurements.

April 21, 1887.

Mr. Marks:

Dear Sir:—I have worn one of your artificial legs with patent india-rubber foot for one year and four months. My leg was amputated above the knee. I have walked five or six miles in a single day and could walk ten. I would advise any body who is so unfortunate as to lose his leg to go to Marks.

Yours truly,

JAMES R. BENHAM.

Prineville, Cook Co., Oregon.

LEG ABOVE KNEE.
Fitted from Measurements.

Buttonwood, Lycoming Co., Pa., Nov. 7, 1887.

A. A. Marks:

Dear Sir:—I have one of your legs, and have worn it three months, and am well pleased with it. I got it by measurements and it fits well. I can recommend it to any one. My leg is off above the knee. I can walk almost as well as ever. I am now doing all kinds of work and have had no repairing.

Yours,

CHAS. MOYER.

LEG ABOVE KNEE.

Nov. 14, 1887.

A. A. Marks:

Have been wearing artificial limbs thirty-eight years. I wore out six in twenty-two years. Costing me from twenty-five to forty-five dollars a year to keep them in running order. Did not enjoy the rattling of them. Have been wearing a Marks leg sixteen years; expense one dollar a year and all the comforts a veteran could wish for in using a first-class leg. My limb is in as good running order now as when I first commenced to wear it. I expect it to last many years. Would not exchange for half a dozen of the best artificial limbs that I have seen. "Nufced."

JAMES T. SAMPLE, Mexican Veteran.

Sewickley, Allegheny Co., Pa.

LEG ABOVE KNEE.

Nov. 3, 1887.

Mr. Marks:

Dear Sir:—I received your letter, and will let you know that I can walk almost as well with my artificial leg as others with both natural legs. I am wearing your artificial leg for the last six months. I do not use a cane unless I go some distance, and I am moving about all day at barbering from early in the morning till late at night. My stump is only six inches long from the body.

Respectfully yours,

JAMES MONTZ.

Weatherly, Carbon Co., Pa.

LEG ABOVE KNEE.

Bethlehem, Northampton Co., Pa., Nov. 11, 1887.

Mr. A. A. Marks:

Dear Sir:—I have been wearing your patent artificial leg for nearly two years, and am exceedingly well pleased with it. The rubber foot is a success.

It maneuvers admirably, and moves soft and nicely as can be desired. I have a four-inch stump from the body. People are astonished that I can get around so well, and often say no one would think that I had a wooden leg. People often rsk which leg is the wooden. I walk every day to school, over a half mile.
Yours truly,
ERVIN P. MILLER,
Cor. High and Geopp Sts.

LEG ABOVE KNEE.

ERIE, ERIE CO., PA., Oct. 28, 1887.

A. A. MARKS, NEW YORK CITY:

MY DEAR SIR :—In response to your letter of 26th instant requesting a statement of my experience as a wearer of artificial legs I will state :

I lost my leg in front of Atlanta, in July, 1864, and came north with a stump but a few inches long, and the end of the stump poorly protected on account of the flesh being eaten away by gangrene. After worrying along for fifteen years, part of the time on crutches, and part of the time on the old style wooden foot legs, of which I had three kinds, I finally made a trip all the way from Santa Fe, New Mexico, to your office and got one of your rubber-foot legs. I was then mining and smelting at Bonanza City, N. M., and the leg gave good satisfaction in that rough business and rough country. In 1881 I entered Uncle Sam's service and since that time have travelled over most of our territory, part of the Rocky Mountains, going in all kinds of weather, and in every conceivable conveyance, as a special examiner of the pension office must of necessity do, and I have found your leg much better than you recommended it. The first leg I got in 1880 never had a cent's worth of repairs on it during the five years I wore it, and is now laid away ready for use in case of an emergency. The one you made me two years ago bids fair to equal the old one. Previous to getting your rubber foot I was constantly annoyed by loose joints and rattling sounds, and the ankle cords were especially aggravating, for they would stretch, break, or wear out just as soon as I got away from shops where repairs could be made. Now I walk several miles each day without any fear of a break-down, and without that unpleasant dead thud that follows that step of a wooden foot on a plank sidewalk or bare floor.

Very respectfully,
MELVILLE DAVIS,
Vet. late of Co. E, 15th Iowa Vols.

LEG ABOVE KNEE.

Fitted from Measurements.

OLIVIA, BLAIR CO., PA., Oct. 31, 1887.

MR. A. A. MARKS:

DEAR SIR :—I received one of your patent artificial legs with rubber foot fitted from measurements some two years ago, and from that time to the present writing I have worn it every day.

I am a farmer living in the country, and have rough roads to travel, but I can walk five miles a day. I would advise all who want a good leg that will not get out of order to get one from you, as my leg has not cost me one cent for repairs yet.

Yours truly,
MILES LEWIS.

LEG ABOVE KNEE.

Dec. 1, 1887.

MR. A. A. MARKS, New York City :

DEAR SIR :—I take pleasure in writing to you in reference to the "Marks Patent Artificial Limb" I received from you eighteen months ago. I have worn it constantly ever since, and have experienced no pain or inconvenience from it. I can walk four or five miles without any trouble. The rubber foot is as good now as the first day. I travel up and down hills during the winter when they are very slippery, and never fall.

I remain, yours respectfully,
JNO. J. CRANE.

GIRARDVILLE, SCHUYLKILL CO., PA.

LEG ABOVE KNEE.

Fitted from Measurements.

MILL VILLAGE, ERIE CO., PA., Oct. 27, 1887.

A. A. MARKS:

DEAR SIR :—I am a telegraph operator and live two miles from the office. I walk that distance every night and morning. I have worn one of your artificial limbs for over two years, and I can cheerfully say that I think it has *no equal*.

My limb was made from *self-measurements* and is a *perfect fit*.

It is just as good to-day as it ever was ; in fact, there is nothing that I can see to wear out. My limb was amputated about six inches from the body. But I can walk almost as good as I could with the natural limb. The rubber foot is a *success*.

Very respectfully yours,
FRANK PORTER.

LEG ABOVE KNEE.

Fitted from Measurements.

Oct. 27, 1887.

A. A. MARKS:

DEAR SIR :—Yours of the 26th to hand and contents noted.

In reply would state that I will endorse any thing you wish to put in the pamphlet, for I think that the rubber foot is the best in the world. I am a segar-maker by occupation. I have stump 10 inches. I have worn leg nine years. I have walked as far as 20 miles in one day, and did not mind it as much as one of the men with me, for he had to go to bed and he had two good legs.

Respectfully yours,
J. F. SOURBEER.

246 Hummel Street, HARRISBURGH, PA.

LEG ABOVE KNEE.

Fitted from Measurements.

WOODBURY, BEDFORD CO., PA., Oct. 29, 1887.

MR. A. A. MARKS, New York City:

DEAR SIR :—The artificial leg which I received of you in October, 1885, with rubber foot is giving me perfect satisfaction in every respect. I have worn four different makes of legs inside of twenty-two years with ankle joints, and can truly say that I would not have a new leg with the ankle joint as a gift since I have been wearing your rubber foot. The first experience I had in wearing your rubber foot was in 1878. It was attached to a leg which I wore for seven years before. Then you made an entire new leg in 1885. I always used to have trouble with the ankle joint. At one time it left me walking on the end of the ankle without a foot. I have often been put out of my wits by having to get the joint repaired, and in fact they are only rattle traps at the best. My limb is a full-length limb. Stump about ten inches long. I am on my limb about fourteen hours a day. My occupation is a barber. Around town I hardly use a cane except in winter time. I can say I am proud of my rubber foot. No flap at each step, and one hundred people gazing at my feet.

I hope this may be the means of many a poor cripple's choosing your rubber-feet limbs to replace those they have lost. They come as near to the natural limbs as can be made.

I claim that from experience, which is the best schoolmaster.

Respectfully your friend,

E. E ROSE.

LEG ABOVE KNEE.

Emanuel Rectory, NEWPORT, R. I., Nov. 7, 1887.

MR. A. A. MARKS:

DEAR SIR:—In answer to your letter I have nothing to add to the letter I wrote you some years ago, save that a larger experience has only served to make me more satisfied with the work that you have done for me. The especial points that have given me satisfaction are three—viz : the leg fits well, it makes no noise, and needs no repairs.

Truly yours,

R. B. PEET, Rector.

LEG ABOVE KNEE.

WESTERLY, WASHINGTON CO., R. I., Nov. 30, 1887.

A. A. MARKS, ESQ.:

DEAR SIR:—I do not see why any one needs a testimonial to convince them that your legs are the best, when they need only to consider their construction to be convinced that it is so.

Yours respectfully,

O. S. CHAPMAN.

LEG ABOVE KNEE.

Fitted from Measurements.

S. J DOUTHIT, Master, Greenville County.

GREENVILLE C. H., S. C., June 22, 1885.

MR. A. A. MARKS:

DEAR SIR:—I received my artificial leg of your make, on the 6th inst., but have delayed acknowledging it, as I preferred to give it a trial. I have been using the leg every day since I received it, and am well pleased with it in every respect. It fits me perfectly; much better, in fact, than any I have had made by other manufacturers who had me present at the fitting. I think I can safely say that you may put me down as one of your customers from this on. I have three legs of other manufacturers, but I doubt that I shall ever use them after wearing yours.

Very truly yours,

S. J. DOUTHIT.
Judge of Probate.

LEG ABOVE KNEE.

Fitted from Measurements.

P. MONSERRAT, Fashionable Boot and Shoe Maker,

CHARLESTON, S. C., Nov. 9, 1887.

MR. A. A. MARKS:

DEAR SIR:—I have much pleasure in stating that the artificial leg I bought from you over four years ago has given me entire satisfaction and I can heartily recommend any one so unfortunate as to require such assistance to you. I have never lost an hour since I put your leg on. I never use a cane unless

going a long distance from home. I wear your leg all day long the year around without trouble.
Yours truly,
SEBASTIAN MONSERRAT.

LEG ABOVE KNEE.

COPPERAS HILL, ORANGE CO., VT., Oct. 31, 1887.

A. A. MARKS:

DEAR SIR:—I am a hard-working farmer, and have worn your artificial limb for over seventeen years, and still prefer it to any other make. I tried several kinds, but never found one that could compare with yours either in durability or comfort.

I have never paid a cent for repairs, and if I were to have another I should not hesitate to send to you. My limb is amputated below the knee. I have always had a perfect fit. If I were to give any advice to the world I would say to all, get A. A. Marks' artificial limb on account of the rubber foot.
Very truly,
CHARLES A. SARGENT.

LEG ABOVE KNEE.

ENOSBURGH FALLS, FRANKLIN CO., VT., Nov. 28, 1887.

A. A. MARKS:

DEAR SIR:—Prompted by a desire to aid any of my fellow-beings who may be afflicted like myself with the loss of a limb, I thought I would write you my endorsement of your artificial legs. During the past six years I have worn one. The point of amputation is about half way between the knee and hip, and although my occupation is very laborious, being that of a tanner, yet I experience very little inconvenience from using an artificial limb, owing to the perfect fit you gave me and excellent manner in which the leg works, especially the rubber foot. I would advise all who are in need of any thing of this kind if possible to get one of your make. You are at liberty to use the above in any manner you deem best in the interest of suffering humanity, while I remain
Gratefully yours,
CHARLES LUCIA.

LEG ABOVE KNEE.

Fitted from Measurements.

LONDON BRIDGE, PRINCESS ANNE CO., VA.

A. A. MARKS:

DEAR SIR:—I hereby testify that I have for a period of five years worn an artificial leg with rubber foot attached, manufactured by you for an amputation above the knee, the fitting of which was from measurements.

I claim it to be superior to any other for durability and comfort; during said five years cost of repairs has been fifty cents for spiral springs. I am, sir,
Yours truly,
JOHN F. DOZIER.

Occupation, Farmer.

LEG ABOVE KNEE.

Fitted from Measurements.

ALMOND & PITMAN, Importers, Manufacturers, and Dealers in Drugs and Medicines.
801 Main St., LYNCHBURG, CAMPBELL CO., VA.,
Nov. 1, 1887.

MR. A. A. MARKS:

DEAR SIR:—I am well pleased with your rubber foot, and find it easier to walk on and less expensive in way of repairs than any limb I have ever seen. I have worn limbs of several manufactures.

My limb was amputated at lower third of thigh. Occupation, Physician and Druggist. I am pleased with your new style of attaching suspenders.

Yours, etc.,
W. E. PITMAN, M.D.

LEG ABOVE KNEE.

Fitted from Measurements.

FAULKNER & CRAIGHILL, DRUGGISTS,
LYNCHBURG, VA., April 6, 1887.

A. A. MARKS, N. Y. :

DEAR SIR :—I have waited to write until a fair report could be made on the artificial leg lately furnished through us for Lloyd Cheatham. It is questionable if in your whole experience you have ever succeeded more perfectly in satisfying in every particular than in this case. All the measurements were taken very carefully, and the proof of their accuracy is evidenced in the fact that the *leg fitted perfectly in every way* and was put on as soon as received and *has been worn every day since.* He had never worn an artificial leg, and as soon as he put it on started off, of course on his crutches, and walked to his home *on the leg* more than a mile away. This was on the 10th of February. I never saw him again until about three weeks later, when he walked in our house, having discarded one of his crutches. In the course of another week he had discarded the other, and used only a cane. He can walk now without that, and with almost imperceptible limp, and there is reason to believe that that will disappear in time. From his appearance in walking or standing any one would never for a moment suppose he had an artificial leg, and when it is remembered that his amputation is above the knee, and that he has worn his leg less than two months, and that *he has never had to leave it off* from tender stump or other cause, his is a most remarkable case. He is perfectly delighted, and at his request this letter is written.

Respectfully yours,
ED. A. CRAIGHILL, M.D.,
of FAULKNER & CRAIGHILL.

LEG ABOVE KNEE.

Fitted from Measurements.

TOLEDO, LEWIS CO., WASH. TER., Oct. 29, 1887.

DEAR SIR :—The artificial leg I received from you in 1886 when at Lititz to replace the one I lost at Pueblo in 1882 has satisfied me fully. I had little confidence in artificial legs, as my stump had been out of use for four years and had become weak and stiff. After a few attempts on your leg I found that I could do very well on it. At this date I never use a cane and travel long distances. In regard to the rubber foot, I am so attached to it I would not consent to wear any other ; its movements are all I can ask for. My leg is in as good condition as when I received it and to all appearances will last six or eight years. I am five feet seven and one-half inches high and weigh one hundred and eighty-nine pounds, and am thirty-four years of age. I heartily urge all in need of artificial limbs to patronize you.

Respectfully,
WM. F. DUNCAN.

LEG ABOVE KNEE.

BOLLER & KUONI, dealers in General Merchandise and Produce, Wool, Seed, Dressed Poultry, Butter, Eggs,
SAUK CITY, SAUK CO., WIS., Dec. 8, 1887.

A. A. MARKS, ESQ., New York :

DEAR SIR :—In answer to your letter of Oct. 26th I state that I have worn an artificial leg of your manufacture since 1881, and so far am well pleased with it.

Respectfully yours,

C. KUONI.

LEG ABOVE KNEE.

FORT ATKINSON, JEFFERSON CO., WIS., Nov. 6, 1887.

A. A. MARKS:

MY DEAR SIR:—Two years ago to-day I put on one of your artificial legs with rubber foot. My left leg is amputated seven inches from my body, and by occupation I am a carpenter. I have worn artificial legs for over twenty-two years of different makes, and I must say that your make of leg beats them all. I hesitated a long while about getting your leg with rubber foot, but after wearing it two years I can say it has given perfect satisfaction. I can go up and down hill or up a ladder with it with perfect ease. It is apparently as sound to-day as it was when I took it from the factory, and I recommend it most highly to all who need an artificial leg.

Respectfully yours,

M. S. MOSES.
Late Corpl. Co. E, 81st N.Y. V. V. I.

LEG ABOVE KNEE.

Fitted from Measurements.

BELMONT, LA FAYETTE CO., WIS., Jan. 26, 1888.

TO WHOM IT MAY CONCERN:

When but eleven years old I had my left leg amputated about four inches from the body, and soon as I was able I purchased a leg from A. A. Marks of N. Y. City. After using it for three years it gives me pleasure to testify to its wonderful utility. When not in school I work on the farm, doing any of the ordinary work found there to do, as chopping wood, pitching grain, etc.

While attending school in Chicago I met many persons wearing different makes of artificial legs, but I can truthfully say that none walk with the ease and agility that I do. Aside from the superior merits of his limbs I recommend Mr. Marks for his very prompt and fair dealings. Any letters of inquiry will be promptly and cheerfully answered.

Respectfully,

O. L. TRENARY.

LEG ABOVE KNEE.

Nov. 12, 1887.

MR. A. A. MARKS:

DEAR SIR AND FRIEND:—I must drop you a few words of thanks. I have worn one of your artificial limbs for twelve years, and I consider it is the best leg made. My occupation is auctioneer and land agent, and some days I stand on my feet all day. I can and do travel from ten to fifteen miles per day.

I have been in company with men for years; and they never knew my leg was off until I told them. My leg is off above the knee. I know of a man who has worn one of your legs for eighteen years. He has bought two since, but he falls back on the Marks leg. Whenever I see a man with a limb off, I advise him to get a Marks limb. I consider the rubber foot a great benefit and also the simplicity of the knee joint. I could say lots more about your legs, but it is not necessary, as your limbs are widely known.

Ever your friend,

J. O. CUSHMAN.

MIFFLIN, IOWA CO., WIS.

LEG ABOVE KNEE.

LACOLLE, CANADA, Nov. 14, 1887.

A. A. MARKS, ESQ., New York City:

DEAR SIR:—I have much pleasure in stating that the artificial leg bought from you over two years ago has given me entire satisfaction, and I can heartily recommend any one unfortunate enough to require such assistance to you.

Yours very truly,
DUGAL CAMPBELL.

LEG ABOVE KNEE.

ST. ROSALIE JUNCTION, QUEBEC, CANADA, Nov. 5, 1887.

A. A. MARKS, ESQ.:

DEAR SIR:—I have been wearing one of your artificial limbs over three years with the utmost satisfaction. Point of amputation about six inches from the hip joint, and I weigh two hundred and sixty-nine pounds. I am a watchman in the G. T. Ry. and work from 7 at night until 7 in the morning. My limb has cost me nothing for repairs in all this time.

Respectfully,
G. P. HAMEL.

LEG ABOVE KNEE.

Nov. 3, 1887.

A. A. MARKS:

DEAR SIR:—It is now seventeen months since you fitted my son Edward (aged at the time eleven years) with one of your artificial legs above the knee. I desire to say that it has exceeded my expectations in every particular, not having had to use a walking-cane in twelve months. My acquaintances frequently express their surprise when they see him walking so well.

He has never neglected your advice as regards the proper care and preservation of the leg. It is as good now as it was the day you fitted it on. My wife and I shall always feel grateful to you for your marked kindness and attention to our boy during his stay at your establishment, and recommend you to any person desiring an artificial limb, as we know by the experience of our son that your rubber limbs are vastly superior to any other kind made. I remain,

Yours very truly,
WILLIAM WALSH.

285 Brussels St., ST. JOHN, N. B., CANADA.

LEG ABOVE KNEE.

Fitted from Measurements.

Dec. 14, 1887.

A. A. MARKS:

DEAR SIR:—Being among the many who have been so unfortunate as to have lost a limb, and tired of going about on crutches, I came to the conclusion to purchase an artificial leg.

Having consulted several makers (you being one of the many) I concluded to give the "rubber foot" a trial. It has since resulted that I made a very wise choice. My leg, as you are already aware, was amputated above the knee (four inches) nearly three years ago. About nine months after amputation had taken place I began to wear one of your patent artificial legs made from measurements sent you. I do not hesitate to state that I could not have had a better fit had I gone to the manufactory.

During the two years which I have constantly worn the leg I have not had to leave it off one hour, and since I have been wearing it it has never rubbed me at the point of bearing.

The advantages which your leg possesses over the other make of legs is, I think, in no small degree due to the rubber foot, because the graceful and almost natural movement is sufficient to deceive the most critical. Since I have been wearing this leg I have met other persons wearing different makes of legs. Before leaving them they wished they had one like mine. The noise made by them when walking was like a wheelbarrow being pushed over a pebbly walk. I am at St. Bonaventure's College, and indeed I think college life a pretty severe test for an artificial leg. I have to ascend over four flight of stairs every time I go to my room, and besides going through all the discipline of the college. I thought

when I had lost my leg I could never become a schoolboy again, but nature well knows "no prodigies remain," and, dear sir, to conclude, I can not but hope that your life may be prolonged for many years to come to be a benefactor to those who are so unfortunate as to be deprived of their limbs. I remain, dear sir,
Yours truly,
RICHARD DWYER.
RIVER HEAD, HARBOR GRACE, NEWFOUNDLAND.

LEG ABOVE KNEE.

Fitted from Measurements.

Dec. 2, 1887.

MR. A. A. MARKS:

DEAR SIR :—I received your kind and welcome letter, and I am glad to hear from you any time, for when I hear your name I feel as though I would like to take you by the hand and call you my friend, for I once thought no man living could do as much for another as you have done for me. About two years ago I caught a heavy chill in my leg, and I tried every doctor near at hand for a remedy. All proved helpless. Doctor Anderson told me that the only chance for my life was to have my leg taken off; I at once gave consent, giving up as I thought all the comforts of this life. I have since found that I was mistaken. While spending a few days in St. John I heard of a man that lost his leg and got another. I sought the man and found it was true, and to inform me further he loaned me one of your books, which I read for myself, and read to others what your artificial leg could do.

I thought it was all a fable; others told me it could not be that a man could skate and walk and jump with an artificial leg, but I have proved it to be true. I have been wearing one of your legs a little over twelve months, and I can do almost anything but fly. I have walked twelve miles in a day. I go shooting, fishing, and I don't care for any man. I have heard so many complaining with corns and with chilblains; I have one leg free from all this. I often wish I could tell to every body what a change I have had in my life since I have worn one of your artificial legs. I am not going to be like the fox who lost his tail and who wanted his brother foxes to cut off theirs; no, just come and see me and you will see about one of the happiest men in the world, who was once one of the most miserable.

I was speaking a little while ago to a man with a leg imported from England; it was made in London; when he saw what I could do he wanted to know how I got it; he told me he was going to condemn his.

Yours very truly,
URIAH BURSEY.
OLD PERTICAN, TRINITY BAY, NEWFOUNDLAND.

LEG ABOVE KNEE.

Fitted from Measurements.

MOUNT PLEASANT, RUNCORN, CHESHIRE, ENGLAND, Nov. 17, 1887.

DEAR SIR :—In answer to your letter I have great pleasure in testifying to the merits of your artificial leg. I have now worn it for five years, and am very glad to say I am quite satisfied with it. Not having worn any other make I am not able to speak from experience of the merits of yours over any other. But from what I have seen other people wearing, I am convinced that it is far in advance of all. The india-rubber foot is quite a marvel to every body, and for neatness and durability of construction it cannot be surpassed. I was fitted from measurements taken by a resident surgeon of the Liverpool Royal Infirmary (Mr. McCormick), and received an artificial leg from you and found it fitted quite comfortably. The point of amputation to which I have been subject is about two inches above the left knee. My occupation is that of a grocer, in a co-operative store, and the longest hours I am on my feet are on Fridays, about ten hours, and on Saturdays, from about 11 A. M. till 10:30 P. M.

I do not feel very tired after my work. I am glad to be able to say the cost of repairing the limbs made by you is so little that I could not attempt to reckon it up. You are at liberty to make whatever use you like of this testimonial, and if it should prove an inducement to any unfortunate fellow-being to try one of your artificial limbs, I should be glad to think I have done something to help relieve suffering humanity.

Yours truly, WALTER LACY.

To A. A. MARKS, ESQ.

LEG ABOVE KNEE.

Fitted from Measurements.

SHAG VALLEY STATION, WAIHEMO, OTAGO, NEW ZEALAND, July 10, 1884.

You may be pleased to hear that Mr. Trapski is successfully using the leg you made for him and can walk easily and quickly. He has every reason to be grateful to you for the trouble taken in his case, and will, I'm sure, readily recommend your firm to any one suffering from a like misfortune. In this recommendation I shall gladly join.

FRANK D. BELL.

LEG ABOVE KNEE.

Fitted from Measurements.

AMSTERDAM, HOLLAND, Nov. 23, 1887.

MR. A. A. MARKS, New York:

DEAR SIR:—In answer to your circular Oct. 26th, I take much pleasure in certifying that the two new legs you furnished me from measurements, give me great satisfaction in every respect. I have never seen legs of better construction, and I do not believe that any other kind would need less repairs.

The rubber foot and the knee joint are far superior to all others I ever saw; hence, I can strongly recommend your highly respectable firm to all others who need artificial limbs. I lost my left leg above knee, in the year 1872, crushed by an engine.

Allowing you to publish the above, if agreeable, I remain, dear sir,

Respectfully yours,

FRANCIS HERCKENRATH.

LEG ABOVE KNEE— STUMP ONE AND SEVEN-EIGHTHS INCHES LONG.

Fitted from Measurements.

Mr. A. A. MARKS:

DEAR SIR:—When thirteen years old, I lost my right leg and used a common wooden leg till I reached 44 years. By this time my attention was called to your artificial legs with rubber feet. I sent you my measure and got a leg from you which I have used ever since, now for about six years. I am very well satisfied with it. It fits me admirably, and has required no repairs worth mentioning. The new suspenders are a real improvement. The stump, though only one and seven-eighths inches, has never been sore since I used the leg, which was formerly a usual occurrence.

Yours gratefully,

COPENHAGEN, DENMARK, Nov. 21, 1887. G. HEINEMAN.

LEG ABOVE KNEE.

Translated from the Spanish.

Private Correspondence of the Postmaster General.

ORIZABA, MEXICO, Nov. 20, 1887.

A. A. MARKS, ESQ., New York:

DEAR SIR:—Five years ago I was afflicted with the necessity of having my right leg amputated four centimeters above the knee joint, and since that time have used one of your patent artificial legs with rubber foot. Up to this time I have not only found it unnecessary to repair the leg, but can, with a few touches of varnish, give it an appearance equal to new, in spite of the constant use I put it to daily, both on foot and on horseback.

It is solid in construction, extremely light, perfect in form, and easily managed. It is difficult by mere sight to distinguish from a natural leg, as it possesses a close resemblance to nature, that is only rivaled by that extreme similarity between one drop of water and another drop. I walk perfectly without a cane every day, and every day congratulate myself more and more on having sent my order to you, because I believe that without any question you are unequaled by any other house in the world in the manufacture of artificial limbs.

I constantly recommend your house on all available occasions, and I listen with pleasure to the praise my leg elicits from persons who admire its simplicity and perfection of workmanship.

In making this statement (in a form suitable for publication) I am merely rendering due homage to the truth and to the indisputable merits of your establishment. I am, sir,

Very respectfully yours,
E. GUASP DE PERIS.

LEG ABOVE KNEE.

Translated from the Spanish.

MEXICO, Nov. 27, 1882.

A. A. MARKS, ESQ. :

DEAR SIR :—I have taken pleasure in recommending your artificial legs to parties needing them, whom I have met in this city during my present sojourn here. I use the leg you made for me daily, and find it more firm and simple than any I have had made elsewhere. I remain,

Yours,
FEDERICO LARRANAGA,
Consul General of Peru in Panama.

LEG ABOVE KNEE.

Fitted from Measurements.

Translated from the Spanish.

Mineral de la Encarnacion, ESTADO DE HIDALGO, MEXICO.
Nov. 28, 1887.

A. A. MARKS, ESQ., New York :

DEAR SIR :—In compliance with your request I would beg to say the leg you made me is much more satisfactory than the one I used before. I can walk perfectly with it, although the ground is very uneven here. I feel very grateful to you, as all should be who have been relieved by you as I have been, after so much suffering. You are at perfect liberty to publish this if desired.

Respectfully,
ADOLFO PEREZ.

LEG ABOVE KNEE.

PEREZ & PARRAGA,
SAN SALVADOR, CENTRAL AMERICA, Jan. 24, 1883.

MR. A. A. MARKS, New York :

MOST ESTEEMED SIR :—I have been for a long time desirous of writing you and expressing my continued satisfaction with the artificial leg you made for me, and now avail myself of the opportunity.

It is six years since I obtained an artificial leg from you ; during this period I have not had an opportunity to find the least fault with it. I walk very much and without a cane or support. I suffer no pain or uneasiness from it.

Since I have returned to Central America I find it necessary to make long journeys on horseback. In this the leg has assisted me very much. I pride myself on my easy and graceful movements and the facility with which I mount and dismount.

The india-rubber foot which is on the artificial leg is a most excellent invention; without it I question my ability to walk with safety in this country, the streets are so very rough and stony.

My leg is my best friend; it is what I love the most, and without it my life would be miserable. I shall always feel grateful to the esteemed inventor, and, wishing him abundant business and a happy new year, I am,

Your attentive friend,
MANUEL A. PARRAGA.

LETTER FROM THE SON OF THE PRESIDENT OF THE REPUBLIC OF PERU.—LEG ABOVE KNEE.

Fitted from Measurements.

Translated from the Spanish.

LIMA, PERU, SOUTH AMERICA, Nov. 25, 1885.

MR. A. A. MARKS, New York City:

MY DEAR SIR:—I take great pleasure in assuring you that the artificial leg which I ordered of you, to replace the one I lost in the engagement of August 27, 1884, has proved to my entire satisfaction.

It is just that I should recommend your work, since I have been enabled to avail myself of it to such advantage.

In tendering to you this testimony of my gratitude I would add that you are at liberty to publish it if you desire. I am,

Yours very truly,
ABSOLON M. YGLESIAS.

LEG ABOVE KNEE.

Fitted from Measurements.

Translated from the Spanish.

LIMA, PERU, S. A., Nov. 24, 1887.

A. A. MARKS, ESQ.:

DEAR SIR:—Words fail to express the gratitude I feel towards you for the great invention you have achieved in your "Patent Artificial Legs"; it would be impossible to conceive of greater perfection in the imitation of nature. The naturalness of movement, simplicity of mechanism, weight, and in fact, everything render it possible to manage them with the utmost ease. I at first despaired of managing my leg, as has been done in some instances cited in your pamphlet, but by dint of untiring perseverance I am convinced now that all you claim for them is true. And to-day no one not in the secret, could tell that I wear an artificial leg, the short time that I have had it notwithstanding. I should like this letter brought before the notice of all those persons who like myself have been unfortunate enough to lose a limb, and for which you are the only person competent to supply a substantial and perfect substitute.

Renewing my expressions of gratitude, I take pleasure in subscribing myself
Yours very respectfully, MIGUEL P. BRAVO.

WEARING KNEE-BEARING ARTIFICIAL LEGS.

KNEE-BEARING AMPUTATION.

Fitted from Measurements.

2057 Delgany St., DENVER, COLO., Nov. 3, 1887.

A. A. MARKS, 701 Broadway, N. Y.:

DEAR SIR:—Your note of inquiry as to the condition of my leg made by you in April, 1883, at hand. In reply will say the limb is in perfect condition. I have worn it constantly since I got it and have not paid one cent for repairs except for the elastic spring. I thought I had made a mistake in taking my measure; at first (as I measured for it myself without any assistance) it seemed too long, but when I became accustomed to it I found it all right, and still so find it.

I am a builder (carpenter by trade) and have as many as twenty-four men in my employ at one time, and can clearly say the men who can do as much work as I can at the bench, or putting work up, are very scarce. Very few people know I have an artificial limb. I can throw my full weight on the limb and lift all I am able to without pain or inconvenience, thanks to the doctor who suggested the point of amputation enabling me to wear the knee-bearing leg.

Very respectfully yours,
M. L. BELL.

KNEE-BEARING AMPUTATION.

Oct. 28, 1887.

A. A. MARKS, New York :

DEAR SIR:—I am writing to express my thoughts about your artificial limbs. I have worn one of them seven years continuously, and have not had it repaired once during that time. I cannot express my delight in having found so great a treasure. I have worked nearly all the time during the seven years, and can safely say that without the leg I could have done nothing. And also if I want another I shall know where to get a good one, and that at the place I got this one. I am,

Respectfully yours,
WILLIAM HICKERSON.

WESTPORT, FAIRFIELD CO., CONN.

KNEE-BEARING AMPUTATION.

Seventeen years on a " Salamander" leg.

P. O. Department, WASHINGTON, D. C., Oct. 27, 1887.

MR. A. A. MARKS :

ESTEEMED FRIEND :—Your favor of the 26th (yesterday) received and read with extreme pleasure, and any thing I can say in regard to your Salamander leg will be said in a few words.

You made one for me in September, 1870, and I have worn it with the exception of about five months up to the present time.

It has cost me about $2.75 for repairs, and I intend to wear it three years longer. The rubber foot is a grand success, and I do not want any better leg (except the natural one).

I wore one of —— legs for five years, and it cost me fifty dollars for the *grand improvement*, and it cost me in the five years nearly sixty dollars for repairs, and I would not wear one of them for a gift. I am a clerk in the post office department.

My leg is off 1¼ inches below the knee, and the leg is knee-bearing.

Sincerely yours,
WELLINGTON GLENN.

KNEE-JOINT AMPUTATION.

Wears No. 115 leg.

SAYBROOK, McLAIN CO., ILL., Nov. 8, 1887.

MR A. A. MARKS:

DEAR SIR :—I have worn your artificial leg for about seventeen years.
I am a shoemaker by trade. Knee amputation.
Repairs amounted in the whole to about four dollars.
I think that the rubber foot is better than any other kind.
It is more pliable.

Yours respectfully,
R. C. CHAINEY.

KNEE-BEARING AMPUTATION.

OAKLEY, LOGAN CO., KANSAS, Nov. 19, 1887.

A. A. MARKS, ESQ. :

DEAR SIR:—In regard to my experience in using an artificial leg will say that I have worn an artificial leg 22 years.

Two of ——, one ——, and one of A. A. Marks' rubber feet.

The rubber foot I have worn for twelve years. Repairs and oil, 25 cents. It cannot be any more and be artificial. It gives a soft-like, safe step. I am a stone mason and builder. My work is on rough ground, with spall, fragments, and rubbish as usually seen about stone buildings while under construction. This is the place to test an artificial leg. No other leg ever did so much good until I tried the rubber foot. I will give a few rough ideas of the common sense of it. 1st, It has a stiff ankle joint which, though apparently a disadvantage, is really its charm.

I can stand on the heel or toe at will; this gives me great advantage in turning about and getting around lively. The joint will flap on all other legs as soon as a little weight is applied to them. They will then be flat on the ground, and it will be impossible to turn until the weight is relieved.

If on a sidehill, roof, or ladder the joint is not safe, but the rubber foot is always safe. I got my leg on Government order. I have twice drawn commutation money, $75 each time; total, $150. Mr. ——'s limbs cost me $25 to $50 every five years in repairs. I might say much more in favor of your limbs, but space forbids. Any person wanting to know about your limb I will cheerfully answer all communications if a P. O. stamp is enclosed. Last year I accepted the foremanship on the Kansas division of U. P. R. R. I had from forty to fifty men. This year I accepted the foremanship of the Pioneer Town Site Co., doing business at Russell Spring, Logan Co., Kansas. I built the court house. It is a fine stone structure, one of the finest buildings in Kansas. I directed all the building for the company, perhaps $100,000 worth. I now have the superintendence of 150 men.

Any thing I can do for you in the loyal State full of old vets will be only a pleasure.

Respectfully yours,

GEO. E. KERNS.

KNEE-BEARING AMPUTATION.

95 Madison Street, GRAND RAPIDS, MICH., Oct. 31, 1887.

A. A. MARKS, ESQ.:

DEAR SIR:—Your leg made for me fourteen years ago I am wearing yet; it has given the best satisfaction.

I have worn it continually and it is in good order yet.

If I should want another leg I would send to you and get it.

I am on the road continually and have given my leg some pretty hard trials.

Yours very respectfully,

HEMAN BLODGETT.

KNEE-BEARING AMPUTATION.

EAST GILEAD, BRANCH CO., MICH., Oct. 31, 1887.

A. A. MARKS, ESQ., NEW YORK:

I have worn artificial legs for twenty-two years, have during that time worn out two, and have had the third one now three years, this last one being of your make. I regard the one I am wearing now as being far superior in many ways to the other two. I wear what is termed a knee-bearing leg, it being so constructed that the superincumbent weight is borne by the bent knee in a socket fixed to receive it in that shape.

Your make of leg gives me a better gait in walking than the others. I have had a great many people ask me why it is that I am not near so lame as I used to be. This leg does not give me near the trouble to keep in repair, as the others, the rubber foot doing away with need of machinery below the knee.

I would state that I regard the rubber foot as being one of the greatest improvements in artificial limbs. In point of durability, from what I can see now, it seems that this leg will outwear the others. I am a country merchant, and actively engaged in the details of my business.

CHARLES CARROLL.

KNEE-BEARING AMPUTATION.

Fitted from Measurements.

Nov. 1, 1887.

A. A. MARKS:

DEAR SIR :—In 1874 I heard of your making rubber feet. I took my measure and sent it to you for one of your knee-bearing limbs. I have worn it every day now for 13 years without any repairs, and I think it will last 3 or 4 years yet. I have examined all makes of artificial limbs both in this country and Europe during the last twenty-five years that I have been wearing an artificial limb, and will say that for practicability, durability, and comfort they surpass any artificial limb made in the world.

Yours truly, T. N. WEEKS.

BUTTE CITY, SILVER BOW CO., MONT.

KNEE-BEARING AMPUTATION.

BRIGHTON, POLK CO., MO., Nov. 2, 1887.

MR. A. A. MARKS:

DEAR SIR :—After wearing one of your artificial limbs for six months and over, I am well satisfied with it and more than pleased with the rubber foot. It works like a charm, far superior to the old-fashioned wooden foot. I wore one of them for five years prior to yours. As to the durability of your leg I think it will last a lifetime. My leg was amputated at the knee joint and is a hard stump to fit, but your artificial leg fits superbly.

I can now walk with ease and enjoy life.

Yours ever,

C. W. SHERMAN.

KNEE-BEARING AMPUTATION.

W. W. ENGLISH,
The Celebrated Door Check.
LINCOLN, NEB., Nov. 1, 1887.

MR. A. A. MARKS:

DEAR SIR :—I have worn artificial limbs for twenty-three years. During that time I have had three different kinds. The leg that you made for me is the boss; I have worn it now for one year, and I like it better every day. The rubber foot cannot be excelled. There is no clank or clatter in the rubber foot, as there are no joints to be wearing out, or springs to break, as in the old style. I walk two or three miles every day, going to and from my office, with perfect ease. My limb is amputated below the knee, and I use a knee-bearing limb.

It fits me splendidly ; I do not have to wear straps or suspenders to keep it on. A lady met me on the street to-day and said : "Why, Mr. English, you walk so well no person would hardly know that you wear an artificial limb." I heartily recommend your limbs made with rubber feet to every person in need, and especially to my old comrades in the late unpleasantness.

Respectfully yours,

W. W. ENGLISH.

KNEE-BEARING AMPUTATION.

Fitted from Measurements.

OMAHA, DOUGLASS CO., NEB., Oct. 30, 1887.

A. A. MARKS, ESQ. :

DEAR SIR :—I beg to add my testimony to the merits and superior qualities of your excellent artificial legs. Having worn one of them long enough to be able to judge, I will say that in my estimation they can not be surpassed in anything that goes to make a perfect artificial substitute, to say nothing of their simple and common-sense construction, which alone should commend them to favor.

I desire especially to speak for the rubber foot, which is truly a great discovery and a blessing to the wearer. The very fact of its being rubber, which is soft, ought to lead to its adoption by every one hearing of it or requiring it, approaching nature as it does more closely than a wooden foot ever can. I also desire to express to you my admiration for you as a skillful artisan, having made a leg for me from measurements only, which fits perfectly, is very comfortable, and enables me to walk about with an easy, natural step, notwithstanding that my case differs somewhat from most others, being an amputation in the knee joint and requiring a knee-bearing leg of special construction.

I shall always take pleasure in recommending your house, and with best wishes for your prosperity, I am,

Very truly yours,

H. G. J. LEHMAN,
1619 Howard St.

KNEE-BEARING AMPUTATION.

LAKEVIEW, PASSAIC Co., N. J., Oct. 27, 1887.

MR. A. A. MARKS:

DEAR SIR:—In complying with your request of the 26th, I hasten to say I will give with pleasure my recommendation of your limbs. I will say that I have worn your legs for the last 25 years, and in that time put them to the severest test. Having worked at my trade, that of a machinist, up to a few years back, I have taken my part in handling the heaviest machinery in all conceivable positions both in marine engine building, locomotive work, and in pedestrianism.

I have acted as a sewing machine agent in this and other cities, and would carry a machine on my back two and more flights of stairs and think nothing of it. The lasting qualities of your leg without repair, in my experience, which I judge to be tougher than most other people's, is on an average seven years. The elastic rubber foot is one of the most charming features of your artificial limbs, doing away with the disagreeable clicking noise which ankle joints give to most legs, also giving a firmer step and more natural tread to the walking, so that you are not in constant dread of breaking down and becoming helpless on some lonely road, as I have been with some of the old-fashioned joint legs. So far as my judgment goes, your legs will last longer, give better satisfaction, and cost as little as any of the legs that are now made or before the public for the use of the unfortunates.

Respectfully yours,

JAMES RAWSON.

KNEE-BEARING AMPUTATION.

Nov. 4, 1887.

MR. A. A. MARKS:

DEAR SIR:—Having worn an artificial limb of your make, I would say that for comfort, ease, and durability they are far superior to any artificial foot I have ever used; this is the second one I have had of yours, and it is in the neighborhood of 13 years that it has been in constant use, and it is much better than Dr. ——'s to-day. I have done all kinds of farming work, and all kinds of lumbering work, hauling logs, etc., and also a great deal of hunting, which is hard on a wooden leg; it is a very honest, upright leg, and as long a time as I have worn it there has been no rattling whatever. I do most heartily recommend them to all, or any one who may be in need of an artificial limb. I expect to take the third one soon, if I am spared to need its use, as I do not intend to wear any other parties' make.

Respectfully yours,

JONATHAN BURRELL.

WASHINGTON, WARREN Co., N. J.

KNEE-BEARING AMPUTATION.

347 West 16th St., New York City, Oct. 29, 1887.

Dear Sir : I have neglected to keep the promise I made a year ago to inform you of my experience with your artificial leg.

The result of our deal was both creditable to you and satisfactory to me. While the artificial limb has been found to be all you promised for it, it has also been the means of enabling me to resume my ordinary work, consequently I may look upon you in an especial manner as my benefactor. The socket of the leg could not be better adapted to my stump; it fits the parts admirably, causes me no discomfort, and still is quite snug. The entire limb apparently remains in as good condition as when first applied, although since then it has been employed without one day's interruption. As far as durability is concerned, the leg shows no wear and bids fair to have as much longevity as the famous "one-horse shay," while the only expense it has entailed for a year has been the price of a couple of stump socks.

You know that "he that is well hath no need of a physician." This may be the reason of my tardiness in making known my appreciation for what you have done for me. I am not ungrateful for favors, although often careless in returning thanks; but had I not been perfectly satisfied with the leg I would have been troubling you long before now. I am employed in the Gas Works at 18th St., North River, and to any person seeking such information I will be pleased to recommend your artificial limbs. In giving this advice I am not prompted by any motive except a wish to render a substantial service. The rubber foot is an invaluable and indispensable part of the leg. I cannot speak too highly of its many advantages. It inspires a certain confidence, a reliability which dispels all fear of falling, and like Davy Crockett one feels that, his position being safe and "all right," he has nothing to do "but go ahead." The application of motion at the ankle, which is at the mercy of a weak pivot of a screw, is only of advantage while the screw lasts. But I feel assured from observation that a movable ankle joint is really an impediment to good locomotion. It acts like a constant menace. A friend of mine bought one of ——'s limbs some time ago, and he says that ever since his perambulations might well be compared with those practiced by a raw recruit of the army who walks by count; that is to say, he goes along muttering inaudibly two words—one, two; one, two. With his foot bobbing up and down, how can a person feel sure of his foothold or expect to walk naturally ?

Besides, the fear of a misstep keeps his mind under a great strain, similar to that of the recruit who stands in fear of rebuke for his awkwardness. There was a fox once that lost his tail and then persuaded all the other foxes to have their tails cut off in order that they might appear to be in the fashion. But I do not want any one to forfeit a natural limb in order that they might enjoy with me the advantages of wearing one of your artificials. A lifelong residence in New York, with a sojourn of several months a couple of years since in Bellevue, the largest hospital on this continent, would seem to qualify me to express an opinion and to use some judgment in the choice of artificial limbs. In conclusion, I beg to state that after careful comparison of artificial limbs offered by four different makers in this city my preference must be awarded to the appliances patented and brought to such perfection by you.

Dear sir, with assurance of my highest respect and esteem,

I am, very truly yours,
DENNIS O'KEEFE.

KNEE-BEARING AMPUTATION.

Oct. 26, 1887.

A. A. Marks :

Dear Sir :—Having worn one of your patent artificial limbs for the past twenty years, I have no hesitation in saying that with the improvements made in my last limb, which I procured a short time since, the rubber foot far surpasses any that I have ever used, one of which was that of the best of other makers, the cost of keeping your leg in repair being but very trifling, as there is nothing about them to require much expense in so doing.

Respectfully yours,
MRS. ALFRED ROBERTS.
506 Hudson St., NEW YORK CITY.

P. S. You are at liberty to refer any of my sex in need of such aid as you can give, to me, and I will give them ocular proof of what I say.

KNEE-JOINT AMPUTATION.

Nov. 14, 1887.

DEAR MR. MARKS : I have worn the leg you made for me nearly six years and I have no fault to find with it. My limb is amputated in the knee joint. I never used any thing to help me to walk, a cane nor any thing else. My occupation was a dressmaker, but now I am housekeeping for myself.

My address is 670 9th Ave., NEW YORK CITY.

MAGGIE DUFFY.

KNEE-BEARING AMPUTATION.

Fitted from Measurements.

PLATTSBURGH, CLINTON CO., N. Y., Oct. 28, 1887.

A. A. MARKS, ESQ.:

DEAR SIR :—In 1864 my right leg was amputated near and below the knee. I procured one of your knee-bearing rubber-foot limbs, one of which I used nearly fourteen years without repair and it is a pretty good limb yet. I walk considerable, and I think, judging from seeing others walk who use a different make of limb, I get around as well if not better than they. I would not exchange for any other that I have seen in use.

Yours respectfully,
J. PARMERTER.

KNEE-BEARING AMPUTATION.

CAZENOVIA SEMINARY, CAZENOVIA, MADISON CO., N. Y., Nov. 8, 1887.

MR. A. A. MARKS :

DEAR SIR :—I have worn an artificial limb of your make for about fifteen years. Previously I had worn one of a different manufacture, but I did not like it. Since wearing one of your make I have walked more easily and with much less noise. The expense of keeping the leg in repair has been very little indeed, and I am confident that no other could have been more satisfactory.

Very truly yours,
I. N. CLEMENTS, Principal.

KNEE-JOINT AMPUTATION.

Oct. 28, 1887.

DEAR SIR :—I have been wearing your make of artificial limb with rubber foot for about nine years, and I must say that I consider them the best that are made for durability, elegance, fit, and movements. The expenses for repairs have been trifling. My limb was amputated in the knee, and the artificial limb assists me in doing my housework. I can do all my work as well as though I had my own natural limb. I can recommend your make of artificial limbs with rubber feet to be the best manufactured.

MRS. ELLA E. MILLER.

2113 E. TIOGA ST., PHILADELPHIA, PA.

KNEE-JOINT AMPUTATION.

Walks up and down Stairs Three Stories High.

SUBLIMITY, MARION CO., OREGON, Nov. 19, 1887.

MR. A. A. MARKS:

DEAR SIR:—I have worn your artificial limbs sixteen years, and I must say that I am entirely satisfied; it is the most durable leg that I have ever had; my leg is amputated at the knee joint, and must say that I have walked as far as fourteen miles in a rough country. I have worked at haying and hoeing, and worked with a threshing machine. I have also been night watchman at the Oregon State Insane Asylum for one year, going up and down stairs in the building, which was three stories high.

I have had three legs from other makers before I tried yours, each one being of a different construction; they were all unsatisfactory. I use a cane very seldom, because I leave it stand or forget when I go about. I recommend your limbs to all who are in need of them.

Yours truly,

ERNST BAKER.

KNEE-BEARING AMPUTATION.

MT. PLEASANT MILL, SNYDER CO., PA., Nov. 2, 1887.

Having had the misfortune to lose one of my legs the 27th of September, 1886, amputated at knee joint with the patella retained, I can now wear one of A. A. Marks' artificial legs, and must say it gives me perfect satisfaction. I consider the india-rubber foot a great improvement. Dispensing with the machinery of the ankle joint, it also gives as much lateral motion on uneven ground as is necessary, and I am delighted to say that he has accomplished the difficult problem of enabling me to get support during progression on the end of the stump instead of entirely on the sides.

His plain and simple mode of constructing artificial limbs is to my mind unquestionably the best, and when asked by poor legless persons as to whose make of artificial limbs would be the best to secure for comfort and utility, I most decidedly say, without any hesitation, A. A. Marks'.

Yours with respect,

MARAND ROTHROCK, M.D.

KNEE-BEARING AMPUTATION.

Fitted from Measurements.

BLACKS, YORK CO., S. C., Nov. 23, 1887.

A. A. MARKS, ESQ., 701 Broadway, N. Y.:

DEAR SIR:—Yours of the 26th to hand. I would say that I am very glad to recommend your artificial limbs to any one, as I have been wearing one of your knee-bearing legs for over twelve months with much ease and no expense to me at all. I am a clerk in a retail store, and do a great deal of walking, but I find your rubber foot the very thing for walking all day on the floor, I can also say that my limb was fitted from measurements and is a perfect fit. I am willing to answer any letter of inquiry that may be sent to me. I am,

Yours truly,

W. B. ANTHONY.

KNEE-BEARING AMPUTATION.

MARTINSBURG, BERKELEY CO., W. VA., Dec. 15, 1887.

A. A. MARKS:

DEAR SIR:—Now as to the merits of your rubber foot I will say they can not be excelled. The leg you made for me in 1870 was in constant use for fifteen years, and I know it did not cost me over one dollar for repairs. I neither used shoulder straps or front strap on it. The leg you made for me in

1875 I only commenced to wear in 1885. I don't retract any thing I wrote you in 1875, which you will find in your pamphlet of 1884, page 52. When the time comes for me to receive another, I shall call on you to make it.

Yours respectfully,
WILLIAM DEAN SMITH.

KNEE-BEARING AMPUTATION.

Translated from the Spanish.

SANTIAGO DE CUBA, Dec. 12, 1885.

MR. A. A. MARKS :
Gratitude is one of the noblest sentiments of the human heart. My duty is not only to express my gratitude to you, but to pay a tribute of justice to merit. While at sea I was thrown from the walking-beam of an engine and lost my leg. During the period of convalescence I learned of your celebrity and procured one of your legs. Thus I find myself with my left leg replaced by your skill to such remarkable perfection that I am actually restored to my usefulness.

Your obedient servant,
JOAQUIN RICALO MUQUERCIA.

KNEE-BEARING AMPUTATION.

Fitted from Measurements.

Translation from the Spanish.

ARROYO, PORTO RICO, Nov. 17, 1885.

MR. A. A. MARKS :
DEAR SIR :—I take great pleasure in stating that the artificial leg you made and sent to me I have worn constantly. It gives me complete satisfaction. Four times daily I walk from one town to another, a distance of four miles, without fatigue.

JOSE MARIE LEBRON.

WEARING BELOW-KNEE LEGS.

BELOW-KNEE AMPUTATION.

Louisville & Nashville Railroad Company, Transportation Department.
MONTGOMERY, ALA., Jan. 9, 1888.

A. A. MARKS, ESQ., New York :
DEAR SIR :—It affords me great pleasure to add my endorsement to your already large list of testimonials. While employed as conductor on the L. & N. R. R., in Oct., 1886, I had my foot so badly mashed as to necessitate amputation about five inches above the ankle. Four months afterwards I called on you in your city, and was fitted up for duty again with one of your rubber feet, and after wearing it as I have I would have no other.

I have now worn it for about one year, and have never lost a single minute on account of it. Two weeks after I left your office I could walk all day without the use of a cane. I have met several persons wearing other makes, and they pronounce my walking the best they have ever seen, and I have never seen any one who could equal it. Persons who have worn legs for years say I can walk better than they can. I meet people every day and associate with them in business for weeks before they find out I wear an artificial. I can keep a good walker busy keeping up with me when walking. I can cheerfully recommend the rubber foot to any who may be so unfortunate as to have to wear them.

Yours truly,
W. K. ATKINSON.

BELOW-KNEE AMPUTATION.

Fitted from Measurements.

TROY, PIKE CO., ALA., Nov. 3, 1887.

MR. MARKS:

DEAR SIR:—I am well pleased with your foot. I have been wearing your leg fourteen months. I have been going to school and preparing for business. Mr. Marks, I walked twelve miles Wednesday night, serenading, all around the neighborhood.

Yours truly,
M. V. THRASHER.

BELOW-KNEE AMPUTATION.

Fitted from Measurements.

PLANO, TULARE CO., CAL., Nov. 15, 1887.

A. A. MARKS:

DEAR SIR:—The leg and foot that you sent for my son in 1876 lasted remarkably well for such an energetic fellow, hardly still a moment, and when he goes he will get there as soon as the best of them. The limb performed to satisfaction in every respect and has lasted ten years.

Respectfully,
WM. THOMSON.

BELOW-KNEE AMPUTATION.

Fitted from Measurements.

TEHAMA, TEHAMA CO., CAL., Dec. 26, 1887.

A. A. MARKS:

DEAR SIR:—My leg was amputated about three inches above the ankle joint. I have worn an artificial leg made by you for more than three years. It has given me entire satisfaction, inasmuch as I am enabled to attend to all my former duties without interruption. I frequently follow a plow all day, often twenty miles, run a header, and do other such arduous work.

The cost of repairs during that time has not exceeded three dollars. I can conscientiously recommend your work to all persons in need of artificial limbs.

J. T. STILLWELL.

BELOW-KNEE AMPUTATION.

Fitted from Measurements.

Dec. 2, 1887.

MR. A. A. MARKS:

DEAR SIR:—The leg you made for me four years ago from measurements which I sent you has given entire satisfaction.

I have seen a great number of people wearing artificial limbs, but I have not met with any one who can get around as well as I can. Have been in rough places in the mountains where any one would think it was impossible for a man wearing an artificial limb to climb around. Can ride horseback or walk long distances almost as good as any man who has two good legs.

Therefore I can recommend it to any person as the best artificial limb made, as I have seen nearly all that are in the market.

I am by occupation an engineer, and my leg has had pretty rough usage at times, but has not cost me a cent in repairs for the four years I have been wearing it.

        Yours truly,   Wm. Willoughby.
 Grass Valley, Nevada Co., Cal.

BELOW-KNEE AMPUTATION.

Nov. 3, 1887.

Mr. A. A. Marks:

Dear Sir:—After using one of your artificial legs for ten years I am glad to give a testimony to its merits—a good fit, perfectly easy, and for durability it has no equal. The cost of repairs is not worth mentioning, and the value of it for one who has lost a leg where I have, which is about eight inches from the foot, can not be estimated. Thousands of dollars could not give me the comfort that my artificial leg has. My occupation since I have had the artificial limb is keeping a clothing store.

       Yours very truly,   John Farrel.
 Grass Valley, Nevada Co., California.

BELOW-KNEE AMPUTATION.

Fitted from Measurements.

Nov. 9, 1887.

Mr. A. A. Marks, New York City:

Dear Sir:—I have worn one of your artificial legs with a rubber foot (below the knee) for over seven years, for which I sent the measurement from this city. It proved a perfect fit, and never gave me any trouble during this time. I have given it a thorough trial, having worked in a hay and grain store and wood and coal yard, where there is heavy lifting, and it has only cost a trifle to repair the shoulder-strap once. I had worn the —— artificial leg for several years, and the springs and cords were continually breaking and needing repairs.

I consider your leg with rubber foot far superior, more durable, easier, and more comfortable to walk with than any artificial leg made at the present time.

I shall certainly recommend your legs in preference to any other as the best. Wishing you success in your business, I remain,

       Yours respectfully,   Daniel W. Holmes.
 390 Francisco St., San Francisco, Cal.

BELOW-KNEE AMPUTATION.

Santa Rosa, Sonoma Co, Cal., Dec. 11, 1887.

To all those who are so unfortunate as to have to wear artificial limbs:

I have been wearing A. A. Marks' legs for seventeen years.

They have always given good satisfaction; for durability they can not be excelled. I have been roughing on them for years, climbing mountains where neither horse or mule could travel, and intend to continue to wear them while I live. I can recommend them to any one that is so unfortunate as to need an artificial leg.

I have been mining and prospecting in the Shasta Mountains, and it tries the metal of artificial legs.

        Yours,   Benj. Speelman.

BELOW-KNEE AMPUTATION.

Fitted from Measurements.

"Run, jump, climb, and skate."

Needles, San Bernardino Co., Cal., Nov. 10, 1887.

A. A. Marks, New York:

Dear Sir:—My son John Jerome Booth, aged ten years, who had the misfortune to lose a foot about five years ago, has used one of your artificial limbs for the past four years with complete satisfaction. Soon after procuring the Marks limb I concluded to try ——, and for that purpose ordered one with lateral motion. Here, then, I had a fair opportunity for competitive trial. As a result, the leg was returned for repairs in six months, while the Marks is at present in use, having been returned but once during the entire time, and that only for lengthening to suit the height of the growing boy. The little fellow runs, jumps, climbs, and skates as well as any of his companions, and the closest observers, when informed of his misfortune, are at a loss to determine which is the real and which the artificial limb.

I would be ungrateful, too, if I did not refer to the universally prompt, polite, and obliging manner which has characterized your dealings with me. Heartily recommending the Marks artificial limbs to the maimed, I am,

Your obedient servant,
JAMES P. BOOTH, M.D.,
Surgeon A. & P. R. R. Co.

BELOW-KNEE AMPUTATION.

Nov. 1, 1887.

A. A. MARKS:

DEAR SIR:—I am now wearing the leg that was made for me in September, and it fits me very well. As you perhaps remember, I purchased a leg from you in 1863, before you used the rubber foot, and since then I have worn the —— leg, and the —— leg, and, as you know, I have used the rubber foot a great deal of the time, since you introduced it in the market, and I think it is far ahead of any leg that I have worn, for durability and economy, and I always feel safe when wearing the rubber foot, as there are no springs or cords to break, no squeaking or clattering sound to attract the notice of people as I pass by, and there is nothing to oil, except the knee joints, which can be done in a few moments, and then my mind is easy, so far as the leg is concerned, for the next two or three days. As for repairs, I would state that I have worn the rubber foot for a straight seven years without spending a nickel, except for oil for the knee joints, and 25 cents will cover that item. My leg is amputated about four inches below the knee, and my occupation is a clerk.

I do considerable walking every day. My weight is about 163 pounds.
Respectfully yours,
THOMAS GIBSON.

561 Mission St., SAN FRANCISCO, CAL.

N. B. You will perhaps remember that the leg I got from you in 1863 was a present from my comrades of Co. B, 5th New Jersey Vol. Infantry.

BELOW-KNEE AMPUTATION.

Fitted from Measurements.

Office of County Coroner,
MANITOU SPRINGS, EL PASO CO., COLO., Jan 14, 1888.

MR. A. A. MARKS:

DEAR SIR:—I wish to state to you that the last leg ordered from you for W. C. Allen, is in every way satisfactory. He can work on his ranch, plow, cut timber, or any other work. Few would know he had an artificial limb.

Very respectfully,
ISAAC DAVIS.

BELOW-KNEE AMPUTATION.

1533 17th St., DENVER, COLO., Nov. 18, 1887.

A. A. MARKS:

DEAR SIR:—It affords me great pleasure to express my views regarding your most excellent artificial limbs with rubber hands and feet. I had the misfortune to lose my left leg while engaged in action in the late war of the rebellion, and received my first artificial limb of Mr. —— in N. Y. City in the fall of 1865. At that time I knew nothing about the different limbs, their good or bad qualities, but took the first one offered to me; although it was a great improvement on crutches, it did not give satisfaction, and 1 soon threw it away. After examining the different kinds of limbs I could see or hear of in the United States, and some from Europe, I secured one of your legs, and have continued to use yours ever since.

During the past 22 years, I have traveled around considerable, and met persons wearing all kinds of legs, but I have yet to see the colors of the banners of those that can walk better than I can, if they use any other limb than yours. Your limbs have given me perfect satisfaction, combining, as they do, easy, comfortable, graceful, and natural motion and durability. I wore one for ten years constantly, and was engaged in rough outdoor work all the time in this mountain country. Several of my acquaintances who have lost their legs, and having seen my leg, sent in their orders and measurements, and have always been highly pleased with the result. Wishing you all the success you can possibly desire, and that your efforts to benefit the disabled may continue to be duly appreciated, I remain,

Yours very truly,
RICHARD McCLOY,
Formerly Private Co. A., 10th Regt., N. Y. Cavalry.

BELOW-KNEE AMPUTATION.

Fitted from Measurements.

PLATTEVILLE, WELD CO., COLO., Nov. 1, 1887.

MR. A. A. MARKS:

DEAR SIR:—I have used artificial legs for over twenty years, and I think I ought to be a good judge. The first two or three weeks I thought I would not like the leg, but since I have got used to it I like it first rate. I can walk easier with your leg and rubber foot attachment than with any other leg I have ever tried, and I have tried four different kinds.

I am a plasterer by trade, and work with your leg on the scaffold every day now, and can safely recommend your leg to any one who is so unfortunate as to need one in preference to any other make I have ever tried. It fits me better than any leg I have ever tried, and it was made from measurements. Any one wishing to ask any questions can write to me at Platteville, Weld Co., Colo.

Very truly yours, JAMES DIMMICK.

BELOW-KNEE AMPUTATION.

Nov. 6, 1887.

A. A. MARKS, New York:

DEAR SIR:—Your favor of the 26 ult. is received.

In August 29, 1884, I lost my right foot, which was amputated ten inches below the knee. Having a large coasting vessel under construction at the time, I wanted to apply the best limb, one that would be the most suitable for my business. I therefore made a careful study of artificial limbs of different makes, and with advice of my doctor selected yours. I applied one of yours on the first of December, thirteen weeks after amputation, and in a short time I was able to walk so well that hardly any one knew I had lost my foot. I have not had any repairs made except what you have done free of cost.

I work and do all my business now with all ease possible for any one with a false limb, and feel as well as ever.

I think your artificial limb with the rubber foot is the best one that is made. There are no cords or joints to break down, and the rubber foot soon gives one all the movement in order to walk, and then one always knows there is no turning-over motion of the foot. I like it better than any other I have ever seen. I have used this one nearly three years, and like it more and more. I always know where to find it.

Hoping you will live many years to bless the afflicted with still other improvements, I am,

Very truly yours,
LUCIUS J. STEVENS.

CLINTON, MIDDLESEX CO., CONN.

BELOW-KNEE AMPUTATION.

E. A. Nellis.
WINSTED, LITCHFIELD CO., CONN., Nov. 8, 1887.

A. A. MARKS, ESQ. :
DEAR SIR :—In answer to your letter of October 28, I would say : In 1864 I lost my leg by amputation below the knee. In 1865 I procured, as I supposed, one of the best artificial legs in use, the wearing of which gave me much pain, and I was often obliged to go back on crutches until the irritated and swollen stump was again in condition to wear the leg. It also annoyed me very much by frequent rattling of the ankle joint. Repair bills were from $6 to $8 a year. I was obliged to use a cane when walking, and walk only when obliged to do so. I wore this leg about two years. I met a great many wearing artificial legs made by various firms, all of whom were laboring under difficulties similar to my own, the same chafed stumps, the same rattle of ankle joints, and heavy thud in walking which distinguished any one wearing an artificial leg with wooden foot and ankle joint. I think it was in 1867 or 1868, while in Watertown, N. Y., I met a gentleman wearing one of your artificial legs with rubber foot. I was surprised to see this man go up and down stairs actually on a run. He also moved about among the guests at the hotel noiselessly and quietly, with the grace and ease of natural motion. I have forgotten the name of this gentleman who advised me to get one of A. A. Marks' artificial legs with rubber foot. I at once wrote to you, requesting you to send me instructions and blanks for taking measurements.

I received a prompt reply, followed instructions, sent in measurements and order for a leg. I soon received notice from you that the leg was ready to be fitted. I went on to New York, and when the leg was fitted and finished I put it on at your office and walked down to Fulton St., after eating supper walked down to Peck Slip, took boat for New Haven, feeling like a new man. I am now wearing the third leg made by you. I have worn your legs constantly from the time I first received one, never having lost an hour's time from its use.

I go up and down stairs, up and down hill, through the brush, hunting and fishing. In fact, I go when and where I please with ease and comfort. I think my repair bills for the last two years amount to about $2.50. I can only say, as the gentleman in Watertown said to me, try one.

Very respectfully,
E. A. NELLIS.

BELOW-KNEE AMPUTATION.

Fitted from Measurements

TALCOTTVILLE, TOLLAND CO., CONN., Oct. 31, 1887.

DEAR SIR : In response to your inquiry as to how I am satisfied with my leg, I would say that it has more than met my expectations.

I am now wearing it my third year and have not had to have it repaired yet. I can play base-ball and other outdoor games, run, jump, climb trees, and skate as well and with as little fatigue as other 14-year-old boys. I spend most of my spare time in the woods hunting and trapping. My leg was amputated below the knee. As soon as I received the leg from the express agent I put it on and walked home. I can heartily recommend your legs to any one needing an artificial leg.

Yours truly, GEORGE G. GRISWOLD.

BELOW-KNEE AMPUTATION.

Nov. 5, 1887.

Mr. A. A. MARKS, ESQ. :
DEAR SIR :—It is with pleasure I give my testimony as to the merits of your artificial limbs. Having had an experience of nine years with them I am competent to say that, for durability, easy movement, and excellent workmanship, nothing better could be desired. Although my case is rather a difficult one,

from the fact that the point of amputation is only three inches below the knee, yet, being of a rather restless nature, I walk on an average about four miles per day, and often a good deal more, without the slightest exertion or pain. In all these nine years I had only one occasion for repairs, and this being necessitated by an accidental fall. I have not the slightest hesitation in recommending the Marks artificial limb to any of my friends who may have to take recourse to a substitute for nature, and shall be pleased to answer questions in detail.

Yours respectfully,
NORRIS E. RUTHER.
24 Hill St., NEW HAVEN, CONN.

BELOW-KNEE AMPUTATION.

PEOPLE'S LINE to Bridgeport—Steamer *Rosedale*.
Dec. 18, 1887.

A. A. MARKS:

DEAR SIR :—On Feb. 3, 1887, I purchased an artificial leg from you. In four days after I commenced work on Steamer *Rosedale*. I am on my feet from 6.30 A.M. to 7.30 P.M., daily. I have lost no time, neither have I experienced any inconvenience in the use of it. I have not spent any thing for repairs, and it remains the same as when purchased. My leg was amputated one and one-half inches below the knee. I would be pleased to recommend them to any person who may be in need of one. I can be found on Steamer *Rosedale*, Pier 24, East River, N. Y., between the hours of 11 A.M. and 3 P.M., or in Bridgeport any evening or Sunday.

I will only be too happy to give any information to any who will call and see me.

Yours truly,
CONRAD PRUTTING.

BELOW-KNEE AMPUTATION.

So. NORWALK, FAIRFIELD CO., CONN., Nov. 2, 1887.

A. A. MARKS, ESQ. :

DEAR SIR :—The artificial limb that I have from you I have worn continually for five years, working in the children's carriage business at Five Mile River, Conn. I think that the rubber foot is a great improvement. The cost in that time has been nothing, no repairs being needed. Point of amputation, four and one-half inches below the knee. My work is rather laborious.

Respectfully yours,
FREDERICK A. SCOFIELD.

BELOW-KNEE AMPUTATION.

"Most substantial leg made."

Nov., 1887.

MR. A. A. MARKS:

DEAR SIR :—It is fourteen years since I bought my artificial leg of you. I did not think I should ever walk as well as I do with it. I have done all the hard work that is to be done on a small farm, even to building a stone wall, of which there was nearly one hundred rods, and some of my neighbors said it was done better than they could have done it for themselves. I am walking and going somewhere all the time, driving the cows and going after them, a mile or more every day.

I think your artificial leg with the rubber foot is the most substantial leg made.

CHARLES E. COMSTOCK.
WILTON, FAIRFIELD CO., CONN.

BELOW-KNEE AMPUTATION.

Oct. 27, 1887.

Mr. A. A. Marks:

Dear Sir :—In reply to your request I would say that my right leg was amputated four inches below the knee. I have been wearing one of your style of legs for about five years without any repairs whatever, except a new shoulder strap, and those I sweat out. The limb bids fair to stand me ten or fifteen years longer; it appears to be as good now as when you made it. I am a laboring man, and have to walk one mile to and from my work, and walk so well that most folks don't know that I wear one. It is a smart walker with two legs that can get away from me. I think there is no artificial foot that comes so near the natural one as the rubber foot, for this reason: it gives either way, and with a shoe or boot on it is hard to detect from the natural one. The boot don't look as if it had a last inside, as one does made of wood. I am an old soldier, and would recommend your artificial legs to all comrades in my condition.

Respectfully yours,

L. C. BECKWITH.

THOMASTOWN, LITCHFIELD CO., CONN.

BELOW-KNEE AMPUTATION.

BRANFORD, NEW HAVEN CO., CONN., Dec. 14, 1887.

Mr. A. A. Marks:

Dear Sir :—It is with a willing hand that I write you these few lines in praise of your artificial leg with rubber foot. Nine years ago I wrote to different firms in the United States, asking for catalogues for artificial limbs, and all responded.

I compared them all, and thought yours would be the best, and I can confidentially say that your artificial leg with rubber foot is the best made in the *world*. I have worn the leg for nine years, and it has not cost me one cent to repair it. My work is of a laborious character, standing all day and lifting heavy work. Nine years ago I went to your place of business and left my measurements, receiving the leg in two weeks, and have been wearing it ever since. By my telling of the good of the leg, I have sent five men to you, and they all speak of them in the highest terms.

The amputation of my leg is four inches below the knee.

Dear sir, if I live long enough to wear out this one, I will surely have another. This is the first letter that you have had from me since I bought the leg, and I am pleased it is not a letter of regret. I know of others whose artificial legs are breaking down all the time, which have cost them more than the first cost of the leg. If there is any one who disputes or does not believe the foregoing, please write to JOHN B. COAKLEY, Branford, Conn., and all letters will be kindly answered.

BELOW-KNEE AMPUTATION.

Fitted from Measurements.

Dec. 14, 1887.

A. A. Marks:

Sir :—In regard to my artificial limb, I got it ten weeks after the amputation and have worn it ever since. My limb was amputated six inches below the knee. I was five weeks in Hartford Hospital; in eight weeks Dr. Parker of South Manchester took my measures for the limb I got from you. I had it in two weeks after, and I have worn it ever since. I can walk twenty miles a day. I work in the N. Y. & N. E. R. R., in New Britain, Conn. I can do any work that ever I did.

Yours very respectfully,

TIM CURTIN.

64 Cleveland St., NEW BRITAIN, CONN.

BELOW-KNEE AMPUTATION.

Oct. 29, 1887.

I have worn one of the legs made by you for the last seven years, and it has not been out of order or caused me the loss of an hour from my work, which is laborious, having to lift coils of copper wire weighing as high as one hundred and thirty pounds. I consider the rubber foot by far superior to all others (having had experience with other manufacturers' legs) for durability and advantage to the wearer. I never dared do any thing outside of light employment while wearing the other style of legs.

My leg was amputated four inches below the knee. I will be pleased to correspond with any body in this matter, and will consider that I have done a deed they should be thankful for to the end of their days for putting before them an article that in my experience ranks next to the human foot. I would not wear one of the previously worn legs if presented to me free, if there was one of A. A. Marks' in market selling for twice its present price.

I am, in gratitude,
A. A. BRIDGEMAN.

84 Central St., ANSONIA, NEW HAVEN Co., CONN.

BELOW-KNEE AMPUTATION.

4 Franklin Block, BRIDGEPORT, CONN., Nov. 8, 1887.

A. A. MARKS:

DEAR SIR :—I have been wearing your patent artificial leg for the past fifteen years; I had previously worn others; but they were not satisfactory to me. In my opinion, your leg is far superior to any other artificial leg made. First, because of its ease, elasticity, and stillness; these are obtained by the use of the rubber foot, and I think it is the only sensible thing to use for this purpose, as it is free from all complications of cords and bolts, such as are used in other legs, and which cause a continual rattling, and is very disagreeable. Second, because of their durability, which is no small item. I have used the one I am now wearing about seven years, and it is good for a long time yet.

I am in the insurance and real estate business, and am continually on the go. There are few who walk as much as I do. My leg is amputated four and a half inches below the knee. The cost of repairs during the fifteen years will not exceed two dollars per year. During this time I have recommended them as the very best leg that could be obtained, and a large number of these parties to whom I have recommended have purchased, and are still wearing them, and in every instance to their entire satisfaction.

Yours very truly,
A. E. BARTRAM.

BELOW-KNEE AMPUTATION.

EAST HAVEN, NEW HAVEN Co., CONN., Nov. 18, 1887.

A. A. MARKS:

DEAR SIR :—The undersigned parents of the child, Mabel, to whom some three or more years ago, when but a little more than one year old, you fitted a lower limb after an amputation, are not only willing but anxious to testify to its merits.

The child uses the artificial limb without the least inconvenience, and we would also sincerely thank you for your attention to her needs.

MR. & MRS. E. S. THOMPSON.

BELOW-KNEE AMPUTATION.

Fitted from Measurements.

WESSINGTON, BEADLE Co., DAK., Oct. 30, 1887.

MR. A. A. MARKS:

DEAR SIR :—I was unfortunate enough, nearly two years ago, to lose my leg, about five inches below the knee. As soon as it was thoroughly healed I received an artificial leg from you, taken from measurements, and I have worn it every day since, without the use of cane or crutch. My occupation is butchering. I do all kinds of shop work, and can carry a quarter of beef, without the least trouble. As for repairs, the cost has been little or nothing, as I have only paid fifty cents in nineteen months. I would not be without the leg for twice the amount it cost me. I can heartily recommend it to any one in want of such an article.

I remain, as ever, yours truly,

WARREN HURST.

BELOW-KNEE AMPUTATION.

Nov. 8, 1887.

MR. A. A. MARKS.

DEAR SIR:—Hearing that you are about to publish a new pamphlet, I will cheerfully write a brief sketch of my experience, regarding the durability and advantage respecting ease, comfort, wear, and natural movement of your artificial limbs. My leg was amputated six inches above the ankle, on the twelfth of June, 1884, and on the twenty-fourth of September, the same year, you fitted an artificial limb, and I have worn it constantly ever since, scarcely missing the loss of my own member; not even the pleasure of skating and dancing is denied me. And, what is better still, the leg in practical use does not get tired or out of order. My occupation is a rough, laborious one, and I *never* favor the amputated limb in the least; in fact, when lifting bags of grain, or heavy boxes, I always place the strain of the load on the artificial limb.

I run and jump as freely as before injury, and I can testify, for a certainty, that your limbs are very durable.

Yours respectfully,

ALVAH E. YOUNG.

1007 C St., S. W., WASHINGTON, D. C.

BELOW-KNEE AMPUTATION.

U. S. Soldiers' Home, WASHINGTON, D. C., Nov. 16, 1887.

MR. A. A. MARKS:

DEAR SIR:—In reply to your favor of the 26th ult. I can state that I have worn an artificial leg ever since the war.

I knew nothing of your leg until about 1868. I had then used two legs of different makes. One did not answer at all.

The other I took to you, and had a rubber foot put on, and was so well pleased with the change that I have ever since used your leg. My experience indicates that your foot is superior in durability, at least to those I have tried. In my judgment, its great merits are its *simplicity*, *durability*, and its *elasticity*.

The material and workmanship have always been good.

Yours truly,

R. CATLIN,

Deputy Gov. Soldiers' Home, late Capt. 5th U. S. Art.

BELOW-KNEE AMPUTATION.

Fitted from Measurements.

NASHUA, PUTNAM CO., FLA., Nov. 4, 1887.

A. A. MARKS:

DEAR SIR:—My leg is all right. I have been wearing it since June 4, about five months. It has cost me nothing as yet for repairs, and I work with other men at farm work.

Respectfully,

JOHN CROUCH.

BELOW-KNEE AMPUTATION.

Fitted from Measurements.

BARTOW, POLK CO., FLA., Nov. 10, 1887.

A. A. MARKS, Esq., New York :

DEAR SIR :—I have purchased two artificial legs from you. The first, in 1881, while living in Albuquerque, N. M., which lasted me five years ; the other, which I am now wearing, I purchased from you last year. I am highly pleased in every respect with your work. I can attend to my business, which is store and office work, nearly as well as I could before I became disabled.

Very respectfully,

D. QUINN,
Clerk and Treasurer.

BELOW-KNEE AMPUTATION.

TALLAHASSEE, LEON CO., FLA., Oct. 29, 1887.

DOCTOR A. A. MARKS :

DEAR SIR :—Your favor of the 26th to hand.

In July, 1863, I lost a foot at the battle of Gettysburg, Pa., amputation just above the ankle. In 1864 I purchased an artificial limb made at Charlottsville, Va., used this limb until 1866, then made purchase of a —— of Philadelphia, which I wore until 1870, and then purchased a —— limb. In 1876 I purchased one of your limbs with a rubber foot. I therefore claim to be in a position to judge as to who is the best maker of artificial limbs.

I unhesitatingly pronounce your artificial limbs the best I have ever seen, and had I the ear of every person needing an artificial limb I would advise them as strongly as possible to purchase one of the Marks limbs. Having worn your limb for over ten years I find the rubber foot as good now as the day when the purchase for the limb was made. During the past ten years I have had occasion to send for only knee bolts and shoulder straps.

About two years ago, you will remember, I sent you an order for an artificial limb for a colored man at this place. His measurements were taken according to directions sent out by you. When the limb was received it was found that you had made a perfect fit, and the party has time and again thanked me for recommending your limb. My occupation is that of a cotton commission merchant, and am forced to do a great deal of outdoor work. I have often been told by acquaintances of ten years' standing that they had known me for some time and had only lately discovered that I was the wearer of an artificial limb, and then had to be told first of the fact. Nothing artificial can be made perfect, but your limb, in my opinion, is the best that can be made. During the war I was captain of Co. M, 2d Fla. Regt. With my best wishes, I remain,

Very truly,

JOHN DAY PERKINS.

[From the Hon. T. W. GETZEN.]

BELOW-KNEE AMPUTATION.

Fitted from Measurements.

FORT WHITE, COLUMBIA CO., FLA., Nov. 5, 1887.

MR. A. A. MARKS :

DEAR SIR :—I have been wearing an artificial leg of different make for over twenty years, and I prefer yours to any I have ever worn. I especially like the rubber foot, as there is no rattling and squeaking, so disagreeable to sensitive ears, and there is plenty of elasticity. I have been wearing one of yours now for the last four years, and have paid not nothing for repairs. It was fitted from measurements taken by myself with instructions furnished on blank form from you. The leg when received had only to be cut in a few places where there was too much pressure. Of course I think it best to visit the factory for fitting, but that is not always convenient.

My leg is amputated two inches below patella or knee-pan.

My occupation is general farming, which I superintend and direct myself.

Respectfully,
T. W. GETZEN.

BELOW-KNEE AMPUTATION.

HENRY L. WILSON, Real Estate Agent,
28 Peachtree St., ATLANTA, GA., Jan. 5, 1888.

MR. A. A. MARKS:

MY DEAR SIR:—I am so much pleased with my artificial limb that I feel like urging every one so unfortunate as to lose a leg to try one of yours. It is light and simple, never getting out of fix. During the seven years I have used mine it has never given me the slightest inconvenience, but is always ready for use.

I went to military school one year and beat the drum, marching in front of the company one hour every day. Coming home, I went into the insurance business, and was an insurance solicitor for over a year, keeping me on the go all day long in rain, snow, and sleet, and I never used a stick. After that I went into the real estate business with my father, and on one occasion walked sixteen and one-half miles on a railroad track, in the rain, to transact some business. In this walk I crossed two tressels over fifty feet high, and over a new road that was very muddy, it having rained for three or four days. I regard the rubber foot as the greatest invention of this century, it being noiseless and filling the shoe so perfectly it is almost impossible to say which is the artificial foot. I have gone with new friends for months, and they never once thought I had an artificial limb. I have been asked by people if my shoe hurt my foot, and when I would tell them I had on an artificial limb they would laugh at me, and I would have to let them feel for themselves before they would believe it.

I can dance, act on the bar, skate on rollers, and even run.

Yours, etc.,
W. T. WILSON.

BELOW-KNEE AMPUTATION.

Fitted from Measurements.

AMERICUS, SUMTER CO., GA., Nov. 4, 1887.

Mr. A. A. MARKS, New York City:

DEAR SIR:—I am happy to have an opportunity of contributing for publication my experience with your patent artificial limbs. I have worn your patent, made from measurements for amputation below knee, for two years with great ease, and without any repairs excepting one suspender, which cost the small sum of $1.50. I consider the rubber foot the greatest wonder of the limb, giving as it does a life-like motion, and rendering the wearer capable of walking on uneven surface with ease and dispatch.

I work on a farm, my occupation being a planter.

I cheerfully commend your make of limbs for their durability, simplicity, and comfort; in fact, I am so highly pleased that I cannot entertain the remotest idea of ever purchasing any other than the Marks.

Most respectfully yours,
JESSE J. WEAVER.

BELOW-KNEE AMPUTATION.

Nov. 9, 1887.

A. A. MARKS, ESQ., Manuf. of Artificial Limbs, New York City:

DEAR SIR:—It is with pleasure that I write you regarding your rubber limb which you applied to my leg.

My occupation is a pretty good test of its qualities, being a traveling passenger agent, and going all the time, and do not use a cane.
I give it my hearty endorsement.

Yours truly,
R. A. WILLIAMS.

T. P. A. M. & L. R. R., ATLANTA, FULTON CO., GA.

BELOW-KNEE AMPUTATION.

Fitted from Measurements.

A. A MARKS, New York City:

DEAR SIR :—In answer to your letter in regard to artificial legs of your manufacture, I would say that I regard them as the best, both in construction and durability. I am wearing the same one that I purchased from you four years ago, and I am pleased to say that it has always given perfect satisfaction. My occupation is that of a stationary engineer. While my duties are not laborious, I think I give your leg as severe a test as could be made, as I do a great deal of walking, having charge of eight engines, 14 pumps, four 125 H. P. boilers and two 40 H. P. boilers, all scattered over five acres of ground.

Yours truly,
SAMUEL E. BIXBY,
ATLANTA, GA.

Care of Atlanta Cotton Mill.

BELOW-KNEE AMPUTATION.

Fitted from Measurements.

Dec. 7, 1887.

DR. A. A. MARKS:

DEAR SIR :—I take pleasure in recommending your rubber foot. The rubber comes nearer imparting the natural elastic motion to the step than any device yet invented.

Yours with respect,
MATTHEW RICE.

632 Broad St. AUGUSTA, GA.

BELOW-KNEE AMPUTATION.

Fitted from Measurements.

PALACE FARM, AUGUSTA, GA., Nov. 9, 1887.

DR. A. A. MARKS:

DEAR SIR :—Ten years ago my leg was amputated below knee. I at once had a leg made and paid a large price for it. I was at the shop where it was made every day to try it. After it was made I could not wear it any length of time for reason of its paining me. I abandoned it in less than three months.

In conversation with a friend he advised me to order a leg from you. I took the measure in Augusta, Ga., sent it on to you in July, nine years ago. One month after I received the leg with rubber foot. I put it on without anything being done to it in the way of adjustment. I have worn it ever since, and have not paid a cent for repairs, and have not done any thing on it myself.

I was in the grocery and butcher business three years, and have been farming ever since, and being a fleshy man, working hard, you know the test I put the leg to. I believe with my present experience in taking care of an artificial leg I could have worn one of your make fifteen years. I have recommended your rubber foot and hand to several. Without exception they have given perfect satisfaction. I ordered an arm with rubber hand for Miss Emma Beaver, who works in Augusta Cotton Factory, and she uses it for any work she has to do. I know one gentleman who wore (or tried to wear) five different make of legs and could not wear any of them. I recommended him to send to you for one. He did so, and now he says he wears it with perfect ease. It was a good day for the maimed when you put the rubber foot into use. You are at liberty to use

this as information to any one who might be in need of artificial limbs. Knowing the value of them myself, it would be a source of comfort to me to know that I had been able to give my experience for the benefit of my suffering friends.
        Very respectfully,
GEO. R. DORSEY.

BELOW-KNEE AMPUTATION.
COLUMBUS, MUSCOGEE CO., GA., Nov. 1, 1887.

MR. A. A. MARKS:
    DEAR SIR :—I purchased from you some time ago an artificial foot, having had my foot cut off below the knee. I can without hesitation recommend it for durability and advantage compared to the old style, and in particular your mode of construction. It causes me no pain and gives entire satisfaction, wherein the old style foot hurt me the whole time of five years I wore it. I am a boiler-maker by trade. I do heavy flanging for the firm. I work and do repairs on boilers throughout the country. A few days ago I took a walk of ten miles across the country, something I never could do with the old style. Any person desiring further information I will kindly give, and recommend your artificial limbs to all persons desiring to purchase such.
Respectfully,
J. S. MCBRIDE.

BELOW-KNEE AMPUTATION.
Fitted from Measurements.
Nov. 8, 1887.

MR. A. A. MARKS:
    DEAR SIR :—I will tell you something about my artificial leg. I wore a leg fifteen years and liked it well. Seven years ago I got one of yours and liked it a great deal better. If I knew I could not get another no money could buy my leg. My occupation is keeping house, such as all country women have to do. You can use my name if you desire.
Respectfully yours,
FANNIE CRITTENDEN,
ELBERTON, ELBERT CO., GA.

BELOW-KNEE AMPUTATION.
Fitted from Measurements.
EXETER, PIERCE CO., GA., Nov. 5, 1887.

A. A. MARKS, Esq., New York :
    DEAR SIR :—The artificial leg received from you has given entire satisfaction. I have been using it for eight years, and can recommend to any one desiring the use of an artificial limb. My limb was amputated above the ankle, and I find the superiority of the rubber foot above all others, and their durability and advantage the same.
        Yours respectfully,
THOS. SPIKES.

BELOW-KNEE AMPUTATION.
STAPLETON, JEFFERSON CO., GA., Nov. 19, 1887.

MR. A. A. MARKS, New York :
    DEAR SIR :—I wish to certify that I have worn artificial legs for twenty-three years, and never could wear one with any ease or comfort until I purchased one of your make with india-rubber foot, which I have worn for eight years with only ten dollars for repairs. My leg was amputated six inches below the knee. I am a farmer ; do not labor, though walk a great deal, and my weight is two hundred and ten pounds. I walk so well as to cause persons

to affirm that I have two good natural legs until they had examined. There is no noise whatever unnatural while in motion with one of your manufacture of legs, and I take the greatest pleasure in recommending them to the public, as I think there is no other that will compare with yours; therefore I never expect to wear any other, as I would not accept of any other as a present.

Yours, etc.,

B. A. HOOK.

BELOW-KNEE AMPUTATION.

Fitted from Measurements.

"Eight years and not a cent for repairs."

JUG TAVERN, WALTON CO., GA., Nov. 3, 1887.

A. A. MARKS:

DEAR SIR:—I beg leave to state that I have been wearing your rubber foot for seven or eight years, that previously I had worn three other different makes of artificial limbs, and that yours excels them in every particular, and that I shall never wear any other leg as long as I can get Marks' leg. I walked last Friday twelve miles on Marks' leg without inconvenience.

It is now in good order. I have examined twenty different makes of legs and feet, and as for power, certainty at the ankle joint (a great desideratum), and durability yours far surpasses them all. The old style ankle joint and cat-gut accompaniments will have to take a back seat. Ours is an age of progress; scientific development will always lay shoddyism in the shade.

The two limbs I have worn of your make, though made from measurements, were perfect fits. Neither of the limbs purchased of you have ever cost me a cent for repairs.

Yours truly,

A. LOUIS BARGE.

BELOW-KNEE AMPUTATION.

Fitted from Measurements.

MONTICELLO, JASPER CO., GA., Nov. 2, 1887.

I have used your artificial foot and leg continuously for three years, and it gives perfect satisfaction. The fit by measurements was perfect. I had no repairs done during the three years, although I was in active business, such as salesman in retail dry-goods and grocery store, and have walked the old field bird-hunting, for one-half day at a time. The rubber foot seems as good to-day as when first bought. Hoping that the above will be of some service to some maimed, and yourself, I am,

Yours truly,

THOS. EZELL.

BELOW-KNEE AMPUTATION.

Fitted from Measurements.

PLANTERSVILLE, GEORGETOWN CO., GA., Nov. 10, 1887.

A. A. MARKS:

DEAR SIR:—I have been wearing limbs of your make for the last sixteen years, and I most cheerfully state that they have given great satisfaction. I prefer your make of leg to any other, for noiselessness, durability, and perfect fit from measurements.

The rubber foot surpasses all others, and wears well. I have had three of your limbs, and have given them severe tests, and recommend them to all who have been unfortunate in losing a limb. I have been wearing artificial limbs for twenty-two years; I have worn one other make, but your make is far ahead. I have not paid one cent for repairs. My leg is amputated six inches below the knee.

Very respectfully yours,

JOHN FORD.

BELOW-KNEE AMPUTATION.

Fitted from Measurements.

VILLA RICA, CARROLL CO., GA., Oct. 29, 1887.

MR. A. A. MARKS, New York:

DEAR SIR:—I wish to say a word of encouragement to you, in regard to your artificial limb. I have been trying one of your rubber feet, for nearly three years, and don't think that there can be too much said in their favor. I think that they are as near a success as can be. I must confess that when I first got my foot, I was very much disheartened with it. I thought that it did not fit, and that I never would be able to wear it at all, but after trying it for a while, I found that I was in fault, and not the foot. Now I can put it on in the morning. I am in the mercantile business, and I have a good trade, and can attend to my sales myself, almost as though I had two natural feet. My foot was amputated just above the ankle.

As to durability, I don't think it can be excelled. There is hardly any cause for it to wear out. There is no rattling or squeaking about it, and if I was not known to be a cripple, people would say that I had a corn on my foot or something of the sort. So I hope that you may live a long life and be able to relieve and comfort a great many in trouble and need your help. Wishing you all the success, I remain,

Yours truly,

W. F. STRICKLAND.

BELOW-KNEE AMPUTATION.

Fitted from Measurements.

DANA, LA SALLE CO., ILL., Nov. 12, 1887.

MR. MARKS:

DEAR SIR:—I have worn your make of artificial limbs three years, and like them very well. I am a farmer, and do a great deal of work. My limb was taken off half-way between the knee and ankle joint. I haven't had any repairs except a new suspender.

Yours truly,

W. HENRY JONES.

BELOW-KNEE AMPUTATION.

Fitted from Measurements.

Nov. 18, 1887.

DEAR SIR:—I am very well pleased with the artificial leg you sent me. I was five years old when I had the first one, and I am now thirteen years old, and I thank you for it.

Yours, very truly,

ROSIE MAY.

SIBLEY, FORD CO., ILL.

BELOW-KNEE AMPUTATION.

Fitted from Measurements.

WENONA, MARSHALL CO., ILL., Oct. 29, 1887.

MY DEAR FRIEND:—I received your letter on the 28th, and am very glad to hear from you. I am getting along very nicely with your artificial limb.
I walk a half a mile every day to school.
No matter how much I walk, it never hurts me a bit.
My leg is all right yet.

From your friend,

MICHAEL MULCAHEY.

BELOW-KNEE AMPUTATION.

Fitted from Measurements.

ARGOS, MARSHALL CO., IND. Oct. 31, 1887.

A. A. MARKS, ESQ.:

DEAR SIR :—I purchased an artificial leg of your manufacture, with the patent jointless rubber foot, about four years ago, and must say that it far exceeds its representations.

I have not had any repairs done on my substitute, but it is a wonder I have not required a new leg, considering the way I have used it. My leg was amputated just three inches below the knee-pan, and I went so long on what is called a peg leg that my stump was shaped badly, but I go just the same, regardless of these drawbacks; can skate on ice or roller skates. My occupation is not laborious, but I do a great deal. I think the rubber foot far exceeds any thing of its kind. I close, wishing you great success.

Yours truly,

WM. H. ROBERTS.

BELOW-KNEE AMPUTATION.

Fitted from Measurements.

ROOK & DENNIS, Brooms and Brushes.
JONESBORO, GRANT CO., IND., Oct. 30, 1887.

DEAR SIR :—I write you in regard to the artificial leg you made for me nearly three years ago. I consider it superior to any other leg I have ever worn; it has not been out of order since I got it. The lightness, easiness, and softness of the rubber foot far excels any other leg I have ever seen, I am a broom maker and our factory is one mile from town. I walk it twice a day and don't tire. I have worn artificial legs for twenty years. My leg was amputated six inches below the knee. I can cheerfully recommend your artificial leg.

Yours truly,	A. DENNIS.

BELOW-KNEE AMPUTATION.

Fitted from Measurements.

JONESBORO, GRANT CO., IND., Nov. 20, 1887.

DEAR SIR :—My left limb was amputated March 10, 1884, four inches below the knee; I was run over by the train near Marshalltown, Iowa. I wore a wooden peg that I fixed myself until March 10, 1887, when one of your artificial limbs with rubber foot was received, made by sending the measurements to you. I had worn the peg so long, and not using my knee joint it became very weak, and I somewhat lost the use of it. I could not quite straighten the stump. For this reason, I could not wear the limb only a part of the time, but after a while I could walk without the use of a cane. I have been a farmer all my life until the past year. I am caring for my afflicted father; he weighs over 170 pounds and is almost entirely helpless; he can walk when he is helped. I can lift and care for him as well as any body. I would advise any one not to put off getting a new limb as long as I did, but advise them to go and get one with a rubber foot.

Yours truly,

HENRY W. ELLIOTT.

BELOW-KNEE AMPUTATION.

KEWANNA, FULTON CO., IND., Oct. 29, 1887.

A. A. MARKS:

DEAR SIR :—I have worn the artificial leg I received of you about four en months; have given it a thorough trial, and think it is the best artificial limb I have ever seen. I have had twenty-two years' experience with other patents,

and yours is superior to all of them. Your leg gives the wearer more of a life-like appearance when walking. I often walk five miles at one time, and can do it with ease and comfort.
Yours respectfully,
T. W. PATTY.

BELOW-KNEE AMPUTATION.

Fitted from Measurements.

LA FONTAINE, WABASH CO., IND., Jan. 13, 1888.

A. A. MARKS, New York City :
DEAR SIR :—Mr. Albert Thomas, the drawing of whose limb I sent you last fall a year ago, is well pleased with his limb, as it is a perfect fit and enables him to walk with but little inconvenience. I have no hesitancy in recommending it as being superior to any with which I am acquainted.
Yours truly,   JAMES L. DICKEN, M.D.

BELOW-KNEE AMPUTATION.

Fitted from Measurements.

Nov. 14, 1887.

MR. A. A. MARKS:
DEAR SIR :—I had an artificial leg made by measure, as you know. It fits all right, and has never cost me a dollar in over three years. I am a farmer, and do as much work as my hired men. I never use a cane to walk with. I have a boy seven years old. He often wants to run me a foot-race, but I can beat him. I wanted a friend of mine in La Porte to buy his leg of you. He got a Chicago leg, and it is not of much service.
Yours respectfully,
ED. HEWS.

LA PORTE, LA PORTE CO., IND., BOX 868.

BELOW-KNEE AMPUTATION.

Fitted from Measurements.

Nov. 5, 1887.

A. A. MARKS :
DEAR SIR :—I take pleasure in testifying to the satisfaction I have derived from the use of your artificial limb.
I have worn it nearly fourteen months, and have not missed a day of school on account of it. I have no hesitation in saying that as far as my knowledge goes they are the simplest and the most useful that are made. Others have expressed the same opinion as myself. My limb was amputated below the knee January 20, 1886, and in about six months afterward I sent my measurement for a limb, which was made without my presence. I have had no repairs. I consider that your appliances fulfill all the conditions called for in providing artificial support after amputation.
Yours respectfully,
W. ALBERT THOMAS.

LA FONTAINE, WABASH CO., IND.

BELOW-KNEE AMPUTATION.

Nov. 19, 1887.

A. A. MARKS :
DEAR SIR :—The rubber foot you made me two years ago is perfectly satisfactory. I can use it just as well as I could the ——. I have strongly recommended it to every one I have met who needed anything of the kind, and hope I have been instrumental in sending you some customers.
If I should ever need a new leg I will have nothing but the rubber foot.
Yours truly,   H. B. LAWRENCE.

TERRE HAUTE, VIGO CO., IND.

BELOW-KNEE AMPUTATION.

In the U. S. Service as Guide and Interpreter.

FORT SUPPLY, IND. TER., Nov. 15, 1887.

A. A. MARKS, New York City:

SIR:—I take pleasure in stating that the artificial leg with rubber foot which I received from you has given entire satisfaction. I consider it near perfection, compared with others I have worn. My leg was amputated just below the knee, and with your appliance I can walk almost as well as I could with the natural limb. I am in the employ of the U. S. Government as guide and interpreter, and am in the saddle a great portion of the time.

I have as yet had no occasion to have any repairs to the leg.

Yours truly,
AMOS CHAPMAN.

BELOW-KNEE AMPUTATION.

Fitted from Measurements.

CHANCY, CLINTON CO., IOWA, Nov. 2, 1887.

Mr. A. A. MARKS:

DEAR SIR:—I have worn two different make of limbs, but neither gave me as good satisfaction as yours. I feel proud in recommending your limbs, as they are the best in the world. I am a great lover of sport, such as fishing and hunting, and can walk all day. My weight is two hundred pounds. I have worn one of Marks' limbs for over eight years, and it has never needed repairs. I had the measurements taken where I live. Yours truly,

JAMES CARTER.

BELOW-KNEE AMPUTATION.

Fitted from Measurements.

MEDIAPOLIS, DES MOINES CO., IOWA, Nov. 3, 1887.

A. A MARKS, ESQ:

DEAR SIR:—In complying with your request I take pleasure in recommending your artificial limbs. I have been wearing your patent rubber foot for fifteen years, having been fitted from a plaster cast for leg amputated five inches below the knee.

During the above time I have had two limbs; during the preceding ten years I wore out four limbs made by other parties.

Am engaged in commercial business, and am on my feet almost constantly, and perform all labor required and stand by my associates in business.

Yours truly,
S. D. FULMER.

BELOW-KNEE AMPUTATION.

EDDYVILLE, WAPELLO CO., IOWA, Nov. 28, 1887.

Mr. A. A. MARKS:

DEAR SIR:—In reply to your letter I will say I have worn your artificial leg for seventeen years, and I regard your patent as first-class in every respect. I wore one leg fifteen years and it never cost me five cents. I should recommend A. A. Marks' legs above all others. My occupation is sewing-machine agent, and I am always on my feet, and the leg is never idle. I have gained from one hundred and thirty-five to two hundred and thirty pounds since I have been wearing the limb.

Hundreds of people in this part of the country don't know that I wear an artificial limb. They are no Sunday leg, like some manufacturers'; they are all the week, the year around. I should advise all persons requiring an artificial leg or hand to try Marks' patent above all others.

Yours with respect,
JAMES M. WELCH.

BELOW-KNEE AMPUTATION.

Fitted from Measurements.

CEDAR FALLS, BLACK HAWK CO., IOWA, Nov. 9, 1887.

A. A. MARKS, New York:

DEAR SIR :—The artificial leg with rubber foot furnished by you for me, now nearly fifteen years since, has been in constant use during all that time, and has not at any time failed to give full and perfect satisfaction. I have been wearing an artificial leg for the past seven years, and had worn out and thrown away two of other makes before procuring one of yours. From my experience and close observation of others I am fully warranted in stating that your leg with rubber foot is in very many essential points superior to any other that has come to my notice. On the score of economy, my experience is that, the first cost being the same, the expense of repairs on other legs, for a term, say of ten years, will increase the cost of their legs to at least double that of yours. During the fifteen years I have worn your leg I have expended in repairs not to exceed seven dollars, less than I often expended in a single year on the other legs. The absence of springs, cords, pulleys, and bolts in the foot is a great improvement, enabling the wearer to step softly without the jar and jerking movement so observable in the more complicated feet. My leg was fitted by you from measurements made by myself on blanks furnished by you. The fit was from the first complete, and I have never had occasion to make any change.

I have known of several others whose experience in this respect is similar to my own. I have recommended your leg to a number of unfortunates, and in no instance have they failed to be well satisfied.

I am, respectfully,
S. H. PACKARD, Atty., etc.

BELOW-KNEE AMPUTATION.

Fitted from Measurements.

INDEPENDENCE, BUCHANAN CO., IOWA, Dec 11, 1887.

A. A. MARKS:

DEAR SIR :—I can very cheerfully comply with your request, and will state that I obtained my first limb of you in the fall of 1877, and wore it eight years, doing heavy farm labor the greater part of the time. It never cost me a cent for repairs.

I have worn my second limb two years. Last year I farmed one hundred acres, fifty of wheat, forty of flax, and ten of corn, and did not hire in all one week's work. The leg is made of the best material, the weight is light, and it is always ready for business.

Both legs were made from measurements and fit like gloves.

The point of amputation is three and one-half inches above ankle joint.

I would advise any one in need of an artificial limb to give Marks a trial.

Very respectfully,
W. A. ROGERS.

BELOW-KNEE AMPUTATION.

SPENCER, CLAY CO., IOWA, Nov. 7, 1887.

MR. A. A. MARKS:

DEAR SIR :—The first artificial limb I had was in 1864, made in Chicago. It did not last over one year till I had to repair it. Since that time I have worn your limbs and have found them to be the most durable of any limbs I have ever seen.

My leg is off eight inches above the ankle. I am a carpenter, and can climb a ladder or go where any others can go; as for me, I would not change it for any one I have ever seen.

The one I have now I have worn three years, and it is as good as ever; if any one wants any reference to your limbs direct them to me.

I am, yours respectfully,
SCOTT CASE.

BELOW-KNEE AMPUTATION.

Fitted from Measurements.

Nov. 2, 1887.

A. A. MARKS, New York City:

DEAR SIR:—On the 26th day of February, 1886, you know I wrote you telling you that my leg was amputated two inches below the knee joint, and asking you if you thought you could make me a leg so that I could use the knee joint in walking. To this you promptly answered that you could, and sending me your formula for taking measure at home. This was done and returned to you with the order. In about ten days the leg arrived with instructions how to put on, etc., and I can say I have been wearing it with satisfaction every day since, not having required any repairs, as there is no machinery about it to become out of order, and no rattling noise to be heard when I walk, because the foot is made of rubber. This not only makes the step silent and natural but also saves wearing out the socks.

Yours truly,
HELGE THOMPSON, Postmaster.
DUNBAR, MARSHALL CO., IOWA.

BELOW-KNEE AMPUTATION.

Fitted from Measurements.

RANDALL, JEWELL CO., KANSAS, Nov. 13, 1887.

A. A. MARKS:

DEAR SIR:—For the benefit of those who have been unfortunate like myself, by the loss of a limb, I would say that I believe the limb with a rubber foot, manufactured by you, to be superior to any limb that I have any knowledge of. I have worn limbs of three different kinds. The limb you made for me by measurements I have worn for over five years, and it has not cost me one cent for repairs during that time. There are no cords, bolts, or other machinery in the ankle, to get out of repair, or cause annoyance. Any one desiring information further, and will write me, I will cheerfully answer.

Respectfully yours,
MANOAH STONE.

BELOW-KNEE AMPUTATION.

Oct. 30, 1887.

I had your feet applied to two of ——'s legs, which proved very satisfactory. I am standing or walking all the time.

Respectfully yours,
T. H. McLAUGHLIN.
ARKANSAS CITY, KANSAS.

BELOW-KNEE AMPUTATION.

Fitted from Measurements.

CONWAY SPRINGS, SUMNER CO., KANSAS, Nov. 2, 1887.

A. A. MARKS:

DEAR SIR:—I have worn the limb made by you from measurements sent you by mail one year, and am well pleased with it. My limb is amputated four inches below the knee.

I work as an operator, and have no trouble in performing my duties, so far as the limb is concerned. I have been crippled ten years, and my greatest regret is that I was induced to wear a peg leg so long. I can cheerfully recommend your limb to any one having had the misfortune to lose a limb.

I will answer any inquiries that may be made concerning the limb.

I am, yours very truly,
C. P. HALE.

BELOW-KNEE AMPUTATION.

Fitted from Measurements.

Santa Fe Town and Investment Company, J. A. GRAYSON, President.

HUTCHINSON, RENO CO., KANSAS, Nov. 15, 1887.

FRIEND A. A. MARKS:

I feel like saying a few words for your most elegant artificial leg. It seems to me there can be no better made. I have thoroughly tested them, to my greatest satisfaction, in all kinds of weather. Their durability can not be questioned in my judgment, and your success in fitting and measuring has proven excellent. I can cheerfully recommend them to one and all.

The present is my third limb, and you have improved on each one.

My occupation has been, for a number of years, looking up good locations and buying o town sites. I do a great deal of walking.

Yours respectfully,
J. A. GRAYSON.

BELOW-KNEE AMPUTATION.

Fitted from Measurements.

Can walk and run with perfect ease.

MONTANA, LABETTE CO., KANSAS.

In February, 1886, my son, Louis S. Bauman, received from A. A. Marks, of New York City, a patent rubber foot, which up to date has given the best of satisfaction, and promises to continue to do so for a long time to come. Casual observers never detect but what the boy has his natural limbs. He walks and runs with perfect ease. My whole family feel it a duty to highly recommend to all in need of artificial limbs A. A. Marks' rubber feet, and in connection with that we feel it a duty to recommend the promptness with which Mr. Marks deals with his customers.

ELD. W. J. H. BAUMAN.

Nov. 3, 1887.

BELOW-KNEE AMPUTATION.

Fitted from Measurements.

HAVANA, MONTGOMERY CO., KANSAS.

STATE OF KANSAS,
County of Montgomery,

J. C. Blair, being duly sworn upon his oath, deposes and says as follows:

I have worn artificial limbs about twenty months.

I wore one manufactured by —— of Independence, Kansas, about eleven months, which was of but little service to me. It was too heavy, did not fit, and was continually getting out of order at the ankle joint, and was a great discomfort to me. I then sent measurements to A. A. Marks of New York City, and in a very short time received one of their artificial legs with rubber foot, which was very light, fitted like a glove. I have worn it about nine months, had no repairs, and it has given general satisfaction.

I have no fault to find, and believe that the rubber foot is the best in the world, and can be surpassed by none.

My leg is off four inches and a half below the knee.

I am in the real estate business, at Havana, Kansas; can take care of my horses, harness and hitch them to buggy. I have walked as far as four and one-half miles at one time, while wearing Marks' artificial leg.

Signed, J. C. BLAIR.
Witness, CAPT. GEO. A. PECK.

STATE OF KANSAS, }
County of Montgomery. } ss.

Subscribed and sworn before me, a notary public, in and for said county and State, this the thirty-first day of October, 1887.

J. R. BLAIR,
Notary Public.

BELOW-KNEE AMPUTATION.

Fitted from Measurements.

Works on a farm.

KIRWIN, PHILLIPS CO., KANSAS, Oct. 31, 1887.

MR. A. A. MARKS:

DEAR SIR:—I had a foot amputated March 19, 1885, and as soon after as possible I began to wear a peg, and continued to wear one until January 1, 1887. Since then I have worn one of your artificial legs with rubber foot fitted to measurements, and I have had no use for the peg. I have worn this leg ten months, and notice that my health is a great deal better than when I wore that strap around me, which belongs to a peg. I can do almost as much on the farm—for that is my occupation—as any one.

The leg is as good as when I received it, and no money could entice me to be without one. As I consider your leg perfect, why should I not testify to its merits? It has put me on my feet again. People that do not know that I have an artificial leg will hardly believe it when told.

Wishing you success, I am,

ELIAS R. ANDERSON.

BELOW-KNEE AMPUTATION.

GARNET, ANDERSON CO., KANSAS, Oct. 31, 1887.

A. A. MARKS, ESQ.:

I avail myself of the opportunity to write you a few lines. In 1864 I received one of Dr. ——'s legs, and tried to use it for years, but could never wear it with any comfort, and finally laid it aside altogether and took to the peg leg.

I then thought I would never try an artificial leg again. But a friend that was wearing one of your legs with rubber foot persuaded me to try your leg. So two years ago I got you to make me a leg, and have worn it ever since, and have had no trouble with it; it is the boss. I would not take a leg with ankle joint as a gift, unless I wanted a leg and music box combined.

My leg is off five inches below the knee. I walk without a cane, and very few notice my being lame; I think I do as much walking every day as any man in our little city, and my leg never gets sore and has never been out of repair since I got it.

Very truly yours,
J. A. BELL,
Co. I, 22d Regt. Ind. Vol. Inft.

BELOW-KNEE AMPUTATION.

PARADISE, RUSSELL CO., KANSAS, Nov. 4, 1887.

A. A. MARKS:

SIR:—It is with pleasure I recommend your artificial leg, knowing by long experience that there is no other limb made that can give the satisfaction your artificial limb gives. I have been using your make for the last fifteen years and am well pleased with it. My occupation is farming. My limb is off from

one and one-half inches below the knee joint. It has never cost me ten cents for repairs since I have been wearing your make of a limb, and the rubber foot is just what makes your limb the best ; no jarring when walking.
Hoping you success, I remain yours,
S. B. ANDREWS.

BELOW-KNEE AMPUTATION.

CALDWELL, SUMNER CO., KANSAS, Nov. 22, 1887.

MR. A. A. MARKS :
DEAR SIR :—I have worn one of your artificial legs for one year and eight months.
My leg was broken nine inches below the knee by falling off a load of hay on August 17, 1885. It was broken so badly that it had to be amputated. I received one of your legs March 9, 1886 ; put it on the next day, but could not make much headway with it ; but I kept trying and conquered at last. I am a farmer and am on my feet all the time ; I have attended forty-five acres of corn this summer, twenty acres of oats, and two acres of potatoes, and have not had any repairs done as yet.
Yours truly,
O. H. BENEDICT.

BELOW-KNEE AMPUTATION.

Fitted from Measurements.

CASEYVILLE, UNION CO., KY., Nov. 5, 1887.

MR. A. A. MARKS :
KIND SIR :—I sent my measurements to you for an artificial leg about three years ago ; it came in about two weeks after I ordered it. The fit was perfect. It has not cost a cent for repairs. I am more than pleased with the rubber foot, which works with perfect ease. It is far superior to the old style foot that has joints at the ankle and always rattling. My work is not very laborious. I have worn artificial limbs for seven years, but have found none to suit me half so well as the one I have now.
My leg was amputated just above the ankle. Any one needing an artificial leg will do well to send measurements to A. A. Marks.
Very respectfully,
DICK RUDY.

BELOW-KNEE AMPUTATION.

Fitted from Measurements.

CONCORD, LEWIS CO., KY., Oct. 3, 1887.

MR. A. A. MARKS :
DEAR SIR :—Having worn one of your artificial limbs for three months I can inform you that I am more than pleased with it.
I am a farmer and can do almost any kind of light work. I would not do without one of your legs for twice the value of it. The rubber foot is so natural ; there is no rattling noise and the step so soft and light. I recommend it to all in need of one as being the best.
Yours truly,
JOHN VANCE.

BELOW-KNEE AMPUTATION.

Fitted from Measurements.

MAYSVILLE, MASON CO., KY., Nov. 14, 1887.

A. A. MARKS :
SIR :—I have used your leg for eight years, and it is the best I ever had. I had three others, but yours is the best of all. It cost me nothing for repairs.
Yours,
MARTIN GRIMES.

BELOW-KNEE AMPUTATION.

Fitted from Measurements.

WINGO, GRAVES CO., KY., Dec. 12, 1887.

DEAR SIR :—I am well pleased with your work, and am willing to testify to the merits of your limbs. I would advise every one in need of artificials to purchase of you. Your rubber foot has no equal. It is more durable than any I have ever tried. I have tried ——'s work, of Cincinnati ; he required me to come to Cincinnati to get a fit. I went, and his fit was nothing to compare with yours from measurements. I am a farmer ; I cultivated twenty-five acres of corn this year, and six acres of tobacco. I did my own plowing. I have been wearing an artificial leg for seven years.

Yours truly,
GEO. G. CARMEN.

BELOW-KNEE AMPUTATION.

NEW ORLEANS, LA., Nov. 10, 1887.

MR. A. A. MARKS :

DEAR SIR :—As soon as my foot was amputated I began to make inquiries as to an artificial limb. I wanted one that was light, *noiseless*, durable, and not always needing repair. After examining four different patents, I concluded that A. A. Marks' patent artificial leg was the one that came up to my wishes ; and I can add that it has far exceeded my expectations. As for the ankle joint movement, I was delighted to have a leg without it. The lack of this movement causes no awkwardness in my gait. I have met acquaintances on the street who, not having heard of my accident, were astonished when I told them I was using an artificial leg. Any one wishing to make further inquiries of me concerning the A. A. Marks artificial leg can obtain my address from you.

I most heartily recommend artificial limbs manufactured by you to any one in need of them, as I feel that it is to the one I am using that I am indebted for being almost as active as before I lost my own limb.

I remain, with respect,
MRS. S. EASTON.

BELOW-KNEE AMPUTATION.

Office of Hurricane Island Granite Co., DAVIS TILLSON, Proprietor.

ROCKLAND, KNOX CO., ME., Oct. 29, 1888.

A. A. MARKS, Esq., New York City :

DEAR SIR :—I have worn an artificial leg for the past thirty-six years, and have had experience in using limbs made by the most celebrated manufacturers. For the past ten years I have worn constantly one of your rubber feet, which has given me entire satisfaction. It very far surpasses all others in durability, absence of disagreeable noise, and freedom from unpleasant concussion in walking. I am,

Yours respectfully,
DAVIS TILLSON.

BELOW-KNEE AMPUTATION.

ORONO, PENOBSCOT CO., ME., Nov. 9, 1887.

MR. MARKS :

I have to say in your favor that I have used your leg for twelve years and that it never cost me one cent for repairing. I am a laborer, and work hard all the time, and go up and down ladders, and it is in good shape yet. As soon as I want one again, I will have one of your make. I think it is the best leg made. I give you great credit for your work. I remain,

Your friend,
THOMAS KELLY.

BELOW-KNEE AMPUTATION.

Fitted from Measurements.

Does all kinds of housework and writes poetry.

SACO, YORK CO., ME., Oct. 31, 1887.

MR. MARKS:

Having worn one of your artificial legs for twelve years, I can truly say they are the best that I have ever seen.

They are very much better than those with ankle joints.

The rubber foot is a marvel of neatness and durability, and I could not wear any other. I wear it with ease and comfort, and have paid but a very small sum for repairs. I do all my housework and go in and out of doors without canes. When I go any distance I take my canes, as my natural leg has broken in two places. People think that I get around remarkably well; when I was hurt I did not think that I could ever walk again, and it is a great pleasure to me to get about my work. I cheerfully recommend you to all in need of limbs.

HOW I BECAME A CRIPPLE, AND WHY I USE ONE OF A. A. MARKS' ARTIFICIAL LIMBS.

As I was riding in town one day
My horse got frightened and ran away;
Into the wheels my feet were caught,
And now a poor cripple is my lot.

For many rods I was dragged, they say,
When a good Samaritan passed that way;
He raised me up with grief to see
Each limb broken below the knee.

To Doctor Warren's he carried me;
Amputation must be done, said he,
A carriage get without delay;
She must be taken home right away.

One leg was taken below the knee,
The other with splints bound up, you see;
The Doctor said, " You will walk again,
On a leg of cork, I think, without pain.

" An Artist, Dr. Marks by name,
Can fit from measure just the same
As though you to him in person went."
To New York, Broadway, I quickly sent.

'Twas made and sent without delay,
By P's Express the seventh day.
I tried it on; it fitted neat,
With rubber foot and straps complete.

I now could walk around the room,
Then o'er the house about my home;
Could cook and wash and iron too,
And do all the work that others do.

For twelve long years I've worn the leg
With ease and comfort, and I beg
That blessings fall from day to day
On Dr. Marks of New York, Broadway,

Yours very respectfully,
MRS. S. E. SILLEY.

BELOW-KNEE AMPUTATION.

Congregational Parsonage, WALDOBORO, ME., Nov. 3, 1887.

MR. A. A. MARKS:

DEAR SIR:—It gives me great pleasure to assure you that the apparatus made by you in 1876 has answered my expectations, enabling me to walk in a natural manner and leave the crutch.

My parish work calls for a great deal of walking, which I can do with great ease. As to durability, strength, and simplicity, I could not compare the same with other manufactures, as I have never had to do with them, but will say I am sure nothing more suitable for the purpose can be found. Hoping many others may find as I have the value of your great work, and that you may be spared many years to continue to benefit others as you have me, I remain,

Respectfully,
RUFUS P. GARDNER,
Pastor of First Congregational Church.

BELOW-KNEE AMPUTATION.

EASTPORT, WASHINGTON CO., ME., Oct. 30, 1887.

MR. MARKS:

DEAR SIR:—The leg you made for me over two years ago is just as good as the day I got it. It is the best leg that I ever wore.

I have been wearing artificial limbs since 1864, and have had many different makes, but I must say your make is the best.

Your legs do not get out of repair as the others did. It used to cost me a great deal to keep the other different makes in repair. Since I have worn your new patent leg I have not been laid up with chafing one day. Of the other makes I never had but one that would not chafe my stump and lay me up.

I like your rubber foot very much and would have no other make.

I have the best fit from you that I ever had. I am a sealer by trade. I work in a sardine factory, and I can make my rubber foot get around with the best of them. I advise all those that are in need of legs to get one of your make. The rubber foot will never play out. Point of amputation, two and one-half inches below the knee.

Yours,
HUGH THOMPSON,
Co. K, 6th Maine Vols.

BELOW-KNEE AMPUTATION,

Fitted from Measurements.

Oct. 29, 1887.

A. A. MARKS:

DEAR SIR:—I take pleasure in writing to you to inform you of the fact that your artificial limb with rubber foot has given me entire satisfaction. I can say for one that your leg is the best leg that is made. I have worn the ankle joint leg. Every little while I had to put in new cords. The noise it made was unbearable. But it isn't so with your rubber foot, which is firm and solid.

I am a laborer, and I work on my leg every day. I have worn an artificial leg for 24 years.

Mine has not cost me a cent for repairs, or given me a moment's trouble since I began wearing it. It is a very decided improvement in artificial feet, and I heartily commend their use to all persons wearing artificial legs. Your fitting from measurements is good. I am,

Yours respectfully,
W. H. THOMAS.

BELFAST, WALDO CO., ME.

BELOW-KNEE AMPUTATION.

Fitted from Measurements.

BELFAST, WALDO CO. ME., Nov. 6, 1887.

DR. MARKS:

DEAR SIR:—I am pleased to speak in the highest praise of the foot you made for me, and which has been in constant use for seven years, without repairs. I do my housework for four in the family, have now one little babe, work hard all the time, and have never used the crutch for the whole seven years.

I go to dances once in a while. I do wish that those that have lost a foot could see me walk and dance. My foot was amputated four inches above the ankle. I would be pleased to write to any one that would like information concerning the foot.

Yours truly,

MRS. C. H. BRIER.

BELOW-KNEE AMPUTATION.

ROUND POND, LINCOLN CO., ME., Nov. 31, 1887.

A. A. MARKS:

DEAR SIR:—I have worn your rubber foot two years, and like it so well I would wear no other. My business is that of a stone cutter, and I am obliged to stand all day. I am very hard on an artificial leg, yet this one has cost me nothing for repairs, and I walk very comfortably with it. My leg is amputated three inches above the ankle joint. I can recommend your make to any one in need of an artificial limb.

Truly yours,

E. Y. BRYANT.

BELOW-KNEE AMPUTATION,

Nov. 3, 1887.

A. A. MARKS, ESQ., New York City:

DEAR SIR:—I have been wearing one of your legs for eighteen months with perfect satisfaction. I was one month learning to walk; since that I have had no trouble. For the last six months I walk to and from work (three miles each way), and often as far at night, without feeling tired. I have had no repairing nor any alterations done since purchasing.

Yours ever,

R. E. WARD.

Clerk B & O. Freight Office, Locust Point, BALTIMORE, MD.

BELOW-KNEE AMPUTATION.

Fitted from Measurements.

Nov. 2, 1887.

MR. A. A. MARKS:

DEAR SIR:—I am still wearing the leg you made me about nine years ago, and I can truly say that it has not been out of repair since I got it. I wear it every day and work at my trade—shoemaking. I think your patent leg is the most durable leg that is made. My weight is 224 pounds, and I have carried three bushels of wheat on the leg. I think I have a right to know the difference between artificial legs, for I have worn several kinds.

I wore one of Mr. ———'s legs with ankle joint about one year, and then it was played out. For my part I never want any other kind of a leg but one with a rubber foot and solid ankle.

I take much pleasure in recommending to my friends and comrades.

Yours truly,
CYRUS RIDENOUR.

HAGERSTOWN, WASHINGTON CO., MARYLAND.

BELOW-KNEE AMPUTATION.

Fitted from Measurements.

Nov. 5, 1887.

A. A. MARKS:

DEAR SIR :—Yours of October 26 is at hand. In regard to your artificial limbs I can say that they are the most perfect I have ever seen. I have worn my leg three years and two months, and have not had to lay out a cent for repairs. I am now working on my farm, do all my mowing by hand. Cut the grass on five acres. Marks' leg is the one to have. You can use my name.

Yours respectfully,
A. N. JAMESON.

P. O. Box 1252, FITCHBURG, WORCESTER CO., MASS.

BELOW-KNEE AMPUTATION.

Nov. 1, 1887.

MR. A. A. MARKS:

DEAR SIR :—I take great pleasure in writing to you, and informing you that I am well, and still continuing to wear your artificial limb. I am happy to state that I still wear the leg you made for me in 1880, and it is in good order yet. I am using it every day. The leg you made for me in 1884 is also good yet.

I have only paid seven dollars in repairs, so far, in all. I have worn legs made by other manufacturers, with wooden feet, and ankle joints, but in all my years of experience I never found myself satisfied until I procured one of your artificial legs with the rubber foot. I walk more naturally and more comfortably than I ever did on the other legs that I have worn with the wooden foot and ankle joints. As I wrote before, I flatter myself that I can walk farther and faster and endure more hard work on your rubber foot than any body can on a wooden foot that I have ever seen. The rubber foot does away with the clattering wooden foot and squeaking ankle joints with cords, bolts, and springs, that I have had the misfortune to wear before I had the chance to hear of your rubber foot, and since I have worn your legs I have had the pleasure of sending to you Messrs. Parker, Conway, Estevez, Kennealy, Frates, and others, and they all join in saying that you have made them legs far better than they expected. I will say that my work is very laborious, as I have to stand on my feet sixteen hours a day, lifting barrels, and climbing up and down stairs constantly every day. I have worn artificial legs now fifteen years. My left leg is amputated four inches above the ankle. I have walked a mile inside of ten minutes. In conclusion, I would say that I consider the leg made by you the best in the world. Particularly the elastic rubber foot. I cheerfully recommend your work, and shall be only too glad to reply to any one who may feel so disposed to write to me on the subject, by mail or in person.

Hoping this may meet the eye of some poor unfortunate like myself, and help to put him on his feet (rubber), I remain,

Respectfully yours,
JOSEPH H. SYLVESTER.

120 Commercial St., BOSTON, MASS.

BELOW-KNEE AMPUTATION.

Fitted from Measurements.

99 Foster St., WORCESTER, MASS.

A. A. MARKS, 701 Broadway, N. Y.:

DEAR SIR:—Having now worn the artificial leg procured from you fourteen months, I can say that after an experience of over twenty years with different makes yours with the rubber foot is the most comfortable I have ever worn, and as it was fitted from measures, and without any alteration whatever, I thought it phenomenal. As to its durability, I cannot say any thing of the future. I have not expended a cent for repairs yet, and it is as good as the first day I put it on. I am on my feet most of the time in the iron business, and can walk home at night (nearly a mile) as well as the best. As my stump is quite short (three and one-half inches below the knee), I have reason to be thankful that I came to you, as I get along with so much comfort.

Yours respectfully,
JAMES P. CROSBY.

BELOW-KNEE AMPUTATION.

FRED E. STROH, bread, cake, and pastry baker,
421 & 423 Hanover St., BOSTON, MASS., Oct. 28, 1887.

MR. A. A. MARKS:

DEAR SIR:—I will cheerfully recommend your leg as being the best. My leg was amputated about half way between the ankle and knee, seven years ago. I wore two legs of different make before getting yours. I have worn your leg fourteen months, and am perfectly satisfied with it. I feel more secure upon it. It makes less noise than a foot with the ankle joint. It is more elastic in walking. I am on my feet a good part of the day. I am a baker, by trade, and take charge of my shop from 4 o'clock A. M. until 1 o'clock P. M. Then often take a long walk among the business houses, buying my goods, and never use a cane.

I give the leg hard wear, and so far have not paid any thing for repairs. I can truly say I am much pleased with your leg.

Yours respectfully,
F. E. STROH.

BELOW-KNEE AMPUTATION.

HOLLISTON, MIDDLESEX CO., MASS., Oct. 27, 1887.

Mr. A. A. MARKS:

DEAR SIR:—The leg I bought of you two years ago this fall has proved more than satisfactory; I cannot speak too highly of it. I would advise any one in need of an artificial foot to get the rubber foot.

In two years I have not laid out any thing for repairs.

My leg was taken off three inches below the knee. With the aid of your leg with rubber foot, I have been able to do quite a business selling goods.

Yours respectfully,
A. APPLETON ADAMS.

BELOW-KNEE AMPUTATION.

READING, MIDDLESEX CO., MASS,, Nov. 25, 1887.

A. A. MARKS, ESQ.:

DEAR SIR:—I have worn one of your rubber feet for the last ten years and like it very much. There is not that disagreeable noise inseparable from the other kinds I have worn.

My foot was amputated just above the ankle. I work at my trade (machinist) nearly all the time. I usually have a good deal of walking and going up and down stairs to do. Shall order another rubber foot if this wears out.

Yours truly,
E. F. RICHARDSON.

BELOW-KNEE AMPUTATION.

113 Main St., NORTH ADAMS, BERKSHIRE Co., MASS., Nov. 4, 1887.

Mr. A. A. MARKS:

DEAR SIR:—I am glad to have an opportunity to testify to the merits of your artificial limbs with rubber feet.

I have worn an artificial limb for twenty-two years. The first five years I wore one with a wooden foot and ankle joint.

I have worn yours seventeen years with very little repairs.

When I laid aside the one with the wooden foot and put on one of yours I felt that I was nearly a sound man again. I am in the furniture and undertaking business, and have been since before I lost my limb. I perform all the parts of business capable of being performed by a man with two natural limbs.

I consider your leg far superior to any other artificial limb made. The rubber foot gives an easy and natural motion to the step.

Yours truly,
J. H. ADAMS.

BELOW-KNEE AMPUTATION.

Fitted from Measurements.

Can run and play ball.

SPENCER, WORCESTER Co., MASS., Nov. 7, 1887.

A. A. MARKS:

DEAR SIR:—My foot was amputated at the ankle joint, about eighteen months ago. About eleven months ago I received a rubber foot from you fitted by measurements and a plaster cast of the stump made by a dentist. It fits perfectly, so that I have not used my crutches for months. During term times I go to school, and vacations I work in the woolen mill. I can run, play ball, and do as other boys do. My age is fourteen. I am perfectly satisfied.

Yours truly,
ALEXANDER ALLEN.

BELOW-KNEE AMPUTATION.

CHARLTON, WORCESTER Co., MASS., Oct. 26, 1887.

Mr. MARKS:

I received yours of the 26th and was glad to hear from you. I have some land to work on, and I make boots. I can walk one mile or two with ease on the leg you made me last year. It is all right, and I am well pleased with it.

It is off below the knee.

EMULUS HARWOOD.

BELOW-KNEE AMPUTATION.

SOUTH WILLIAMSTOWN, BERKSHIRE Co., MASS., Nov. 11, 1887.

MR. A. A. MARKS:

DEAR SIR:—You ask me to say a word for your artificial limbs. I can say that I have worn one eight years and it has given me perfect satisfaction. The rubber foot gives more of a natural step—elastic. I can walk farther and easier than with any other kind. I can go on the floor and dance with the best of them with good limbs.

Yours,
W. M. FIELD.

BELOW-KNEE AMPUTATION.

Nov. 1, 1887.

Mr. A. A. Marks:

Dear Sir:—I take great pleasure in writing you a recommendation. I have worn the artificial leg you made for me for over ten years, during which time I have worn no other.

I am now twenty-two years old. I went to school until I was eighteen. Running, playing ball, skating, and dancing were the sports I frequently indulged in. Your rubber-foot leg enabled me to do this and keep every one in ignorance as to my condition.

I have been working in a shoe shop in Brockton for four years and stand on my leg ten hours a day. I have not been obliged to pay a cent for repairs yet.

Yours truly,
VICTOR BEAUREGARD.

26 Huntington St., BROCKTON, MASS.

BELOW-KNEE AMPUTATION.

Nov. 28, 1887.

Mr. A. A. Marks:

Dear Sir:—After five years' experience with three artificial legs with ankle joints from well-known makers, and seventeen years' constant use of the rubber foot, I can honestly recommend the rubber foot as the *best*, being simple in construction, firm, natural and easy in motion. I have worn the leg you made me nine years ago every day in that time and without any repairs whatever. I will cheerfully answer all letters from comrades and others in regard to the leg.

Respectfully yours,
J. W. FARNSWORTH,
Late 3d R. I. Vols. and 57th Mass. Vet. Vols.

5 Orange St., WALTHAM, MIDDLESEX Co., MASS.

BELOW-KNEE AMPUTATION.

" You have done more for cripples than any one else in the land."

Nov. 2, 1887.

Mr. A. A. Marks:

Dear Sir:—Accept my thanks for the rubber-foot leg you made for me. I have used two artificial legs with ankle joints and have had no comfort with them. But since I got your rubber foot October, 1886, I am able to run and walk. I weigh two hundred and thirty-five pounds, and I have had a great deal of walking to do. I consider you have done more for cripples than any one else in the land.

Yours with respect,
ROBERT KENNEALY.

Business place, No. 65 Atlantic Ave.
Residence No. 22 Sawyer St., BOSTON, MASS.

BELOW-KNEE AMPUTATION.

Fitted from Measurements.

Nov. 4, 1887.

Mr. A. A. Marks:

Dear Sir:—I have worn one of your artificial legs for the last three years, and my work is of such a nature that it necessitates my standing or walking nearly all day, so I am competent to judge of its efficacy and durability, and I can cheerfully recommend it to any person who may need one, and I am especially pleased with the rubber foot. I would say that it has not cost me a cent for repairs since I purchased it, and it is likely to last a number of years yet.

DANIEL MURPHY.

57 Furnace St., No. ADAMS, MASS.

BELOW-KNEE AMPUTATION.

Nov. 24, 1887.

MR. MARKS:

DEAR SIR:—I received my leg, and feeling so much pleased with it that I wish to say it is a great deal better than I ever expected. I can do very nearly as well with it as I could with my own leg, and would be pleased to recommend them to all in the need of artificial limbs of any kind.

Yours respectfully,
WILLIS A. TAFT.

NORTHBRIDGE CENTRE, WORCESTER CO., MASS.

BELOW-KNEE AMPUTATION.

WILLIMANSETT, HAMPDEN CO., MASS., Nov. 14, 1887.

MR. A. A. MARKS:

DEAR SIR:—Your favor of the 26th ult. duly received.

I have worn one of your artificial legs with rubber foot for ten years, and it is still giving satisfaction.

During the ten years it has cost me nothing for repairs, except one or two suspender bands.

Yours respectfully,
J. G. SPITZLI.

BELOW-KNEE AMPUTATION.

MAZEPPA, WABASHA CO., MINN., Jan. 16, 1888.

I go to school. I have worn your artificial leg three years, and it gives me entire satisfaction.

Yours truly,
EMMA AUGUSTIEN.

BELOW-KNEE AMPUTATION.

Fitted from Measurements.

Nov. 13, 1887.

MR. MARKS:

DEAR SIR:—I have been wearing your patent artificial leg nearly three years, with the utmost satisfaction. My occupation is farming. I have been to no expense since purchasing.

I would not part with your leg on any account if I could not get another of the same make. I can heartily recommend it to any one in need of artificial limbs.

Yours truly,
JAMES E. JOHNSON.

DORR, ALLEGAN CO., MICH.

BELOW-KNEE AMPUTATION.

WHITE LAKE, OAKLAND CO., MICH, Nov. 7, 1887.

MR. A. A. MARKS:

DEAR SIR:—I have been wearing your artificial leg for nearly seventeen years. I have no occasion to find fault with it. The rubber foot in my judgment is the best in the market. I especially recommend it for its simplicity and durability, compared with the old style. I have worked at my old business as a farmer ever since I got your leg. I feel grateful to you for the service rendered me.

Yours very respectfully,
CHARLES HIBNER,
Co. K 5th Regt. Michigan Infantry.

BELOW-KNEE AMPUTATION.

Fitted from Measurements.

Nineteen years in use and good yet.

Dec. 12, 1887.

A. A. MARKS:

DEAR SIR:—I wish to inform the public of the superiority of your patent limbs. My limb was taken off below the knee. I took my own measurements and sent for your patent limb; got it all satisfactory in February, 1869, and have worn in ever since. I never had any repairs on it only what I could do myself.

It is good yet and nineteen years old next February. My work is all kinds of farm work. If I thought I could not get another limb, money could not buy the old one. I feel confident no other patent limb could do any more than this has done for me. If this is of any use to you you are at liberty to publish it.

Yours with respect,
L. H. NORRIS.

ELM HALL, GRATIOT CO., MICH.

BELOW-KNEE AMPUTATION

Fitted from Measurements.

SOUTH BAY CITY, MICH., Nov. 4, 1887.

A. A. MARKS:

DEAR SIR:—I take pleasure in assuring you that the artificial leg you made for me from measurements now nine years in use is in every way satisfactory to me. It is far superior to any I have ever seen. I work in a saw-mill filing. I wear it from morning till night, week in and out. I think the rubber foot far superior to any I have ever seen, for there is no machinery to oil and keep in repair. I have never paid any thing to have my limb repaired. I would recommend you to every one in need of artificial limbs.

Yours respectfully,
JOHN STEWART.

BELOW-KNEE AMPUTATION.

Fitted from Measurements.

MARLETTE, SANILAC CO., MICH., Oct. 26, 1887.

Mr. A. A. MARKS:

SIR:—I hear that you are about to publish a new pamphlet of your legs and arms with rubber hands and feet.

Seeing I have a leg of your make myself, I will tell you in as few lines as possible how useful mine has been to me. I have worn my leg for about six months and it is as good as when I got it. Some people say that the rubber foot will not last long, but I think it will, for I have worked on the farm, and bound wheat after the reaper, and bound as much as any of the other men.

I got $1.50 per day, and I only had worn the leg two months. I have worked with men for weeks and they would not know that I had an artificial limb on. I can walk about as good as before. The rubber foot is a great thing; it gives such a natural step. I have an uncle that has one of the

Detroit legs and he cannot walk nearly as well as I can. Mine is more firm and natural. I am going to school now, but I work Saturdays.

I tell you for a fact my leg is better than my uncle's.

I can step as quietly as any one. I danced on the Fourth of July a long time. I can get around about as good as ever.

Well, I can't think of any more to say to benefit the public, so I will close, feeling pleased to render them all the help I can. I remain,

Yours truly,
THEO. WELCH.

BELOW-KNEE AMPUTATION.

Fitted from Measurements.

SAULT STE. MARIE, CHIPPEWA CO., MICH., Oct. 30, 1887.

MR. A. A. MARKS, New York City:

DEAR SIR :—I had the misfortune to lose my leg some three years ago ; as soon as I could I began to look around for a good substitute. I applied to a good many manufacturers of limbs, but none satisfied me until I got hold of one of your catalogues. As soon as I had read it I at once made up my mind to order one of your patent legs with rubber foot.

I sent for instructions how to measure ; as soon as the blanks were received I had my leg measured and I ordered one. I can assure you that I am more than pleased with the leg. My leg is cut off about six inches above the ankle. I am an engineer on a steamboat by occupation, but this season I have been foreman of public works, where I had to be constantly on my feet, and I am sure had I not had your rubber foot I could not have stood the fatigue. I can lift, jump, run, and walk as fast as most any ordinary man. I am fifty years old. I have worn your leg constantly since last April. You are at liberty to use my name at any and at all times.

Yours,
J. R. COOK.

BELOW-KNEE AMPUTATION.

Fitted from Measurements.

Nov. 8, 1887.

MR. A. A. MARKS:

The leg I got from you I am well pleased with.

It was a first-class fit. I have worn it two years and a half, and it is in good condition yet. I can recommend that your limb with the rubber foot is much easier than a wooden one. When I get another leg I shall get one of yours.

Yours truly,
HIRAM GIBSON.

GREENVILLE, MONTCALM CO., MICH.

BELOW-KNEE AMPUTATION.

Fitted from Measurements.

Nov. 13, 1887.

MR. A. A. MARKS:

DEAR SIR:— I am very well pleased with my leg, as I have had it about seven years or more, and it has given perfect satisfaction in every respect. I am a farmer, and can do all the work required of a man on a farm with ease for one that has had the misfortune to lose a limb.

Yours with respect,
ADAM HEMSTEAD.

INDIAN LAKE, OSCEOLA CO., MICH.

BELOW-KNEE AMPUTATION.

Fitted from Measurements.

Nov. 4, 1887.

MR. A. A. MARKS:

DEAR SIR:—In compliance with your wish I can say this for the leg: The artificial leg you made for me two years ago I have used every day since. My occupation is that of a watchman, which requires a great amount of walking, and I have never experienced any inconvenience whatever. It is giving entire satisfaction.

OLE LARSON.

GULL RIVER, CASS Co., MINN.

BELOW-KNEE AMPUTATION.

Fitted from Measurements.

HASTINGS, DAKOTA Co., MINN., Nov. 23, 1887.

A. A. MARKS, ESQ.:

DEAR SIR:—I have worn an artificial leg made by you for nearly two years. My leg is amputated about six inches below the knee. Our family physician, A. H. Steen, took my measure.

It fits very nicely, and has not cost me any thing for repairs.

I am very well pleased with it. My occupation being farming, I can do very nearly as much work as before losing my leg.

I always do and will speak a good word for your work when an opportunity offers.

Yours truly,

S. J. ORR.

BELOW-KNEE AMPUTATION.

Fitted from Measurements.

FRAZEE CITY, BECKER Co., MINN., Nov. 3, 1887.

MR. A. A. MARKS:

DEAR SIR:— Sixteen years ago you first started me out with one of your artificial limbs fitted to my leg amputated just above the ankle. My experience has always been satisfactory, and since coming West and putting it to severe test I have been especially pleased. I have worn my present limb over four years, and not once during that time has it needed repairs. I actually forget at times that I am lame. The rubber foot, which makes your limb superior to others, meets all the requirements, stays longer in the race than any competitor, and does not make any noise about it. Your limbs cannot be too highly recommended for their comfort, durability, and naturalness. And certainly the avoidance of the cost and trouble of repairs makes them the economical limbs.

Yours sincerely,

JOHN F. SCHENK.

BELOW-KNEE AMPUTATION.

Fitted from Measurements.

WASHINGTON, FRANKLIN Co., Mo., Nov. 10, 1887.

MR. A. A. MARKS:

DEAR SIR:—With pleasure I will say that I am satisfied with your artificial leg. I have been using an artificial leg for 14 years, and have had one from several factories, but none so well pleased me as yours. It was made by measurement, which proved satisfactory. I have used yours three years, and no repairing. I use it every day. The rubber foot is more durable than any other. My occupation is President of Washington Clay Manufacturing Company.

Respectfully,

ROBERT H. HOFFMANN.

BELOW-KNEE AMPUTATION.

Fitted from Measurements.

MISSOURI CITY, CLAY CO., MO., Oct. 27, 1887.

DR. A. A. MARKS, New York City:

DEAR SIR:—In answer to your favor of the 26th, I will say I have been using one of your artificial limbs with rubber foot for nine years, and it has given entire satisfaction in every particular. For the last three years I have been superintending a farm of 500 acres, and it is the wonder of every one how I get around on the farm, and more especially when you take into consideration the fact that I weigh 225 pounds.

I have used two other makes, and consider the rubber foot far superior to any I have used. There is one point I wish to call your attention to; that is, I was fitted exactly from measurements the first trial, and have not had any trouble since. Yours respectfully,

A. M. GRIFFITH.

BELOW-KNEE AMPUTATION.

Fitted from Measurements.

KAHOKA, CLARK CO., MO., Nov. 2, 1887.

Mr. A. A. MARKS, New York City:

DEAR SIR:—I hope you will pardon me for not letting you know sooner that I received my artificial leg in good shape some time ago. I have changed my address since I ordered it, but it came to me all right at this place. To say that I am well pleased with it is just putting it mildly, as every thing fits so well and measurements were so accurate. Would advise those wishing comfort, ease, and gracefulness to get one of you. I have not used it more than a month, and therefore cannot say any thing as to its durability, but thus far it works to perfection.

Yours respectfully,

R. B. JENKINS.

BELOW-KNEE AMPUTATION.

Fitted from Measurements.

"Taken for his brother."

HUMPHREYS, SULLIVAN CO., MO., Nov. 18, 1887.

Mr. A.A. MARKS:

DEAR SIR:—It has been about two and one-half years since I received one of your artificial limbs. It has proved exactly as represented, a perfect fit, and has given entire satisfaction. Those who need limbs need not fear that you can give a perfect fit by sending measures as you direct.

My leg is amputated just below the knee, and I walk without crutch or cane. I have attended school with students who knew of my misfortune in losing my limb, who, when they saw me walking with my artificial limb, often mistook me for my brother.

I have several times walked four or five miles at a time.

I know nothing about the old style of limbs, but the new india-rubber foot is a great success. My limb has needed no repairs. This recommendation is given cheerfully.

Respectfully,

B. F. DONOHO.

BELOW-KNEE AMPUTATION.

SYRACUSE, MORGAN CO., MO., Oct. 28, 1887.

MR. A. A. MARKS, New York City:

DEAR SIR:—I am a merchant. I have been wearing your artificial limb for four months. My leg is amputated nine inches below the knee. I am well pleased with my leg. I think it quite an improvement over the old style.

Respectfully yours,
DAVID CROWE.

BELOW-KNEE AMPUTATION.

Dec. 15, 1887.

MR. A. A. MARKS:

I have been a constant wearer of your make of limbs since April, 1870. I worked at various kinds of work, at home on a farm, and shop work also. My limb proved to be one of the best.

My amputation was my right leg, two and one-half inches below knee joint, which serves me well, and I can work with any one and walk easy and well. Seven years ago I thought I would go West. I have traveled a great deal through the western territories. I started from Washington Territory across the mountains, on horseback most of the time. I could get off and on alone as easy as ever. I have had men watch me to see me spring into my saddle, and say, "You beat any thing I ever saw, you will beat some of our old riders." My journey lasted from the fourth of August until the first of November. I stopped and visited the natural curiosities of the West. When I reached the eastern part of Montana in Custer County I went to herding. I herded for two years every day. In the winter I went on foot. I am certain that I made from six to eight miles a day, through the winter. In the summer I used a horse all the time. There was a young man there ; we used to ride and hunt together a great deal last spring. I went and staid with him, and that revealed to him what he never thought.

He said I used to go a little lame at times. He wanted to know who made that limb. I said Mr. A. A. Marks of New York.

"Well, that beats any thing I ever saw. I can't hardly believe my own eyes." He asked a hundred questions or more about how I got along for repairs. I said I have none, only what I do myself. It does not cost me more than $1 a year outside of what I can do myself. They are so simple and easy and comfortable.

I have seen men that had limbs fitted in Chicago, and got a botch job.

I have just had a new leg fitted, one of your natural cork legs. I think it will be a complete success. I would like to say to those that are beginning to wear a limb to do as I did. After wearing my limb all day, at night some place would be chafed and sore. I used to wash it in cold water out of a well ; then in the morning I would put a piece of paper around the tender part, and the result was, I was as good as new. Cold water is the best remedy for toughening my limb of any thing I ever tried. "Where there is a will there is a way." to get along, not sit down and say I can't. I should like to say a great deal more. A letter addressed as below will reach me.

JOHN G. NICHOLS.

POWDERVILLE, CUSTER CO., MONT.

BELOW-KNEE AMPUTATION.

Fitted from Measurements.

OTTO FOSTER, Deputy County Treasurer and Notary Public.
CENTRAL CITY, MERRICK CO., NEB., Oct. 29, 1887.

A. A. MARKS, ESQ. :

DEAR SIR :—Having been a wearer, for the last six years, of one of your artificial limbs with rubber foot attached, I wish to say that in lightness and *durability* your limbs are unparalleled.

My own, I am using yet, will last me for a good time to come.

My position as Deputy County Treasurer requires standing on my feet the most of the time, and very much walking from desk to desk.

I have used artificial limbs for thirteen years, but your make is the best in regard to lightness and durability. My stump holds ten and one-half inches below the knee, and if any one of our suffering community requires an artificial limb I will and shall recommend your limbs highly.

Very truly yours,
OTTO FOSTER.

BELOW-KNEE AMPUTATION.

Fitted from Measurements.

BENJ. SANDERS, Attorney at Law,
EUREKA, EUREKA CO., NEVADA, Dec. 26, 1887.

A. A. MARKS, ESQ.:

DEAR SIR :—I have had some experience with artificial legs. I have worn one for thirteen years, and there are people living with me in the same town who do not know that I have lost a leg.

I can walk as fast and as well as any of them.

I think your leg is the best that is made. I can walk about the office and court room just as still as any one. I can walk down the street as fast, and no one can detect from any noise that my leg makes that I have one on, and I am not at all lame.

Yours respectfully,
BENJ. SANDERS.

BELOW-KNEE AMPUTATION.

Fitted from Measurements.

CLAREMONT, SULLIVAN CO., N. H., Oct. 31, 1887.

A. A. MARKS:

DEAR SIR :—I have worn the rubber foot you made for me nearly two years and I am very much pleased with it. My foot was taken off about five inches above the ankle, and my weight is two hundred and forty pounds. I am a machinist by trade, and can stand on my leg at the vise or lathe all day with ease. I was surprised to get it so soon after I sent my order. I think the workmanship superior to any other make. I can recommend your rubber foot to all in need of a false limb as being the best fitting. I was surprised to have such a good fit by measure, as you never saw me, but you made the leg by measure just as well as it could be if I had been at your place. I thank you very much for your promptness in filling my order. I have never seen any other make that I would swap mine for, and if I ever want another I shall come to you for it.

Very respectfully yours,
F. A. WATRESS.

BELOW-KNEE AMPUTATION.

Fitted from Measurements.

MARLBOROUGH Depot, CHESHIRE CO., N. H., Oct. 29, 1887.

A. A. MARKS, ESQ.:

DEAR SIR :—I lost my foot by the cars the 27th of May, 1886.

My limb was amputated about six inches above the ankle joint.

I began wearing an artificial limb of Mr. Marks' make, August 19, 1887, which was fitted by measurements, and have worn it every day since with satisfactory results. It is a great benefit to the human race that there is such an invention for those that are unfortunate to lose a limb. I am persuaded that Marks' leg is the best, as there is no ankle joint to get out of order, and the rubber foot, being elastic, relieves the stump from the jar in walking. Having never worn limbs of other makes, cannot say as much as others, but would advise those who are unfortunate to lose a limb to get an artificial of Marks.

Yours respectfully,
E. A. FULLER.

BELOW-KNEE AMPUTATION.

Oct. 28, 1887.

A. A. MARKS:

DEAR SIR:—I have worn one of your artificial limbs for more than four years. I am well satisfied with it and can recommend it, to all in want of the same. I have never worn any other.

I walk three-fourths of a mile to my work and go over the road four times a day. I think your rubber feet are the best, from what I can learn from my own observation.

Yours truly,
CHARLES W. WALLINGFORD.
Station Agent, SOMERSWORTH STATION, GREAT FALLS, STRAFFORD CO., N. H.

BELOW-KNEE AMPUTATION.

Fitted from Measurements.

EAST WOLFEBORO, CARROLL CO., N. H., Jan. 10, 1888.

A. A. MARKS:

DEAR SIR:—I cannot see how you made such a good fit for me from measurements. The fit is so perfect the leg does not even feel strange to my stump. The leg enables me to walk so naturally my most intimate friends can hardly tell which is the artificial. I cannot find words in the English language expressive enough to convey my feelings of satisfaction and gratitude. The leg is worth its weight in gold.

Respectfully yours,
Mrs. CORA B. ADJUTANT.

BELOW-KNEE AMPUTATION.

Fitted from Measurements.

PITTSBURG, COOS CO., N. H., Oct. 31, 1887.

MR. A. A. MARKS:

DEAR SIR:—The artificial leg which I received of you some three months ago is giving good satisfaction. I wear it all the time. It is a good fit and works well in every way.

I work on a farm and do a great deal of traveling and go hunting and trapping as though I had two natural feet. I have never worn a patent limb until yours was received. Although I have seen a number of persons that have worn them with ankle joints, I think the rubber foot is far ahead of any I have ever seen.

There are three men in my place that wear legs with ankle joints, and I can walk with the most natural step and greatest ease of any of them. The amputation was about four inches above ankle joint.

Very truly yours,
EDWIN S. KEACH.

BELOW-KNEE AMPUTATION.

Locomotive Engineer.

Nov. 1, 1887.

MR. A. A. MARKS:

DEAR SIR:—I have worn your artificial leg for the past sixteen years, and have found it entirely satisfactory.

I have been employed as locomotive fireman, and at present am locomotive engineer, and have never found any difficulty in performing my duties.

Yours respectfully,

JAMES GOOD.

178 Pavonia Ave., JERSEY CITY, N. J.

BELOW-KNEE AMPUTATION.

Nov. 17, 1887.

A. A. MARKS:

DEAR SIR:—Having had your style of artificial limb in use for twenty years I find, after using it all these years, that I would not under any circumstances use any other make. I find it durable, easy, soft, and comfortable to wear. I have to put your limb to a very severe test, and it stands it nobly and satisfactorily.

I am employed as gate tender at street crossing, rolling up two heavy gates, up and down every few minutes in the day, with perfect ease to my amputated limb, which I consider a very severe strain and test to your artificial limb. This I do from day to day, rain or shine. My amputation is five inches below the knee.

I find the comparative cost of limb to be very slight. I would highly recommend to those unfortunates like myself to use the same as I am using. They will never regret it, and use no other. Hoping this may be of some use to you, I remain,

Yours,

WILLIAM WICK.

132 R. R. Ave., JERSEY CITY, N. J.

BELOW-KNEE AMPUTATION.

93 Harrison Ave., JERSEY CITY, N. J., Nov. 27, 1887.

MR. MARKS:

I can cheerfully say that I have had the use of patented artificial legs for six years, next February 14, and I can say that your artificial leg has given me the highest satisfaction.

I lost my right leg about fourteen years ago; it was amputated three or four inches above the ankle joint, and ever since I have had your artificial leg I have followed the kalsomining trade for more than five years. I put my leg on every morning, and continue my daily trade, going up and down my ladder from morning until night, both winter and summer.

Yours truly,

J. B. COLE.

BELOW-KNEE AMPUTATION.

BERGEN POINT, HUDSON CO., N. J., Nov. 8, 1887.

MR. A. A. MARKS:

DEAR SIR:—It being several years now since I have had to call on you even for the slightest repairs on my leg, I beg to say that I travel several miles every day and do it with comparative ease. I have now worn your leg over eighteen years, and am thoroughly convinced that it is the best leg that is made. Knowing this to be a positive fact, I take great pleasure in congratulating you in your great success.

Yours truly,

W. DANFORTH.

BELOW-KNEE AMPUTATION.

Oct. 18, 1887.

A. A. MARKS, ESQ.:

DEAR SIR:—After wearing my artificial leg which you made for me over three years ago, I wish to tell my story for the good of those who are in need of a substitute.

I have been to Europe this summer, and I tell you it was surprising to see how amazed people were on board the steamer both ways when I told them that I had only one leg, because this artificial leg is so lifelike that nobody ever takes notice of it when I am walking.

In Germany I met a couple of invalids of the Franco-German war who lost their legs. They had artificial legs, but they could not walk very well with them. After showing them my leg they acknowledged it to be the best. It is so much lighter; it does not make any noise, and there is no troublesome machinery to it. Who made the leg? was generally the question. I answered it with the greatest of pleasure. You ought to have seen my father and friends, how full of joy they were to see me walk so natural and easy, and not only walk, but climb hills and mountains also. To make it short, this leg gives the best of satisfaction, and speaks for itself. I only wish I could tell this to every one who is in need of a substitute.

Very respectfully yours,
GEORGE C. GRAU,
Late private of Co. E, 7th Regt. U. S. Infantry.
108 Springfield Ave., NEWARK, N. J.

BELOW-KNEE AMPUTATION.

CHARLES VAN BRUNT, OF LONG BRANCH CITY, N. J., says:
Write any thing you wish in testimony of my satisfaction with the artificial leg you made for me in 1885 and I will endorse it. I am delighted with the rubber foot.

BELOW-KNEE AMPUTATION.

ROSELLE, UNION CO., N. J., Nov. 3, 1887.
DEAR SIR :—I take pleasure in writing to inform you that your artificial limb has more than filled my expectations in the time I have been wearing it, now almost two years. I can wear it with comfort and walk miles without feeling tired. I can also run quite readily, and often play ball with the boys. I had my foot taken off a little above the ankle joint, and have worn your leg now almost two years. I am employed by the Central Railroad of New Jersey, as delivery clerk on their docks at New York, and I am constantly on my feet. When I first went to work there I left home at 5:48 in the morning and generally got home 10:22 at night ; I was on my feet four-fifths of that time, and my limb is as sound as a dollar to-day, and I have not had a cent's worth of fixing done to it since I had it. There is a friend of mine who has got a new leg since I have gotten mine. I don't remember the name of it, but it is going to pieces, and makes a rattling noise when he walks. If you want a leg that will *stand* by you, or rather under you, go to Marks.

Your fit is as perfect as if it had grown there, and I will with pleasure give attention to all you may refer to me. I remain,
Yours truly,
M. H. CAMPBELL.

BELOW-KNEE AMPUTATION,

Nov. 1, 1887.
A. A. MARKS :
I wish to say that I am very much pleased with your artificial limb. I can walk without a cane around the house and out to church, quite a distance.

I live in Phillipsburg at present. I am seventy-four years old and live with my youngest son. I had the best doctor in the United States and the best care. I have worn my limb one year and one-half. With due regards,
MALINDA GILLEN.

PHILLIPSBURG, WARREN CO., N. J.

BELOW-KNEE AMPUTATION.

Fitted from Measurements.

ROCKSBURG, WARREN CO., N. J., Nov. 5, 1887.

MR. MARKS :

SIR :—I am highly delighted with your leg. I have used an artificial limb since 1865, and about three years ago I got your patent, and I have more comfort than I ever had before. I can get around better, hunt the mountains, and feel at ease.

I would not give it for all the limbs I ever saw.

Yours with respect,
S. B. DANLEY.

BELOW-KNEE AMPUTATION.

ELIZABETHPORT, N. J., Nov. 1, 1887.

MR. A. A. MARKS :

DEAR SIR :—I have worn one of your artificial limbs for three years, and it has proved to be what you recommended.

My business requires me to be walking around all day from half-past six A. M. to five P. M., and during that time I have not had a single repair.

I remain, yours truly,
H. JENKINSON.

BELOW-KNEE AMPUTATION.

Oct. 28, 1887.

DEAR SIR :—Having worn one of your artificial limbs for over eight years, I would recommend it above all others for its strength and durability. I have worn my first limb for over seven years, and in that time it has cost me just $1.50 for repairs.

I have not a bit of trouble with my new limb, which I have four months. I can use your limb and do nearly as well with it as if it were my natural one.

Yours, etc.,
JOHN J. KEILY.

435 Court St., ELIZABETHPORT, N. J.

BELOW-KNEE AMPUTATION.

TRENTON, N. J.; Oct. 31, 1887.

MR. A. A. MARKS :

The artificial foot you made me last May, I am more than pleased with, having worn it every day since, from six A. M. until nine and ten P. M., with much ease. My work is that of a mill machinist and engineer. I can do as much work now as ever before.

Yours, etc.,
EDWARD KURTZ.

BELOW-KNEE AMPUTATION.

RARITAN, SOMERSET CO., N. J., Nov. 14, 1887.

MR. A. A. MARKS :

DEAR SIR :—I have worn one of your artificial legs for fourteen years with very little repair. It has given me good satisfaction. Stump seven inches. I like the rubber foot very much.

Yours,
J. A. VAN NEST.

BELOW-KNEE AMPUTATION.

Long Branch City, N. J., Dec. 14, 1887.

Dear Sir:—I have been walking on one of your limbs two years, and I like it very much, especially the rubber foot. It is the best, and I would recommend it. My limb is off two inches below the knee, and I can walk all day without any pain.

Yours, etc.,

D. C. Wood.

BELOW-KNEE AMPUTATION.

Long Branch City, N. J., Nov. 19, 1887.

A. A. Marks:

I am a carpenter by occupation and work steadily. I procured my limb in 1864; point of amputation six inches below the knee; the cost of limb on an average has not exceeded $2 per year; the rubber foot is the best I have yet seen, and can recommend your make of limb as the most durable and easiest to wear.

Yours respectfully,

Jos. S. Van Dyke.

BELOW-KNEE AMPUTATION.

Oct. 28, 1887.

Mr. A. A. Marks:

Dear Sir:—I take great pleasure in addressing these few lines, in order to express the satisfaction which I have had with your make of artificial leg. This is the second of your make I have worn, and very few can tell I have an artificial leg.

At present I am attending to the Laurel House Bowling Alley, and can bowl as well as the most of them. I have done farm work, running express, and most kind of hard work, since I have had this leg. I do heartily recommend your patent foot to any and all that are in need of same.

Respectfully,

Thos. J. Sprowl.

Lakewood, Ocean Co., N. J.

BELOW-KNEE AMPUTATION.

70 Mechanic St., Paterson, N. J., Oct. 27, 1887.

Mr. A. A. Marks, Manufacturer Artificial Limbs:

Dear Sir:—I have used legs of other makes and am at present wearing one of yours, and will say that it gives as good satisfaction as any other that has been presented to my notice, probably more. There are several things which recommend it.

Of course the rubber foot is the principal point of difference between your leg and that of other manufacturers. This foot combines to make the leg much simpler, consequently rendering it of less trouble to the wearer, and to keep the shoe always neater in appearance, preventing it from becoming bent and ugly looking.

It is also cleaner than the other foot, and of course there is no danger of any noise or rattling, etc., occasioned by its use.

But aside from the question of superiority of your make as compared with others, I would like to record the fact that treatment at your office is, as far as my knowledge extends, exceptionally courteous and even kind. Patients, whether male or female, need not be afraid that when dealing with your establishment they will be treated otherwise than in a gentlemanly and considerate manner. I have always found it so, receiving the kindest attentions on every occasion of my visits.

Yours very truly,

JOHN PARK.

BELOW-KNEE AMPUTATION.

Worn one leg seventeen years.

Oct. 29, 1887.

MR. A. A. MARKS :

DEAR SIR :—I would just say I am still wearing the leg I got from you in March, 1870, and I want to know if any other soldier has had one in use over seventeen years.

I would recommend your work to any one wanting an artificial leg, for they are the best leg made, and I would not do without one of them for a hundred dollars of any man's money.

FRANKLIN S. MONCRIEF,
Co. D, 10th Regt. New Jersey Volunteers.

BOX 856, VINELAND, CUMBERLAND CO., N. J.

BELOW-KNEE AMPUTATION.

ELIZABETH, N. J., Oct. 29, 1887.

MR. A. A. MARKS :

DEAR SIR :—I have had eight years' experience with one of your artificial limbs. I am very well pleased with your work, and am only too willing to testify to the merits of the same.

Furthermore, I can cheerfully recommend them to those whom necessity requires to make use of them.

Yours respectfully,

FRED. V. MEEKER.

BELOW-KNEE AMPUTATION.

ENGLEWOOD, BERGEN CO., N. J., Nov. 2, 1887.

MR A. A. MARKS :

SIR :—I am well pleased with the limb and willing to testify to its merits. My work is felling and hewing timber, which is very laborious. The point of amputation is about seven inches below the knee. The cost of repairs has been comparatively nothing. So far I have had it two years this month.

Yours respectfully,

JONATHAN A. BAKER.

BELOW-KNEE AMPUTATION.

FRANKLIN PARK, MIDDLESEX CO., N. J., Nov. 12, 1887.

A. A. MARKS:

DEAR SIR :—In reply to your letter of Oct. 26, will say that I had my first artificial leg and foot when I was eight years of age, and have had three in all. The present one I got in 1876 ; I think that your artificial limbs could be made to last with proper care from twenty to thirty years. I never have seen any better.

Yours truly,

JOHN H. BEEKMAN.

BELOW-KNEE AMPUTATION.

NEW YORK CITY, Nov. 17, 1887.

To all who are unfortunate to have lost a limb, I, John G. Collins, have had twenty-four years' experience in wearing limbs.

I have worn Dr. ——'s limb, and have seen the legs of many makers, but believe that none are to be compared with the Marks.

As to ease in walking or standing, I cannot ask for any thing better. There are many people who have known me for years and don't think that I wear an artificial limb. If there are any one-leg gentlemen that would like to have a walk with me call around at 565 West 37th Street; let me know two days ahead of time, and I will be ready to give him a tramp.

Yours truly,
JOHN G. COLLINS.

BELOW-KNEE AMPUTATION.

One leg in use over twenty years and still in order.

Society of the Army of the Potomac.
Nov. 14, 1887.

MR. A. A. MARKS:

DEAR SIR :—I have been wearing one of your artificial legs with patent rubber foot (amputated below the knee) over twenty years. I have never worn any other make of artificial leg and cannot therefore say from personal experience that your artificial limbs are better than those of other makes, but I can say from observation and inquiry with those who are wearing artificial legs, and I know many, that the one I wear (your patent) is in every respect superior, more durable, less liable to get out of order than any artificial leg I have seen or have any knowledge of.

Truly yours,
SAM'L TRUESDELL,
18 Broadway, N. Y.   Brvt. Lt. & Col. 65th N. Y. Vols.

BELOW-KNEE AMPUTATION.

Washington Avenue, near 167th St.,
NEW YORK CITY, December 5, 1881.

MR. A. A. MARKS:

DEAR SIR :—After an experience of over eight years in the use of your patent artificial leg with rubber foot, I desire to say that it has given me first-rate satisfaction. About four years ago I was induced to purchase a leg of Mr. ——'s make, with his wooden foot and ankle joint. After using it for nearly two years with constant repairs, I abandoned it, and am now using yours again. That trial was enough for me; I want no more ankle-jointed wooden feet for me on an artificial leg, so long as yours are to be had, as my own experience proves their superiority. I cheerfully recommend yours above any and all other makes.

CHAS. LIBENAU, M.D.

BELOW-KNEE AMPUTATION.

211 West 31st St., NEW YORK CITY, Oct., 1887.

I hereby certify that I have used one of the Marks artificial legs for several years past, and I know of no other that I prize so highly, and I cheerfully recommend it. It has caused me no trouble or expense since I have worn it.

Respectfully,
P. R. PALERMO.

P.S. I have worked in a machine shop, and the leg has had no need for repairs.

BELOW-KNEE AMPUTATION.

Jan. 28, 1888.

A. A. MARKS:

DEAR SIR :—In answer to your circular in regard to rubber limbs, would say that I have worn one of your rubber limbs for about fifteen years with entire satisfaction and at a nominal cost for repairs. My occupation is that of a truck-

No. 287.

man for the New York Belting and Packing Company. I help in loading my own truck and frequently lift bales of several hundredweight.

The limb has been in constant use. Leg amputated below the knee.

Respectfully yours,

C. H. BREWSTER.

15 Park Row, N. Y. CITY.

BELOW-KNEE AMPUTATION.

448 W. 19th St., NEW YORK CITY, Oct. 27, 1887.

MR. A. A. MARKS:

DEAR SIR :—Having worn one of your patent artificial legs for nearly five years, and will make application for a new one from the government just as soon as the time comes, seems that I am satisfied with it. I have only about three inches below the knee. I have been working as night watchman on the Erie Railroad dock for the last two years, and am on my leg twelve hours every night, and it does not trouble me at all. I have seen several other kinds, and recommend yours above all others.

I wish to say a few words for two of my friends that I sent to you for a leg; one has got a stump above the knee; he is working for the Manhattan Gas Company at pretty hard work, and gets along splendidly on his leg, which he has had about four months.

The other one has got a stump below the knee. He is on his feet all day long as brakeman on the elevated railroad. He has been wearing his artificial leg about sixteen months.

Yours truly,
JOHN J. WILSON,
Company G, 3d Infantry U.S.A.

BELOW-KNEE AMPUTATION.

Fitted from Measurements.

201 W. 44th St., NEW YORK CITY, Nov. 3, 1887.

DR. MARKS:

DEAR SIR:—In reply to your questions concerning my leg, I would say that in the six years I have used your legs in no case have they failed to give satisfaction. I find the leg extremely light and durable, and a leg that a person is not afraid of breaking by hard usage, an advantage of importance to me, for I am very hard on a leg. Last winter I worked in a printing office, and was the boy of all work, having to run a number of errands and to be on my feet a great deal; in every case I could depend on the leg as well as my good one. It has been said that long and continued standing is more tiresome than walking. It may be so, but while out hunting last fall I had to stand up all day in a rather tipply hunting boat, where balancing added to the fatigue of standing. This was due I believe to the rubber foot, which accommodates itself so well to uneven and unlevel surfaces.

I found I could stand as long as the rest of the hunters.

My leg is amputated two and one-half inches below the knee.

I have worn your legs for six years and shall always continue to wear them.

I am, sir, yours very truly,
GEO. W. SHERIDAN.

P. S. I would further say that I can skate both on ice and rollers, and enjoy it hugely.

BELOW-KNEE AMPUTATION.

120 W. 23d St., NEW YORK CITY, Jan. 18, 1888.

I have worn your leg for about four years, and can recommend it highly.

T. W. CARROLL.

BELOW-KNEE AMPUTATION.

BARRETT, NEPHEWS & Co., 5 John St., N. Y., Oct. 31, 1887.

SIR:—I have used the Marks leg for twenty-six years.

It cannot be excelled; I have used one continuously for ten years without having any repairing. Your legs have given me the greatest satisfaction; as for durability, they have no equal.

There is no foot in my opinion that can compare with the rubber foot.

Respectfully yours,
JOHN S. BOWNE,
Care of the above address.

BELOW-KNEE AMPUTATION

Nov. 3, 1887.

A. A. MARKS:

I received your circular, and in answer would say that I have worn my leg since October, 1869, and have had no repairs done. The leg is off below the knee.

I am perfectly satisfied with it, but will soon have to have another. Wishing you much success, I am,
Yours truly, F. NICHOLS.
13 William St., New York City.

BELOW-KNEE AMPUTATION.

27 Jones St., New York City, Jan. 2, 1888.

A. A. MARKS :

I lost my leg below the knee from gunshot wound received in the late war. As soon as my stump healed, the United States Government presented me with one of ——'s legs with an ankle joint. I wore it for a short time, and thought I liked it, but when I had one of your rubber feet applied to it I at once discovered that I had bettered my condition, and that the ankle joint in an artificial leg was as useless as "wings on a pig." I have worn your rubber foot now

No. 288.

about twenty years, am a machinist, and work at the lathe, and forge ten hours a day as steadily as the days come and go. For ten years I worked on a foot lathe, doing the treading with my rubber foot.

Sundays I take my family out for a walk, and frequently jaunt about all day. I have been so thoroughly restored by your patent that really I cannot see or feel that I am different to persons in possession of their natural limbs. I do not take a second place to any body, either on the walk or at the bench.

WILLIAM DIETZE.

BELOW-KNEE AMPUTATION.

Nov. 2, 1887.

Mr. A. A. MARKS :

DEAR SIR :—The six years' experience I have had with your artificial limb I have found it most satisfactory in every respect. The rubber foot works to perfection. I have done hard, laborious work for about four or five years with it without any repairs. I cannot recommend it too highly for the great service it has done me, and I can say without contradiction that it is impossible to make a better. Hoping, sir, that you may have long life and success to successfully fit up many an unfortunate man, as you have me,

Yours, with gratitude,
PETER NEENAN.

165th St. and 10th Ave., NEW YORK CITY.

BELOW-KNEE AMPUTATION.

75 West St., NEW YORK CITY, Nov. 10, 1887.

A. A. MARKS, ESQ.:

DEAR SIR:—I am pleased to report that with your patent rubber-foot leg I have been especially pleased. I am not only able to attend to my business, but can indulge in a good long walk occasionally, and enjoy myself in other respects. I can walk better and further on your legs than on any of the old styles I have worn, the action of the foot being natural and noiseless, sufficiently so to deceive the closest observers. I seldom use a cane, and feel no actual need for one. I have never met any one wearing your make of legs that has not spoken highly of it.

Mr. F. V. Meeker long ago advised me to buy your leg, as well as Mr. J. P. Kenny. Both these gentlemen were known to me, and were operating satisfactorily on your leg. I yielded to their advice, and have never since regretted it. I can walk on smooth and rough walk with perfect safety, unattended by disagreeable noise or danger of breaking or tripping.

Respectfully yours,
J. J. EAGAN.

BELOW-KNEE AMPUTATION.

Nov. 16, 1887.

A. A. MARKS, ESQ.:

DEAR SIR:—I have taken great pleasure in recommending your artificial legs to parties needing them, whom I have met in this city and abroad. I have been wearing your make for twenty years, and if the good One spares me I will say I will keep on for twenty years more. My stump is one inch below the knee. I have marched in a parade in this city from 59th Street to the Battery, and return, when the streets were in a bad condition for men to walk in with both legs. Phil. Kearny post, to which I belong, in this city, can vouch for the above.

I remain, yours truly,
A. HAUSBECK.

14 St. Luke's Place, NEW YORK CITY.

BELOW-KNEE AMPUTATION.

24th Ward, WOODLAWN, NEW YORK CITY, Nov. 8, 1887.

MR. A. A. MARKS:

DEAR SIR:—I wish to say through your pamphlet that I have been wearing one of your patent artificial legs for over nineteen years, and it gives me much pleasure to record my testimony in favor of it. I have worn it in all kinds of laboring work, and it has proved to be every thing you claimed it to be, durable and lasting. It has no equal. I shall always wear your patent leg, and at all times recommend it to others.

Yours respectfully,
MICHAEL DOOLEY.

BELOW-KNEE AMPUTATION.

Twenty-two years on the rubber foot—Experience is the best teacher.

Nov. 2, 1887.

A. A. MARKS, ESQ.:

DEAR SIR:—On the 27th day of April, 1865, I had the misfortune to lose my right foot, and all the toes of the left foot, up close to the ball of the foot, by a railroad accident on the Harlem Railroad, and after lying in the hospital three months or more, in the month of September of the same year, I got one of your artificial legs with the rubber foot, and to say it has given me entire satisfaction is not saying half enough for it; in fact, I don't know what I could have done without it, being a poor man and having a large family depending upon me for support. I only had my trade to fall back on, which is heavy and laborious work, ship-caulking, which keeps me on my feet the most of my time. I weigh 204 pounds. This I think very trying on perfect limbs, let alone false limbs. As to the durability of your limbs, I have had the one I use now in constant use the last seven or eight years, and you have got the first dollar to get yet for repairs, in my 22 years of experience with your artificial legs. I can safely say that I have seen a couple of hundred persons with artificial limbs of other makers, and from my own experience will say without fear of contradiction that none of them are as perfect as yours with the rubber foot. "Experience is the best teacher." Hoping this will meet the eye of some poor unfortunate like myself, I remain,

Yours respectfully,

JOSEPH BATEY.

553 E. 143 St., NEW YORK CITY.

BELOW-KNEE AMPUTATION.

Oct. 30, 1887.

MR. MARKS:

DEAR SIR:—I recommend every person who has lost a limb to get one of your patented limbs with the rubber hand or foot, or both if required. My wife lost her left foot about three years ago, which was amputated about five inches below the knee, and in three months after the accident I got one of your limbs with the rubber foot attached. It has had constant wear in all kinds of housework, as well as for walking long distances, ever since, and it is just as good to-day as it was the day I received it.

The fitting is perfect, never causing any soreness or lameness of the stump whatever. My wife says she scarcely realizes that she ever lost a limb, and strangers, even experienced doctors, seeing her walking, or at work, can never detect that she is wearing a false limb, and some when told do not believe until they see for themselves. A friend of my wife, a Mrs. K——, knows of a doctor in Morrisania who has lost one of his limbs, and got one of some other make, and can not wear it without causing soreness and lameness, and if possible we will direct him to you or get some of his friends or acquaintances to do so.

Very respectfully yours,

WILBUR S. STUDWELL.

721 East 169th St., NEW YORK CITY.

BELOW-KNEE AMPUTATION.

73 Taylor St., WILLIAMSBURG, KINGS CO., N. Y., Oct. 28, 1887.

MR. A. A. MARKS:

DEAR SIR:—As you are to publish a new pamphlet, I wish to add my name to your list of patients who use your rubber feet.

After using one of yours for several years I was induced by Mr. —— to purchase one of his make with ankle joint and wooden foot. It was not satisfactory, and after a thorough trial I had to condemn it and came to you again. The limb I am wearing at present time I have been wearing for the last eight years constantly without one cent of expense, and I think there are very few who use an artificial leg as much as I do. For three years I was messenger for the New York and Brooklyn Ferry Co. I had a great deal of walking to do, I often hear friends and acquaintances express great surprise upon learning that I am wearing an artificial limb. You are at liberty to use my name as occasion requires for reference.

Yours truly,
WM. C. DITMAR,
Ferrymaster New York and Brooklyn Ferry Co.

BELOW-KNEE AMPUTATION.

Oct. 26, 1887.

MR. A. A. MARKS:

DEAR SIR:—I learn that you are going to print a new pamphlet; if so, I would like to express my thanks for your wonderful leg. About 12 years ago I was run over by an 8th Avenue horse-car and had my right leg so mutilated that it had to be amputated five inches below the knee, and just as soon as my leg got well I got one of your artificial legs, and have used it for ten years with but a very little expense. Now I can walk so well, strangers do not believe I have an artificial leg.

My weight is 225 pounds. I stand at my work (a marble turner) all day, and often for weeks I work fifteen hours a day.

I do not know what I would do without your leg. I always recommend your limbs to those I meet who are compelled by misfortune to use an artificial leg. I am,
Yours most respectfully,
THEODORE W. SCOTT.
335 Graham Ave., BROOKLYN, E. D., N. Y.

BELOW-KNEE AMPUTATION.

Oct. 27, 1887.

MR. A. A. MARKS:

DEAR SIR:—I have been wearing artificial limbs for thirty-eight years. I have been wearing one of your limbs with rubber foot about one year, and for general comfort and ease in walking I can cheerfully say it is superior to any I have ever worn. Point of amputation above ankle.
Yours respectfully,
THOMAS McCAULAY.
292 Flatbush Ave., BROOKLYN, N. Y.

BELOW-KNEE AMPUTATION.

Dec. 29, 1887.

DEAR SIR:—I have been wearing one of your artificial legs for three or four months and find it a great comfort to me.

I can play ball and run like the others. I can poney down the hill like the other boys. I think your leg the best in use, and no mistake.
Yours respectfully,
HENRY OETJEN.
565 Third Ave., BROOKLYN, N. Y.

BELOW-KNEE AMPUTATION.

Worn one leg twenty years, night and day.

614 Bergen St., BROOKLYN, N. Y., Nov. 17, 1887.

MR. A. A. MARKS:

DEAR SIR:—This is to certify that I have been using one of your improved artificial legs for over twenty years with the greatest satisfaction. As to its durability and ease over others I have no doubt. I had seven years' experience with ankle-joint legs, and they were almost useless to me, as my business has always been laborious. I follow the occupation of contractor and builder. The improved rubber foot is, I believe from my experience, the best made. I have worn the one you made me over 20 years night and day. The cost of repairs in all that time is for an occasional pair of knee-joint bolts, and an occasional back strap, that I always put in myself. I am still wearing the same leg, and now with a little repair would be as good as new. I remain,

Respectfully yours,
PATRICK McCARTY.

BELOW-KNEE AMPUTATION.

177 Flatbush Ave., BROOKLYN, N. Y., Nov. 14, 1887.
DEAR SIR:—In reference to your artificial limb, I can simply say that I do not think its equal exists. I am a bartender by occupation, have worked eighteen hours out of the twenty-four, and have never had any cause to remove the limb for ailings, or lost time or money for repairing; it is not quite two years since I lost my limb, the amputation being made above the ankle. I am now wearing one of your artificial limbs one year, and can honestly say that my stump has always been healthy. It has never troubled me in the least. As I am personally acquainted with such people who are compelled to wear artificial limbs, I have had a good opportunity to see the difference in them, and I should truly say that I would never recommend any other, as I am fully convinced that yours are the best and most durable. For further information I can be seen personally at my residence.

Yours sincerely,
LOUIS F. BEHNKE.

BELOW-KNEE AMPUTATION.

Oct. 27, 1887.
I have now been wearing Marks' artificial limbs for over twenty-one years, and proclaim their superiority over all others.

Previous to using his I tried those of three other makers, but from none of them have I derived the comfort and satisfaction which I have from those of Marks. In my opinion they are the nearest approach to the natural limb of any that has yet been invented. I consider his rubber foot far ahead of any other contrivance to replace the natural foot. They are noiseless, reliable, and lasting. I have put them to the severest test, for during fifteen years of the time I have worn one of them my occupation was of a very laborious character, and taken in connection with my weight, which always averaged two hundred pounds, was such as to try the merits of any limb. It has stood the test beyond my expectations, and I confidently give the Marks limbs the preference before all others.

JAMES BOYLE.
271 Berry St., BROOKLYN, E. D., N. Y.

BELOW-KNEE AMPUTATION.

69 6th Ave., MOUNT VERNON, WESTCHESTER CO., N. Y.
MR. MARKS:
DEAR SIR:—Having used one of your legs for a number of years, I am glad to say that I must give you credit for making the best and most durable leg that I have seen. I work at most everything that gives it a hard trial, such as working on a thirty-foot ladder at painting in the warmest of weather. Last winter I drove a wagon and was out all kinds of weather, but it still holds well. I would be pleased to talk and give all the information I can about

your leg. I could not say too much for you. I can be seen at any time at my residence, Mount Vernon, and I defy any one not knowing me to tell that I have one of your limbs. My limb is off six inches below the knee. I remain,
Respectfully yours,
JOSEPH PUGMIRE.

BELOW-KNEE AMPUTATION.

Fifteen years in constant use.

W. PEPPER, Miller and Dealer in Grain, Feed, Coal, etc.,
Feed Mill, Saw Mill, and Cider Mill,
TOWNERS, PUTNAM CO., N.Y., Oct. 27, 1887.

MR. A. A. MARKS:

DEAR SIR:—The leg you made for me in 1872 has been in every-day use from that time till now, and is a good leg yet.

The expense for repairs has been less than a dollar per year.

I think as it stands my business no one need fear to put your rubber foot to the severest tests.

Yours, etc.,
W. PEPPER.

BELOW-KNEE AMPUTATION.

CHEMUNG COUNTY CLERK'S OFFICE,
ELMIRA, CHEMUNG CO., N. Y., Nov. 7, 1887.

MR. A. A. MARKS:

DEAR SIR:—I desire to say in the fewest words possible that after wearing three different legs I am prepared to certify that for ease, comfort, and durability your legs with rubber feet are and of right ought to be placed at the head of the list.

One matter that should never be lost sight of is its durability.

I have worn your leg over nine years, and have paid out just twenty-five cents for repairs, and the old thing seems to be good for another nine years. My experience, covering a period of twenty-four years, is that, with other legs, the item of repairs is from $5 to $10 per year, to say nothing of the inconvenience of waiting for repairs.

THEO. G. SMITH, Deputy.

BELOW-KNEE AMPUTATION.

Nov. 1, 1887.

MR. A. A. MARKS, New York:

DEAR SIR:—It is with pleasure that I can endorse your artificial leg after seven years' use constantly in my occupation, railroading, where I have an opportunity of testing thoroughly its durability and efficiency, particularly your rubber foot.

It never deceived me. Being heavy upon my feet, weighing 220 pounds, jumping on and off moving trains about the same as before losing my leg, and have had no occasion to lay out a cent for repairs. My leg being amputated below the knee brings a first-class foot into prominence and hard to counterfeit, which my experience proves to me you have succeeded in doing. I am,
Yours truly,
HENRY N. SMITH.

1308 Hall St., ELMIRA, CHEMUNG CO., N. Y.

BELOW-KNEE AMPUTATION.

N. REYNOLDS, Undertaker.
DELPHI, ONONDAGA CO., N. Y., Dec. 4, 1887.

A. A. MARKS:

DEAR SIR :—Yours of October 26th is at hand. I have worn your legs nearly twenty years and have worked at nearly all kinds of work. I think they are the best leg made. I am by occupation an undertaker. The leg I am wearing at present I have worn over eight years.

Respectfully yours,
N. REYNOLDS.

BELOW-KNEE AMPUTATION.

MATTEAWAN, DUTCHESS CO., N. Y., Nov. 16, 1887.

MR. A. A. MARKS:

DEAR SIR :—I wish to give my testimony in recommending your patent artificial legs with rubber feet. I have used four of your legs and find them satisfactory in every respect.

I want no ankle joints. The rubber foot is the best improvement yet. As for repairs, it has not cost me over $3 for all.

I am standing all day at my work. I have used patent artificial legs since 1864 and yours give the best satisfaction of any.

Amputation below the knee.

Yours truly,
RUFUS TILBE.

BELOW-KNEE AMPUTATION.

Fitted from Measurements.

VAN ETTENVILLE, CHEMUNG CO., N. Y., Nov. 1, 1887.

MR. A. A. MARKS:

DEAR SIR :—It gives me great pleasure to state that after having used one of your patent artificial legs for over three years I find it to be superior to the legs of other makers that I have used before. It is safe to stand or walk on. It does not produce the creaking and rattling noise which greatly annoyed me in the others. It is easily kept clean and in good working order. It has not cost me one cent for repairs. I am on my feet every day. My business is harness making, and I cannot see but that my leg is as good now as it was when I commenced wearing it. I particularly recommend your success in fitting from measurements. My leg is amputated below the knee. My stump is eight inches long. I cheerfully recommend all who inquire about artificial limbs to you as the place to get the best.

Respectfully,
GEO. W. HARVEY,
Co. I, 14th N. Y. H. A.

BELOW-KNEE AMPUTATION.

Oct. 27, 1887.

MR. A. A. MARKS:

DEAR SIR :—I have used one of your patent limbs for eighteen months, and have found it perfectly satisfactory, and would recommend it to any one who wants one.

Yours truly,
JOHN M. MILSPAUGH.

WALDEN, ORANGE CO., N. Y.

BELOW-KNEE AMPUTATION.

Oct. 28, 1887.

Mr. A. A. Marks:

Dear Sir:—In answering your request I will state as follows: On the 23d of March, 1887, I had my foot so badly crushed that amputation was necessary. The accident happened at eleven o'clock in the forenoon; at three o'clock in the afternoon my foot was gone forever. I felt that my affliction was great, but when I was recovering my doctor told me about your artificial legs and how I could use one. I then felt encouraged. I was only nineteen days in bed with my leg, when it was all right, so as to allow me to go all around the room, with the use of two chairs.

In four months I had one of your artificial legs with rubber foot, which I can recommend to anybody. I can work at anything almost and can walk with ease and comfort. Any one desiring to communicate with me, in regard to your foot I will cheerfully answer. I owe my recovery to Dr. John T. Howell, who attended me and recommended your leg. I remain,

Yours truly,

PATRICK C. CASEY,

Cor. of Veness and Carpenter Aves., NEWBURGH, N. Y.

BELOW-KNEE AMPUTATION.

71 South St., NEWBURGH, N. Y., Oct. 28, 1887.

A. A. MARKS:

Dear Sir:—Having had considerable experience with your artificial limbs I take pleasure in testifying to their merits.

On April 9, 1865, I lost my right leg at Sumterville, S. C. and have used artificial legs for twenty-two years.

In September or October, 1865, I was furnished with an artificial leg made by Dr. ——; the leg fitted and was well made, but the continual squeaking of the ankle joint, requiring it to be oiled very often, and the heavy thud of the foot in walking annoyed me so much that I concluded to have one of your rubber-foot legs.

I was so well pleased with it that I had a rubber foot applied to the old ankle-joint leg, and in 1882 had you make me a new leg with rubber foot.

I have seen about all the different kinds of legs made and must say that I consider yours the best. My amputation is two and one-quarter inches below the knee, and my business requires me to be on my feet from 5 A. M. to 10 P. M. daily. I use a cane only when I am on the street, and walk so well that many have no idea that I have an artificial leg.

During the twenty-two years that I have used artificial legs it has cost me about $75 for all repairs and supplies, an average of less than $3.50 per annum. I am well pleased with the legs you have made for me, and take pleasure in testifying that yours with patent rubber foot is the best and most durable artificial leg made.

Very respectfully,

JOSEPH LOMAS.

Late Sergt. Co. B, 56th N. Y. S. V. Vols., Ex-Postmaster, ex-Collector and ex-member of Assembly.

BELOW-KNEE AMPUTATION.

ELLENVILLE, ULSTER Co., N. Y., Oct. 27, 1887.

Dear Sir:—My occupation is harness maker. I have worn your artificial leg almost sixteen years. The actual cost for repairs in that time was not more than ten dollars. I am satisfied that for endurance your patent artificial leg can not be beat.

Yours truly,

AUGUST GROSCH.

BELOW-KNEE AMPUTATION.

HUDSON, COLUMBIA CO., N. Y., Nov. 18, 1887.

To MR. A. A. MARKS:

DEAR SIR:—Agreeable to your wish, and desirous of adding a word of cheer to the unfortunate, I most gladly give my experience in the use, durability, and ease of your rubber foot.

I am a farmer, which has always been my principal business. For the past twenty-five years or more I have worn the rubber foot constantly about farm work. I think I have had it repaired three times, though in neither case was it absolutely necessary. The elasticity of the rubber foot no doubt added much to its durability, and at the same time gave a more natural movement in walking, obviating the disagreeable thumping that attended the other foot I had used, and at the same time the jar to the natural limb, making it more comfortable and easy. In a word, I think for grace of movement, easiness, use, and durability the rubber foot is as near the action of the natural limb as can be hoped for, and a substitute of incalculable blessing to those using it. To move about like other men, and capable of doing any kind of business, does to a large extent mitigate the loss sustained, and gives hope and cheer to those who have met with the loss of a limb. Let no one therefore be despondent; the future is equally hopeful for them. I should have said that I use the short leg, having about six inches of stump below the knee.

I am, yours most truly,

H. R. HOSFORD.

BELOW-KNEE AMPUTATION.

DE GRASSE, ST. LAWRENCE CO., N. Y., Nov. 7, 1887.

MR. A. A. MARKS:

DEAR SIR:—I feel as though I ought to thank you for the success you have had in fitting me with an artificial limb. I believe no other limb that I have seen could take the place of the rubber foot. I have worn an artificial limb for the past twenty-two years; the first ten years I wore Dr. ——'s. It was a good limb for about two years, and then the foot became worn and worthless; to-day I am wearing one of yours, and have worn it almost seven years, and it is a good limb now.

I have not laid out one cent for repairs yet. I am a laborer and often lift heavy articles, such as barrels of sugar and all kinds of freight. I would advise all who are so unfortunate as to be obliged to wear an artificial limb to try the rubber foot. I remain,

Yours very respectfully,

A. H. ARMSTRONG.

BELOW-KNEE AMPUTATION.

WATKINS, SCHUYLER CO., N. Y., Nov. 8, 1887.

MR. A. A. MARKS:

DEAR SIR:—It is with pleasure that I add my testimony to the number who have and are giving your artificial limbs their due reward. I have worn your make of leg for three years. I have never worn any other, and have no desire to, as I believe your rubber foot is easier to walk on, more durable, and much more natural than any other kind. I never use a cane.

I go up and down stairs the same as people with natural feet. I can run and skate on ice and roller skates. I walked three miles in forty-five minutes with the greatest of ease. I had my leg fitted from measurements, and it works like a charm. My leg is off about four inches below the knee. The cost for repairs on the leg is too slight to mention.

Yours respectfully,

EDWARD BERTHOLF.

BELOW-KNEE AMPUTATION.

Fitted from Measurements.

LOCKPORT, NIAGARA CO., N. Y., Oct. 28, 1887.

A. A. MARKS, New York:

DEAR SIR:—The leg you furnished me from measurements sent you, fitted perfectly and has given the best of satisfaction.

Yours truly,
PATRICK CLARK.

BELOW-KNEE AMPUTATION.

WHITEHALL, WASHINGTON CO., N. Y., Nov. 10, 1887.

MR. A. A. MARKS:

DEAR SIR:—Your letter received, asking me to tell of my experience with artificial limbs. I am very glad of a chance to speak a word in favor of the limbs of your make, one of which I have worn constantly for the last ten years. My business (boating) is at times very laborious, besides requiring me to be up night and day a great deal of the time. I think the solid rubber foot is the best thing of the kind made ; it is more like the natural foot and is not liable to get out of order. You are at liberty to refer any one to me for further information.

Yours truly,
C. M. JILLSON.

BELOW-KNEE AMPUTATION.

Louisiana Street Freight Depot, BUFFALO, N. Y., Oct. 27, 1887.

I have worn your legs for twenty-eight years, and commend them to all.

REUBEN HALL.

BELOW-KNEE AMPUTATION.

PORT RICHMOND, RICHMOND CO., N. Y., Nov. 7, 1887.

A. A. MARKS:

DEAR SIR:—In reply to yours would state that I have worn an artificial limb for the last fifteen years, and for the last four years have been wearing one of yours with rubber foot.

With my experience I consider your artificial limb with rubber foot far superior to any I have used, and recommend it to my patients. I can walk much better than I ever could before. Expenses for repairs are almost nothing. I can safely say I consider your artificial limbs the best in the market. You can refer any one to me in regard to your limb.

Yours, etc.,
DR. G. W. NELSON.

BELOW-KNEE AMPUTATION.

Fitted from Measurements.

ITHACA, TOMPKINS CO., N. Y., Oct. 3, 1887.

A. A. MARKS:

DEAR SIR:—It gives me pleasure to recommend an article that proves a success after a fair and impartial test.

I have worn your artificial leg since November, 1880. My stump is four inches below the knee. Three years this fall I purchased a second leg of you, my stump having shrunk so much that the first leg had to have a new socket. I sent to you to have a new socket put on the foot, which you did by measurement and I must say the fit was perfect. I now have the two legs, which I hope will last me for the next twelve years. The only repairs aside from the new socket are new bolts in the knee joints, which I put in myself. My business is that of foreman of machine works, which requires a great deal of walking up and down stairs; in fact, I am on my feet from ten to thirteen hours a day. It is quite a relief when I get home to change legs; one experiences about the same relief as in changing shoes when very tired. As for durability, the rubber foot can not be excelled. Wishing you continued success, I am,

Very truly,
EDGAR O. GODFREY.

BELOW-KNEE AMPUTATION.

Fitted from Measurements.

CLAYVILLE, ONEIDA CO., N. Y., Nov. 1, 1887.

MR. A. A. MARKS:

DEAR SIR:—It is with great pleasure I recommend your patent artificial legs. Having used others with ankle motion I am able to judge the difference and the advantages of your patent rubber foot. There is no rattling or breaking down. I have given yours nearly twenty years' trial without extra cost, and in so doing have proved the real merits and great satisfaction it has given me. I have done all kinds of heavy shop work on it with comparatively no difficulty, with amputation five inches below the knee. My leg was fitted from measurements. I can work on the roof of a building with ease.

Yours respectfully,
D. M. GREEN,
Late Co. A, 97 Regt. N. Y. V.

BELOW-KNEE AMPUTATION.

PRATTSBURG, STEUBEN CO., N. Y., Dec. 7, 1887.

MR. A. A. MARKS, New York:

DEAR SIR:—Accept a few lines from me in favor of your artificial limbs October, 16, 1886, I had my leg amputated five and one-half inches below the knee. February 18, 1887, I commenced wearing one of your make of limbs I surprise many by the way I get around.

The deception is so complete that a person will often mistake in telling which is my artificial leg. I sometimes walk four or five miles, and often work on my feet all day. I can do most any kind of work. I have followed the plow some, not from necessity, but for the novelty of the thing. It seems almost superhuman that there could be a substitute made for the natural limb which would have the natural movement and lightness of step that your rubber foot has. With the rubber foot a person steps fully as light as with the natural foot. The cost of repairs, which I have heard so much complaint from those wearing the ankle joint movement, is certainly done away with by the rubber foot. Your invention is in fact a great boon to all who have had the misfortune to lose a limb, and truly there is many a dark cloud with a silver lining. Refer to me at any time, and I will gladly respond.

Yours respectfully,
G. WELFORD DEAN.

BELOW KNEE AMPUTATION.

Oct. 10, 1887.

MR. A. A. MARKS:

DEAR SIR:—I have been using one of your artificial limbs for several years, and find it answers *fully* to every thing you claim, durability, neatness, etc. I am on my feet the most of my time, and walk a great deal, and find no inconvenience.

My leg is amputated about five inches below the knee. The cost for repairs is very small. It is a grand success. I remain,
Truly yours,
HUGH DICK.
WALLKILL, ULSTER CO., N. Y.

BELOW-KNEE AMPUTATION.

Nov. 3, 1887.
MR. A. A. MARKS:
DEAR SIR:—I am glad to have a chance to give testimony of your artificial legs with rubber feet. I have worn one of your artificial legs four years and eleven months, and it has not cost me a cent for repairs, and it will last me a number of years yet. I am yard-master of the Ulster and Delaware Road, and on the go from twelve to fourteen hours every day, and have not lost a day since I got your leg. I would have no other as long as I can get one with rubber foot. . . . My leg is amputated about four inches above the ankle. Mr. Marks fitted me by measurement, and it fitted like a kid glove, and I have not had any trouble with the stump since I have worn his leg. I will be pleased to answer any letter that may be sent to me for information. I remain,
Yours truly,
JOHN LOUNSBERRY.
RONDOUT, ULSTER CO., N. Y.

BELOW-KNEE AMPUTATION.

Fitted from Measurements.

PALMYRA, WAYNE CO., N. Y., Oct. 26, 1887.
A. A. MARKS, ESQ.:
DEAR SIR:—Your letter of the 26th inst. at hand.
I answer as follow : Fitting by measures good. Cabinet maker by occupation. Have worked at farm work. I have used artificial legs twenty-two years. I have three of Marks', one of ——, and like yours much the best. Leg off eight inches below the knee. I have worn your leg eighteen years at a cost of less than one dollar and fifty cents a year. I like your leg well enough to buy when this gives out.
Yours very truly,
P. P. LAIRD.

BELOW-KNEE AMPUTATION.

HORNELLSVILLE, STEUBEN CO., N. Y., Oct. 28, 1887.
DEAR SIR:—I have worn your artificial leg five years with entire satisfaction. I have been at all kinds of occupations.
I have had no repairing. Amputation just below the knee.
Last year I was in a grocery business where I was on my feet continually.
Yours respectfully,
P. DONNELLEY.

BELOW-KNEE AMPUTATION.

MR. A. A. MARKS:
DEAR SIR:—This is to testify that I have used one of your artificial legs fourteen years with a trifling expense, and the second one you fitted me with I have used three years without any expense. After using other artificial legs with ankle joint, attended with large expense and inconvenience of the ankle-joint breaking and rattling, I am convinced that your patent leg with rubber foot is the best artificial limb manufactured in this or any other country. Point

of amputation, six inches below the knee. Occupation, harness-maker. I have used artificial limbs twenty-four years.

Yours truly,
ABRAHAM EVANS,
Late of Co. H, 66th N. Y. Infantry.
WALKER VALLEY, ULSTER CO., N. Y.

BELOW-KNEE AMPUTATION.

Nov. 4, 1887.

MR. A. A. MARKS, New York:

DEAR SIR:—As a testimonial of the excellence of your patent artificial limbs, I would say for the benefit of those who are so unfortunate as to need an appliance of the kind, I am a farmer and it is now nearly two years since I have worn one of your artificial legs. October 6, 1885, I had my right leg amputated six inches above the ankle joint, and in the following February you applied the artificial one.

I have worn it every day since, and must say that I am well pleased with it. I do most all kinds of work on a farm, can handle all kinds of machinery, can get in and out of a wagon and drive ten or fifteen miles by day or night nearly as well as ever.

I get on so well that I myself and all my friends are surprised.

They think it very remarkable. Since my misfortune, I have carefully inquired about all the different patents of artificial legs and feet. I find none to compare with your solid ankle joint and rubber foot. After nearly two years wear, mine seems as good as new, and never had any repairs. I can wear a sock on it as long as I can on the natural foot. It makes no unnatural noise in walking, and no ankle joint getting out of repair.

From my experience, I would advise any one needing an artificial leg to procure one of A. A. Marks, with solid ankle and rubber foot, by all means.

Respectfully yours,
J. EYSAMAN.
EDWARDSVILLE, ST. LAWRENCE CO., N. Y.

BELOW-KNEE AMPUTATION.

Oct. 30, 1887.

MR. A. A. MARKS:

DEAR SIR:—The artificial leg you made for me gives good satisfaction, and I don't think there is any other foot made as good as the rubber foot. I have my leg going on three years, and have had no repairs done to amount to anything. I had the socket lined and the foot re-covered once. The cost has been nothing. I am a miner, and the work is very hard on an artificial leg, but my leg has stood the work well, and I can't see but that it is as good now as ever.

Yours, etc.,
EUGENE FITCH.
CARMEL, PUTNAM CO., N. Y.

BELOW-KNEE AMPUTATION.

McGRAWVILLE, CORTLAND CO., N. Y., Oct. 29, 1887.

MR. A. A. MARKS:

DEAR SIR:—I will say to you in regard to the limb, I am greatly pleased. I can do any kind of work. I am in a hotel and restaurant, and am on my feet from six in the morning until ten at night. I would not exchange for any other.

I have worn the limb about two years without repairs, and my weight is 191 pounds.

GEO. R. GARDNER.

BELOW-KNEE AMPUTATION.

Fitted from Measurements.

CANAAN FOUR CORNERS, COLUMBIA CO., N. Y., Oct. 31, 1887.
MR. A. A. MARKS :
DEAR SIR :—Yours of the 26th received, and in reply would say that after wearing limbs of your make for some sixteen or seventeen years, and having worn the old style with ankle joint, I can say that yours with rubber feet are far the best in all respects.
The one that I now wear you made some two or three years ago from measurements. It was a good fit, and is as good to-day as when I first put it on, I think. My limb is off below the knee ; I am a harness-maker, but give my leg some pretty rough use sometimes.

Respectfully yours,
C. H. GROVES.

BELOW-KNEE AMPUTATION.

PORT JEFFERSON, SUFFOLK CO., N. Y., Nov. 2, 1887.
For the last twelve years I have used one of A. A. Marks' artificial limbs with rubber foot with satisfactory results.
No rattling hinges or squeaking joints to annoy me. I can recommend your leg to all who contemplate getting a limb.

Yours,
GEO. W. KIMMER.

BELOW-KNEE AMPUTATION.

Nov. 2, 1887.
A. A. MARKS :
DEAR SIR :—I am more than pleased with my leg, and I gladly add my testimony to its superiority. I have worn your celebrated leg with rubber foot for the last nine years, giving satisfaction.
I have had severe trials ; my leg could stand them, and I am certain that I can appreciate it as the best artificial leg ever patented. I occupy myself in going to school every day, so I can cheerfully recommend your patent limb to all needing substitutes for lost limbs.

Yours truly,
HIRBEN H. OSTRANDER.
ELIZAVILLE, COLUMBIA CO., N. Y.

BELOW-KNEE AMPUTATION.

Dec. 18, 1887.
A. A. MARKS :
DEAR SIR :—My experience, in wearing your leg, is such that I cannot say too much in its praise. In 1872 I first got my artificial leg from you. For twelve long years I wore that leg every day ; the first four years I built bridges, graded streets, and dug sewers in the city of Utica. The next three years I kept a hotel. The next five years I boated on the Erie Canal.
During the twelve years it did not cost me a dollar for repairs, but at the end of that time it was nearly worn out. I had to repair it myself. Finally, I was compelled to replace it by a new one. Having been persuaded to try the Rochester leg, I bought one and paid $50 for it. Now I am without a leg, and out of pocket $50. I have not worn the leg much more than half the time since I had it, and it is all to pieces. I want to know how much you will charge me to put a foot on this leg I got from ——. I think, if you put a foot on it, I could

wear it until my circumstances would allow me to come down and get one of your legs.

While I worked in Utica, there was no man who could out-walk me or out-work me.

Respectfully yours,

JOHN McCUE.

WATERLOO, SENECA CO., N. Y.

BELOW-KNEE AMPUTATION.

Fitted from Measurements.

823 River St., TROY, N. Y., Nov. 3, 1887.

DEAR SIR :—Replying to your circular letter of the 26th ult., I have to say that for over five years I have used one of your artificial limbs with rubber foot, and I am frank to assert that I would use no other than those manufactured by you, so satisfactory has the purchase been. My leg is amputated between the ankle and knee, and I very much doubt if any other artificial limb would have served me so well. I have worked on it every day, and my employment is of a very laborious character. During the five years I have expended for repairs less than two dollars, and the limb is still in excellent condition. It affords me great pleasure to furnish this testimonial, because the limb has proved to be all that you claimed for it at the time of the purchase. You can refer to me at any time. I appreciate a good article, and have enough of the milk of human kindness in my composition to advise unfortunates like myself where to go to get the best.

Very respectfully yours,

WILLIAM McFARLANE.

BELOW-KNEE AMPUTATION.

MONT MOOR, ROCKLAND CO., N. Y., Nov. 5, 1887.

MR. A. A. MARKS :

DEAR SIR :—Having used one of your patent artificial legs with rubber foot some twelve or thirteen years, I consider that a fair trial. I am a farmer, and have had little or no expense attending the use of the leg. I cheerfully recommend your work.

Truly yours,

C. R. MERTINE.

BELOW-KNEE AMPUTATION.

LLOYD, ULSTER CO., N. Y., Oct. 27, 1887.

A. A. MARKS :

DEAR SIR :—I have the pleasure of adding my testimonial to the great many already in your pamphlet. My wife had her limb amputated in Roosevelt Hospital in New York City, July 15, 1882.

One year afterwards she commenced wearing one of your limbs, and is wearing it now with ease, doing all her housework up and down stairs. In four years it has cost her four dollars, one dollar per year. Limb was amputated below the knee joint. I am

Respectfully yours,

M. R. NILAN.

BELOW-KNEE AMPUTATION.

Fitted from Measurements.

DE FREESTVILLE, RENSSALAER CO., N. Y., Oct. 31, 1887.

A. A. MARKS, ESQ.:

DEAR SIR :—Your letter mailed to Mr. M. J. Whalen of Bath on the Hudson, New York, bearing date October 26th, was duly received by him. At his request I reply to the same in reference to his experience with your artificial legs. On the 21st of September, 1885, I first wrote you in regard to Mr. Whalen's leg. Within a few days I received a reply from you inclosing a chart with instructions for measurements. On the 7th of October following I measured his leg according to your system and forwarded the same with drafts to you. About three weeks afterward the leg arrived by express. We can simply say *the fit is perfect*, and you have Mr. Whalen's thanks for your system of fitting by measurements, which *saves the expense and loss of time* of visiting your office.

The leg has now been worn every day for a period of two years, and thus far cost *nothing for repairs*.

The amputation was performed March 28, 1884, at a point four inches below the knee joint. His occupation is not laborious, but requires a vast amount of walking, and it is necessary for him to be almost constantly on his feet. The leg has in every way been satisfactory, and we can heartily and conscientiously recommend it to any who may need such an appliance.

With good wishes for your continued success, and thanking you for your prompt and honorable mode of dealing, I am

Respectfully yours,
A. TEN EYCK, M.D.

BELOW-KNEE AMPUTATION.

BANK OF CHATEAUGAY,
CHATEAUGAY, FRANKLIN CO., N. Y., Oct. 31, 1887.

A. A. MARKS, ESQ.:

DEAR SIR :—It is with pleasure that I add my testimony to the value of the improvements you have made in artificial limbs. I have worn an artificial leg for the past twenty-two years. During the first fifteen years I tried various makes, but was always annoyed after wearing one but a short time by the joints in the foot becoming loose, and "rattling," or "clicking" at every step. Your rubber foot is entirely noiseless, and does away with the above very serious objections to all other makes.

The elasticity of the rubber fully takes the place of joints in the foot and ankle. But more than any thing else I value your make because of its perfect fit and stability. While standing on a moving wagon, car, or ferryboat, there is none of that "waving," or "see-sawing" motion so common and noticeable in wearers of all other makes. I am now wearing the same leg I bought of you about seven years ago, and during that time I have not paid out a dollar for repairs. I weigh 175 pounds, and for four years was salesman in a dry goods store, and on my feet from twelve to fifteen hours a day. For the purpose of benefiting any in need of an artificial limb I will gladly answer any personal letters addressed to me. Yours very sincerely,

ISAAC M. WARREN.

BELOW-KNEE AMPUTATION.

NAPLES, ONTARIO CO., N. Y., Oct. 29, 1887.

A. A. MARKS, ESQ. :

DEAR SIR :—My left limb was amputated eight inches below knee in 1876. Since November of that year I have worn limbs with rubber feet, manufactured by your house, and my annual expense for repairs is probably about $1.50 to $2, including new lacings. I will simply say your limbs are *absolutely satisfactory*.

The rubber foot so perfectly imitates the motion of the natural one that I take pardonable pride in walking on the streets, as I always do, without a cane. My work in the bank keeps me on my feet most of the day at the teller's desk, and also requires considerable walking in making our street collections.

You may feel free to refer any one in western New York to me at any time.

Yours respectfully,
L. E. MUNSELL.

BELOW-KNEE AMPUTATION.

19 FORBUS ST., POUGHKEEPSIE, N.Y., January 11, 1888.

MR. A. A. MARKS:

DEAR SIR:—The artificial leg that you made for me three months ago has proved perfectly satisfactory, and far exceeds any thing I ever anticipated in taking the place of the limb I lost about one year ago while on duty, as brakesman, for the New York Central & Hudson River R. R. Hoping you will be able to help others as you have helped me, I remain, yours,

CHAS. WING.

BELOW-KNEE AMPUTATION.

Twenty-four years on one rubber foot.

GREENBUSH, RENSSELAER CO., N. Y., Nov. 1, 1887.

A. A. MARKS, ESQ., New York City:

DEAR SIR:—In answer to yours of the 26th, I will say that it gives me great pleasure to recommend your artificial limbs, for, from my long experience in wearing your limb, I can do so honestly. I have worn the limb that you made for me in 1863 every day up to the present date, or about twenty-four years.

It has not cost me to keep in repair during all that time $25, and as I weighed only about 140 pounds when I first commenced wearing it, I have for the past twelve or fifteen years weighed over 220 pounds, and it is yet a good limb. My business has been as laborious and active as any man in my condition in the State of New York, for I had to earn my own living since I was ten years of age, and any man who has to earn his living, and does it, can not sit down all the time.

MICHAEL VAUGHN.

BELOW-KNEE AMPUTATION.

Oct. 27, 1887.

A. A. MARKS, ESQ., New York:

DEAR SIR:—I have been wearing one of your artificial legs, with rubber foot, for the past ten years, and now have my second leg. My foot was ground off at the ankle joint, and then amputated half way between the knee and ankle. I well remember how discouraged I was, and that life seemed to have but few chances for me, as I supposed I would have to peg my way through life, as I had never given artificial limbs a thought. But, I am happy to say, through your invention I am able to perform my duties without any inconvenience whatever. I use no cane or other assistance in walking, and can walk a mile in fifteen minutes. I frequently go trout-fishing, and walk ten miles. I am perfectly at home on roller-skates, and in fact can perform any work I ever could before amputation.

I have known persons three years who never knew I wore an artificial limb, and would not believe it until they saw it, as there is nothing in my walk to indicate my misfortune. I would say to all those who are so unfortunate as to lose a limb, do not be discouraged, brighter days will come, and when you get to promenading on one of Marks' artificial limbs you will wonder at the possibility of such restoration. The cost for repairs has been but a trifle for the ten years, not to exceed $5. Parties who desire to ask any questions, or for information in regard to artificial limbs, will receive a prompt reply by enclosing a two-cent stamp.

With best of wishes, I am, yours truly,

IRA W. SCHAFFER,
Pumping Engineer.

SCIO, ALLEGANY CO., N. Y.

BELOW-KNEE AMPUTATION.

LANSINGBURGH, RENSSELAER CO., N.Y., Oct. 31, 1887.
A. A. MARKS, ESQ, New York City:

DEAR SIR:—Your letter of the 26th inst. received. I take pleasure in testifying to the satisfaction your artificial limbs have given me, having failed in my attempts to walk satisfactorily on an ankle joint leg purchased some years previous. The first leg I purchased of you was in 1878. I continued to use it until 1886. During most of that time my labor was such as to compel me to stand fully half the time. This I did with comparative ease. The cost to keep it in repair was practically nothing, probably not $2 for the whole time.

In 1886 I purchased a second leg of you, which has given me even better satisfaction than the first one. I account for this from the fact that I stand but very little now, and that my stump, which is about six inches long below the knee, shrunk all it ever will while I was using the first leg. From the fact that I bought of you the second time shows what make of leg I preferred.

Yours truly,
JAMES H. ROGERS.

BELOW-KNEE AMPUTATION.

BERKSHIRE, TIOGA CO., N. Y., Nov. 1, 1887.
Mr MARKS:

SIR:—I have worn one of your artificial limbs with rubber foot for two years and found it one of the greatest blessings this world can afford for one afflicted as I am. For after nearly six years of suffering I had my foot amputated, and in three weeks from that day I came to you and was measured for another, and as soon as I received it I was walking without the aid of anything, in less than half an hour. I have done the work of six in the family and taken care of the milk and butter of nine cows this summer. I have not been to any expense for my foot since I got it. My leg was amputated about one inch and a half above the ankle joint.
Yours respectfully,
MRS. G. M. SMITH.

BELOW-KNEE AMPUTATION.

WINSTON, FORSYTH CO., N. C., Nov. 28, 1887.
A. A. MARKS, New York City:

DEAR SIR:—Your letter asking for a testimonial received a few days ago. I hardly know what to say, or how to start, as it is impossible for me to say enough about the good qualities of your leg. My leg is cut off two and one-half inches below the knee, yet with one of your legs I am able to lead a very active life, being in the mill business (flour and meal), and have to be from the cellar to the garret constantly. I am just twenty-one years old, and have had one of your legs for about four years, and it is good yet. I weigh 175 pounds, and it seems to me I have been unusually hard on it, but it seems to meet every strain and abuse and still stands. Yours is the only leg I have ever worn, and I am perfectly satisfied with it, and I am sure I will never wear any other make.
Respectfully yours,
KLEBER DENMARK.

BELOW-KNEE AMPUTATION.

Fitted from Measurements.

North Carolina Talc and Marble Co.,
JARRETTS, SWAIN CO., N. C., Nov. 7, 1887.
A. A. MARKS:

DEAR SIR:—In reply to your favor of October 26th, will say I have been wearing one of your legs since 1882. I am a miner by occupation, and have been

rushing over the mountains of North Carolina. My leg was made by self-measurement, and is a little short, but it is all my fault, as you proffered to remedy it without cost. This I should have had done, but could not possibly spare the leg.
W. S. THOMAS.

BELOW-KNEE AMPUTATION.

North Carolina Board of Health,
WASHINGTON, BEAUFORT CO., N. C., Jan. 11, 1888.

DEAR SIR :—I have now been using your make of artificial limbs for sixteen years with the greatest comfort and satisfaction, and am fully convinced that it possesses great advantages over any other form or make of limb. The conviction has been forced upon me after a full and free investigation of the others offered for the same purpose. It is simple, strong, durable, light, easily moved in walking, and perfectly noiseless. In fact, it thoroughly embodies all the qualities desired by a person who needs an appliance of this kind. I can walk just as well as when I had two good, sound limbs, and only those who know of my misfortune can tell that I use an appliance of this sort. I am constantly reminded by even them as to how well I walk and run about.

Very truly yours,
JOHN McDONALD, M.D.

BELOW-KNEE AMPUTATION.

Fitted from Measurements.

PAINESVILLE, LAKE CO., OHIO.

MR. A. A. MARKS:

DEAR SIR :—I am in receipt of your letter. Much honor is due you for your relief of the disabled. I don't know that I can express more than hundreds have of your excellent inventions. My own experience is, for durability, ease, comfort, and applicability, no artificial can compare with yours. My amputation is below the knee. I have worn a leg of your make fourteen years constantly. Foot repaired once during that time. It is easy and quiet to wear, no unpleasant sound, always ready, so reliable, with an elastic step. An important point of economy is this: patients can be measured at their own homes, and be fitted by you in their absence, saving time and expense of traveling. I am happy to recommend the limb to all who need an easy, well-fitting, and finely formed limb.   Yours respectfully,

MRS. E. R. GAGE.

Nov. 18, 1887.

BELOW-KNEE AMPUTATION.

Fitted from Measurements.

Office of the *Bryan Press*, SIMEON GILLIS, Publisher,
BRYAN, WILLIAMS CO., OHIO, Oct. 29, 1887.

A. A. MARKS:

DEAR SIR :—I have been wearing your make of artificial limbs since 1868. Previous to that I had worn one of the highest-priced legs in this country, and consider yours much the better. Its points of superiority are chiefly in the doing away with the loose toget joints found in all other artificial legs at the ankle and toe. Your rubber foot does away with the necessity for these joints, and gives the step a certainty of action that no other leg has. It also gives a springy, light step that is impossible in a wooden foot. Your knee joint irons are much better than those of the other leg I wore. I have had three of your legs, and one was fitted from measurements furnished by myself, and I went to the shop and had the others fitted.' The one made from measurements was as good as any of the three. I am very hard on a leg, as I am active and not careful to favor it, and weigh 186 pounds. My point of amputation is two and one-half inches below the knee. I think the most difficult point to fit, for the

reason that the bones are movable and change the form of the stump, and the prominence of some bones in standing and others in sitting makes it difficult to secure a perfect fit. Wishing you may have the opportunity to lighten the step of many more unfortunates, I am, truly yours,
SIMEON GILLIS.

BELOW-KNEE AMPUTATION.

Fitted from Measurements.

ZANESVILLE, MUSKINGUM CO., OHIO, Oct. 29, 1887.

A. A. MARKS:
DEAR SIR:—In reply to yours, I can say I never had any experience with the old style, but I believe the rubber foot to be the best, and from my experience in this I am very grateful to you for the one I now have. My occupation is clerk in coal-yard, and I am on my feet half the time. I have worn my leg six months and have no pain. My leg was cut off six inches below the knee. No cost for repairs. I am well pleased in every way, and most cheerfully recommend your artificial limbs to all who may need them.
Yours truly,
JAMES COFFEY.

BELOW-KNEE AMPUTATION.

General Freight Department,
THE LAKE SHORE AND MICHIGAN SOUTHERN RAILWAY CO.,
CLEVELAND, OHIO, Nov. 5, 1887.

A. A. MARKS, ESQ., New York City:
DEAR SIR: During the "late unpleasantness" I donated one foot as a slight token of my regard for the "Sovereign and Independent State of Georgia." For the past eighteen years I have used as a substitute one of your limbs. Have found the same to answer the purpose about as nearly as art can approach nature. It has proved safe, reliable, and durable in all kinds of services, and under all circumstances, and with the exception of substituting a new socket once when the old one had become too small, total cash for repairs has not equaled $1 per year.
As I weigh about 190 pounds and see considerable of active life, my impression is that I have done the square thing by it, so far as testing its qualities is concerned.
Yours truly,
JNO. G. JAMES,
Late of Co. B. 57th Reg. Ill. Vol. Infantry.
Have worn artificial limbs of different make twenty-two years.

BELOW-KNEE AMPUTATION.

Oct. 31, 1887.

A. A. MARKS:
I have had one of your artificial legs with rubber foot some ten years. I have not been able to wear it all the time on account of salt-rheum. I have worn it, however, as much as five to six years steady. It will doubtless wear much longer; I am a farmer by occupation, and have worn the leg to do all kinds of farm work. I think it is the best leg made.
I like the rubber foot because it is durable; it is firm; when you put it down it is there, and you feel safe on it.
You can put your weight on it, and cary a bag of wheat to the granary and feel safe on it. The rubber heel makes a spring to come down on. The rubber foot supplies all necessary ankle motion.
My experience is that side ankle motion is useless.
Then the foot comes down easy without that jar there is to a wooden foot. The cost of repairs is nothing when compared with other artificial limbs. There

are no joints, springs, or cords to be wearing and breaking every few weeks. The first leg I got was in 1865. I paid $50, besides the government order to get the best. I got it, ankle joint and all. It cost me several dollars a year for repairs, besides being obliged to do without it a week or two at a time while it was being repaired at the shop. But then the music of it was worth something. Sometimes you could hear it screech and scream forty rods; one would think that Sitting Bull was coming sure. With the rubber foot you lose all that charming music. My leg is off below the knee.

Yours truly, J. C. CHELLIS.
BURTON, GEAUGA CO., OHIO.

BELOW-KNEE AMPUTATION.

Fitted from Measurements.

VERNON JUNCTION, RICHLAND CO., OHIO, Oct. 31, 1887.
MR. A. A. MARKS:

DEAR SIR:—I can safely testify to the merits and superiority of your artificial limbs over all others which it has been my privilege to notice, in my own case and in that of others.

I have worn three limbs made in Philadelphia, but received scarcely any benefit from their use; but when I got you to make one for me in June, 1880, I found I had hit the mark. I am still wearing that limb, and to all appearance will continue to do so, if I live for three or four years longer. It has not cost one cent so far for repairs; the great trouble with the other limbs was the wooden foot with artificial joints in them, which never lasted longer than two years, and then I had to pay $20 for a new foot or throw the leg away; but your rubber foot does away with all that trouble, and although I am receiving almost every day letters from other firms, I will never as long as I live have any other than yours. My limb is amputated 4 inches below the knee, and although the joint is stiff strangers will not believe that I have lost a limb until I show it to them.

I am tilling the soil on a small scale, and am on my feet from morning until night, and feel no inconvenience from the use of your limb. The measurements I sent you secured a good fit, which shows that you can make as good a fit as if I had come to you, and you had taken the measure yourself.

If any one wants any information I will gladly give it to them, if they will write to me or call on me and see for themselves.

WM. C. CRESSWELL.

BELOW-KNEE AMPUTATION.

Nov. 3, 1887.
MR. A. A. MARKS:

DEAR SIR:—Having been wearing artificial legs for the period of twenty-one years, the first fourteen years I wore out two of Mr. ——'s legs manufactured at Indianapolis, Ind. The next five years I wore out one of Dr. ——'s artificial legs made in N. Y. C. and the two last years I have been wearing your artificial leg with the rubber foot. It gives good satisfaction. I think that the rubber foot is the best artificial foot that is made.

Yours truly, J. W. HUNTZINGER.
KOOGLE, VAN WERT CO., OHIO.

BELOW-KNEE AMPUTATION.

Fitted from Measurements.

CONNEAUT, ASHTABULA CO., OHIO, Oct. 29, 1887.
A. A. MARKS, ESQ, New York City:

SIR:—In answer to your circular letter of the 26th inst., relative to the artificial limb bought of you some eight years ago, it is with pleasure I heartily assure you the limb has answered very satisfactorily and has been in continuous use since first received. My left leg was amputated below the knee and your substitute therefor has been worn to my great convenience and safety. I feel grateful that you have been so fortunate as to produce so exceedingly valuable and satisfactory a limb.

I can recommend your limb under each and all circumstances, and though I have worn it so long it has not occasioned me any expense in repair. My occupation is painting, necessarily standing a great deal, ascending ladders, climbing buildings, etc.

The limb has never failed to be all I required in my business.

I may need another limb very soon and will order one from your house.

I am, respectfully, your obt. servant,
WILLIAM H. LEROUX.

BELOW-KNEE AMPUTATION.

ONTARIO, RICHLAND CO., OHIO, Nov. 7, 1887.

A. A. MARKS, ESQ. :

I have been wearing your rubber foot for the past three years, and I must say it gives me satisfaction in every respect.

I walk so natural on it that some persons that I come in contact with daily do not know that I have a limb off or suspect that I wear an artificial limb.

Respectfully, W. P. WESTON.

BELOW-KNEE AMPUTATION.

Oct. 30, 1887.

MR. A. A. MARKS :

DEAR SIR :—I have worn your artificial leg for two years and I find it to be a good substitute for my natural leg,

I can most emphatically say that it is the best I can get, and far superior to any I have ever seen for comfort and durability.

The fact of the matter is, too much praise can not be given to them. I would advise any one so unfortunate as myself to provide themselves with Marks' superior leg.

Yours respectfully, C. H. HAYES.
P. O. Box 66, ZALESKI, VINTON CO., OHIO.

BELOW-KNEE AMPUTATION.

Oct. 28, 1887.

A. A. MARKS, New York :

DEAR SIR :—I presume you think it strange not to have heard from me sooner, but I have been giving the leg a good fair trial. I have been wearing it for eighteen months, and can now say that it gives *perfect satisfaction*. I had worn the wooden foot for eight years previous to this one of your make, and it is a great relief to be able to walk on the street without attracting the attention of every one you meet. The rubber foot does not make any more noise than the natural one. I am a compositor.

I shall be very happy to answer any letter or show the leg to any one who may apply. J. V. MERWIN.
130 Lake St., CLEVELAND, OHIO.

BELOW-KNEE AMPUTATION.

Fitted from Measurements.

NELSONVILLE, ATHENS CO., OHIO, Nov. 8, 1887.

MR. A. A. MARKS :

DEAR SIR :—I am a coal miner by trade and have worn your patent rubber foot for about one year, and from what I can find out I don't want any other than yours. It costs me comparatively nothing for repairs. I have walked ten miles in a day with ease.

Yours truly,

JOHN E. MILLER.

BELOW-KNEE AMPUTATION.

Fitted from Measurements.

ASHLAND, ASHLAND CO., OHIO, Oct. 30, 1887.

MR. A. A. MARKS:

DEAR SIR :—My experience with artificial limbs has not been very long, but I think that the rubber foot is just the thing, for there is no ankle joint to get loose and rattle, and there is no jar when you walk. For durability I think that they will last as long as any thing you can get, for I am on my feet all day. Every day I walk from five to ten miles. The fitting from measurements I am perfectly satisfied with; mine has had no repairs. Amputation below the knee.

Yours truly,

M. H. SHILLITTO.

BELOW-KNEE AMPUTATION.

Fitted from Measurements.

75 State St., West Side, CLEVELAND, O., Oct. 30, 1887.

DEAR SIR :—It gives me pleasure after wearing your artificial limb fourteen years, to write you of the satisfaction it has given me. I have never used a cane since I have worn it. I have been to dances several times since I have had the limb. I am teaming and handling pig iron and stone every day. People I am working with do not know I wear any thing of the kind. The point of amputation is below knee.

Yours very truly,

J. THOMPSON.

BELOW-KNEE AMPUTATION.

Fitted from Measurements.

FRIENDSVILLE, MEDINA CO., O., Nov. 10, 1887.

MR. MARKS:

DEAR SIR :—You made me a leg in 1879, and I wore it ever since. I like it first rate. My repairs were seventy-five cents in eight years. I have worn a —— leg but I did not walk as well as I can with this one. When this one is worn out I intend to get another of your make, as they are the best. My leg is amputated four inches above the ankle. My occupation was a farmer and salesman, but since last spring I am in a grocery store and am postmaster. I weigh two hundred pounds. The rubber foot is just the thing—no cords to break.

Yours respectfully,

S. A. FLICKINGER.

BELOW-KNEE AMPUTATION.

Fitted from Measurements.

Dec. 8, 1887.

MR. A. A. MARKS:

DEAR SIR :—I am a carpenter and joiner. I am wearing your artificial limb, made from measurements, which secured a good fit. I have been wearing the limb for the past nine years with little or no repairs. I know it is the best in the market ; as I have worked in the wood business, I know the limb is made of the best of wood for that purpose, with the rubber foot.

Yours truly,
J. C. KEEF.

416 Hamilton St., CLEVELAND, OHIO.

BELOW-KNEE AMPUTATION.

Fitted from Measurements.

A. A. MARKS, New York City :

DEAR SIR :—Leg received a few days ago. I am well pleased with it. It is the second one I have worn of your make. I prefer yours to any other. They are durable and strong. I am doing all kinds of out-door work,. horseback riding, teaming, chopping, etc. The first one I wore five years with but a few dollars' worth of repairs. Had it not been for an accident that happened by a horse falling on frozen ground would have lasted a few years longer. Both legs made from measurements.

Respectfully yours,
W. GROVER.

JORDAN VALLEY, MALHEUR Co., OREGON, Nov. 5, 1887.

BELOW-KNEE AMPUTATION.

Can climb trees.

Oct. 31, 1887.

A. A. MARKS :

DEAR SIR :—For the benefit of those in need of an artificial limb or limbs, and as an expression of esteem towards and confidence in you as the maker and inventor of the best artificial limbs in the world, I write this, hoping it may be of service to you as well as valuable information to those in search of a durable, comfortable, and lifelike substitute for nature.

I had the misfortune to lose my left leg eight inches below the knee in the late war, and July 27, 1884, I received an artificial limb from the U. S. government made by —— of your city, which I wore for ten months, when it literally went to pieces, compelling me to get another substitute. I purchased in October, 1865, one of Dr. ——'s ball and socket limbs, which I wore with considerable vexation on account of breaking down. In 1870 I procured one of your limbs with a rubber foot, which I wore with ease and comfort for five years at a cost of $1.70 for repairs in the five years. In 1875 I received the second limb with the rubber foot ; have worn the two limbs for fifteen years with comfort, at a nominal cost for repairs.

This I regard as a big saving over the other limbs ; the rubber foot gives all the motion required in walking, and is noiseless, having no bolts in the ankle joint to get loose, rattle, give people warning that one is coming. I walk so perfectly that any one who is not acquainted with my misfortune can not detect that I am a wearer of an artificial limb. I am a tinner, and for the last ten years I have been engaged constantly in putting on tin and iron roofs, and will defy any man with good sound limbs to beat me climbing a ladder or getting over the roof of a building, regardless of pitch of roof. Having worn your limbs constantly since 1870, I know whereof I speak when I say that your limbs with the rubber feet are the best. As for fitting limbs, I have found that you understand that art to perfection, and with a perfect fit there is ease and comfort. I can skate on ice and roller skates, walk on the roughest of roads, and climb good-sized trees, and shake hickory nuts. Should any one want any particular information, I will be pleased to furnish it. Hoping this will reach the attention of every one in need of an artificial limb.

I remain, yours truly,
E. F. BENNETT,
Co. B. 76th Reg't Pa. V.

GREENVILLE, MERCER Co., PA.

BELOW-KNEE AMPUTATION.

CARBONDALE, LACKAWANNA CO., PA., Nov. 7, 1887.

MR. A. A. MARKS:
I have recommended your artificial limbs to all whom I have met in need of them, for I am exceedingly well pleased with mine. I lost my foot in February, 1883; I applied your leg in July, 1883, and have worn it ever since. My advice to those who have lost their limbs is to wear the rubber foot.

I will walk any ankle joint motion in the country from six to twelve hours' walk. My occupation is a miner. I wear your leg every day, and the cost for repairs has thus far been nothing. Your friend,

K. BRENNAN.

BELOW-KNEE AMPUTATION.

Fitted from Measurements.

Nov. 2, 1887.

A. A. MARKS, ESQ.:
DEAR SIR:—Having worn an artificial foot for nineteen years I think your system is perfect. The foot you made for me, October, 1877, from measurements, was and is yet as good a fitting foot as any I ever had made. I like it just as well as the one I had fitted on at your office some years later, and which I am wearing to-day. I thought when I gave you a second order I was giving a practical endorsement of the superiority of your artificial feet over the old style of ankle joints, one of which I was wearing when I gave you my first order. Speaking of ankle joint limbs, I wore one for nine years, and in comparing the cost for repairs, not taking into account the time occupied in running to the maker, I find that I spent in nine years $113 against something short of $10 for my rubber foot in ten years, and as to running to the maker I have not had that to do. If you have any inquiries from Philadelphia, or vicinity, just refer them to the watchman at the Frankford Boiler Works, who is satisfied that there are no limbs manufactured equal to those of your establishment.

I remain yours, respectfully,

JOHN CHILD.

1838 Buckins St., PHILADELPHIA, PA.

BELOW-KNEE AMPUTATION.

LEHIGHTON, CARBON CO., PA., Nov. 8, 1887.

A. A. MARKS, New York City:
DEAR SIR:—My artificial limb is all that can be expected. Indeed, a great deal more than I had a right to expect. I seldom use a cane, only in wet weather or on very rough roads. My friends all say that any one not knowing me could not tell that I am wearing an artificial. I consider myself under lasting obligations to you for the perfect fit you made me, and take great pleasure in recommending your limbs to all the unfortunate. Very truly yours,

A. W. RAUDENBUSH.

BELOW-KNEE AMPUTATION.

FRIEDENSVILLE, LEHIGH CO., PA., Nov. 6, 1887.

MR. MARKS:
DEAR SIR:—Yours of October 26th is received. You invite me to write a testimonial for publication, and as I have had some experience with your artificial leg, I therefore desire to let the public know my appreciation of your work. I had my leg amputated, four inches above the ankle joint, at St. Luke's Hospital at Bethlehem, Pa., November 29, 1884. I was at that time eleven years of age. Five months after amputation I applied to you for one of your rubber-foot artificial legs. And I am proud to tell the public that I am getting along

first-rate with it. I only used a cane one day after receiving the leg; two weeks after I walked the distance of two miles to a camp-meeting, and I enjoyed myself there during the afternoon as well as any of the rest. I walked home again in the evening. I felt no effects from the walk.

I thank my parents for purchasing the rubber foot. I must give you credit for the good fit of the leg, as I do not suffer any thing from wearing it. I am

No. 289.

No. 290.

thankful to say that I can walk about as good as ever; any one that does not know that I have lost my leg would not notice it by my walking. My artificial leg at present is as good as new. I had it lengthened twice and repaired once, the amount for which was in the total only $6.

I have two photographs of myself, one standing naturally with the leg on, and the other one standing with the leg by my side; I will send them to you. As I do not know that I can say any thing more at present,

I remain, yours truly,

EMILY J. BENNETT.

BELOW-KNEE AMPUTATION.

TOPTON, BERKS CO., PA., Dec. 5, 1887.

A. A. MARKS, New York City :

DEAR SIR :—I have the greatest pleasure in addressing you these few lines, in order to express the satisfaction I have with the artificial leg you manufactured for me. To its comfort and stability I owe the invaluable treasure of walking almost naturally. I never use a cane. My occupation is laborious. I have used your make of legs since 1866. I have used this one sixteen years, and it has proved most satisfactory, never having required any repairs. I claim to be capable of judging of its merits. Hoping you may live long to benefit others as you have me, I remain, your obedient servant,

G. W. REIFER.

BELOW-KNEE AMPUTATION.

GLEN ROCK, YORK CO., PA., Nov. 3, 1887.

MR. A. A. MARKS:

DEAR SIR:—Let me state to you that the artificial limb I purchased from you in the month of August, 1887, gives satisfaction. I have had it on from the day I got it, except when I am in bed. Trusting that every one who may be so unfortunate as I have been may take my advice and purchase from you, which I am most assured they will never regret,

I am, yours respectfully,
J. L. ROHRBAUGH, Telegraph Operator.

BELOW-KNEE AMPUTATION.

GENERAL STEAMSHIP AGENCY, J. H. WILSON, AGENT,
CARBONDALE, LACKAWANNA CO., PA., Oct. 27, 1887.

A. A. MARKS, ESQ.:

DEAR SIR:—On September 30, 1876, I met with an accident which necessitated the amputation of my left leg about four inches below the knee. At that time I weighed 182 pounds. After getting well my weight increased to 208 pounds. I thought then that I was too heavy to wear an artificial limb, so I concluded that the rest of my life (as I was then 49 years of age) would be spent walking upon crutches, until I came across a gentleman from out west by the name of Cole, who was a much heavier man than myself, and had worn one of your artificial legs with rubber foot for over 10 years, and was then on his way to New York to order an extra leg. He told me that it had not cost him any thing for repairs during that time, as they were made so durable, not having any machinery about them to get out of order. This being a very good, and at the same time substantial recommend (as he showed me his artificial leg), from an entire stranger, I came to the conclusion that I would have one made also.

I had one made in October, 1881, and have now worn it six years without any expense for repairs, and it looks as if it would be good for another six years.

I would further state from my own experience that I am well pleased with it, and consider that Marks' artificial legs with rubber feet are the best as regards durability and comfort.

Mine never troubled me a particle since I had it made. I have worn it constantly ever since. As further evidence of the durability of your make of artificial limbs I will here state that in the fall of 1882 I saw a man by the name of Kearney Brennan who had lost one of his legs. I told him of the comfort I experienced in wearing one of your make. He went to New York and had one made for himself. He has continually worn his limb; as a brakeman on one of the trains on D. & L. R. R., at this place, his work is such as would soon spoil an artificial limb if not very durably made, and when he is off his train it is surprising to see how well he uses his limb; a stranger could not tell he had one on.

JOHN H. WILSON.

BELOW-KNEE AMPUTATION.

YORK, YORK CO., PA., Oct. 27, 1887.

MR. A. A. MARKS:

DEAR SIR:—I have great pleasure in addressing you these few lines to express the satisfaction I have with my artificial leg. It is now three years since I fell from a building. My left foot was so badly crushed that amputation was necessary a few inches below the knee. I have been using an artificial leg of your make ever since. I am a tinner by trade. I can climb ladders and work at tin roofing, hanging spouts, etc.

The leg fits me to perfection, and the first time I put it on I walked without a cane, and do not use a cane now.

My step is perfectly easy. I consider the rubber foot superior to any other, as there is no ankle joint to get out of order. I want none but of your manufacture. Gratefully yours,

JACOB W. SELAK.

BELOW-KNEE AMPUTATION.

LEWISTOWN, MIFFLIN CO., PA., Oct. 31, 1887.

A. A. MARKS:

DEAR SIR:—I take much pleasure in stating that the artificial leg I bought of you over a year ago has given entire satisfaction, and can recommend any one in need of such assistance to you.

Yours respectfully,

F. J. ZERBE.

BELOW-KNEE AMPUTATION.

Fitted from Measurements.

G. H. WHITE'S WAVERLY BAZAR,
WAVERLY, LACKAWANNA CO., PA., Nov. 9, 1887.

MR. A. A. MARKS:

DEAR SIR:—In 1866 I bought one of your artificial legs with rubber foot, and wore it for fourteen years without one dollar for repairs, and never had to resort to crutches one day during all of this time. In 1880 I ordered another one of your legs, and have worn it continously ever since without one dollar expense.

And it seems just as good as ever. I have received seventy letters of inquiry from all parts of the country in regard to your rubber legs. My leg was amputated two inches below the knee.

By occupation I am a barber, and have worked at the chair for the last ten years. I cannot see how any one wanting an artificial leg would think of trying any other kind, taking durability and neatness of build into consideration, no rattle box, do not have to carry crutches or kit of tools to keep it in repair.

Yours truly,

G. H. WHITE.

BELOW-KNEE AMPUTATION.

HONESDALE, WAYNE CO., PA., Oct. 28, 1887.

MR. A. A. MARKS:

DEAR SIR:—Yours of October 26th received. I work hard every day. I have worn one of your artificial legs fourteen years. My leg is amputated seven inches below the knee.

I think it has cost me not over $1.50 for repairs in that time, except for straps. I am wearing the same leg yet.

I handled one afternoon this week 160 barrels of apples, which would be a fair half-day's work for a sound man.

My leg is not new now by any means, for I have worn it continually for fourteen years,

Yours truly,

C. A. CORTRIGHT.

BELOW-KNEE AMPUTATION.

121 Garfield Ave., HYDE PARK, LACKAWANNA CO., PA., Oct. 28, 1887.

DEAR FRIEND:—I am glad to have a chance to uphold your artificial legs as the best leg I have ever worn in my life. It fits nicely and neatly, and for walking it is the best.

I am glad to let you know that in the third month that I wore my leg I walked twenty-four miles in one day without raising a blister on my stump.
Yours truly,
GEORGE HOPKINS.

BELOW-KNEE AMPUTATION.

EASTON, NORTHAMPTON, PA., Nov. 28, 1887.

I have worn an artificial leg with rubber foot for twenty-three consecutive years. The repairs during that time have been slight, total cost not exceeding $35 for the entire period.

I have been thoroughly satisfied with the action of the leg and cheerfully recommend it to all.
JOHN H. MEBUS.

BELOW-KNEE AMPUTATION.

PITTSTON, LUZERNE CO., PA., Oct. 28, 1887.
MR. A. A. MARKS, New York :

DEAR SIR :—Yours of October 26th is at hand,

It is with pleasure that I give my testimony in regard to your make of limbs. I have been wearing one of your legs for seven years and in that time have never lost a day's work.

My occupation is shipping clerk for a sash and door factory. It is a three-story building and my business calls me up and down the stairs a great many times a day. I can go up or down a pair of stairs as fast as any one that has both legs. The cost for repairs on my leg in the seven years of constant use has been about $5. In my estimation there is no limb made in the wide world that will give the wearer the satisfaction that yours will. I have tried some other makes with the joints in the ankle, but they are useless to me. They may answer for some if they want always to sit down and never get on their feet. But if a man wants a limb that will be of some use, he must buy the rubber foot.
Yours truly,
G. E. CARPENTER.

BELOW-KNEE AMPUTATION.

Fitted from Measurements.

SHENANDOAH, SCHUYLKILL CO., PA., Oct. 31, 1887.
A. A. MARKS, ESQ.:

DEAR SIR :—It is with pleasure I write you adding my testimony of the excellence of your artificial legs. The one I purchased of you four years ago is giving me entire satisfaction and comfort. It is almost as good to-day as when I bought it.

It has not cost me $1 for repairs, although it has been subjected to a very severe test. I am an engineer, consequently am on my feet nearly all day long. There are three engines and sixteen boilers in our plant, which I have to keep in working condition. So you can see I have a great deal of running around to do. Yet I have worn this leg every day and all day ever since the first day I went out with it. Is not this remarkable when you come to consider that I have only 1½ inches of stump below the knee? I consider your artificial limbs with rubber feet the most durable and superior limb manufactured.

Also your system of self-measurement perfect, as the leg I wear is a perfect fit made from measurements sent you.
Yours very respectfully,
JOS. HINKS.

BELOW-KNEE AMPUTATION.

Fitted from Measurements.

Nov. 1, 1887.

Mr. A. A. Marks :

Dear Sir :—I have been wearing one of your artificial limbs from the 26th of December, 1885, which I got by sending measurements to you, and it gives satisfaction. My age is fifty-five years.

I would recommend your artificial limbs to all that need them.

Mrs. Rees T. Davies.

Ashland, Schuylkill Co., Pa.

BELOW-KNEE AMPUTATION.

Fitted from Measurements.

Deyarmon & Galley, Dealers in Groceries, Confections, etc., Dawson, Fayette Co., Pa., Oct. 28, 1887.

Mr. A. A. Marks :

Dear Sir :—Am now wearing the second artificial leg manufactured by you. I take pleasure in bearing testimony to merit, etc., of said limb. Will answer kindly all inquiries addressed to me as to point of amputation, fitting from measurements, durability, cost of repairs, occupation, etc.

Yours truly,

T. Robb. Deyarmon.

BELOW-KNEE AMPUTATION.

Oct. 31, 1887.

A. A. Marks :

Dear Sir :—In reply to your communication of the 26th inst. would state that I have been wearing artificial limbs, of different makes, for the last nine years. My right limb was amputated about seven inches below the knee joint. Your gum foot has given entire satisfaction, and I believe it to be superior to any artificial foot in existence. My occupation for the last several years has been in an upholstering and awning establishment.

I do my share of the work equal with any of the hands employed by the firm, sometimes carry a ladder and heavy iron rods more than half a mile, handle heavy furniture, and make myself generally useful. I take great pleasure in recommending your artificial limbs to all persons who are in need of the same.

Very respectfully,

James K. P. Dumars.

206 Locust St., Harrisburg, Pa.

BELOW-KNEE AMPUTATION.

Fitted from Measurements.

Oct. 27, 1887.

Received yours of the 26th and am pleased to be allowed the privilege of expressing my opinion of your limbs.

I am by occupation an accountant, and am put to pretty hard tasks, such as standing half the time and walking a distance of three miles twice a day. I have worn Marks' artificial leg for nine months, and it has not cost me one cent for repairs.

Above all other improvements made on artificial limbs is the rubber foot, which is more durable than any other.

I remain yours truly,

Wiley S. Devore.

Steelton, Dauphin Co., Pa.

BELOW-KNEE AMPUTATION.

Oct. 31, 1887.

Mr. A. A. Marks:

Dear Sir:—I have worn one of your legs since the 3d of July, 1884, and it has cost me only for a new socket, which is no fault of the leg or the maker, as it was occasioned on account of the stump shrinking. I am a laboring man in a shop and have seen several different makes of legs. I would advise any man that has to wear an artificial leg to get your leg—that is if he wants a good substantial limb. My limb is just as good to-day as the day I got it, so I can cheerfully recommend it as being a good substantial limb. I remain,

Yours respectfully,
Patrick Foote.

Susquehanna, Pa.

BELOW-KNEE AMPUTATION.

South Bethlehem, Northampton Co., Pa., Nov. 18, 1887.

Dear Sir:—I have worn your artificial leg one year and I have had full satisfaction. I can say for truth that the rubber foot cannot be excelled in the world. I am sorry that I am not capable of giving your artificial leg half its merits. I can say for a perfect fit, and ease and comfort in wearing, it is the greatest invention I know of. I have a half a mile to go to work, and walking every day. I weigh all the stuff the company buys and sells, so I am all the time on my feet, and I can walk as good as ever I did.

I remain, yours truly,
Michael Fox.

Fourth Street.

BELOW-KNEE AMPUTATION.

Riverside Hotel, A. G. Gregory, Proprietor,
Meshoppen, Wyoming Co., Pa., Oct. 31, 1887.

Mr. A. A. Marks, New York City:

Dear Sir:—I recommend your artificial limb that I purchased of you six years ago next March to be far superior to any thing I ever expected to get, giving the very best satisfaction, not costing me one cent for repairs, and has had very hard usage. I belong to the baseball club here, play every season, go hunting winters with the rest of the boys, and can walk as far in a day, through the woods, as any of them. The rubber foot suits me and I want no other.

Very respectfully,
A. G. Gregory.

BELOW-KNEE AMPUTATION.

Nov. 1, 1887.

Mr. A. A. Marks:

Sir:—I am in receipt of your favor, asking for my experience in regard to the artificial leg purchased of you.

I have worn your work for the last seven years with great satisfaction. The cost of repairs is hardly worth mentioning.

I have been for some time past working as an outside laborer in the coal mines, where I am most of the time on my feet and do some quite hard lifting. My artificial leg has far exceeded my expectations. I can walk, run, and even dance a good figure on a ball-room floor. You have my best wishes for your success.

Amputation eight inches below knee. I think no other material equal to your rubber foot.

John Maxie.

1002 Jackson St., Scranton, Pa.

BELOW-KNEE AMPUTATION.

Office of G. W. JACKSON, Alderman,
3½ Fourth St., HARRISBURG, PA., Oct. 27, 1887.

MR. A. A. MARKS:

DEAR SIR:—It affords me pleasure to give my testimony in favor of your rubber foot as being far superior to all others.

I have worn limbs with ankle joints, and I have worn the rubber foot for ten years, and I speak from experience. I am a practical machinist, and am opposed to complicated machinery when it can be avoided, and that you have done in the rubber foot. My foot has cost me nothing in ten years for repairs, and is sound yet. One day while I was wearing the limb with the ankle joint I was on the street when a bolt broke in the ankle and stuck in the end of my stump, and that satisfied me that I wanted no ankle joints while I could get the "Marks rubber foot," and I am still of the same opinion. My amputation is just above the ankle.

My advice to all brother cripples is to get a "Marks rubber foot," and they will never regret it.

Yours truly,
G. W. JACKSON.

BELOW-KNEE AMPUTATION.

PORT CLINTON, SCHUYLKILL CO., PA., Nov. 4, 1887.

MR. A. A. MARKS, ESQ.:

DEAR SIR:—Hearing that you are preparing another pamphlet, I will cheerfully give my endorsement. My right leg is amputated seven inches below the knee. In August, 1886, you made me an artificial leg which gave entire satisfaction then, and has proved a great friend to me since. The "rubber foot" gives the leg its advantage over others. I was measured and fitted the same day, and wore the leg the tenth day after being measured.

I canvassed for books, etc., from April to August, walking twenty miles or more a day, and did not feel any more fatigue than I would if I had my two sound legs. One evening a young man and I were caught in a thunder-storm, and he told me not to walk so fast, that he could not keep up with me. I do not use a cane, and did not from the start. The leg has not cost any thing for repairs yet, and it is in good condition now. In regard to the artificial leg, I will cheerfully answer any letters addressed to me on the subject.

Yours very respectfully,
GEO. W. KUTCH.

BELOW-KNEE AMPUTATION.

BEAVER MEADOW, CARBON CO., PA., Oct. 29, 1887.

MR. A. A. MARKS:

DEAR SIR:—I feel it my duty as a wearer of one of your artificial limbs to send you a testimonial concerning the advantage and durability of your patents. I have been wearing other makes of artificial legs with iron joints in the feet with a great deal of trouble for four years. I had to be repairing them all the time. I have seen legs worn that came from Philadelphia and Pittsburg, and they did not satisfy me, so I resolved to visit you. I found what I wanted. I found that your make of limbs was far superior to those I have used or seen used. My experience with it since has justified me in my conviction.

I think it is almost equal to the one I had amputated, for I can walk quicker and work with more ease than I used to do.

My occupation is that of a coal-miner, and the people say, "just think of it, that a man with one leg will go into the bowels of the earth and climb up and down on an incline of from forty to forty-five degrees the same as a man with two legs." My friends, you need not wonder, for that gentleman, A. A. Marks, has got his patent rubber hands and feet down so fine that those that wear them can do any kind of labor. My leg is amputated below the knee. Those

who are crippled, should they chance to read this, I hope they will remember the above-named firm. I am
Yours respectfully,
JAMES J. McBRIDE.

BELOW-KNEE AMPUTATION.

CENTRALIA, COLUMBIA CO., PA., Nov. 3, 1887.

A. A. MARKS, ESQ.:

DEAR SIR:—I have been wearing artificial limbs for twenty-four years. I wore one of yours twelve years without any repairs. It was a good limb when I cast it aside to try another manufacture. I made nothing by the change.

My occupation was that of a country schoolmaster in the winter and a miner during the summer months. I can recommend the india-rubber foot as an improvement on clashing ankle joints.

Wishing you the full measure you deserve,
I am faithfully yours,
DANIEL W. LENIHAN.

BELOW-KNEE AMPUTATION.

J. W. MERSHON & Co. Undertakers,
WAVERLY, LACKAWANNA CO., PA., Nov. 7, 1887.

MR. A. A. MARKS:

DEAR SIR:—Having for the past twenty years been wearing one of your artificial legs I desire to add my testimony to the already long list of those benefited by your admirable patent rubber hand and foot. I wore one of your feet every day for fourteen years with but one dollar's expense for repairs. None but those who know of my having lost a limb will believe that I wear a patent leg, so naturally and easily do I walk. I never use a cane and make no rattling noise when I walk on the sidewalk.

I worked for six weeks in a furniture manufactory with twenty men ten hours a day, and not one of them knew I lost a limb until I told them. I am a cabinet maker and undertaker by trade. I am on my feet all the time. I know the rubber foot is the most durable of any leg made, and the fitting is perfect. Any one wishing to write to me will address as above.

J. W. MERSHON.

BELOW-KNEE AMPUTATION.

Oct. 30, 1887.

DEAR SIR:—I now seat myself to answer your letter inquiring after the leg I got from you with rubber foot. I have worn it three years in mud and water. It has been wet for three days at a time. It has been very satisfactory. If any person requires one and will keep it dry, it will last him ten years without any repair, for I have had no repairs to mine yet, and use it every day. I have walked fourteen miles one day and walked in mud one-third of the way. My leg is cut off below the knee. I am an oysterman, and have to wade in water and mud, for we pick the oysters up by the hand and carry them to the boats in baskets, which is hard work for a man that has two legs. Any person who wants to know whether this is true or not, let him write to the proprietor of Cobb's Island Hotel, and then they can get all the references that they want.

Yours truly,
SAMUEL L. MATTHEWS.

CHERITON, NORTHAMPTON CO., PA.

BELOW-KNEE AMPUTATION.

WEATHERLY, CARBON CO., PA., Oct. 17, 1887.

MR. A. A. MARKS:

DEAR SIR:—In reply to your request I would say that I am more than pleased with the leg I purchased of you. I can get along very well—so well in fact strangers will not believe me when I tell them I have an artificial leg. I am a member of the brass band of our place and can travel with any of them. My occupation is a laborer in the car-shops of this place. I will do all I can to help the sale of your artificial limbs.

Yours sincerely, WM. C. NUSS.

BELOW-KNEE AMPUTATION.

Fitted from Measurements.

Oct. 28, 1887.

MR. A. A. MARKS:

DEAR SIR:—I have used your artificial limb for five years, and find they give perfect satisfaction in every respect. My right leg was amputated about four inches below the knee. When I received the limb I was agreeably surprised at the perfect fitting by self-measurement. One dollar will cover all the money I have expended for repairs. For lightness, durability, and especially your rubber foot, they are unexcelled. I am a shoemaker by trade. To any one obliged to use artificial limbs I can confidently recommend yours.

FRANK P. NEWMYER.

DAWSON, FAYETTE CO., PA.

BELOW-KNEE AMPUTATION.

Nov. 3, 1887.

MR. A. A. MARKS:

DEAR SIR:—Your letter of October 26th on hand and its contents carefully noted. As regards my case in your letter of inquiry, I would say that in July, 1880, I had the misfortune to lose my leg by an accident, and it was amputated six inches below the knee ; six months afterward I went to Philadelphia to get a leg, but was told that it was too soon, as my leg would shrink.

I went to Pittsburg and got one. Ten days after I got it my limb was so chafed that I was obliged to use my crutches for six months. I sent it back to have it made smaller. When it was returned it was too small, and I abandoned it. I then called on you at your office. You kindly told me that you could make me one, but the stump would shrink, but in one year I should return and you would make me a new socket. I can find no words to express my admiration for the limb that was furnished by your house.

I suffer none by its use—and the rubber foot, what shall I say for it. Nothing but *excelsior*. I have never seen any thing to equal it. I write the testimonial only in the hope that some one as unfortunate as myself may read this and profit by my experience. Any communication addressed to me as regards your house, your work, and dealings, will be cheerfully answered.

I am, sir, your obedient servant,

CHARLES WOLLERTON,
Foreman of the Construction Shops, P. R. Road, HARRISBURG, PA.

BELOW-KNEE AMPUTATION.

Fitted from Measurements.

SPARTANSBURG, CRAWFORD CO., PA., Nov. 7, 1887.

A. A. MARKS:

DEAR SIR:—In reply to your inquiry concerning my limb which was made six years ago from measurements sent for amputation below the knee, will say that it is entirely satisfactory, especially for durability, simplicity, and nominal cost of repairs.

My occupation is running a planing mill, which is laborious and heavy on the limbs and feet, handling lumber most of the time.

My weight is over two hundred pounds. The rubber foot prevents any jar and makes the tread light and elastic.

Yours respectfully,
W. W. WHITE.

BELOW-KNEE AMPUTATION.

Oct. 31, 1887.

MR. MARKS: With regard to my experience of artificial limbs, I am well pleased with your work, and am willing to testify to the merits of your limbs. I have worn artificial limbs for the past nine years; some have been of other make, and I can testify that yours is decidedly the best for comfort and ease, and does not make that rattling noise when walking, or that ugly sound on the pavement, as other limbs do. As to fitting, I do say that mine fits as well as I could expect. I am willing to testify to all this if you send any person to me. I am a dressmaker by occupation. My amputation is seven inches below the joint; I have a great deal more comfort from your limbs than from the others. Your limb is all and every thing that a person can expect.

Yours respectfully,
MISS M. A. CARR.

1349 Vine St., PHILADELPHIA, PA.

BELOW-KNEE AMPUTATION.

Fitted from Measurements.

Nov. 9, 1887.

A. A. MARKS, ESQ.:

DEAR SIR:—In answer to your letter of the 26th ult. asking me to state my experience in the use of your artificial limbs, I would say it has been very satisfactory indeed.

As I am a hatter by trade, I have considerable walking to do, and sometimes heavy lifting and out of five different makes of artificial legs which I have used I find yours to be the most durable, combined with ease and comfort. My point of amputation is below the knee. Your success in fitting me from measurements has been very satisfactory indeed. In regard to the cost of repairs, I have used your make of limb five years, and as yet it has cost me nothing for repairs. I shall at any time be pleased to impart any information in regard to the above to those who may wish to consult me personally.

I remain, yours respectfully,
WM. WILLIAMS.

No. 682 Florence St., PHILADELPHIA, PA.

BELOW-KNEE AMPUTATION.

Nov. 3, 1887.

DEAR SIR:—I wore three artificial limbs before I received yours.

Yours is the finest leg I ever wore for fitting and easy walking.

The rubber foot is the best I ever used.

All the expense for repairs is $1.50. My leg is off four inches below the knee and my weight is 216 pounds. I wore your first leg for over five years, and I have just started to wear the second one, and the first is good yet. I am janitor, and I have a great deal of walking to do.

Respectfully yours,
JOHN REYNOLDS.

256 Manton Ave., PROVIDENCE, R. I.

BELOW-KNEE AMPUTATION.

229 Pine St., Providence, R. I., Oct 27, 1887.

Mr. Marks:

Dear Sir:—I have received your circular asking me to testify to the merits of the leg you made for me, which I will gladly do, as I am well pleased with your make. My leg is off five inches below the knee, and I have worn it for nine years. I expect to have another of your make very soon.

Respectfully yours,
Francis Slaiger.

BELOW-KNEE AMPUTATION.

Oct. 29, 1887.

Dear Sir:—I have worn the artificial leg that I purchased of you last June every day since, and I am glad to tell you that I am very much pleased with it in every way. Why, it actually surprises some of my friends to see the way that I get around with it without the use of a cane. I tell you that you don't want a cane at all. I don't want one. It is in the way.

Yours truly,
H. C. Mowry.

Manton House, Manton, Providence Co., R. I.

BELOW-KNEE AMPUTATION.

Fitted from Measurements.

Congaree, Richland Co., S. C., April 20, 1887.

Mr. A. A. Marks, New York:

Dear Sir:—Artificial foot received in good order, and am well pleased with it. Have been wearing it one week yesterday. Had no trouble whatever in fitting it. I am attending to my business now, and have not stopped an hour since I put it on, only on Sundays. I would not do without it for three times the cost.

Yours very truly,
W. H. Motley.

BELOW-KNEE AMPUTATION.

Fitted from Measurements.

Fort Mott, Orangeburgh Co., S. C., Nov. 21, 1887.

Mr. A. A. Marks:

Dear Sir:—In reply to your letter as to how I am pleased with the artificial leg I bought of you, I will say I do not know how I could get along without one. I am fifty years old, and have been wearing an artificial leg for twenty years. During that time I wore two other make of legs besides yours, which I consider worthless compared with yours. One of the other make of legs I wore about three months, and the other about six months; the balance of the twenty years I have been wearing your make with rubber foot. During that time I have bought two new legs; both were fitted by measurement. I found no trouble in wearing them after wearing the first one for a while.

The superiority of your leg is the rubber foot. It does not matter how long you wear it it does not have any of that screaking when you walk which all the others that I have had any experience with had. For durability it will outlast a half dozen of any other feet I ever saw. I am a farmer by occupation, and weigh about 200 pounds. I attend to all of my business myself, and do any kind of work on a farm that any other man can do. Amputation about four inches above ankle joint. I remain,

Yours very respectfully,
P. W. FAIREY.

BELOW-KNEE AMPUTATION.

SCARBOROUGH, ANDERSON CO., TENN., Dec. 6, 1887.

MR. A. A. MARKS:

DEAR SIR:—I want to say to you that I am well pleased with the artificial leg furnished by you. I received a leg on government order in the fall of 1865, which lasted me about five years, with some repairs. I received one of your legs in 1870, and wore it fifteen years with less expense.

I consider your rubber feet and hands the best thing yet invented for artificial limbs. I received a leg from you two years ago, fitted from measurement sent to you. It only lacked a very little lining to make it all right, and I think if I had taken the measures as tight as directed it would have lacked nothing. I have used your make of legs at nearly all kinds of work, such as plowing,

No. 291.

spading, hauling logs, and other hard work. I have walked twenty-five miles in a single day. The rubber foot lasts longer and takes less repairs than any thing I know about. Yours respectfully,

LEWIS C. COX.

BELOW-KNEE AMPUTATION.

Dec. 17, 1887.

Mr. A. A. Marks:

Dear Sir:—I will always feel thankful to you for your skill in fitting the artificial leg to me. I lost my right leg at the battle of Nashville, Dec. 15, 1864. I had used a wooden one until you attached the artificial one, and it would have amused you to see me back home among my people, to see them eyeing me with curiosity, wondering how my right leg should have grown out so suddenly with a foot on it. They were not aware that I had gone to New York to have you fit such to me. I walk like any other man, and with as much ease. A thousand thanks to you, and my hope is you may get all the work you can do, and live long to enjoy the fruits of your inventions.

Yours, with great respect,
CARROLL CHILDERS,
Late private Co. D., 13th Col. Inf., Nashville, Tenn.

BELOW-KNEE AMPUTATION.

Fitted from Measurements.

Hiwasse College, Monroe Co., Tenn., Nov. 2, 1887.

Mr. A. A. Marks, New York:

Dear Sir:—Your favor of the 28th inst. reached me this eve, and in reference to your patent limbs, I am very highly pleased with mine. I have been wearing one of your artificial legs, with rubber foot, about two months, and the more I wear it the better I like it. I am going to school at Hiwasse, and I have about one half a mile to walk four times a day. The cost of repairs has been nothing. I am certain that the rubber foot is superior to the wooden foot in every way, and then it is much more reliable, for there is no iron in the rubber foot to make it wear and get loose like there is in the wooden foot.

Respectfully yours,
A. F. TURRENTINE.

BELOW-KNEE AMPUTATION.

Fitted from Measurements.

Able to do some tolerably heavy carrying and lifting.

Haenel & Martens, Grocers, 1700 Lavacca St., Austin, Texas.

A. A. Marks:

Dear Sir:—The artificial leg (below knee) you made for me some time ago fits nicely, and I am well pleased with it.

I am attending to business every day from morning till late at night, without tiring much, and without the assistance of a cane, and am able to do some tolerably heavy lifting and carrying (as we do all the work ourselves). Your patent rubber foot comes as near being natural as any thing I ever saw, and the whole appearance is almost lifelike. I have not had any repairing done to it since I am wearing it, and would not do without it for any thing.

The longer I use it the better I like it.

Yours respectfully,
GEORGE MARTENS.

BELOW-KNEE AMPUTATION.

Fitted from Measurements.

Llano, Llano Co., Texas, Nov. 8, 1887.

Dear Sir:—I have been wearing your patent artificial leg for over seven years with the utmost satisfaction. I can go anywhere I want to. I can run, jump, and climb—in fact, any thing that any body can do. I would not give your leg for any other two legs that I have seen. I never use a cane, even when going a long distance from home. I would advise all who want to feel like a new person to get one of your patent legs.

Yours truly,
W. E. SIMPSON.

BELOW-KNEE AMPUTATION.

EMORY, RAINS CO., TEXAS, Jan. 30, 1888.

A. A. MARKS, New York City:

DEAR SIR:—We will ever remember you as a benefactor of the human race. The leg made and sent by you to Samuel M. Jackson is not only a beauty in make and durability, but is so well adapted and fitted that it is impossible, without a knowledge of the fact, to tell that he has lost a leg. It is the best leg that I have ever seen. The whole medical profession and citizens agree to these facts. When Jackson put on the leg, then walked a few steps, he exclaimed : "I'm all right now," and the big tears fell from his cheeks, with the reply that, "I can't tell you how grateful I am to Mr. Marks for this wonder."

Yours respectfully,
GEO. R. KIMBROUGH, M.D.

BELOW-KNEE AMPUTATION.

Fitted from Measurements.

SURGEON-GENERAL BARNES, U.S.A., SAID THE MARKS LEG GAVE THE GREATEST SATISFACTION.

CORPUS CHRISTI, NUECES CO., TEXAS, Nov. 1, 1887.

A. A. MARKS, ESQ., Manufacturer of Artificial Limbs, New York City.

DEAR SIR:—After using one of your artificial legs for about seven years, I deem it proper to inform you as to my opinion of the limbs of your manufacture. I lost my leg on April 8, 1881, by the accidental discharge of my pistol, while in the discharge of my duties as deputy collector of customs at Carizo, Texas. While the stump was healing, I asked Surgeon General Barnes, U.S.A., whom he thought was the best manufacturer of artificial limbs. He replied that there were several bonded manufacturers for the United States, but that A.A. Marks of New York City gave the greatest satisfaction. So I stated my case to you by mail, and was informed that you could make a good fit by my taking the measurements according to instructions mailed me, without my going to New York. I forwarded you the measures and received the limb.

I commenced using it at once, and soon laid aside crutches and cane, and do all my walking without the aid of a cane, notwithstanding the amputation was made about two inches below the knee joint. I have never tried any other make, but I prefer the rubber foot, as it is pliable and free from noises.

It, in fact, resembles the original so well that persons do not dream of my being a cripple, until told and the proof shown them.

As to strength, I don't think there can be a stronger, for it carries me all right with a weight of 280 pounds.

I am pleased with your artificial limbs, and take pleasure in recommending them to others who have been unfortunate like myself. I am, very respectfully,
JAMES DOWNING.

BELOW-KNEE AMPUTATION.

Fitted from Measurements.

A. R. GOSSARD, Machinery and Supplies,
AUSTIN, TEXAS, Nov. 31, 1887.

A. A. MARKS, New York:

DEAR SIR:—I am using one of your legs with rubber foot, and like it better than the old style. I have used artificial limbs for six years. My limb is off about half-way from ankle to knee.

Respectfully

A. R. GOSSARD.

BELOW-KNEE AMPUTATION.

Fitted from Measurements.

GILMER, UPSHER CO., TEXAS, Feb. 15, 1876.

Mr. A. A. MARKS:

DEAR SIR:—I have been using one of your patent legs since 1871; it has never given me any trouble; I can walk with an ease that is surprising to myself. The india-rubber foot is, in my opinion, the next thing to life itself, obviating the necessity of an ankle joint.

I have used other artificial legs that had ankle joints, heel-cords, &c., that were clacking, breaking, and making a noise very obnoxious to the ear of one who has the misfortune to be mutilated. I take this opportunity to say to those who have met the missiles of the late unhappy war that the inventions of A. A. Marks excel every thing of the kind that I have ever met with in the way of substitutes for a lost limb.

Yours very truly,

B. T. HUMPHREYS.

BELOW-KNEE AMPUTATION.

Fitted from Measurements.

UINTAH, WEBER CO., UTAH, Nov. 11, 1887.

A. A. MARKS:

DEAR SIR:—I have used one of the artificial legs manufactured by you for over three years and a half, and therefore I can say I have had some experience with it. The rubber foot works almost as well as the natural one, and after I got used to it and got it well fitted to the stump I was surprised how easy it was to get along with my usual work on the farm. I have never used any other kind of artificial leg; I am well satisfied that nothing can be better than the one I got from you with a rubber foot, and I would say to any one who has the misfortune to lose a limb, by all means, partner, get a new one from A. A. Marks, and you will soon forget your misfortune, as after a short while you will get used to the artificial one and work as easily with it as you did with the natural one. I am working on a farm and do all my work myself, besides going around with my machine and cutting hay for my neighbors. I had my left leg broken by a wagon loaded with lumber running over it. It was amputated below the knee, and I can say that, from the measurements I sent to you according to your directions, you made a perfect limb, with joints so easy and solid, at the same time, that it has not cost me scarcely any thing to keep it in good order.

Yours respectfully,

TIMOTHY O'NEIL.

BELOW-KNEE AMPUTATION.

CLARENDON SPRINGS, RUTLAND CO., VT., Oct. 30, 1887.

DEAR SIR:—On March 20, 1884, I was engaged in sawing wood with circular saw; I slipped and fell with my foot under the saw, which sawed through the ankle. It was so badly injured that the doctors had to amputate it four inches above the ankle joint.

I went to your establishment and purchased a limb; on the first of April I went to work in a cheese factory, and worked seven months, and never lost one day, and ever since then my occupation has been cheese-making. From the first the leg has never given me any trouble. I walk with safety and comfort.

Have never had any repairing done. I walk very much, and labor constantly, and none except those who know of my condition would imagine that I am wearing an artificial leg. I have seen other kinds, but I prefer yours to any other. I take pleasure in recommending yours to those that are in need of artificial legs. I can say those that once try your limbs will never use any other.

Yours respectfully,
MYRON D. SEARLES.

BELOW-KNEE AMPUTATION.

EAST ARLINGTON, BENNINGTON CO., VT., Nov. 2, 1887.

MR. A. A. MARKS:

DEAR SIR:—I most cheerfully add my testimony to the great worth of your artificial limbs. I have been using one of your patent limbs since 1869. The india-rubber foot is in my opinion the next thing to life itself, obviating the necessity of an ankle joint. I have used artificial limbs with ankle joints and cords which were continually breaking and getting out of repair until I lost all confidence in them. My occupation is a forger, running trip hammers, and hand forging, doing very heavy jobs. I am constantly on my feet, and can walk with perfect ease and safety anywhere. It never gets out of repair.

I would not have any other, especially one with an ankle joint, as the rubber foot gives all the motion required. I cheerfully recommend all who inquire about artificial limbs to get Marks', the best made.

Respectfully yours,
A. A. GRANT,
Late of Co. A, 2d Vt. Vols.

BELOW-KNEE AMPUTATION.

Oct. 31, 1887.

MR. MARKS:

DEAR SIR—I am glad to have an opportunity of placing in your hands for publication my experience with and my views of your patent artificial limbs. From my thirteen years of constant labor on your patent limb on a farm, and doing all kinds of work with ease and comfort, I can truly say yours is the best in my views. I had one of ——'s before I got yours, and it did well for a year. It was the old style leg with ankle joint. It was out of repair very often, and it got so I did not dare to go out on the street with it. But yours is good yet. I wish no better leg than yours with patent rubber foot. My leg is off six inches below the knee.

Yours truly,
WM. B. GILL.

No. 172 North Willard St., BURLINGTON, VT.

BELOW-KNEE AMPUTATION.

WEST RANDOLPH, ORANGE CO., VT., Oct. 31, 1887.

MR. A. A. MARKS:

DEAR SIR:—Before wearing your artificial leg I wore two with ankle and toe joints, cords and springs. They were constantly out of repair. Have worn yours with rubber foot twelve years. It has not cost me $2 for repairs in that time. My leg is amputated four inches below the knee.

Respectfully yours,
L. H. GOODRICH.

BELOW-KNEE AMPUTATION.

NORTH HYDE PARK, LAMOILLE CO., VT., Oct. 29, 1887.

A. A. MARKS, ESQ., New York City :

DEAR SIR :—Yours of the 26th inst. came duly to hand. I take pleasure in answering your inquiries in regard to how I like your rubber limbs. I have worn one of your artificial limbs for fourteen years, and during that time I did not have to pay out any thing for repairs except for a strap to go over my shoulder, and for that length of time it worked very nicely.

My business for four years was farming, doing all kinds of work that farmers have to do. Two winters I worked on the mountain cutting and skidding logs, which was a very trying test for the limb. The limb that I am now wearing is one of your make, and I have worn it two years, and it has never given out or failed in any particular, and I am well pleased with it. I think the rubber foot is the best artificial that can be got up, as there is no ankle joint to wear out and rattle at every step I take, and be all the time failing, as is the case with other artificials.

I think they are far more durable than any other manufactured that I have seen yet ; I can walk five or six miles without any trouble. By sending you my measurements I got a good fit, and am wearing it very comfortably.

Yours very truly,

EDWIN A. GALLUP, Late of Co. L., 2d Vt. Vols.

BELOW-KNEE AMPUTATION.

BELLOWS FALLS, WINDHAM CO., VT., Oct. 27, 1887.

DEAR SIR :—I have been using one of your artificial limbs for the past three years, and am pleased to say it has given entire satisfaction. My limb was amputated five inches below the knee. My occupation as fireman in Moore and Arms' paper mills gives my limb a thorough test. It has required very little repairing, the repairs having cost less than $10. With my best wishes for your future, I remain, Yours truly,

CHAS. M. DODGE.

BELOW-KNEE AMPUTATION.

Fitted from Measurements.

UNION RIDGE, CLARKE CO., WASH. T., Nov. 6, 1887.

MR. A. A. MARKS :

DEAR SIR :—I have worn one of your artificial limbs for the last six years, made from measurements. I am well satisfied with it in every way. My trade is dressmaking.

Amputation below the knee. I remain,

Yours truly,

HANNAH CARTY.

BELOW-KNEE AMPUTATION.

Fitted from Measurements.

CHEHALIS, LEWIS CO., WASH. T., Sept. 3, 1887.

A. A. MARKS :

DEAR SIR :—In reply to your request, I will state that I am very well satisfied with the limb you sent me. My labor is heavy. It has cost me nothing for repairs so far, which is fortunate, as there is no place to take it to here, and I could not spare it long enough to send it to you.

Yours truly,

A. C. ST. JOHN.

BELOW-KNEE AMPUTATION.

Fitted from Measurements.

314 Commercial St., SEATTLE, WASH. TERR., Nov. 4, 1887.

A. A. MARKS:

DEAR SIR:—During the last ten years I have been obliged to wear a substitute. I tried the ——, then the ——, and got fairly disgusted with both of them, owing to the cords breaking or the bolts wearing and creaking, and, worse than all, echoing from the hills beyond, made me mount a peg leg of my own make, and one day I met a friend of mine, an old army captain, who persuaded me (in spite of my prejudice against artificial limbs) to get one of your patent. Finally I consented, and have worn it ever since.

Every step I take brings 183 pounds to bear on it, and still the foot is as flexible as ever; in fact, it has given me entire satisfaction, and I can heartily recommend your patent artificial feet. Truly,

THOS. E. HUGHES.

BELOW-KNEE AMPUTATION.

Fitted from Measurements.

A lumberman riding horseback and walking over logs.

GLENVILLE, GILMER CO., W. VA.

MR. A. A. MARKS, New York City:

DEAR SIR:—Allow me to say, for the benefit of those needing artificial limbs, that I have worn your patent leg with rubber foot for fifteen years, and in the fifteen years' constant use I have not paid $5 for repairs. I walk with ease and alacrity.

I have been engaged in lumbering for the last ten years, riding horseback as much as four to five days out of each week from place to place, and then walking over logs to measure, etc.

I have examined several different kinds of limbs, but think that for comfort and durability your limbs are superior to any I know of. The first leg that I wore was a leg made in Cincinnati; it did not prove satisfactory. I cheerfully recommend you to all those who need artificial limbs, and also I am glad to state that in my case you have been successful in fitting from measurements.

Yours most respectfully,

JOHN S. BRANNON.

BELOW-KNEE AMPUTATION.

WESTON, LEWIS CO., W. VA., Oct. 31, 1887.

A. A. MARKS:

SIR:—I want to write you a short testimonial which you may use in your pamphlet for the benefit of those cripples who may desire to use an artificial limb. I was wounded in 1864, which resulted in the amputation of my left foot four and half inches above the ankle joint, which left a very tender stump by sloughing.

After that time I ran a saw and grist mill for ten years.

Afterward I was engaged in the mercantile business, and am now a photographer. The first order that I gave was for one of ——'s legs, which was tolerable. The next I ordered was one of yours; it was very good. But, like all others, thinking there might still be a better one, I ordered one of —— and it was a perfect nuisance, and then 1881 I fell back on your old stand-by leg. This I am still wearing. I recommend you, and will wear no other in the future.

JACOB STEALEY,
Co. E. 10th W. Va. Infty.

BELOW-KNEE AMPUTATION.

WILSONBURG, HARRISON CO., W. VA., Nov. 4, 1887.

To WHOM IT MAY CONCERN :

I have worn an artificial limb of Marks' patent for two years, and I find it superior in every respect to any other. As merchant I am on my feet almost all day long, and do not suffer any inconvenience from the limb. This I think is owing to the fact that the foot is of rubber. My foot was amputated just above the ankle, and during the time I have worn the artificial limb, I have no cause for complaint or repairs.

Respectfully,

M. J. FRANCIS.

BELOW-KNEE AMPUTATION.

Fitted from Measurements.

ADDISON, WEBSTER CO., W. VA., Nov. 22, 1887.

MR. A. A. MARKS, :

DEAR SIR :—I am well pleased with your artificial leg. It hides the deformity, and enables me to walk with comfort and ease. My walk is natural. I can ride with the same comfort that I did with my natural leg. Occupation is farming, and by the help of your artificial leg I perform the same amount of labor I ever did ; fitting from measurements ; amputation below the knee.

Yours respectfully,

LEVI SKIDMORE.

BELOW-KNEE AMPUTATION.

Fitted from Measurements.

Nov. 80, 1887.

I am a farmer and lumberman. My amputation is eight inches below the knee. My leg was fitted by measurements and works first rate. I am much pleased with it.

S. D. KNOWLES.

WAUSAU, MARATHON CO., WIS.

BELOW-KNEE AMPUTATION.

Fitted from Measurements.

Nov. 13, 1887.

MR. A. A. MARKS :

DEAR SIR :—I have worn one of your artificial limbs for six years, and am highly pleased with it. I think the rubber feet are just the thing and do away with the old style of springs ; they are more durable and far better in every respect.

As to your success in fitting from measurements, my limb fits me to a T. My occupation is farmer, and my limb is amputated four inches below the knee, and I have never paid out a cent for repairs yet, and I think if I ever buy another limb I will give you my order. I think your limb is far superior to any I have ever seen.

Yours respectfully,

EDWARD R. SMITH.

DOWNSVILLE, DUNN CO., WIS.

BELOW-KNEE AMPUTATION.

BROWNTOWN, GREEN CO., WIS. Dec. 15, 1887.
MR. A. A. MARKS:
DEAR SIR :— I have worn your patent leg for over two years with perfect satisfaction. I want no other kind. I have worn an artificial leg nearly twenty-five years, and was always bothered with the springs and ankle joint giving out. Yours has never troubled me any, and is apparently as good as new. The rubber foot is almost like the natural one. No dropping of toes, no swinging side-wear, but straight forward over rough ground or on sidewalk, or up and down hill. I would cheerfully recommend it to all in need of a substitute.
Very respectfully yours,
BENJAMIN WICKS.

BELOW-KNEE AMPUTATION.

CROSS PLAINS, DANE CO., WIS., Oct. 30, 1887.
A. A. MARKS:
DEAR SIR :—As you have made three artificial limbs for me and they have all given complete satisfaction, I believe it my duty to inform you how I am getting along. The first leg I wore was a ——; before I had worn it two years you could hear the ankle rattle for a long distance. The ankle joint in an artificial limb is a nuisance. I believe the rubber foot to be the best and safest yet invented. I am a farmer by occupation, and own and manage a farm of 160 acres. I have been standing husking corn to-day, and kept up my row with two able-bodied men from 7 A.M. to 5 P.M. I have been wearing an artificial limb for twenty-three years, and have not been without one on for thirty days in that time.

My leg is amputated four inches below the knee. I have investigated the "artificial problem" pretty thoroughly, and believe there is nothing made to beat the rubber foot for comfort and durability. I am so thoroughly convinced of the superiority of your limbs that I always recommend them to all inquirers.
Yours respectfully,
HARRISON SAYLES.

BELOW-KNEE AMPUTATION.

Fitted from Measurements.

BELLE PLAIN, SHAWANO CO., WIS., Oct. 30, 1887..
A. A. MARKS, New York:
DEAR SIR :—Your letter with a request for statement is at hand. My leg was taken off seven inches below the knee. I got an artificial one with rubber foot a year ago last winter; since then I have done the same work as I did before, and that is farmwork. I am eighteen years old now, and can lift as much as the best of boys at that age, and walk eight or ten miles without any trouble. Last winter I used the leg very hard while driving teams and hauling timber.
Yours, etc.,
FRANKLIN L. ROUSE.

BELOW-KNEE AMPUTATION.

Office of J. W. WINN, City Marshal,
RIVER FALLS, PIERCE CO., WIS., Oct. 28, 1887.
A. A. MARKS:
DEAR SIR :—It is with great pleasure I reply to yours of October 26. I have been wearing artificial limbs since June, 1863, having lost my natural limb in September, 1862. I have since used three different kinds, yours making four, and when I say that your limb is pre-eminently ahead of them all, I speak the

truth. It is nearly one year since I got you to fix my limb, and I have worn it every day since with perfect ease ; no binding, no chafing or blistering ; no dread to put it on in the morning, for I feel confident that when I do put it on it will fit, and fit as easy all day, which is more than I ever had one do before.

Since last May I have been marshal of our city, and have been constantly on my feet from 8 o'clock A.M. until 11 o'clock P.M ; so you see I have proved it thoroughly.

My limb was amputated five inches below the knee. I have not been to one cent of expense as yet. When I purchased your limb, I was prejudiced against your stiff ankle, but am now thoroughly convinced that I was wrong, and would be willing to certify that, in my opinion, you make the best artificial limb in the market, and have advised my comrades and others to purchase of you.

Yours truly,

J. W. WINN.

BELOW-KNEE AMPUTATION.

AVOCA, IOWA CO., WIS., Nov. 22, 1887.

MR. A. A. MARKS :

SIR :—I will state to you that I never had such a good fit for the last twenty-one years. My leg is off nine inches below the knee. Two years ago I was in your office. I have worn three legs from —— at Philadelphia and none of them equals yours.

The rubber foot cannot be excelled.

Yours truly,

DANIEL LYNCH.

BELOW-KNEE AMPUTATION.

Fitted from Measurements.

WARREN MILLS, MONROE CO., WIS., Nov. 17, 1887.

MR. A. A. MARKS :

DEAR SIR :—I have worn the leg you made for over five years and am exceedingly well pleased with it. In that time it has not cost me one cent for repairs, and it is good for a long time yet. This is very well considering that I have been laboring very nearly every day since I got it. My leg is amputated below the knee. I can heartily recommend your artificial limbs to any one in need of such an article.

Yours respectfully,

JOHN OLSON.

BELOW-KNEE AMPUTATION.

Fitted from Measurements.

BELMONT, LA FAYETTE CO., WIS., Dec. 14, 1887.

A. A. MARKS, ESQ., New York :

DEAR SIR :—Yours of October 26 at hand, and I would say in reply I am doing all my housework, carrying wood, water, etc.

I have worn artificial limbs since 1872. I am now wearing the fourth limb which I purchased of you on or about July, 1885.

It is giving me much better satisfaction than any of the other three which I purchased from different firms. My limb is amputated five inches above the ankle joint. You fitted me perfectly from measurements.

Respectfully yours,

MRS. WM. KRACKE.

BELOW-KNEE AMPUTATION.

The Globe Milling Co., Merchant Millers,
WATERTOWN, JEFFERSON CO., WIS., Dec. 1, 1887.

MR. A. A. MARKS :

DEAR SIR :—It is now over twenty years ago since I bought my first artificial leg from you. I have tried several other makes in the meantime, but none of them have given me such satisfaction in any way. I have found yours the easiest and most comfortable, both for wear and walking, and also the most durable. Have been engaged in the stave and lumber manufacturing business all this time. I had to be around on my feet all day. I could not favor the leg or foot, but used it hard, my leg being taken off about six inches below the knee. I have always recommended your leg as the best I have ever used or seen.

Yours truly,

CHRIS. MAY.

BELOW-KNEE AMPUTATION,

Fitted from Measurements.

Seventy-one years of age—can walk without a cane.

OSHKOSH, WIS., Nov. 19, 1887.

A. A. MARKS, ESQ., New York :

DEAR SIR :—In reply to your circular of October 26, would say that I think your artificial limb is the best that can be made. I have used one since 1881 and it has given perfect satisfaction. My leg was amputated below the knee June, 1881, and measures for the same were taken before the stump had healed.

I have worn the leg every day since. I am seventy-one years old, and can walk without a cane or crutch. I am on my feet in the store from six o'clock in the morning till eight o'clock in the evening, and never think of using a cane except when I go on the street.

The cost of repairs are nominal ; a few dollars covers all expended on it. I think the rubber heel and toe and no ankle joint a great thing for people obliged to wear artificial limbs.

Yours very truly,

K. DICHMAN.

I weigh from one hundred and ninety to two hundred pounds.

BELOW-KNEE AMPUTATION.

Fitted from Measurements.

KINGSTON, ONT., CANADA, Dec. 27, 1887.

A. A. MARKS, New York :

DEAR SIR :—The artificial limb procured from you some five years ago has proved satisfactory. I have worn it constantly ever since without any inconvenience. It has only cost me a trifle for repairs so far, and it will last for a good while yet.

I think the rubber foot a great improvement on the ankle joints.

Respectfully yours,

MATILDA ALBERTSON.

BELOW-KNEE AMPUTATION.

COW BAY, CAPE BRETON, N. S., CANADA, Nov. 30, 1887.

A. A. MARKS, ESQ.:

DEAR SIR :—In reply to your question as to how I like your artificial limbs, I am happy to say that, having worn one for the last six years, I feel convinced that no better can be made. The stump of my leg has given me more or less trouble from causes not remediable, but apart from these drawbacks, at times, I have been for quite a while in the company of people who never suspected that I was dependent on a "cork leg" (as they *will* call it) for support. The limb you furnished the boy Daniel McLean from measurements taken by me has given good satisfaction, and he runs around with his playmates almost as if he had never met with a misfortune.

Yours truly,
R. A. H. MacKeen, M. D.

BELOW-KNEE AMPUTATION.

Fitted from Measurements.

49 Charlotte St., Winnipeg, Manitoba, Canada, Nov. 5, 1887.
A. A. Marks, Esq.:
Dear Sir:—In reply to yours I beg to inform you that I am getting on fine with my leg. It is a first-class fit.

You deserve much credit for it being so, as you had only my own measurements to go by.

The day I put it on I walked four miles across the prairie, and the second day I was at a picnic from eight o'clock in the morning till 10 o'clock at night, and I did not feel the least bit tired. Thanking you for your courtesy to me,

I remain, yours truly,
Wm. Scott.

BELOW-KNEE AMPUTATION.

Fitted from Measurements.

Kingston, Ont., Canada, Dec. 27, 1887.
Mr. A. A. Marks, New York:
Dear Sir:—I procured a leg from you in 1876, for amputation four inches below the knee. I have worn the leg almost constantly ever since. I have had it repaired, of course, at a moderate cost. It will wear for two or three years yet.

I am well pleased with it in every way. I think the rubber foot a great improvement on the ankle joint. As you are aware, I bought a second leg from you about a year ago. It suits also very well. I have not been a whole day on crutches in ten years.

Wishing you the compliments of the season, I remain,
Yours respectfully,
F. S. Rees.

BELOW-KNEE AMPUTATION.

Fitted from Measurements.

St. John, N. B., Canada, Oct. 20, 1887.
Mr. A. A. Marks:
Dear Sir:—I learn that you are going to write a new pamphlet; if so, I would like to tell my story.

In July last I was accidentally caught on an elevator, and my left leg was so fearfully mangled that it had to be amputated above the ankle. In December, after looking around very thoroughly, I purchased my artificial leg of you. I am compelled to say that after one year of constant use I felt confident that I made no mistake in taking your patent. I take pleasure in stating that the leg you sent me by measurement gives me perfect satisfaction. Four times daily I walk from one place to another, and get in and out of my wagon very comfortably, and transact all my business; when walking about I generally use a cane, but often forget it and go about for hours without any, and I get around much better than any one would suppose under the circumstances.

Yours, etc.,
James Delay.

BELOW-KNEE AMPUTATION.

MELBOURNE, QUEBEC, CANADA, Dec. 1, 1887.

MR. MARKS:

DEAR SIR:—I have been wearing an artificial leg for the last twenty-three years. Some thirteen years ago I met one of your patients and was induced to try one of your legs with patent rubber foot, which I have been wearing constantly for the last twelve years, and it has not cost me fifty cents a year to keep it in repair.

My occupation is very laborious, as you must know that farmers have a good deal of heavy work to do. The other limbs which I used were constantly getting out of order, and it cost me a good deal of time and money to keep them in order. In my opinion your artificial leg with rubber foot is the best substitute for the natural that are manufactured on the continent of America. I know by experience that your limbs are the cheapest in the market, for I paid more for repairs in ten years for the other two legs that I wore than the original cost of one of them.

Respectfully yours,

THOS. H. NIXON.

BELOW-KNEE AMPUTATION.

Fitted from Measurements.

WINDSOR, NOVA SCOTIA, CANADA, Dec. 20, 1887.

A. A. MARKS, ESQ.:

DEAR SIR:—I had the misfortune of losing one of my legs on the railway in 1870. Through the kindness of a friend of mine I was recommended to try one of your artificial legs.

For your satisfaction and mine I will say that for the past six years I have worn the same leg, and it has given me good satisfaction. For durability and for comfort I can recommend your make of legs to all those who have been so unfortunate as to lose their natural legs. I am a butcher by trade, and have a great deal of walking and jumping in and out of my wagon, and many people express wonder and astonishment that I can get around so well. I weigh now one hundred and eighty-eight pounds, and had my leg fitted from measurements. I would heartily recommend those in need of an artificial leg to go to you. Hoping you may live long to benefit others as you have me, I remain

Yours very truly,

WILLIAM MARR.

BELOW-KNEE AMPUTATION.

NAPANEE, ONT., CANADA, Nov. 11, 1887.

A. A. MARKS, ESQ., New York, N. Y.:

DEAR SIR:—Having worn one of your artificial legs for about eighteen years, having worn two others by different makers also, I can speak from experience, and I am satisfied there is no leg made to equal yours, particularly so for its durability, as there is no ankle joint (which usually becomes a rattle-box) or springs of any kind to give way, and the wearer always feels perfectly safe against a break-down, which is often a continual dread with wearers of other limbs. The rubber foot in a great measure takes the place of the ankle joint, it being so soft and elastic that there is none of that *pounding sound* usually heard by wearers of legs with ankle joint movements, etc.

Cost of repairs to your limbs are a mere trifle. My amputation is about three inches below the knee. I walk so well that many of my acquaintances have known me for years, and were not aware that I had lost a limb until informed of it. I have much pleasure in recommending your artificial legs with rubber feet to any one so unfortunate as to need a substitute.

Yours sincerely,

J. P. HANLEY, G. T. R. Agent.

BELOW-KNEE AMPUTATION.

TREHERNE, MANITOBA, CANADA, Nov. 10, 1887.

DEAR SIR:—After wearing one of your artificial legs for five years continuously, giving it the hardest of usage, and having worn one of the movable ankle-joint artificial legs previous to getting one of yours, I am in a position to give an opinion on the merits of each. I can recommend your artificial legs with rubber feet in preference to any thing that I have seen or heard of as a substitute for the natural limb, and intend, when this one that I am wearing now is worn out, to order another.

Yours respectfully,

CHAS. O. EVANS.

BELOW-KNEE AMPUTATION.

LOWER PRINCE WILLIAM, N. B., CANADA, Nov. 3, 1887.

A. A. MARKS:

DEAR SIR:—It is with pleasure that I testify to the merits of your artificial leg. I have used one of your make for over two years, and it has proved satisfactory in every respect.

Although my work is quite heavy, yet the leg has stood it remarkably well. You could hardly tell it had been worn.

The expense in that time for repairs has not reached one dollar.

In conclusion I would recommend it to all as the best limb manufactured in America.

Yours truly,

J. R. VAN WART.

BELOW-KNEE AMPUTATION.

247 Ottawa St., MONTREAL, CANADA, Nov. 2, 1887.

Mr. A. A. MARKS:

DEAR SIR:—Having had the misfortune of losing my left leg by being run over by a passenger train on the Grand Trunk Railway, and having had it amputated six inches above ankle joint, I was induced by the earnest solicitation of a friend to get one of your artificial limbs with patent rubber foot. After having worn it for three years constantly without having it repaired, and as my duties require me to be walking from six A. M. until from nine to ten o'clock P. M., and being a heavy man (I weigh over two hundred pounds), I can safely say that the artificial leg manufactured by your firm has no equal for perfect fit and durability. It has passed my most sanguine expectations, and it gives me great pleasure to testify to its general excellence.

Yours respectfully,

WM. CLARK.

BELOW-KNEE AMPUTATION.

Fitted from Measurements.

ST. THOMAS, W. I., Nov. 22, 1887.

I have worn one of the Marks artificial legs with rubber foot for three years, and must accord to him all the merits in the line of the manufacturing of artificial limbs, its durability, its ease and simplicity. I have not had repairs to the value of one cent since wearing the leg, and I have given it test enough to speak of its superiority. I walk for miles without a cane.

I take my usual pleasure in sporting, going over hills and dales without the sign of fatigue or inconvenience.

I must not omit to say that I read in the reports of another artificial limb maker in New York of one of his patients who used one of Mr. Marks' legs with rubber foot, and he had three new feet to the leg in eighteen months, and bold enough to say each foot lasted only six months. I cannot understand it, for I am a carpenter and do a large amount of walking, and my artificial leg has a great deal of wear and tear; and that patient stated he was a groom; impossible, for from my case I do not believe it. I give Mr. Marks leave to publish this in his pamphlet.

R. D. MOTHERSILL.

BELOW-KNEE AMPUTATION.

Fitted from Measurements.

49 Norwood St., BELFAST, IRELAND, June 27, 1884.

DEAR SIR:—On November 24, 1874, I fell from the mast of a ship in Delaware Bay and broke both of my legs, one of which was so badly smashed that Dr. O'Neill of the University Hospital, Philadelphia, advised amputation, which was done a few inches below the knee. I came out of hospital in 1875, and went to reside with a friend in Baltimore. About the latter end of May, 1875—I am not sure of the date—I gave some money I had scraped together to a clergyman named Rev. C. McIlfresh, who took an interest in seafaring men. He advised me to purchase an artificial limb, and took me to an agent of yours in Baltimore, who took the measurements and said he would send to you for the leg. The leg arrived some time about the latter end of June, 1875, and I have been wearing it ever since. I would like to get another just like it. The limb I have has a rubber foot for amputation below the knee. It is a pity you have not an agent here, for there is only one party in this city who makes artificial legs, and they are not to be compared with yours for durability, neatness, and comfort. This party made a botch of mine trying to repair it; before that I could go distances without any difficulty, but now I am afraid to go far for fear of breaking down.

Trusting to hear from you soon,

Yours respectfully,

DR. MARKS. SAMUEL McKEE.

BELOW-KNEE AMPUTATION.

Fitted from Measurements.

Danced at his wedding.

(*Translated from the Spanish.*)

SANTA ROSALIA, MEXICO, Sept. 5, 1887.

A. A. MARKS, New York:

DEAR SIR:—Having had the misfortune to lose my left leg, and being informed by my friend Dr. C. H. Fisher that artificial limbs were manufactured in your city, I made arrangements with the same gentleman to get one of these important members, and was favored with an excellent one, manufactured at your establishment, and which I have used ever since.

When I gave my order I never imagined that an artificial leg could form so perfect a substitute for the natural one in walking, riding on horseback, and even dancing; I supposed it would merely serve to hide the defect, and to preclude that unpleasant impression that is always felt on seeing a mutilated man.

For your satisfaction and my own I would beg to state that experience has demonstrated to me the superiority of the artificial legs with the rubber foot, because they combine simplicity of construction with stability and ease in walking, aside from the consideration of their extreme durability. I seize this opportunity of expressing my gratitude towards yourself for having devoted your energies to the alleviation of mankind in a branch so important as that of

manufacturing artificial limbs, the construction and adaptation of which you so thoroughly understand.
Very sincerely yours,
ANTONIO ALARCON.

C. H. Fisher, M.D., in his letter of November 12, 1887, says :
"Antonio Alarcon was married last week ; he danced a great deal at his wedding."

BELOW-KNEE AMPUTATION.

Fitted from Measurements.

CERRO BLANCO, CARRIZAL BAJO, CHILE, S. A., August 24, 1887.
MR. A. A MARKS, New York :

DEAR SIR :—As no doubt you are aware, the existence of cholera on some of the Chilian posts some six or seven months ago closed all communications between this country and the northern republics, and the artificial leg for my son was thereby a good deal delayed in arriving, reaching me only in April. I wished to give it a fair trial before writing, and I have now much pleasure in telling you that the fit is perfect and that my son is able to use it with the greatest comfort. I have also to thank you for your kind instructions as to bandaging, all of which have been faithfully carried out with great success.

My son begs me to tender you his most earnest and heartfelt thanks for the blessing that you have been the means of rendering to him, and for my part I have only to say that my gratitude is unbounded. I remain, dear sir,
Yours very faithfully,
E. T. MARTIN.

WEARING LEGS FOR ANKLE-JOINT AMPUTATIONS.

ANKLE-JOINT AMPUTATION.

WEST SIMSBURY, HARTFORD CO., CONN., Nov. 4, 1887.
A. A. MARKS :

DEAR SIR :—I had my foot so mangled in a mowing machine four years ago that it was necessary to have it amputated just in front of the ankle. Since then I have been compelled to wear a stump shoe and, having constant trouble with the same, the first of September I had you fit one of your artificial limbs, and since then I have had no trouble. I do not think any thing about having an artificial limb ; it is so easy and comfortable.

I can not say enough in praise of your artificial limbs.
BERTIE R. TULLER.
Eleven years old.

ANKLE-JOINT AMPUTATION.

HARTFORD, CONN., Oct. 30, 1887.

DEAR SIR :—In reply to your letter, I think your feet are the best in the world. I have worn mine for about six months, and have been to dances and a good many social gatherings. I have worn one of the New Haven man's feet, and I could not find the comfort I do with yours. Your feet give more support to the ankle than any other I have seen. I work for I. J. Stein, the silver-plater.

I had my foot taken off four years last March on the Hartford and Connecticut Western R. R. I can recommend your feet as the best in the country.
Yours truly,
EUGENE D. FOX.

INSTEP AMPUTATION.

SAVANNAH, GA., Nov. 1, 1887.

DR. A. A. MARKS, New York:

DEAR SIR:—Yours of October 26 is at hand. Six years ago I was injured by a car of the Central Railroad at Savannah.

Since that time I have been wearing one of your artificial feet for amputation at the instep. My occupation is very laborious, being assistant warehouseman for M. Maclean and Co. I can truly say that your rubber feet are very durable and comfortable and convenient, and I am very much pleased with it.

Yours respectfully,

JNO. L. SPIVEY.

ANKLE-JOINT AMPUTATION.

Fitted from Measurements.

June 27, 1887.

MR. A. A. MARKS:

DEAR SIR:—The rubber foot you made me is doing splendid.

Yours very truly,

WILLIAM POWELL.

EWENSVILLE, GIBSON CO., IND.

ANKLE-JOINT AMPUTATION.

Fitted from Measurements.

WEST GARDNER, WORCESTER CO., MASS., Nov. 13, 1887.

MR. MARKS:

DEAR SIR:—I have worn one of your artificial limbs for three years. I have had no repairs of any kind, and it is just as good as when I bought it. I think your rubber foot the best thing in the market, and far more durable than the old style.

My work has been all standing for the past three years.

Yours respectfully,

O. F. STONE.

ANKLE-JOINT AMPUTATION.

Fitted from Measurements.

KANSAS MEDICAL SOCIETY (STATE), OFFICE OF SECRETARY.
TOPEKA, KANSAS, Nov. 15, 1887.

A. A. MARKS, ESQ.:

DEAR SIR:—I have worn an artificial foot since 1879. The point of amputation is at the ankle, with a portion of the heel remaining. It is a modification of Symes' operation.

I had great difficulty in getting an appliance, and I found it a point very difficult to supply with a comfortable and useful foot. I made many unsuccessful trials and about despaired ever being able to walk without the aid of a crutch. A friend advised me to apply to you, as he had some knowledge of the rubber hands and feet. I did so and received directions from you how to take measurements for the appliance. I sent on the measurements and soon received by express the limb and rubber foot. It was a perfect fit and was comfortable. I could walk with ease and with scarcely a perceptible limp.

I have worn this appliance since September, 1882, and without repairing it.

I am more than pleased with it, and know from experience that you are the only manufacturer of a comfortable and useful limb for the amputations know as Symes' or Chopart's operation. I am a physician, and see quite a number of people wearing artificial limbs, and am well satisfied that the limbs manufactured with the rubber hands and feet, are far superior to any other. Thanking you for the comfortable and useful limb invented through your genius and benevolence, I am,

Yours sincerely,
S. G. STEWART, M.D.

621 Kansas Ave.

ANKLE-JOINT AMPUTATION.

Fitted from Measurements.

WALNUT HILL, NORWALK CO., MASS., Oct. 29, 1887.

A. A. MARKS:

DEAR SIR:—I have worn an artificial limb for twelve years. I have worn one of another kind that had the ankle-joint; it was worn out in three years; and I purchased one from you.

I wore it seven years; it cost me $1.50 for repairs. Two years ago I purchased another limb from you. I think it is the best limb that is made. I would not be without one. I am a wool sorter and have to lift and truck bales that weigh from one hundred to one thousand pounds. My limb is amputated at the ankle joint.

Respectfully yours,
JOHN W. SMITH.

INSTEP AMPUTATION.

TURNER'S FALLS, FRANKLIN CO., MASS., Nov. 26, 1887.

MR. A. A. MARKS:

DEAR SIR:—I desire to inform you that the artificial leg you made for me in 1886 has given me entire satisfaction.

You have my regards for the service you have done me.

Respectfully yours,
JOSEPH PERINET.

ANKLE-JOINT AMPUTATION.

Nov. 10, 1887.

A. A. MARKS:

DEAR SIR:—My foot was amputated at the ankle joint. I have worn a rubber foot of your make for over six years. I find that for perfect fit and durability they cannot be surpassed.

Respectfully yours,
JOHN HILLIARD.

39 7th St., HOBOKEN, N. J.

ANKLE-JOINT AMPUTATION.

Skated twenty miles in one day.

LYNN, ESSEX CO., MASS., Nov. 21, 1887.

MR. A. A. MARKS:

DEAR SIR:—I am pleased to have the chance to write you a testimonial. I am much pleased with my limb. I can say that it is the best limb that I have ever seen for ease and durability. I have worn one of your limbs nearly four years, and it has proved satisfactory in every respect. I am an iron-molder by trade, and am on my feet the most of the time. I can work just as well as if I had my own foot. My amputation is ankle joint. Repairs have been trifling. For walking it is easy. People that know me cannot tell which one is artificial by my walk, and oftentimes I am asked which is my good foot.

I can skate and dance nearly as well as ever I could, and last winter I skated about twenty miles in one day, and that is almost as much as any one wants to do with natural feet. I will answer any correspondence referred to me for information on the subject of the rubber foot.

Yours respectfully,
A. GIFFORD SHUMWAY.

94 Pleasant St.

ANKLE-JOINT AMPUTATION.

Wears No. 137 leg.

LONG BRANCH, N. J., Oct. 29, 1887.

A. A. MARKS:

DEAR SIR:—I take great pleasure in stating that I have used the foot purchased from you for seven years without any expense whatever. I think it the best in use, as I have examined others and find this to be far superior in durability and comfort.

I am janitor of a large school and do all the work pertaining to that office, such as scrubbing, etc. I am also night watchman for a large dry-goods firm.

Very respectfully yours,
CHAS. VAN BRUNT, Sr.

ANKLE-JOINT AMPUTATION.

Editorial Rooms *Irish World*,
17 Barclay St., N. Y., Oct. 15, 1887.

DEAR SIR:—Two years ago I got from you an artificial foot for Pirogoff's operation—the amputation of the foot at the ankle joint. I have worn it constantly since. I have walked some four or five miles a day on it, been on my feet speaking at public meetings for an hour at a time, attended to my duties in this office regularly, and even taken part as a parader in two public demonstrations, not merely without any extraordinary sense of fatigue, but positively without any person not acquainted with me suspecting that any thing was the matter with my nether extremities.

It even amuses me occasionally to challenge intimate friends to pick out the artificial foot by watching my walk, and they generally fail to do it, when they succeed only doing so by guesswork. I have the more pleasure in testifying to the success of your rubber foot from the fact that I had tried artificial feet from two different makers before (one in Dublin, Ireland, and one in Manchester, England), and both were such lamentable failures that I had made up my mind to waste no more money on any thing of the kind, but to hobble through life as best I could on crutches. With your foot I do not require so much as the friendly services of a walking-stick.

You are at liberty to make whatever use you like of my testimony, for I feel that the mere cash payment for the foot is not sufficient recompense for the new life you have given me, and if my evidence induces one similarly situated to try your artificial limbs he will thank me all the days of his life for giving it.

Yours, etc.,
ARTHUR M. FORRESTER,
Asst. Editor *Irish World*.

ANKLE-JOINT AMPUTATION.

Oct. 27, 1887.

MR. MARKS:

DEAR SIR:—I had the misfortune to lose my foot while serving as an engineer on a steamer in 1868. It was amputated at the ankle joint, called the Symes amputation. I have worn several different kinds of artificial limbs, but prefer yours to any I have had. I would not wear a foot with an ankle joint if it were given to me. I have worn yours and worked with it every day for nine years in the Delamater Iron Works, foot of West 13th St., New York City, and not paid a cent for repairs in that time, and found it perfect in every respect, and prefer it to any other make. I cheerfully recommend it to any one of the unfortunate in need of an artificial limb.

Yours respectfully,
F. W. FUNCH.

712 Washington St., NEW YORK CITY.

ANKLE-JOINT AMPUTATION.

177 3d Ave., NEW YORK CITY, Dec. 8, 1887.

MR. A. A. MARKS :

DEAR SIR :—In 1883 I suffered the amputation of my left foot at the ankle joint. I had an artificial leg and foot made for me in England, which I thought served my purpose well, but about a year ago I had you fit me with one of your natural crook legs with rubber foot, which I have since worn with comfort and delight. I am able to walk, run, go up and down stairs and attend to my engine without the least inconvenience or pain. I heartily recommend the rubber foot. Respectfully yours,
EDWARD HANLON.

INSTEP AMPUTATION.

GEO. M. EDDY & Co., Manufacturers of Tape Measures,
351 & 353 Classon Ave., BROOKLYN, N. Y., Nov. 15, 1887.

A. A. MARKS, ESQ :

DEAR SIR :—It gives me a great deal of pleasure to say that the last artificial foot you made for me is probably as near perfection as is possible to make one ; certainly the arrangement of the socket in the front of the leg with the rubber foot attached is far superior to any other I have had made of wood socket, steel joints, and wood foot, all of which have been expensive, have broken easily, and got out of order so as to lose the elasticity which always remains in the rubber foot.

I have had five different appliances for my stump, and I am in honor bound to say that the one you made for me last summer even exceeds your effort of five years ago, and that gave me no expense in the five years. It was a good foot when I put it off for this one, but I did so because I was sure your latest and improved method for Chopart's amputation would prove, as it has done, superior to any other I have ever used. The advantage of this latest appliance by having the wood socket passing up the front of the leg instead of back are, that the leverage is so much reduced that there is no liability of breaking. Second, it may be fitted to feel more comfortable than any other way, giving protection to the sharp edge of the shin.

The rubber foot is more elastic than any other, and makes no noise, does not slip so easily as others. The whole appliance is as simple as any thing possibly can be, and so reduces the liability of breakage and expense. Permit me to renew my expressions of satisfaction with the patient care and fair treatment you have always shown me. Now, if any person has a Chopart's amputation, and wants the benefit of my experience, he may come to me and I will show him my gallery of artificial appliances, and point out the superiority of your latest style to that of any of the other five.

I am, truly yours,
W. P. EDDY.

INSTEP AMPUTATION.

Oct. 27, 1887.

MR. A. A. MARKS, New York :

DEAR SIR —I take the liberty of writing you a few lines in regard to the artificial foot (for Chopart's amputation) I bought of you some time ago. Previous to my buying the foot I visited all the principal makers in New York, but found nothing I liked so well as the foot I saw at your place, and have not as yet had any cause to regret my choice. I am now employed as salesman, and do a great deal of walking and standing, and now, after five months' wear of your foot, I get along almost as well as ever I did, without any limp or halt whatever, and a person not knowing the fact would never suspect there was any thing wrong.

After constant use the foot is in as good condition as it was the day I bought it, not having to be repaired or fixed in any way, the fit being particularly good.

Hoping that all those so unfortunate as to require the use of artificial limbs may call upon you, as I feel they will strike the right man in the right place.

I am, yours truly, ROBERT LOEB.
409 E. 85th St., NEW YORK CITY.

ANKLE-JOINT AMPUTATION.

76 Pacific St., BROOKLYN, N. Y., Nov., 1887.

MR. A. A. MARKS:

I have worn the rubber-foot leg you made for me fourteen years. It has given me perfect satisfaction. I heartily recommend it. I lost my foot in the U. S. Navy.

JAMES CONNELL.

ANKLE-JOINT AMPUTATION.

Fitted from Measurements.

ROCKWELL'S MILLS, CHENANGO CO., N. Y., Nov. 9, 1887.

MR. A. A. MARKS:

DEAR SIR:—My foot was amputated when but a child of thirteen, and as soon as it was sufficiently healed I had one of your admirable rubber feet applied from measurements, and it fitted me as perfectly as though I had gone to New York and had the foot fitted by your own hand. I have used the foot four years now to the untold satisfaction of myself and the utmost gratification of my friends, who often tell me they would never notice any thing peculiar about my walk. I have lived with people for months without their discovering that I was lame.

During the greater part of the time since I have worn your artificial foot, I have attended a boarding school, with its usual number of stairs, which I have run up and down with the greatest ease. I am at present doing a daughter's part of the housework, standing upon my feet the larger portion of the time.

My rubber foot seemed to be a part of me, and I think more of it than any thing I possess. As to repairs, they have been next to nothing, only about $2 during four years. Upon looking over your pamphlet before purchasing my foot I was greatly depressed to find so few testimonials from girls who had worn your limbs, while the pages were filled with endorsements of men and boys. I was almost afraid the limbs were not adapted to the girls. I have long ago proven the fallacy of that notion, however, and to any girl who has lost her limb I would say get one of Marks' limbs with the easy, elastic rubber foot, and thereby be transformed into a happy, useful, and light-hearted girl.

Very gratefully yours,
HATTIE L. MOORE.

ANKLE-JOINT AMPUTATION.

MR. MARKS:

DEAR SIR:—I am a farmer; in March, '86, I cut one of my feet so badly with an axe that amputation was necessary. On March 29 a Symes amputation was performed. In August following I purchased one of your artificial limbs, and must say it gives me entire satisfaction. I am now able to do almost all kinds of farmwork, and walk a mile very comfortably. Indeed many strangers are surprised when they find that I am wearing an artificial limb.

Very respectfully, THEO. HULSE.
CALVERTON, SUFFOLK CO., N. Y., Oct. 31, 1887.

ANKLE-JOINT AMPUTATION.

MT. VERNON, WESTCHESTER CO., N. Y., March 22, 1883.

MR. A. A. MARKS :

DEAR SIR :—I sell morning papers on the R. R. trains, get on and off while the train is in motion, and wear one of your rubber feet ; very few of my

No. 292.

friends know of the fact, and those who do regard me as the possessor of a remarkable foot. I experience no inconvenience ; I heartily recommend your leg as the best made.

JOHN SCHARFF.

ANKLE-JOINT AMPUTATION.

RHINECLIFF, DUTCHESS CO., N. Y., Nov. 29, 1887.

MR A. A. MARKS :

DEAR SIR :—I have the greatest pleasure in addressing you these few lines in order to express the satisfaction which I have with the artificial foot you made for me.

I have worn it constantly for two years and three months.

I walk with safety and comfort, and no repairs needed ; yet I do a great deal of walking. Four years ago I had my foot amputated in the ankle-joint. Not being able to get an artificial foot, I thought of the helpless life that was before me, but through the aid of Dr. Gage I got one of your rubber feet, which I am well pleased with. Hoping you may live long to benefit others as you have me,

I remain, very truly yours, JULIA EMERY.

INSTEP AMPUTATION.

SLATEDALE, LEHIGH CO., PA., Oct. 28, 1887.

MR. A. A. MARKS:
The foot I had made by you gives very good satisfaction. I am well pleased with the material, and also the fit, which is perfect. I would not do without it for any consideration.

Yours truly,

IRA COFFIN.

INSTEP AMPUTATION.

1509 Wallace St., HARRISBURG, PA., Nov. 2, 1887.

MR. A. A. MARKS, ESQ.:
DEAR SIR:—I am glad to testify in this way that your appliance for my foot, a Chopart's amputation, is one of the finest articles in the market. I am a fireman on the P. R. Road and can do my work. I am putting in a sewer seventy feet long, and five deep, besides my work on the road. The cost has been nothing. This is the foot above all others.

I am, very respectfully yours,

C. P. HUTCHINSON.

NIANTIC, WASHINGTON CO., R. I., Oct. 31, 1887.

A. A. MARKS:
DEAR SIR:—Yours of the 26th inst. at hand.
I would say your foot is far superior to the one I have used.
In 1880 I had my foot amputated at ankle (Symes operation).
In 1881 I commenced wearing one of ——'s artificial feet; it made a great deal of noise and was all the time breaking down, which was very expensive to a poor man like myself.
In October, 1885, I received one of your make of feet; the same month I met with an accident breaking my left or well leg; did not get to wearing your foot until March, 1886; have worn it constantly ever since; have worked at my occupation this summer running a stationary engine. People are surprised to see how well I get around. All the expense it has been to me is to have it shortened to correspond with the broken leg. Cost about $3; very reasonable I thought. Your foot is neatly gotten up, light, and makes no noise. Any unfortunates that are in want of artificial limbs would do well to correspond with you.

Very respectfully yours,

F. T. BRIGHTMAN.

APPARATUS.

NO. 160 EXTENSION.

NEW HAVEN, CONN., Oct. 27, 1887.

A. A. MARKS:
DEAR SIR:—The extension with rubber foot manufactured for me has been in constant use for one year. I can recommend it for durability, neatness, and a comfort that a person with a shortened limb should not be without. Not being able to do you justice enough for the comfort that I have derived from it,

I remain, respectfully yours,

W. C. A.

NO. 152 LEG.

PUTNAM, WINDHAM CO., CONN., Nov. 7, 1887.

MR. MARKS;

DEAR SIR:—In answer to your request, I will say that I am very much pleased with the apparatus (with rubber foot) that you fitted to my deformed foot. I have worn it one year and think more and more of it. I would not take any amount for it, if I could not get another. I hope this will induce others in my condition to try your apparatus and walk easier.

I am in a millinery store, and am standing part of the time.

Respectfully yours,
MISS H. S. KENNEDY.

NO. 152 LEG.

Oct. 31, 1887.

MR. A. A. MARKS:

DEAR SIR:—It gives me sincere pleasure to inform you that the apparatus made by you for my son Freddy has my appreciations. It conceals his deformity, and enables him to walk in a natural manner.

Yours very truly,
G. A. WILLIAMSON.

EAST WEBSTER, WORCESTER CO., MASS.

P.S. I would say that the apparatus was applied when nineteen months old. The boy will be three years old the 24th of December, 1887.

NO. 152 LEG.

GROTON, MIDDLESEX CO., MASS., Nov. 3, 1887.

MR. MARKS:

SIR:—In regard to the apparatus, I would say I have worn one nearly a year and it gives entire satisfaction; and I would advise any one in need of any thing of the kind to consult with Mr. A. A. Marks. I am an engineer, and my leg gets pretty hard usage sometimes, and does not get out of order.

Yours respectfully,
E. H. CLARK.

NO. 157 FOOT.

W. C. LEWIS, dealer in Stoves, Hardware, etc.,
GLOBE VILLAGE, WORCESTER CO., MASS., April 1, 1887.

MR. MARKS:

Cady wears his foot all day, with the exception of an hour during the middle of the day. If he had his say it would not be taken off then. He speaks of you every day. It would do you good to see how he runs around on it. I think this is doing pretty well, as it is less than two weeks since he began to use it.

Yours respectfully,
W. C. LEWIS.

NO. 167 FOOT.

275 So. Water St., NEW BEDFORD, BRISTOL CO., MASS., June 15, 1887.

A. A. MARKS:

DEAR SIR:—The boot was received all right and fits perfectly. I have worn it steadily and don't think it can be improved. I feel very grateful that you and your workmen have been gifted with the spirit of wisdom to know what would suit me so well.

I am, yours respectfully,
BELLE GRAY.

APPARATUS.

A. A. MARKS, New York City:

DEAR SIR :—The apparatus furnished by you on government order five years ago has given satisfaction, and I regard it as the very best that could be made for the purpose. My left leg is completely paralyzed in the loss of motion caused by sciatic rheumatism in the U. S. service. I shall need another apparatus in the spring. Please send blanks for order and transportation.

Yours very courteously,
THOS. H. SAUNDERS,
Attorney at Law and Ex County Judge.

OSCEOLA, POLK CO., NEB., Nov. 4, 1887.

NO. 152 LEG.

PEEKSKILL, DUTCHESS CO., NEW YORK, October 24, 1877.

MR. A. A. MARKS:

DEAR SIR :—Some time ago you wrote to me with regard to how much I was benefited by the artificial limb (or apparatus rather) you had adapted to my deformity.

In reply, I would beg leave to state that during the whole time that I have

No. 293.   No 294.

been afflicted with this deformity (37 years) I have never found relief before. I have been operated upon, surgically, three times during my life, the Tendon Achilles cut each time, with no favorable result. At times I have been compelled to use a crutch, and always a cane, upon which I took much of my weight.

Since I have been using the apparatus, my walk has improved almost to perfection, and my comfort more than I can express in words. I now walk with comparative ease, sometimes using a cane, more from force of habit than necessity.

I only wish it had been applied years ago. I should thereby have saved myself much distress and suffering, as well as mortification. Nothing could reach my case to do me any good but your elastic rubber foot, that comes in here so complete, where there is no room for a joint (if one was needed, even in any case). My nearly two years' experience with this apparatus has fixed me up so completely that nothing could induce me to dispense with it. Hoping that your life may be spared for many years to continue to benefit other unfortunates as you have me,

Yours very truly, A. T. CUZNER. M.D.

NO. 150 LEG.

Nov. 10, 1887.

DEAR SIR :—Allow me to express my gratitude for the relief given me by your artificial limb. I have worn artificial limbs for the last twenty years, but not until August, 1886, had I the good fortune to receive your assistance. Formerly the complicated adjustment to my limb hindered me from walking without the aid of a crutch, but since I am in the happy possession of your rubber foot walking becomes a pleasure. The rubber foot without ankle joint gives me the elasticity needed by the pedestrian.

Your artificial limb can certainly be recommended with the utmost confidence.

Yours truly, CHAS. F. SCHANZ.
295 E. 10th St., NEW YORK CITY.

NO. 152 LEG.

SOMERS CENTER, WESTCHESTER CO., N. Y., March 23, 1883.
A. A. MARKS, ESQ.:

DEAR SIR :—Your apparatus for limbs shortened by hip disease I have used for the past two years with satisfaction ; the rubber foot aids the weak limb and gives almost the same elasticity as the natural foot and ankle. Its durability is beyond question, and surpasses those with the ankle joint, in my experience and estimation.

Yours very truly, SAMUEL P. WRIGHT.

NO. 152 LEG.

PENN. RAILROAD OFFICE, 233 S. 4th St., PHILADELPHIA, PA.
A. A. MARKS:

DEAR SIR :—Having used your apparatus for deformed foot constantly for the past ten years I can cheerfully say that it has answered the purpose intended, by concealing my deformity and enabling me to walk in a natural manner and without tiring.

On account of its strength and simplicity of construction, in connection with your rubber foot, I could not conceive any thing more suitable for the purpose.

Yours respectfully, HENRY SASSAMAN.
Dec. 16, 1887.

ABOVE-ELBOW ARMS.

ABOVE-ELBOW AMPUTATION.

Fitted from Measurements.

FARILL, CHEROKEE CO., ALA., Feb. 27, 1887.

I have been wearing one of A.A. Marks' artificial arms, and am much pleased with it, and would say that it is all he claims for it.

MISS MARY CUMBY.

Endorsed by J. W. FARILL, M.D.

ABOVE-ELBOW AMPUTATION.

PUTNAM, WINDHAM CO., CONN., Oct. 29, 1887.

A. A. MARKS, ESQ:

DEAR SIR:—At the age of seventeen years, I met with an accident necessitating the amputation above the elbow of my right arm. I desired after the elapse of a few years to procure the best false arm made, and as your artificial limbs were recommended to me by a neighbor similarly afflicted as being the best, I gave you my order. I have worn the arm a year and six months, experiencing no difficulty whatever, but find it useful to me in my business as well as an improvement in my appearance. During the time I have expended nothing for repairs on same, excepting three dollars for a new pair of straps. No small sum would tempt me to part with it. Thanking you for your kind interest in my behalf, I remain,

Yours truly,
CLARENCE M. FRENCH,
Telegraph Operator.

ABOVE-ELBOW AMPUTATION.

Fitted from Measurements.

HARLEM, COLUMBIA CO., GA., Nov. 3, 1887.

A. A. MARKS, ESQ., New York City:

DEAR SIR:—The artificial arm with rubber hand manufactured for me by you gives perfect satisfaction. My arm is amputated above the elbow. You made perfect fit by measurement taken by my father under your direction. I received the arm last April, and have been wearing it every day since, without the least inconvenience and without any repairs. I do not know how I could do without it. I can use it much better than I expected. I can hold my needles in knitting, and by its aid can do various kinds of fancy work.

Very respectfully yours,
ALICE LAMKIN.

ABOVE-ELBOW AMPUTATION.

Fitted from Measurements.

IDA GROVE, IDA CO., IOWA, Nov. 4, 1887.

MR. A. A. MARKS:

DEAR SIR:—The artificial arm purchased of you three years ago has given good satisfaction. I am a farmer by occupation, and the arm has been in hard and constant use with very few repairs except straps and webbing. The stump of my arm is but six inches long, but the arm fits well, and is all one could expect of an artificial limb, and I can heartily recommend them to any one so unfortunate as to be in need of one.

Yours truly,
CHAS. L. DEWEY.

ABOVE-ELBOW AMPUTATION.

Fitted from Measurements.

Nov. 4, 1887.

MR. A. A. MARKS:

DEAR SIR:—In reply to your request, will say for the benefit of those who are unfortunate enough to be without the use of two arms, that I have a left stump five and one-half inches in length, on which I wear one of your arms with rubber hand; the same was fitted from measurements. I have worn it every day since 1881, and treble the amount of cost would not induce me to be with-

out it. Repairs have been comparatively nothing. A new strap occasionally, that is all; and, further, I know the rubber hand is far superior to any other I have ever seen in use. My hand is as good as the day I received it. I am a newspaper man by occupation. My arm keeps me balanced nicely and fills the vacancy so perfectly that many people associating with me do not know that I am a one-armed man. I am out on a collecting tour through Missouri. My address is 1907 W. 6th St., KANSAS CITY, KANS.
R. A. KOPE.

ABOVE-ELBOW AMPUTATION.

130 Conant St., BOSTON, MASS., Oct. 29, 1887.

A. A. MARKS, ESQ. :

DEAR SIR :—I am thirteen years of age and have been wearing one of your rubber hands for about eighteen months. It has been of such assistance and use to me that I would not be without it for a day. I am able to help myself at table and in many other ways by its means, and most heartily recommend any one in need of artificial limbs to investigate the merits of your inventions.
Yours truly, JOSEPH T. MOONEY.

ABOVE-ELBOW AMPUTATION.

Fitted from Measurements.

KENT CITY, KENT Co., MICH., Nov. 11, 1887.

A. A. MARKS :

DEAR SIR :—In reply to your invitation of the 26th. The artificial arm I bought of you two years ago is in every way satisfactory. The rubber hand is of special benefit. I would not have any other kind of hand. I have only five inches of stump ; was fitted by measurements sent by mail ; don't think it possible to have a better fit. Your arm is all you claim for it. No repairs yet, and don't need any.
Very respectfully. C. S. PARKS,
Agent C. and W. M. R. Co.

ABOVE-ELBOW AMPUTATION.

Fitted from Measurements.

HANOVER, GAGE Co., NEB., Nov. 20, 1887.

DEAR SIR :—I want to inform you that I am able to work well with the artificial arm you made for me. I have had no expenses with it yet with the exception of a shoulder strap. I can use any of the farming tools in attending to eighty acres of land. I can pitch grain and hay, can plow and cultivate. I regard your arm as the best in the market.
Yours, WILLIAM PARDEE.

ABOVE-ELBOW AMPUTATION.

MORRISTOWN, MORRIS CO., N. J., Nov. 7, 1887.

MR. MARKS :

DEAR SIR :—I am perfectly satisfied in every way with the artificial arm I procured of you, two years and over. During that time it has not cost me one cent for repairs. As to the fit, all I can say is to repeat what my friends say, that nobody would know it was artificial unless I told them. The rubber hand is a great saver of gloves, and a vast improvement also. My arm is off between the elbow and shoulder.
Yours respectfully, P. C. ROONEY,
Telegraph Operator.

ABOVE-ELBOW AMPUTATION.

387 Grove St., JERSEY CITY, N. J., Oct. 30, 1887.

DEAR SIR:—It was my lot to meet with an accident by which it became necessary to have my left arm amputated two inches above the elbow. I have been wearing one of your artificial arms for nearly two years. I am well pleased with it. My position is book-keeping, and it is of great service to me, and as an ornament it is next to nature itself. I would certainly recommend your patent.

Respectfully yours,

MAMIE RYAN.

ABOVE-ELBOW AMPUTATION.

220 Garfield Ave., SCRANTON, PA., Oct. 26, 1887.

MR. A. A. MARKS:

DEAR SIR:—Your letter to hand. I gladly comply with your request. I wish to congratulate you on the arm that I received from you, both for its completeness and excellent fit; also for its durability. My two years' experience reflects to your credit. I hope all unfortunates like myself may receive the same benefit that I have had by patronizing you.

The cost of repairs for the two years that I have worn your artificial arm has been too trifling to mention. I earnestly recommend any one that needs any limb to apply to Mr. A. A. Marks.

If any one should wish to refer to me for further proof, kindly apply to the above address. I remain, Yours truly,

D. R. ALLGOOD.

ABOVE-ELBOW AMPUTATION.

Fitted from Measurements.

BARTONVILLE, MONROE CO., PA., Nov. 25, 1887.

MR. A. A. MARKS:

DEAR SIR:—I am wearing one of your patent arms and can say that they are very strongly made and very durable.

My arm was amputated close to the shoulder, with scarcely stump enough for use. I am satisfied with the rubber hand.

Respectfully yours,

S. BUSH.

ABOVE-ELBOW AMPUTATION.

Fitted from Measurements.

GREENVILLE, MERCER CO., PA., Oct. 31, 1887.

MR. A. A. MARKS:

DEAR SIR:—I have used an artificial arm made by you for seven years. During that time it has cost me $2.25 for repairs.

There was no difficulty in obtaining correct size from your system of measurements. My arm is off half-way between elbow and shoulder. I have used no other manufacture, consequently can make no comparison, but like this one well enough to make no change.

Yours truly,

REV. S. H. EISENBERG.

ABOVE-ELBOW AMPUTATION.

WOODSFIELD, MONROE CO., OHIO, Feb. 4, 1888.

A. A. MARKS, New York :

DEAR SIR :—I have been wearing one of your artificial arms (with gum hand) since July, 1883, without one penny of expense to me. I would not have any other kind.

I have been in the mercantile business for four years and can do any thing that is to be done in the store, such as weighing out sugar, coffee, etc., measuring off dry goods, and tying the same up, about as well as if I had my natural hand.

Respectfully,

H. F. BURKHEAD.

ABOVE-ELBOW AMPUTATION-

Fitted from Measurements.

JOHNSTOWN, CAMBRIA CO., PA., Oct. 28, 1887.

A. A. MARKS, ESQ.:

DEAR SIR :—Your arm proved satisfactory. I advise all likewise afflicted to correspond with you.

JAS. C. DARBY, 300 R. R. St.

ABOVE-ELBOW AMPUTATION.

ATLANTA, GEORGIA, March 29, 1883.

MR. A. A. MARKS :

DEAR SIR :—I have been wearing an artificial arm of another manufacturer with your rubber hand attached for several years, and must confess that I am delighted with it, especially the improved adjustable finger. For convenience I keep two rubber hands, one which my wife carefully takes charge of, with my party or opera glove on it, and the other I keep for every-day use; all I have to do is to touch a spring and the hands are changed.

Allow me to mention the fact that in all my dealings with you you have fulfilled your contracts to the letter. You have given satisfaction to me and all my friends in every instance.

One thing I wish to mention : that is, I have more than paid for the extra cost of rubber hand procured from you by the saving in the wear of kid gloves. On the hard wooden hands and fingers a glove will not last over a month ; on your hands they do not wear out in six or eight months. This, together with the soft and natural feel, would commend them with me in preference to others if for no other reason.

Truly yours,

J. S. TODD, M. D.,
Prof. Therapeutics and Materia Medica,
Atlanta Medical College.

ABOVE-ELBOW AMPUTATION.

ST. ALBANS, FRANKLIN CO., VT., Nov. 12, 1887.

DEAR FRIEND MR. MARKS :

I lost my arm by the cars when I was very young, and I have only five or six inches of the arm left from the shoulder. I know it was a very difficult matter to fit an arm on me. I can never half thank you for the perfect fit you made me.

It works just as natural as my good arm, and it is so perfect and natural that I defy any one that don't know me to tell which arm I have lost. It is very durable and useful. I can carry a heavy satchel, and I can do many things that make the arm worth many times the cost of it. I would not want any one to see me now with it off, I have got so accustomed to it. I have had my arm fourteen months, and it has never hurt me or bothered me.

It has not cost me any thing for my arm since I got it, and I know it is just as good as the day I got it. Some people may think it would cost them a lot for gloves. I have bought only two pair in a year, and the last pair is very good yet.

If any one that has lost a limb knew the merits of an artificial limb they would never go a minute without one. I am a telegraph operator in the train dispatcher's office at St. Albans, Vt.

As every one knows that operators have to write very rapid, I do not know what I would do if it was not for the hand. I can not half testify to the merits and comfort and pleasure I have taken in your arm.

Yours very truly, HOMER MCGRIGGS.

ABOVE-ELBOW AMPUTATION.

SEATTLE, KING CO., WASH. T., Nov. 3, 1887.

A. A. MARKS, ESQ., New York:

DEAR SIR:—The arm which I received from you in March, 1885, gives me every satisfaction.

Yours respectfully,

DANIEL MAHONEY.

ABOVE-ELBOW AMPUTATION.

Fitted from Measurements.

SAN JOSE, COSTA RICA, C. A., Dec. 3, 1887.

A. A. MARKS, New York City, N. Y.:

DEAR SIR:—In reply to your favor of the 26th October last, I have the pleasure of stating that immediately after having sent you the measurements for my left hand, amputated two inches below the shoulder, I received from you in the month of January, 1885, an artificial rubber limb, which fits me perfectly well, and serves me up till now (during three years) without any repairs at all. By reason of my occupation necessitating my frequent appearing in public places, I can fully appreciate what a boon your work is doing to humanity.

I am, gentlemen, yours thankfully,

JOSE MONGE REYES.

BELOW-ELBOW ARMS.

BELOW-ELBOW AMPUTATION.

Employed in a grocery store.

IRONATON, TALLADEGA CO., ALA., Nov. 14, 1887.

A. A. MARKS:

DEAR SIR:—In regard to your new rubber hand I will say that it is far superior to any thing I have seen. The first hand I got from you did good service. I wore it seven years in a grocery store. I think the last one I got from you will last much longer in the same business. I have seen many different makes of artificial limbs, but have never seen any thing yet to come up with yours. As for durability, I cannot recommend it too highly.

Yours truly,

JOSEPH ARPIN.

BELOW-ELBOW AMPUTATION.

Jan. 10, 1888.

A. A. MARKS, ESQ.:

DEAR SIR :—The rubber hand received in good time. Words cannot express my opinion ; I am so well pleased with it. I find it very useful in handling things around the office, besides appearing so natural.

Respectfully yours,

JAS. E. KEATING.

PAXON, WHITE CO., ARK.

BELOW-ELBOW AMPUTATION.

Office of WESTBROOK & BRO., Dealers in General Merchandise, MCNEIL, COLUMBIA CO., ARK., Nov. 22, 1887.

MR. A. A. MARKS :

DEAR SIR :—Having worn one of your artificial arms for more than three years, I cheerfully recommend it as being a good substitute. It can not be surpassed for its durability, and cost of repairs is scarcely nothing. It is a great help to me measuring off and wrapping up goods.

Yours respectfully,

A. J. WESTBROOK.

BELOW-ELBOW AMPUTATION.

Fitted from Measurements.

PINE BLUFF, JEFFERSON CO., ARK., Nov. 14, 1887.

MR. A. A. MARKS, New York City:

DEAR SIR :—The arm I ordered of you last April gives perfect satisfaction. The rubber hand is immense. I do not think there could be anything gotten up to equal it. It looks perfectly natural; in fact, some of my friends did not know that I had lost my arm. Being a machinist and engineer, it enables me to follow my profession as ever. I can file, hold the chisel, hold the reins to ride or drive, cut my own meats, and many things that one would not believe could be done with an artificial arm. I have seen several kinds of artificial arms, but none so equal yours with rubber hand. It is very durable, easily adjusted, and soft to the touch. I can write very well with it, though I do not as a general thing use it for that purpose. The hook attachment is very valuable in doing rough work. I would advise those that have to wear artificial limbs to give you a trial before purchasing elsewhere.

Yours truly,

W. E. SNIPES.

WRIST AMPUTATION.

Fitted from Measurements.

NEW ALMADEN, SANTA CLARA CO., CAL., Nov. 2, 1887.

A. A. MARKS :

DEAR SIR :—I have been using one of your most valuable artificial rubber hands. I am greatly pleased with it. I have had it for one year, and I can use a knife and fork, carry a satchel, etc. My occupation is engine-driving. My hand was cut off at the wrist.

I am, respectfully,

THOMAS TONKIN.

BELOW-ELBOW AMPUTATION.

Fitted from Measurements.

Law Division, Department of the Interior, Bureau of Pensions,
WASHINGTON, D. C., Oct. 28, 1887.

A. A. MARKS, ESQ.:

SIR :—Yours, dated the 26th inst., is received and contents noted. I desire to state that four years ago I was so unfortunate as to lose my left hand. I at once became master of the arts of stenography and type-writing, being at present able to compete with the most expert in either of the aforesaid branches.

I am engaged in clerical work of a character that makes it necessary that a person should have the use of his left hand, such as to hold his paper in place while writing, etc.

My artificial member has been as servicable to me in this respect as I could wish. I have worn it since the purchase of you a short while after the accident about four years ago, only removing it at night. It is to-day just as good as the day I bought it, with the exception of one of the straps which secure it to my arm ; you will infer from this that it has not received repairs of any nature from the date of its reception.

Relative to my occupation you are advised ; first, that I perform clerical work entirely, but at times have found it necessary to use my hand in lifting, and, in fact, use it for any thing I choose, without injury to it of any kind ; secondly, my arm was amputated a little above the wrist bone ; thirdly, as stated above, I have not contributed one cent towards its repair ; and, fourthly, I can truly say that it is exceedingly comfortable. It has surely proven its superiority over any artificial limb manufactured. Answering your last inquiry, it can be said that though manufactured from measurement, it fitted accurately.

The steel hook, knife, fork, and nail-brush included in the purchase have been of considerable advantage to me in the different uses to which they have been severally applied.

I am, very respectfully yours,
R. E. MATTINGLY, Stenographer.

475 F ST., S. W., WASHINGTON, D. C.

BELOW-ELBOW AMPUTATION.

Fitted from Measurements.

Nov. 8, 1887.

MR. A. A. MARKS :

DEAR SIR :—I would say, for the benefit of the unfortunates who have to use artificial limbs, that your make is the best I have ever used or seen. I have seen all that are manufactured in the United States.

Yours truly, GEO. W. PELTER.

LEADVILLE, COLO.

BELOW-ELBOW AMPUTATION.

Fitted from Measurements.

JAMESTOWN, STUTSMAN CO., DAK., Nov. 26, 1887.

A. A. MARKS, ESQ., New York City :

DEAR SIR:—I received my arm on the 29th ult., and am more than pleased with it. I think it is, in every particular, a grand success, and I will always be pleased to speak in its praise to my fellow-unfortunates. No doubt you will be greatly surprised to know that I wrote this entire letter and addressed envelope with my hand. I think that if you will compare this with former letters of mine now in your possession you will pronounce this the better writing of the two. Will soon write again. Yours truly,

GEO. H. PURCHASE.

BELOW-ELBOW AMPUTATION.

Fitted from Measurements.

HUFF, SPENCER CO., IND., Nov. 7, 1887.

GENTLEMEN :—I received an artificial hand on the 9th of November, 1885. It was fitted in the city by A. A. Marks, and I have worn it ever since with satisfaction. I have had no repairs on it of any description. The rubber hand is light and durable, and can be used in holding light things. My occupation is that of a teacher.

I would not be without the hand for any price. The arm is a great protection, especially during winter.

THOS. SAUNDERS.

BELOW-ELBOW AMPUTATION.

Fitted from Measurements.

LOGANSPORT, CASS CO., IND. Dec. 20, 1887.

A. A. MARKS, ESQ., New York City :

DEAR SIR :—The rubber hand I bought of you two years and a half ago has been a continual source of satisfaction.

The rubber feature makes it preferable to any other artificial hand with which I am acquainted. I heartily recommend it to any one who may be so unfortunate as to require such assistance. Respectfully yours,

REV. E. S. SCOTT.

BELOW-ELBOW AMPUTATION.

HAYSVILLE, DUBOIS CO., IND., Nov. 8, 1887.

MR. MARKS :

DEAR SIR :—I can recommend your artificial limbs. They are almost perfection. They possess very great durability.

I speak from experience, as I have had one of your artificial arms for three years, and have never had any repairing yet.

My occupation is school teaching.

A. M. ABEL.

BELOW-ELBOW AMPUTATION.

Fitted from Measurements.

GREENE, BUTLER CO., IOWA, Nov. 7, 1887.

MR. A. A. MARKS, New York City :

DEAR SIR :—Having lost my right hand while I was employed as brakeman on the railroad, June 14, 1887, I am now in receipt of the rubber hand of your make. I am well pleased with it. It has every way proved a success. I can do all ordinary work. I have been to no expense on the hand, and I see no need for any repairs. Your humble servant,

W. BERT ROWRAY.

BELOW-ELBOW AMPUTATION.

Fitted from Measurements.

MAYFIELD, GRAVES CO., KY., Nov. 3, 1887.

MR. A. A. MARKS, New York City :

DEAR SIR :—I have been using an artificial hand made by you in June, 1884 : I have been wearing it every day, and it has given me entire satisfaction, at a cost of $4 up to date. I can recommend your rubber hand to any one that is unfortunate enough to need one. My occupation is groceries, and very laborious, for I handle some very heavy goods, such as salt, lime, cement, and flour.

Respectfully yours, PRENTICE PAYNE.

BELOW-ELBOW AMPUTATION.

Fitted from Measurements.

Can carry water, cut wood, and write.

Nov. 3, 1887.

MR. A. A. MARKS:

DEAR SIR:—Having used your artificial limbs for several months, I can unhesitatingly say they are far superior to any I have ever used, and rendered me more service. My occupation as a miller is very laborious. I feel myself under many obligations to you. I can carry water, cut wood, and write very satisfactorily. Yours very respectfully,

GEO. BARNES.

STANFORD, LINCOLN CO., KY

BELOW-ELBOW AMPUTATION.

Fitted from Measurements.

May 2, 1887.

My right arm was amputated six inches below the elbow November 10, 1886. I write this with the aid of an artificial arm made for me by A. A. Marks, N.Y.

WM. HOLLIDAY.

Care of JORDAN, MARSH & CO., BOSTON, MASS.

BELOW-ELBOW AMPUTATION.

FINCHVILLE, DORCHESTER CO., MD., Nov. 4, 1887.

A. A. MARKS:

DEAR SIR:—In the year 1881 I met with the misfortune of having my left hand torn off, and of course the machine that did it took no pains to make a clean job of it, consequently left fair work for the surgeon's knife and saw. I have about half of the forearm left, and with the use of one of your artificial arms I astonish all. My occupation is steam-fitting and I can do any thing that is done in saw mills, file, saw, fire, engineer, and any thing you could mention.

I have been using the arm for three years constantly without any expense. I don't know of any better and don't want to. Mine cost $50. I would not be without it for twenty times fifty.

I can not tell any one how much advantage it is to me. People wonder how I file circular saws and do so many other things. Take away my arm and hook and I feel as much at a loss as when I first lost my hand.

J. F. WHEATLEY.

BELOW-ELBOW AMPUTATION.

Fitted from Measurements.

Oct. 30, 1887.

MR. A. A. MARKS:

DEAR SIR:—I ordered a hand of you in 1882, and must say that I am well pleased with it. It has done good service and is good yet. It has cost nothing for repairs. My occupation is a clerk in a store. I would not part with it for any thing. Yours respectfully,

MR. GEORGE SNYDER.

1121 Thompson St., BALTIMORE, MD.

BELOW-ELBOW AMPUTATION.

Fitted from Measurements.

JACKSON, JACKSON CO., MICH., Oct. 28, 1887.

A. A. MARKS:

DEAR SIR:—My left hand is off just above the wrist. A little over two years ago I had one of your artificial hands made from measurements and have worn it every day since.

It fits perfectly, and were it not for the glove could not be distinguished from the natural hand. I find it very useful, and if compelled to, could learn to write with it.

I have had no experience with other makes, but consider this one fully equal to all that is claimed for it.

I am night gatekeeper in prison.

Yours truly,
CHARLES HAMMOND.

BELOW-ELBOW AMPUTATION.

Nov. 3, 1887.

MR. A. A. MARKS, New York City:

DEAR SIR:—Your artificial hand which you sent me about four years ago is to my best satisfaction. I would not do without it.

Yours truly,
N. LARSON.

CADILLAC, WEXFORD CO., MICH.

BELOW-ELBOW AMPUTATION.

Fitted from Measurements.

Nov. 31, 1887.

Mr. A. A. MARKS:

DEAR SIR:—I take pleasure in testifying that I am more than pleased with my artificial arm with rubber hand. I have worn it for over four years and would not go without it now.

I heartily recommend it to any one who requires such assistance.

Yours respectfully,
JOHANNA L. ELFERDINK.

HOLLAND, OTTAWA CO., MICH.

BELOW-ELBOW AMPUTATION.

Fitted from Measurements.

Can pitch hay.

FREMONT, DODGE CO., NEB., Nov. 4, 1887.

A. A. MARKS:

DEAR SIR:—I wish to say for the benefit of those who, like myself, have to use artificial limbs that it affords me great pleasure to recommend your patent limbs with rubber hands or feet in preference to any I have ever seen in use. My arm I purchased about three years ago has far surpassed my expectations.

My arm was amputated so close to my elbow that I have but very little control over the joint; notwithstanding I can make considerable use of the artificial arm, the fitting is so well and the joints work so nicely. I was somewhat doubtful as to getting a fit from taking the measure myself.

Results have shown that with ordinary care in measuring, following your instructions, one can be positively assured of a perfect fit. The rubber hand is something to be proud of; with gloves on both hands it is almost impossible for a stranger to distinguish the difference. The hook, knife, fork, and brush accompanying the arm are very convenient. With the hook and ring I can pitch almost as much hay as I ever could.

I handled lumber about two years in a lumber yard here, and never had a man in the yard that could handle a stick more in a day than I could. I therefore take great pleasure in recommending your arms to all who are so unfortunate as to need them.

Any one wishing any further advice and will write me I will cheerfully answer. Yours very respectfully, A. W. FORBES.

BOTH ARMS AMPUTATED BELOW ELBOW.

Written with a rubber hand.

Lincoln Neb Nov 10th 1887

Mr Marks

Dear Sir I can cheerfully recommend your artificial hands I have found them very useful money could not buy them if I could not get another pair I can go out in company and no one ever thinks of me being a cripple my hands are so natural.

I write this with my artificial hands and I am preparing to take a position as writer in the Register of Deeds office I am a widow and have to earn my living It makes me shudder to think what my life would be if it were not for your artificial hands they are truly a great blessing to those who have had the misfortune to lose their hands

I am well pleased with mine in every way wishing you success in your great work I am

Respectfully

Mrs Rosella Fox

(No. 295.)

BELOW-ELBOW AMPUTATION.

PLAINFIELD, UNION CO., N. J., Nov. 6, 1887.

A. A. MARKS:
DEAR SIR:—I ordered a hand from you about the 13th of August. I find, from the two months' experience with the hand, it to be a great benefit. I can use your hand quite at ease, and I highly recommend your arm and hand. I would not part with it if I could not get another. I remain,
Yours truly, FREDERICK L. WALKER.

BELOW-ELBOW AMPUTATION.

366 Bergen St., JERSEY CITY, N. J., Nov. 7, 1887.

A. A. MARKS, ESQ.:
DEAR SIR:—On the second day of March, 1880, I lost my right hand in a mill, but with the artificial arm you made for me I am working at my trade as miller, and have not lost a day on account of the arm. Without the arm I would not be able to write these few lines to you.
Respectfully yours,
LOUIS LUEDDECKE.

SECTION OF HAND No. 211.

Mitchell St., ORANGE VALLEY, ESSEX CO., N. J., Nov. 3, 1887.

A. A. MARKS:
DEAR SIR:—Allow me to give my testimony in regard to your rubber hands, one of which I have worn two years.
While out gunning I shot my right hand off nearly to the wrist.
I gave up in despair, thinking my work was done for life, I being a hatter and my work being done almost entirely with the right hand; but after getting one of your rubber hands find I can do my work as well as ever with no inconvenience whatever. I have had it repaired once at a trifling cost. I wish to say I cheerfully recommend them to any who may be so unfortunate as I was in losing a hand. Yours truly,
GEO. GRAY.

WRIST AMPUTATION.

NEW YORK CITY, Oct. 28, 1887.

MR. A. A. MARKS:
DEAR SIR:—It gives me great pleasure to add my testimony and personal experience in regard to the rubber hand made by you.
My right hand was shattered by the accidental discharge of a shot-gun, making amputation at the wrist joint necessary; and as the accident occurred in a section of the western country where it was impossible to obtain efficient surgical aid, the operation was poorly performed, leaving my arm very tender and sore to the touch. This painful condition continued for so long a time after the wound had healed that I had entirely despaired of ever being able to wear an artificial hand until I procured your celebrated rubber hand, which I have now used for a year and a half to my utmost satisfaction. Its distinguishing characteristics are, its durability, natural appearance, and especially its lightness in weight, making it more pleasant and less tiresome to wear than one made of wood or other heavier material. My profession (that of Sanitary Engineer) requires me to use it constantly, and I have already found it equal to any use it has been necessary to put it to., I can carry a hat, cane, or umbrella with perfect ease, and do not have any difficulty in eating or writing with it. The cost of keeping it in order is comparatively nothing, as the one I have has kept in perfect order. Yours truly,
GEO. F. SHRADY, JR.

BELOW-ELBOW AMPUTATION.

11 New St., New York City, Nov. 5, 1887.

A. A. Marks:

I have worn one of your artificial arms with rubber hand for seven years, and found it very satisfactory in every respect.

Until a short time since I was manager of a large branch telegraph office, and I found the arm a great help to me in my duties at times when necessary to work at the key, sending telegrams.

I put a pencil in the rubber hand, between the fingers, and used it to time the message, while sending with the other hand.

To any one who understands that it's necessary to time a message while sending the same will see that the arm was a great help to me. My left arm is gone about four inches below the elbow.

The arm and rubber hand has not cost me to exceed $3 for repairs during the seven years' wear, and that has been for new straps and webbing. I take pleasure in giving my experience.

Yours very truly,
L. Leslie Lathrop.

BELOW-ELBOW AMPUTATION.

352 E. 50th St., N. Y. City, Nov. 10, 1887.

Mr. A. A. Marks:

Dear Sir:—Your letter to Edward Wiley received by me yesterday. I think his address is Gunnison, Colo. I well know he was satisfied with his hand, knowing full well that he is able to drive a team of horses and do other farm work.

Should you wish any more information will be pleased to give it. As you notice, I am permanently located at the above place.

Yours obediently,
Samuel Rapp, M.D.

Oct. 31, 1887.

Dear Sir:—I received your letter on the 28th inst. I send you a few lines in behalf of your artificial arm. My occupation is a sawyer. I lost my hand at the wrist on April 12, 1882, by sawing timber. Two months after I lost my hand I got one of your artificial arms, which I found very valuable. All it has cost for repairs is $1, and I recommend it very highly to any one who is afflicted that way.

So I close these few lines to you.

Respectfully,
Leonard Ryerson.

893 Grand St., Brooklyn, N. Y.

WRIST AMPUTATION.

Brooklyn, Nov. 15, 1887.

Mr. Marks:

Dear Sir:—After using your rubber hand for the past year I take great pleasure in stating that it is far superior to what you claim. I am more than satisfied and would cheerfully recommend your hand to any one who has been unfortunate enough to have lost one.

Respectfully, etc.,
John B. Bradshaw,
Engineer Str. Gov. Hill.

PART OF HAND AMPUTATED.

Nov. 7, 1887.

Mr. A. A. Marks:
 Dear Sir:—I have worn your artificial hand about two months, and I feel very much pleased with it, and I would not be without it.
 Yours truly,
 Tuckahoe, Westchester Co., N. Y. Geo. W. Sloat.

BELOW-ELBOW AMPUTATION.

Fitted from Measurements.

Nov. 3, 1887.

Mr. Marks:
 Dear Sir:—I am wearing one of your artificial hands made from measurements. It gives me complete satisfaction.
 My hand was amputated just above the wrist. My occupation at that time being switchman in the Erie yard at Hornellsville.
 I can recommend any one to you, as your work gives good satisfaction.
 Yours truly,
 Hornellsville, Steuben Co., N. Y. Thomas Robbins.

BELOW-ELBOW AMPUTATION.

Oct. 27, 1887.

Mr. A. A. Marks:
 Dear Sir:—The artificial arm you made me about four months ago is giving complete satisfaction; I would not know how to do without it. I find it very useful in my work.
 Yours respectfully,
 H. A. Leese,
 Secretary D. L & W. Dept. Y. M. C. A.
 Elmira, Chemung Co., N. Y.

BELOW-ELBOW AMPUTATION.

N. Kurz, Jr., Dealer in Groceries, Dry Goods, Hardware, Notions, etc.,
 Callicoon Depot, Sullivan Co., N. Y., Oct. 29, 1887.
Mr. A. A. Marks:
 Dear Sir:—I am very much pleased with my arm. It is so light, convenient, and is worth thousands of dollars to me.
 The new attachment that you have made is so comfortable that I can keep it on day and night. I keep a general country store and do all the work myself. You know that in such small country towns where profits are so small and every thing driven out to the point it does not pay to hire much help, so I buckle right in and do it myself. When I first put on the artificial arm, which was seven years ago, I weighed one hundred and sixty pounds, and I now weigh two hundred and twelve pounds. Isn't that doing good enough?
 I remain, yours very respectfully,
 N. Kurz, Jr.

BELOW-ELBOW AMPUTATION.

Copake, Columbia Co., N. Y., Nov. 9, 1887.

Mr. A. A. Marks:
 Dear Sir:—I respectfully state that I am now using, and have used for the last five years, one of your patent artificial arms with rubber hand. I have never

worn any other, and was advised by a doctor to purchase one of your arms, and was so well satisfied with it that I did not want to try any other. I can recommend any one that has had the misfortune to lose an arm to get one of your artificial arms, the cheapest and most durable for all purposes. I gladly say to all those who have lost an arm that they do not know the benefit of one until they try one. I would not do without mine by any means as long as I can get one of your artificial arms.

Yours respectfully,
WM. B. HOLSAPPLE.

BELOW-ELBOW AMPUTATION.

Fitted from Measurements.

Superintendent of the Poor, Chemung County, BREESPORT, N. Y., Nov. 9, 1887.

A. A. MARKS, ESQ.:

DEAR SIR :—I take great pleasure in testifying to the merits of your artificial limbs. I am wearing one of your rubber hands, and from my experience and in comparing it with others which have come under my notice, I heartily recommend its superiority.

I am obliged to use my hand a great deal and find it as near perfection as it seems possible for an artificial hand to attain.

I have worn it every day for nearly four years, and with the expense of a few dollars upon the suspenders have kept it in such good repair that many have been surprised upon learning that I have an artificial limb. My arm was amputated just above the wrist, and your appliance fits exactly.

Yours very respectfully,
EUGENE ATKINS, Supt.

BELOW-ELBOW AMPUTATION.

Fitted by Measurements.

SANDY CREEK, OSWEGO CO., N. Y., Nov. 13, 1887.

MR. A. A. MARKS:

DEAR SIR :—I have been wearing the artificial arm you made for me now for two years, and am very much pleased with it. Your rubber hand is very convenient. I do not know how I would get along without it. I can farm the same as ever.

The hook arrangement is just the thing for the farmer.

Respectfully yours,
IRVING WILLIAMS.

BELOW-ELBOW AMPUTATION.

CANANDAIGUA, ONTARIO CO., N. Y., Nov. 5, 1887.

A. A. MARKS, ESQ.:

DEAR SIR :—I take pleasure in testifying to the satisfaction I have derived from the use of your artificial arm, my arm being amputated two inches above the wrist joint. I have worn the arm you made for me nearly five years, with perfect ease from the first day, and the cost of repairs is nothing to speak of. I have worked for the N. C. R. Co. as freight inspector and car sealer ever since I purchased my arm. I could not do my work without the hand. I believe your rubber hand and arm to be the most perfect and most durable of any I have ever seen. I am more than pleased with it, and money could not buy it could I not get another. I would advise every person in need of artificial limbs to purchase of you.

I remain, respectfully yours,
J. E. CARR.

BELOW-ELBOW AMPUTATION.

Case of Van Dyke Van Alstyne.

DE FREESTVILLE, RENSSALAER CO., N. Y.

On the 20th of August, 1878, I procured from your office an artificial arm for Van Dyke Van Alstyne. Right arm, two inches above the wrist joint. He is a laborer, and has worn the arm constantly from the time he received it. He uses the hook, with which he is able to do almost any kind of work. The arm has been very satisfactory. It has cost but a mere trifle for repairs.
Truly yours,
Nov. 5, 1887.
A. TEN EYCK, M.D.

BELOW-ELBOW AMPUTATION.

Nov. 10, 1887.

DEAR SIR :—The artificial hand that you made for me is as good a job as I could expect. The more I wear it the better I like it, and the more natural it seems. Any one wanting anything in the artificial line can do no better than consult you. You are at liberty to publish this if you choose, and if ever I come to New York I shall be pleased to call and see you, as I appreciate the way you treated me when I called on you.
Yours truly,
JAMES L. BLOOD.

GLEN, MONTGOMERY CO., N. Y.

BELOW-ELBOW AMPUTATION.

SUMMIT, SCHOHARIE CO., N. Y., Nov. 1, 1887.

MR. A. A. MARKS :

DEAR SIR :—I am well pleased with my artificial arm I bought of you four years ago. I use the nickel-plated hook to great advantage. It costs but a trifle to keep in repair. I am a farmer, and can do nearly all kinds of work.
Respectfully,
MATTHIAS TERRELL.

BELOW-ELBOW AMPUTATION.

Fitted from Measurements.

ALLIANCE, STARK CO,, Ohio, Nov. 5, 1887.

MR. A. A. MARKS :

DEAR SIR :—Yours of the 26th ult. at hand. In reply to your inquiries I can say that I have worn one of your artificial arms for twenty years. About eight years ago I changed the hand, which was somewhat worn, for a rubber one, simply sending measurements, as I did in the first place for the arm, and both arm and second hand were perfect fits. The rubber hand seems to be just as good, after eight years of use, as it was at first.

My arm, the right one, is amputated midway between the wrist and elbow. During the twenty years that I have worn your artificial arm it has not cost me a cent for repairs, except the change of hand. The arm and hand look so natural that strangers never know but that it is natural till told the difference. In view of these facts I can cheerfully, and do most heartily, recommend you to all who may need work in your line. Your many years of experience have eminently qualified you in all respects to be the friend of the unfortunate.
REV. GEO. BOSLEY.

BELOW-ELBOW AMPUTATION.

Fitted from Measurements.

ZANESVILLE, Ohio, Oct. 28, 1887.

A. A. MARKS, ESQ.:

DEAR SIR :—Am pleased to say the arm I bought of you six months ago has proved satisfactory in all you claim for it. I am now able to fill regular desk in freight office, doing all kinds of work requiring use of both hands.

My arm was amputated just below the elbow and before purchasing your arm, I was unable to get any thing to do better than night watchman.

Yours truly, BRUCE McWALKER.

BELOW-ELBOW AMPUTATION.

Fitted from Measurements.

HOUSTON, SHELBY Co., Ohio, Oct. 31, 1887.

MR. A. A. MARKS:

DEAR SIR :—I take pleasure in recommending the artificial hand of which you are the patentee, as, in my opinion, it is the best in use. I have worn the one you made and fitted from measures for seven months, without the cost of one cent. The rubber hand is very agreeable with its flexibility. It resembles more nearly a natural hand than the old style. You are at liberty to use my name as occasion may require. Yours truly,

JAMES S. DEYE,
Telegraph Operator.

BELOW-ELBOW AMPUTATION.

Fitted from Measurements.

KERN & REAMER, Proprietors of the Humboldt Poultry Yards,
Buff Cochins and Light Brahmas a specialty.

Nov. 2, 1887.

A. A. MARKS, ESQ.:

DEAR SIR :—I think it no less than a duty to present to the public and to yourself my estimation of the merits of your artificial limbs. I have my right hand amputated just above the wrist joint, and have been using one of your rubber hands for four years, and must frankly confess that words can not express the satisfaction and benefit I have derived from it. I have seen many other makes, but think that for durability, convenience, and appearance your rubber limbs excel them all. Your method of fitting from measurements can always be relied upon.

The four years with one of your hands made from measurements has given me no trouble, as it now fits as perfectly as when first made, and the cost for repairs on mine for this time has been but a trifle. From experience I can heartily recommend your limbs to any who have the misfortune of needing them.

Respectfully yours,

88 Cherrs St., TOLEDO, OHIO. JOHN J. REAMER.

BELOW-ELBOW AMPUTATION.

Fitted from Measurements.

Oct. 28, 1887.

MR. A. A. MARKS:

DEAR SIR :—I cheerfully endorse your artificial limbs, as they have done me lots of good. I ordered an artificial hand from you some two years back, and have been wearing it every day since. I have never spent a cent for repairs in the two years I have been wearing it. I wear it day and night. I don't even take it off to go to bed. I work at A. E. T. Works, laboring, and can do as much work as any of the men with two hands who work in the same room with me. My hand was amputated at the wrist joint, and your arm could not have fitted better if I had been right there and had it measured. It feels just as comfortable as a good, genuine hand. I have been in company with persons for months, and they never suspected I had an artificial hand, I can use it so well. I cannot say too much for it, and recommend it to any person who has the misfortune to need any.

Yours respectfully,
CLARENCE UPHOLD.

MARIETTA ROAD, ZANESVILLE, Ohio.

BELOW-ELBOW AMPUTATION.

WELLSVILLE, COLUMBIANA CO., OHIO, Nov. 5, 1887.

A. A. MARKS, ESQ, New York:

DEAR SIR :—It gives me great pleasure to inform you that the rubber hand you made for me is entirely satisfactory, and pleases me greatly, as I hold the position of ticket agent at a prominent point on the Pennsylvania Company's

No. 296.

lines, and having a large number of tickets to stamp daily with the rubber hand, and having used the same for about five years, I am in a position to know the value of the hand. I have seen a great many artificial hands, yet I never have seen one to compare with mine for a good fit, serviceability, and durability. My hand was amputated at the wrist.

Yours truly,
JNO. WOOLLEY.

BELOW-ELBOW AMPUTATION.

Fitted from Measurements.

NEWPORT, BENTON CO., OREGON, Jan. 1, 1887.

MR. MARKS:

DEAR SIR:—I received your letter of October 26. I am engaged as night watchman for the government works at Yaquina Bay. My work is not very laborious. I have used an artificial hand four years. Point of amputation two inches below the elbow.

I have not paid any thing for repairs during that time.

I am well satisfied with the hand for handling brush, knife and fork, etc.

Yours truly,
JAS. FOSTER.

BELOW-ELBOW AMPUTATION.

Canton, Ohio, Wrought Iron Bridge Company,
ISAAC VANCE, Special Agent for Western Pennsylvania,
PITTSBURG, PENN., Nov. 5, 1877.

MR. A. A. MARKS:

DEAR SIR:—I would say, for the benefit of the unfortunates who have to use artificial limbs, that I have tried four or five of the leading manufacturers' patents of artificial arms.

There are none that I have tried that gives me the satisfaction that yours have. All of these clap-trap, cat-gut arrangements will get out of order in a very short time. They are about half the time at the manufacturers for repairs and fixing the machinery, which makes it very unhandy when you are three or four hundred miles away from where they are made. Yours need no repairs.

Yours very truly,
ISAAC VANCE,
Late First Lieut., Co. E., 140th Regt., Penn. Vols.

WRIST AMPUTATION.

Oct. 31, 1887.

A. A. MARKS, ESQ, New York:

DEAR SIR:—It gives me great pleasure to say that I am wearing one of your patent arms. My arm was amputated at the wrist joint on the 4th of May last, by being caught in a planing machine, and I procured one of your patent arms with the rubber hand, and on the 28th of September went to my work as a laborer, feeding a planing machine, handling from eighty to one hundred feet of heavy yellow pine lumber in one minute without any inconvenience.

I am using the knife and fork to feed myself with, so that you would hardly know that my hand was artificial. I am so well pleased with it that I am willing to show it and explain its well-deserved merits to any one who is so unfortunate as to be placed in the same position as I am. Respectfully yours,

JOSEPH SHERIDAN.

1530 Carnarvon St., PHILADELPHIA, PA.

BELOW-ELBOW AMPUTATION.

EASTON, NORTHAMPTON CO., PA., Oct. 30, 1887.

A. A. MARKS, ESQ:

DEAR SIR:—I can recommend your artificial arms. Mine gives me great satisfaction. I have seen many other arms, but none of them are equal to the one you have made for me.

I have the arm just five years to-day, and in that time the cost of repairs has not exceeded eighty-five cents, and the arm is good for five years more. I would not do without it under any consideration. I have worn it continually every day during that time. I would not go out of doors without it on. My amputation is between the wrist and elbow. I am working in the office of the L. V. R. R. Co., and my artificial arm comes in very good in holding and folding all kinds of paper which is required in my profession. The arm works like a charm and is a good help for me. I can fully recommend it to any one who wishes to purchase an artificial arm.

I am, yours truly,
JOHN A. SEIBEL.

BELOW-ELBOW AMPUTATION.

Fitted from Measurements.

Oct. 31, 1887.

MR. A. A. MARKS:

DEAR SIR:—My right arm was cut off right below the elbow on the P. & R. Railroad, on the 28th of March, 1883.

I received one of your artificial arms and labored with it ever since the 22d of December, 1883, and it is now just as good as the day I got it. I have not had any repairing done to it. I like it well and would not be without one.

Yours respectfully,
JAMES FROMHARTZ.

SOUTH BETHLEHEM, NORTHAMPTON CO., PA.

BELOW-ELBOW AMPUTATION.

Oct. 28, 1887.

DEAR SIR:—Your circular has been received. Cheerfully I comply with your request and herewith give my indorsement of every thing you claim for your artificial limbs.

For the last ten years I have worn a rubber hand of your manufacture, and during that period it has suited me in every particular, not requiring during the time the least alterations or repairs. With pleasure, therefore, I recommend your rubber hands and feet to whoever is in condition to require the use of the same.

Very respectfully yours,
JOHN KROTZER.

PITTSTON, PA.

BELOW-ELBOW AMPUTATION.

Fitted from Measurements.

NORMANDY, BEDFORD CO., TENN., Oct. 25, 1887.

MR. A. A. MARKS:

DEAR SIR:—After four years of constant use in wearing your patent artificial arm with improved rubber hand I am prepared to give testimony as to its merits. It has never cost a cent for repairs. As to usefulness, it equals my anticipation.

Right arm amputated four inches below the elbow. The fit by measurements is perfect. I am a farmer, and can do almost any kind of farm work. You do not say enough for your arms.

They are much better than you claim for them.

Regards, etc.,
GEO. E. WAITE.

BELOW-ELBOW AMPUTATION.

Fitted from Measurements.

CUERO, DE WITT CO., TEXAS, Nov. 23, 1887.

MR. A. A. MARKS:

DEAR SIR :—I can cheerfully bear testimony to the durability of your artificial arms, having worn one of them for seven years. I visited establishments in person in New Orleans, and am satisfied that you can make a better and more durable arm, from measurements, than those made when the applicant is present.

Indianola was totally destroyed by storm, August 20, 1886.

The county seat was removed to Lavaca, in the same county (Calhoun), as well as the post office, many of the citizens locating in this town. I was transferred to this place by the railroad company, who retained me in their employ after purchasing the Morgan Line.

Hoping the above will prove satisfactory,

Respectfully,

This gentleman's name will be sent upon request.

BELOW-ELBOW AMPUTATION.

Fitted from Measurements.

STAUNTON. AUGUSTA CO., VA., Oct 29, 1887.

A. A. MARKS:

DEAR SIR :—This is to certify that I have been wearing an artificial arm for ten years ; have been wearing one of your improved rubber hands for nearly two years. It has given entire satisfaction both in wear and comfort. I consider it one of the best artificial limbs I have ever seen. I wore an arm of another make for eight years, which gave very good service, but I consider yours of a much superior quality, both in workmanship and durability. I would advise all who are so unfortunate as to need a limb to write for your catalogue and examine your styles before buying elsewhere. My arm was amputated about three inches above the wrist joint. My occupation is book-keeping and teaching. It is my right hand that I lost.

Yours truly,

J. H. SWORTZEL.

BELOW-ELBOW AMPUTATION.

Fitted from Measurements.

A. A. MARKS:

DEAR SIR :—Having understood you were about to publish another pamphlet, will tell you what my opinion is of your work.

When quite a young boy I lost my right hand. I have had several artificial ones, but nothing which suited me as well as the one made by A. A. Marks. My hand was made by sending you my measures and a kid glove. It is as natural as life.

I can truly say it has given perfect satisfaction. It is just what you recommended it to be. I have recommended your work to others, and one young man who lives here has had an arm and hand of your make. He is also pleased with your work.

Wishing you prosperity in your labors, and that you may live to a good old age, that the afflicted may enjoy the fruits of your labors, is the earnest wish of

P. C. CUNNINGHAM.

ST. ALBANS, VT., Nov. 4, 1887.

BELOW-ELBOW AMPUTATION.

Fitted from Measurements.

OCONTO, OCONTO CO., WIS., Dec. 5, 1887.

A. A. MARKS, ESQ., New York City:

DEAR SIR:—I take pleasure in stating that the arm you sent me was far beyond my expectations, and I do cheerfully recommend your artificial limbs to

No. 297.

any one who may need them. I am a painter by profession, twenty years of age, and have worn the arm you sent me four years, without any cost for repairs, and consider it as good now as the day I got it.

My arm was amputated at the wrist joint, and I have never felt any ill effects from it since adjusting the arm.

Yours respectfully,

JOS. E. KEEFE.

BELOW-ELBOW AMPUTATION.

PRAIRIE DU CHIEN, CRAWFORD CO., WIS., Nov. 21, 1887.

A. A. MARKS, New York City:

DEAR SIR:—In July, 1886, I bought of you an artificial hand, for amputation below the elbow. I have worn it constantly since. On many occasions it has been mistaken for a natural hand. As a glove is constantly worn, the hand suffers little from wear. I am satisfied with it, and would willingly answer any questions. Yours,

J. H. FRIAR.

BELOW-ELBOW AMPUTATION.

Fitted from Measurements.

Dec. 28, 1887.

A. A. MARKS, ESQ., New York:

DEAR SIR:—It is about eight months since I got a hand of you, but this time has been sufficient to show me some of its advantages. I have been at a number of public gatherings and there has scarcely one noticed that I had hands other than Nature's own. The arm is perfectly comfortable, and I operate it to good advantage. I am in the employ of the M. C. Railroad Company, where there are many who have had the misfortune to lose a hand.

I have taken pleasure in comparing hands with those who have worn artificial ones for a long time, and they invariably give your rubber hand the credit. A great feature in this hand is the different positions you can place the fingers in. Yours truly,

CORNELL, ONT., CANADA. C. H. CHURCHILL.

BELOW-ELBOW AMPUTATION.

Fitted from Measurements.

FOLLY VILLAGE, COLCHESTER CO., N. S., CANADA.

MR. A. A. MARKS:

DEAR SIR:—I received the arm you manufactured for me. I am quite pleased with it. It fits nicely, and I do not feel it to be awkward. My neighbors and friends are also much pleased to see me once more looking in my natural state. Yours, etc.,

S. E. EGAN.

BELOW-ELBOW AMPUTATION.

Fitted from Measurements.

Roeck Street, No. 19 a LUBECK, GERMANY, Nov. 12, 1887.

A. A. MARKS, ESQ., New York City:

DEAR SIR:—Yours of October 26 is at hand. You can see by my address that I moved from my former home to the city of Lubeck. In regard to the artificial hand I got of you a year ago, I can say it exceeds my expectations.

In consequence of blood-poisoning in the fall of 1883, my right hand had to be amputated on the forearm in April of the following year. I thought that all the pain in the stump had to subside before I could wear an artificial hand, so I waited until I arrived in Germany, a year ago last summer. Having heard of the superiority of the rubber limbs by my arrival in the city of Hamburg, I tried to get an artificial hand of that kind, but had to take a wooden one instead, as the others were not manufactured there. Some years after, I saw your firm advertised, so after wearing the wooden hand some months without any benefit to me, except the look of it, I sent the measure of my left hand to you, and had a rubber hand made, which I fixed on the forearm of the wooden one. It works all right.

If I were compelled to work for my living the rubber hand would be of great use in any occupation. I recommend the rubber limbs to any one who has had the misfortune to become crippled.

As to simplicity and durability they are excellent.

Yours respectfully,

N. MILDENSTEIN.

EXPRESS CHARGES FOR CARRYING AN ARTIFICIAL LEG FROM NEW YORK CITY TO ANY PART OF THE WORLD.

The transportation of an artificial leg or arm from New York City to any point in the world is so greatly facilitated by modern methods, and the expense for the same is so reasonable, that one can not regard that as a hindrance to the purchase of a superior article. Especially since our methods of constructing and fitting from measurements secure every advantage to the wearer without assuming the least risk.

The following schedule of express charges to both, domestic and foreign central offices is based on one artificial leg of the largest size, thoroughly packed in a full-length box, and having a gross weight of twenty pounds. The transportation of an artificial arm costs about two-thirds that of a leg. This calculation is made on a large margin.

The actual cost will rarely reach the amount quoted, as the gross weight of box, packing, and limb, reaches twenty pounds only in exceptional cases:

Alabama: Birmingham, $1.20; Huntsville, $1.20; Mobile, $1.25; Montgomery, $1.20; Selma, $1.25.
Alaska: Sitka, $4.50.
Arizona: Casca Grande, $3.95; Flagstaff, $3.20.
Arkansas: Arkansas City, $1.65; Fayetteville, $1.50; Helena, $1.25; Hot Springs, $1.65.
California: Eureka, $4.20; Los Angeles, $3; Sacramento, $3; San Francisco, $3.
Colorado: Denver, $2; Durango, $3.25; Fort Collins, $2; Gunnison, $2.75.
Connecticut: Bridgeport, 35 cts.; Hartford, 40 cts.; Litchfield, 40 cts.; New Haven, 40 cts.; Willimantic, 40 cts.
Dakota: Bismarck, $1.75; Deadwood, $3.70; Fargo, $1.65; Sioux Falls, $1.50.
Delaware: Dover, 50 cts.; Georgetown, 50 cts.; Wilmington, 35 cts.
District of Columbia: Washington, 50 cts.
Florida: Jacksonville, $1.50; Key West, $2.10; Orlando, $1.65; Tallahassee, $1.65.
Georgia: Atlanta, $1.10; Albany, $1.65; Augusta, $1.10; Savannah, $1.20.
Idaho: Boise City, $3; Ketchum, $2.85; Lewiston, $3.40; Montpelier, $2.75.
Illinois: Cairo, $1.05; Chicago, 75 cts.; Danville, 95 cts.; Freeport, $1; Quincy, $1.05; Springfield, 90 cts.
Indiana: Evansville, 80 cts.; Indianapolis, 75 cts.; Jeffersonville, 75 cts.; Laporte, 80 cts.; Richmond, 75 cts.; Terre Haute, 80 cts.
Indian Territory: Adair, $1.25; Colbert, $1.50.
Iowa: Council Bluffs, $1.20; Davenport, $1.05; Des Moines, $1.20; Dubuque, $1.05; Mason City, $1.20; Sioux City, $1.25.
Kansas: Dodge City, $2.10; Leavenworth, $1.20; Norton, $1.85; Parsons, $1.25; Topeka, $1.25.
Kentucky: Covington, 70 cts.; Lexington, 75 cts.; Louisville, 75 cts.; Owensboro, 95 cts.; Paducah, $1.
Louisiana: Alexandria, $1.65; Lake Charles, $1.65; New Orleans, $1; Shreveport, $1.20.
Maine: Augusta, 75 cts.; Bangor, 80 cts.; Eastport, 80 cts.; Houlton, $1.05; Portland, 65 cts.; Skowhegan, 80 cts.
Maryland: Annapolis, 50 cts.; Baltimore, 40 cts.; Cambridge, 60 cts.; Cumberland, 55 cts.
Massachusetts: Boston, 40 cts.; Fall River, 35 cts.; Fitchburg, 60 cts.; New Bedford, 35 cts.; Pittsfield, 40 cts.; Springfield, 40 cts.; Worcester, 40 cts.
Michigan: Detroit, 70 cts.; Grand Rapids, 90 cts.; Kalamazoo, 90 cts.; Sault Ste. Marie, $1.10.
Minnesota: Duluth, $1.50; Fergus Falls, $1.65; Minneapolis, $1.20; St. Paul, $1.20.
Mississippi: Bay St. Louis, $1.65; Columbus, $1.50; Jackson, $1.20; Vicksburg, $1.20.
Missouri: Jefferson City, $1.05; Kansas City, $1.20; Springfield, $1.20; St. Joseph, $1.20; St. Louis, 90 cts.

Montana: Bozeman, $2.75 ; Butte City, $2.75 ; Glendive, $2.50 ; Helena, $2.50.
Nebraska: Hastings, $1.65 ; Lincoln, $1.50 ; North Platte, $1.75 ; Omaha, $1.20 ; Valentine, $1.90.
Nevada: Carson City, $4.25 ; Elko, $4 ; Eureka, $4.50.
New Hampshire: Concord, 70 cts.; Dover, 65 cts.; Keene, 60 cts ; Lancaster, 85 cts.
New Jersey: Atlantic City, 40 cts.; Millville, 60 cts.; Morristown, 25 cts.; Trenton, 25 cts.
New Mexico: Las Cruces, $2.85 ; Santa Fé, $2.50.
New York: Albany, 30 cts.; Binghamton, 85 cts.; Buffalo, 50 cts.; Elmira, 40 cts.; Hornellsville, 50 cts.; Jamestown, 60 cts.; Ithaca, 50 cts.; Poughkeepsie, 25 cts.; Plattsburgh, 60 cts.; Riverhead, 35 cts.; Rochester, 70 cts.; Syracuse, 40 cts.; Watertown, 60 cts.; Walton, 50 cts.; White Plains, 25 cts.; Utica, 40 cts.
North Carolina: Asheville, $1.20 ; Charlotte, $1 ; Raleigh, $1 ; Wilmington, 95 cts.
Ohio: Cincinnati, 65 cts.; Cleveland, 55 cts.; Columbus, 60 cts.; Dayton, 65 cts.; Steubenville, 60 cts.; Toledo, 65 cts.
Oregon: Portland, $3 ; Roseburgh, $4.05.
Pennsylvania: Easton, 25 cts.; Erie, 60 cts.; Harrisburgh, 40 cts.; Hollidaysburgh, 60 cts.; Philadelphia, 25 cts.; Pittsburg, 55 cts.; Scranton, 35 cts.; Williamsport, 50 cts.
Rhode Island: Newport, 40 cts.; Providence, 40 cts.; Westerly, 40 cts.; Woonsocket, 40 cts.
South Carolina: Charleston, $1.05 ; Columbia, $1.05 ; Greenville, $1.05.
Tennessee: Chattanooga, $1.05 ; Knoxville, $1.05 ; Memphis, $1.20 ; Nashville, $1.05.
Texas: Austin, $1.65 ; Denison City, $1.50 ; El Paso, $2.50 ; Fort Worth, $1.65 ; Houston, $1.65 ; Laredo, $2.
Utah: Salt Lake City, $2.50 ; Milford, $2.85.
Vermont: Bennington, 50 cts.; Burlington, 50 cts.; Rutland, 50 cts.; St. Albans, 55 cts.; St. Johnsbury, 85 cts.
Virginia: Danville, 75 cts.; Lynchburg, 65 cts.; Norfolk, 55 cts.; Richmond, 70 cts.
Washington: Seattle, $3.40 ; Spokane Falls, $3.20 ; Walla Walla, $3.
West Virginia: Charleston, 75 cts.; Martinsburgh. 55 cts ; Wheeling, 60 cts.
Wisconsin: Eau Claire, $1.20 ; La Crosse, $1.20 ; Madison, $1.05 ; Milwaukee, 90 cts.; Oshkosh, $1.05 ; Wausau, $1.20.
Wyoming: Cheyenne, $2 ; Evanston, $2.50.
Canada: Victoria, B. C., $3.60 ; Winnipeg, Man., $2 ; Port Arthur, Ont., $1.55 ; London, Ont., 85 cts.; Toronto, Ont., 80 cts.; Ottawa, Ont., 85 cts.; Montreal, Que., 55 cts.; Quebec, Que., $1 ; St. John, N. B., $1.10 ; Fredericton, N. B., $1 ; Halifax, N. S., $1.50 ; Charlottetown, P. E. I., $1.80 ; St.
Newfoundland: St. Johns, $2.50.

EUROPE.

England: Liverpool, $1.50 ; London, $1.75.
Ireland: Dublin, $2.25.
Scotland: Edinburgh, $2.25.
France: Paris, $3 ; Havre, $2.
Germany: Berlin, $2.
Holland: Hague, $3.
Belgium: Brussels, $2.75.
Switzerland: Berne, $3.
Austria: Vienna, $2.75.
Italy: Rome, $4.50.
Sweden: Stockholm, $3.25.
Norway: Christiana, $3.25.
Denmark: Copenhagen, $3.
Russia: St. Petersburg, $4.50.
Turkey: Constantinople, $4.50.
Greece: Athens, $5.
Spain: Madrid, $4.50.
Portugal: Lisbon, $4.75.

WEST INDIES, MEXICO, AND CENTRAL AMERICA.
Cuba : Havana, $2 ; Sagua la Grande, $2.50 ; Cienfuegos and Matanzas, $3.
Principal Ports of
Antigua, Bahamas, Barbadoes, Bermuda, Curacoa, Dominica, Grenada, Guadeloupe, Hayti, Jamaica, Martinique, Porto Rico, St. Domingo, St. Kitts, St. Thomas, Trinidad, $3 ; Mexico, Guatemala, British and Spanish Honduras, Nicaragua, Costa Rica, Salvador, $6 ; Mexico *via* Railroad Monterey, $2.90 ; Chihuahua, $3,50 ; City of Mexico, $5.

SOUTH AMERICA—Principal Ports of
United States of Colombia, Venezuela, British, Dutch, and French Guiana, Brazil, Argentine Republic, Uruguay, Ecuador, Peru, Chili, also Falkland Islands, $6.

ASIA—Principal Ports of
Arabia, Asiatic Turkey, British India, Ceylon, China, Cochin China, Cyprus, Japan, Malacca, Penang, Pondicherry, Singapore, $6.

AFRICA—Principal Ports of
Morocco, Algeria, Tunis, Tripoli, Egypt, Gambia, Sierra Leone, Liberia, Guiana, Angola, Madeira, Canary, Cape Verde, Fernando Po, St. Helena, Cape Colony, Natal, $6 ; Madagascar, Mauritius, Reunion, Seychelles Islands, $11.

OCEANICA VIA SAN FRANCISCO—Principal Ports of
Australia, Borneo, Celebes, Fiji Islands, Java, New Caledonia, New Zealand, Philippine, Samoan, Sandwich, and Society Islands, Sumatra, Tasmania, $7.

www.ingramcontent.com/pod-product-compliance
Lightning Source LLC
Chambersburg PA
CBHW030426300426
44112CB00009B/878